10.95

Mean Things Happening in This Land

Mean Things Happening in This Land

The Life and Times of H. L. Mitchell
Co-Founder of the
Southern Tenant Farmers Union

by H. L. MITCHELL
Foreword by Michael Harrington

Allanheld, Osmun MONTCLAIR

ALLANHELD, OSMUN & CO. PUBLISHERS, INC.
Published in the United States of America in 1979
by Allanheld, Osmun & Co. Publishers, Inc.
19 Brunswick Road, Montclair, New Jersey 07042

LIBRARY OF CONGRESS CATALOGING IN PUBLICATION DATA

Mitchell, Harry Leland, 1906–
    Mean things happening in this land.

    Includes index.
    1.   Southern Tenant Farmers' Union—History.   2.   Mitchell, Harry Leland, 1906–
I.   Title.
HD1511.U5M57   331.88'13'0975   78-65660
ISBN 0-916672-25-5

Printed in the United States of America

"There is mean things happening in this land
But the Union's goin' on
The Union's growin' strong . . . "

Dedication

John L. Handcox was the young black sharecropper, union organizer, and composer of folk songs of the Southern Tenant Farmers Union in 1935–37. One of his song-poems, "There is Mean Things Happening in This Land," provided the title of this book.

Mean Things Happening in This Land is dedicated to John L. Handcox and the hundreds of other black, brown and white sharecroppers and farm workers who laid their lives on the line in making their real contributions to this movement of theirs, only to disappear later into the barrios and ghettos of the cities. It has been my privilege to be their hired hand and spokesman.

H. L. Mitchell
March, 1979

Contents

Foreword

This book is an extraordinary contribution to the history of the American labor and socialist movements as well as to an understanding of indigenous southern radicalism. It is also a fascinating personal narrative which should reach a broad, non-scholarly audience with an engrossing, true-life tale.

Let me declare an interest at the outset. I am not sure exactly when I first met H. L. Mitchell. I suspect it was in 1953 when I was organizational secretary of the Workers Defense League, one of the many groups in which H. L. was a grass roots militant. Whatever the exact date, I have worked with him over the years in a broad range of causes. In 1973, when a handful of us who were outraged that the leadership of the Socialist Party was supporting the war in Vietnam formed the Democratic Socialist Organization Committee, H. L. was a founding member. But even though I thus openly and enthusiastically confess my long association with him, my judgment about his book is not based on sentimentality or friendship. The reader need only begin the first chapter to understand that fact.

Secondly, and more to the political point, it is no accident that H. L.'s autobiography shows how ordinary people, many of them with little formal education, are capable of great perception and courage. For him and for me, one studies history as objectively as possible precisely because one is so subjective about it, i.e., wants to grasp the lessons of the past which will allow us to shape the future. That cannot be done by interpreting popular struggles as if they were left-wing Westerns in which the good guys always win. In one sense, the Southern Tenant Farmer's Union (STFU), whose creation is chronicled here, was defeated and there is no use trying to walk around the fact. But in that defeat, pressure was generated which left its mark on American history—and which provides a link to the southern and rural radicalism of the future. So I take this autobiography as a book which helps us know what happened in the past *and* what should happen and must happen in the years to come.

Let me pick just three themes out of the many which H. L.'s narrative evokes: history from "the bottom up"; southern and southwestern radicalism; the South and labor today.

The impact of the New Left in the 1960s was somewhat ambiguous. The chief radical organization of that decade destroyed itself in a matter of five or six years (taking the Port Huron meeting of Students for a Democratic Society as the effective starting point). Many of the fantasies about instant revolution now seem foolish; and there were genuine tragedies, like the handful of militants who turned to terrorism and, in some cases, death. Yet the American atmosphere, the cultural mood, was profoundly and permanently altered. In the '50s, college courses on the left, or socialism, were usually taught under the rubric of "Know Your Enemy." But the '60s not only changed the present, they opened up a new American past. The academy not only discovered the relevance and depth of Marxist and other socialist ideas; it also became aware of the role of the rank and file in history.

There have been many scholarly attempts to go back and to reconstruct what happened at the grass roots by examining diaries, letters or, more recently, oral histories which have been recorded by researchers. H. L. Mitchell was a leader—but a leader in a movement in which, out of the necessities of southern life, there was practically no distance between those out in front and those who followed, except that the former were likely to be shot at first. His memoir is of history as it was lived at the base, the story—not as untypical as one might think—of the eleven-year-old who watched with horror as a black man was lynched and went on to read the radical classics in the famous edition from Girard, Kansas.

That personal story coincides with an historic moment in the South: the emergence of a movement of class-based radicalism which threatened the dominant racism. The populists were, of course, the first to pose this threat, but the example is somewhat ambiguous (there was a kind of "separate but equal" participation in which the black and white populists joined in the common defense but never actually merged their efforts). The STFU was less well known. A handful of socialists, with the aid of the lion-hearted leader, Norman Thomas, helped energize a movement which built a sharecroppers' strike and struck terror among the powers that be. The dream that then became a brief reality—of black and white united on the basis of their mutual economic and social needs—is, we will see, still alive. And, almost needless to say, H. L. is still traveling the road trying to bring it back in force.

That leads to my second point: the enormous power of southern radicalism. For many, the South is purely and simply the home of racism and reaction, a region of somnolent conservatism from the end of the populist movement (and of the influence of Booker T. Washington) to the rise of Martin Luther King, Jr., in the mid 1950s. In fact, as H. L. Mitchell so vividly documents, the area has a deep and vital radical tradition. The highest percentage state vote the Socialist Party ever achieved was in Oklahoma and, as H. L. records, the militants of that state staged a "Green Corn Rebellion" to demonstrate opposition to World War I. In northern Louisiana, Huey Long's father was a member of the Socialist local and the Industrial Workers of the World—the "Wobblies"—sank roots there.

Thus, this account of an indigenous, American, southern and rural radical is not the description of an individual's aberration. It illuminates one of the richest traditions of protest and struggle in the United States, one which thus far has been beaten back by a system of entrenched economic power made all the more secure by the manipulation of race prejudice. But, it might be objected, this past is totally past; there is a "new South," part of the affluent Sun Belt, growing at the expense of the industrial North and without any need for H. L.'s kind of leftism. In this view, the Southern Tenant Farmer's Union is a faded episode like the Confederate States of America. That leads me to my last point: the relevance of H. L. Mitchell's fascinating life to the future of the South and, indeed, of the United States.

The Sun Belt/Snow Belt distinction has probably resulted in more careless thinking than any other recent theory. The fact of the matter is that the South—and particularly the part of it in which H. L. fought his battles—is much poorer than the North. This is not to say that New York and Detroit and Cleveland have not been hurt by run-away shops. They have been. It is to argue that the beneficiary of that unplanned process, with its enormous human and social cost, has not been the people of the South, but corporations which have found relatively docile, unorganized and low-wage workers and mean and pinch-penny welfare systems.

That is why the terribly long and difficult battle to organize the workers in the J. P. Stevens plants has such enormous significance. If that effort, carried on against the concerted power of one of the most anti-union companies in the United States, could succeed, it could open the way to the dream of H. L. Mitchell and those hard-headed, practical, and everyday utopians who followed him: of an integrated social class movement fighting for democratic and economic rights and transforming the very structure of the South and of the nation in the process. If that were to happen—and I do not merely speculate about this but, like H. L., try to hurry up history—then the third southern movement of that kind would be the culmination of a hundred years of battle.

But even though I find that vision, that possibility, exhilarating, I do not want to conclude this introduction on an analytic, or even a political, note. What I find so powerful in this book is the testimony to the grandeur of ordinary people in those moments, all too rare up until now, in which they are their best selves. Reading this book is like having a conversation with history; not the history of presidents and princes, but the history of those who do the dying—and the living. We are enormously in H. L. Mitchell's debt.

Michael Harrington
New York, May 1979

Introduction

I never intended to write an autobiography. It seems to me that most of those written are self-serving and not worth the cost of the paper they are written on. These days, they are often produced by ghost writers and are worth even less. The most I had intended to do was just to make available to historians things I alone knew, leaving it to someone else perhaps to write a biography of my life, or tell fully the story of the STFU and its successor organizations. I had tape-recorded talks that I gave on college campuses and had interviewed on tape many old friends and associates. The first thing I knew, I had damn near as many tapes as Richard Nixon when he got caught in the Watergate scandal. So I had many of the tapes transcribed, edited them, and persuaded the Microfilming Corporation of America to film them along with some newly discovered correspondence and documents not previously included in the "Archives of the Rural Poor, or the STFU Papers (1934–1970)." The supplement is called *The Green Rising*.

However, I was persuaded by several historians who had heard me tell my tales to start my own book early in 1977. There was also an outstanding woman educator, Miriam Wolf-Wasserman, who said I must do it. She interested Matt Held, who had recently started his own publishing house. In the early stages, I consulted with Evan Thomas of Norton & Co., the son of my old friend, Norman Thomas. He advised me to go along with Held, rather than to a big publishing house. Some of my other friends, among them Sidney Hertzberg, Beth and George Biderman, had also sounded out other publishers in my behalf. The Bidermans put me in touch with Lynn Davis, a literary agent in New York, who became my agent and finally worked out a contract with Allanheld, Osmun & Company.

On a plane, returning from a speaking engagement, I met a "young lady," Leona M. Torode, whom I told about my newly proposed book. She offered to type it for me. She was about to retire as a civilian employee of the U.S. Army at Redstone Arsenal, only because the Army had compulsory retirement at 70. This would leave her with nothing to do but take courses at the University of Alabama in Huntsville, plus others at the Universities of Clermont-Ferrand, France, and Seville, Spain, and between courses to take trips to see the country and the world. Leona has patiently typed the manuscript *over* and *over*. She has more energy than all the Arabs in the OPEC oil cartel. Her help, including some preliminary editing, was indispensable.

I also owe a debt of gratitude to Joyce Kornbluh for reading the manuscript, dictating a critique, and making suggestions for its organization and presentation. Joyce Kornbluh is an old friend with whom I worked in Washington in the late 1950s. She is now at the University of Michigan, Ann Arbor, specializing in oral history of women workers. She is also the author of *Rebel Voices: An Anthology of the I.W.W.*, published by the University of Michigan Press in 1964.

Anne Loftis became the final editor of *Mean Things*. Anne is the daughter of Allan Nevin, the founder of the Columbia University Oral History Program, and wife of John Loftis, a professor of English at Stanford University. She was a newspaperwoman. Along with Dick Meister, a San Francisco reporter, she wrote the book *A Long Time Coming*, published by Macmillan in 1977, about the origins and development of the United Farm Workers of America, led by Cesar Chavez. Anne Loftis had researched the papers of the STFU on microfilm at Stanford University, in preparation for writing her book. Anne had previously offered me her services as an editor, but it was not until the fall of 1978 that she found the time needed to put *Mean Things* into its final shape. She worked under considerable difficulties.

Finally, I want to express my appreciation to Dorothy, who helped with encouragement, suggestions and corrections of all kinds. Usually such books as *Mean Things* are dedicated to someone like her, but she understands why I wanted to dedicate it to John L. Handcox, the troubador of the Southern Tenant Farmers Union.

1 Growing Up in the Rural South

The Lynching

It was a dark, damp, cold December day in 1917 when I, Harry Leland Mitchell, then eleven years old, stood on the platform in Halls, Tennessee, waiting for the arrival of the excursion train to take me to Dyersburg, twelve miles away. The Illinois Central Railway was transporting people to a lynching. The round trip fare was 25 cents. I had the money, as I was the newsboy at Halls. In less than half an hour we were there. We all rushed uptown to join the crowd gathered on the Dyer County courthouse lawn.

Chained to an iron stake was Scott Lignon, a delivery boy for a local grocery store. He had been accused of making improper advances to a white woman at whose home he had delivered groceries the day before. He had been arrested, jailed, and then turned over to a mob.

Since I was quite small, I soon worked my way through the crowd of perhaps 500 men, women, and children, some younger than I was. Wooden shipping boxes, excelsior, and other kinds of junk were piled about the young black man. It was all saturated with kerosene or gasoline. Scott Lignon was crying for help. I heard later that he was giving the Masonic distress call: "O God, is there no help for the widow's son?"

One of the two large, white, middle-aged men who were in charge of the burning, hesitated, saying, "We can't do this, that boy is a Mason." The other replied, "Oh hell, he's just a nigger Mason. Let's burn him." With that, a match was put to the tinder. The flames rose high, and the odor of burning flesh permeated the air. The black man's body sagged against the iron post and chains. Nauseated, I broke through the crowd and rushed back to the railway station where I stretched out trembling, on the cold ground. This was the only lynching I ever witnessed, but all my life I've heard such episodes recounted in gory detail by family, neighbors and friends.

Another violent incident had occurred earlier that year, also near

1

Halls. Two blacks had escaped from prison. They made their way to a wooded area in Lauderdale County, and were reported to be in an abandoned shack on the Forked Deer River, near town. A posse was formed, and the band of white men set out on horseback, in buggies, and in the few cars then available. This mob was led by Deputy Sheriff Jeff Yarbrough, and was doubtless fortified with moonshine whiskey furnished by the town bootlegger. Yarbrough ordered his men to stand back at a safe distance, while he went into the shack to bring out the convicts. He knocked down the front door and went in with two guns blazing. He shot both men, but Jeff Yarbrough died there with his chest full of buckshot. The posse brought one wounded man back to Halls and proceeded first to lynch him and then to shoot his body to pieces. The other prisoner somehow managed to escape.*

I recall visiting the hardware store where Jeff Yarbrough's body was laid out and seeing the bloody gunshot wounds in his chest. This was the first dead person I had ever seen. I could never forget these killings, the violence between blacks and whites, the savagery of mob spirit. Certainly these early impressions helped to determine the course my life was to take.

Another violent incident had occurred when I was only five years old. My father, James Young Mitchell, whom I called "Jim," had a job in a lumber camp at Tigertail, near where the Obion River flows into the Mississippi. Jim was a kind of strawboss in the millyard. He and one of the black employees got into an argument one day. Jim picked up an axe, and his fellow worker grabbed a cant hook and struck Jim a blow on the head. For days, Jim lay unconscious, near death. Relatives and friends came to help my mother Maude care for him. Among these was Uncle Ed Stanfield from Halls. Half drunk, he told me and my mother that the "nigger" that hit Jim had been caught, tied to a tree, "shot to pieces," and his body—weighted with log chains—dropped into the Obion River. Jim Mitchell recovered and moved back to Halls.

---

*The year 1917 was not a "big year" for lynchings: only 38 people—3 whites and 35 blacks—were reported lynched throughout the nation. In 1919, the number rose to 83. According to Tuskegee Institute records, 4,716 people were lynched in the United States between the years 1882 and 1947. Of these, 1,291 were white. Mississippi headed the list with 574; Georgia and Texas followed, with Alabama, Arkansas, Florida, and Tennessee not far behind. Every state in the union was represented. Arizona lynched only 29—all whites, and Delaware was represented by just one, a black.

Lynching was defined as an illegal act carried out by more than three persons, under the guise of protecting the rights or traditions of the majority. To be counted, the lynching had to be confirmed by newspaper account or another form of reporting, identifying the victim as well as the "crime" with which he was charged. Undoubtedly many such killings took place that were never reported.

Thereafter he was a striking figure with a two-inch streak of white setting off his dark brown hair. Women were attracted to him, and he made the most of their admiration.

It was in Tigertail that I had a black playmate about my age. He was Johnny Jackson. Our mothers gave us food when we were hungry, no matter which home we were in. One day we found a dugout, a kind of boat made of a hollow log. With two short poles, we pushed off into the swift-flowing Obion. Both mothers missed their boys about the same time, and they sounded the alarm when they spotted us headed for the big Mississippi. The men from the lumbermill launched a boat and rescued us.

Another day Johnny and I were playing at my house. The weather was cold and rainy. I announced that Johnny was going to spend the night with me. My mother tried to explain that Johnny could not stay overnight. Since we played together all day long, neither of us could understand the reason why we could not spend the night together if we wanted to. "There is no place for Johnny to sleep," Maude said. "But Johnny can sleep with me," I said. "I got lots of room in my bed." No, Maude explained. It was all right for children to play together, but a black boy could not stay overnight, much less sleep in the same bed, with a white boy. Then, to make us forget the whole thing, she made up a rhyme I still remember, "Johnny will sleep on the floor, and cover with a door." So all three of us made a game of the silly rhyme and we forgot the idea of Johnny sleeping over.

Family Origins

The first member of my branch of the Mitchell family to arrive in America came in the early 1800s. James Alexander Mitchell, a ship-builder and Baptist preacher, left Belfast, Ireland, with a wife and several children, for South Africa to work in a shipyard there. The sailing ship was wrecked off the Cape of Good Hope. Mitchell held onto his Bible and a small chest filled with gold pieces. He clung to a spar, but his wife and children drowned. He soon had to drop the gold, but his Bible is still in the family. The salt water and his teeth marks still show on it. Mitchell was picked up by a ship bound for Charleston, South Carolina. After the loss of that chest of gold, no Mitchell ever had any money, but they always held on to the Bible, and nearly every generation produced at least one Baptist preacher.

A later James A. Mitchell, my grandfather, was just 16 when the Civil War broke out. He was drafted into the Confederate States Army and assigned to an Alabama regiment as a replacement. He was at the Battle of Shiloh, and he lost his hearing at Chattanooga: The story goes that he was the last man in the line of sharpshooters, and he never heard the order to retreat. Suddenly he found himself alone, and facing the whole Yankee Army. He turned, gun in hand, heading south through the woods while Yankee bullets nipped at his heels. J. A. enjoyed telling his grandchildren how he outran the entire Union Army.

In April 1865, J. A. Mitchell signed the oath of allegiance to the United States of America and got married to Miss Mary Hall of Georgia, all on the same day. He took up the trade of harness and saddle maker, and they lived a few years in Alabama, where sons Nat, John, Jim, Foster, and daughters Theodosia and Mary were born. J. A. kept an account book from the day he got out of the Confederate Army and was married. In it, he listed all the money he received and all the purchases he made. He also set down the date of each child's birth, the time he got the call to preach, when he moved from Reform to Gordo to Anniston in Alabama and on to Arkansas, to join his brother John O. in Waldron. Although J. A. was a Baptist, and very much opposed to such things as dancing and drinking, all through the journal there appear notations referring to "a half gallon of whiskey for medicine."

The memorable trip to Arkansas was made by wagon, drawn by a fine pair of oxen. The family apparently prospered in Arkansas, with J. A. ministering to several churches but eventually they moved again. In Tennessee they purchased a large farm near Brownsville, located in Stoggins Bottoms on the Hatchie River. Later they moved to Halls and lived on a small farm about a mile north of town.

Son Jim—destined to become my father—married Maude Stanfield soon after his mother, "Miss Mary," passed away. Maude, a young bride of sixteen, lived for several years in her father-in-law's home. She thought highly of "Brother" Mitchell, as the Baptists called their ministers, but she had a different opinion of other preachers who came visiting. They would sit and argue day and night over what Paul really meant in his letter to the Corinthians. Maude heard so much about the Apostle Paul that she often wondered when he would come calling on Brother Mitchell, and if she would have to wash and iron and cook for *him* too. Being young, most attractive, in a house full of strange men, she was likely turned off by evil-minded visiting preachers, although she never admitted as much. Later she told me that all preachers were hypocrites; Brother Mitchell being one exception, and the blind preacher Harry Leland Martin, for whom I was named, another. Later developments proved that her own husband, my father, was one of the hypocrites.

Maude Ella Stanfield's family were among the first settlers in the town of Halls. Her father was "Eph" (for Ephraim) Stanfield, who came from somewhere up in Pennsylvania. The family of her mother, Amelia Ford Stanfield, had been in the county since it was first opened to settlement. David Ford was the head of the slave patrol before and during the Civil War. Since he was in the Home Guard, he was exempt from serving in the Confederate Army. He owned a large plantation and eighty slaves.

Maude's mother, Amelia, was a great story-teller and delighted in gathering her grandchildren about her to talk of the time when the Yankee soldiers came, and about her evil stepmother, who made her sleep with the little black slave children. One night the Yankees came, searched high and low for money, silver, anything of value, but found nothing but a hogshead of sugar the family had been saving. The Yankees scattered the sugar all over the floor, and Amelia and the slave children had a high old time eating it. Amelia also told of her early marriage to "Mr. Stanfield." When Maude was born, Amelia had childbed fever, and the doctor prescribed opium to relieve it. Thereafter she could not live without her "medicine."

Dr. Young, who treated Amelia, was also a cousin of the Fords. The good doctor had a black family as well as a white one. When he died, he willed most of his property to his black children. Amelia and Sally Young (who was black) always addressed each other as "Cousin." In the late 20s when Amelia was dying, she was visited by members of the family from far and near. Among those who came to pay his last respects was Josh, a former slave, who said, "Now Miss 'Melia, we is the onlyest ones of the Fords that's left."

One of Amelia's daughters, Bess Chisholm, lost her mind, allegedly because she was disturbed by reading a book about white slavery, or prostitution. The book, which was called *The White Rose of Memphis*, was mainly about riverboat gamblers and whores who plied their trades on big paddle-wheel steamers on the Mississippi. Bess was in and out of the asylum at Bolivar, Tennessee. She too was a great story-teller, making up stories as she went along or repeating what she had read. Her son Raynor and I would sit by the hour, fascinated by the knowledge displayed by this remarkable woman.

After the death of her husband Ephraim Stanfield, the storekeeper of Halls, Amelia married William A. Carney, an itinerant timber cutter. One day I was in the house with Grandma Amelia when an unusual noise was heard outside the house. I asked, "What is that?" Amelia replied, "That's just that old Gorilla rubbing his back on the corner of the house." Puzzled and somewhat tactlessly, I later asked Granddaddy Carney why he should be called an ape? "Oh, Miss 'Melia wasn't calling me names," he replied. "She was just talking about what I did in the war." Turned out that he was one of Quantrill's guerrillas, and he showed me his hand with missing fingers. He had lost them in a saber duel with a Yankee cavalryman. Which, maybe, was why he had trouble scratching his back.

William Quantrill was the guerrilla chieftain who was nominally a Confederate irregular, but who actually robbed and killed anyone having money or valuables, without regard to which side of the war he was on. Long before Alf Carney joined the gang, Quantrill led his band in committing the most infamous deed of the Civil War. On August 23, 1863 Quantrill and his men raided the town of Lawrence, Kansas (the present site of the University of Kansas) and burned the town and slaughtered 150 men, women and children. Quantrill prior to the Civil War had lived in Kansas and earned his living at different times as a school teacher and as a gambler. When the war started, he organized his band of desperadoes. After the Lawrence raid Quantrill was declared an outlaw by the U.S. authorities and a reward was offered for him, dead or alive. He died of battle wounds following a skirmish in Kentucky in May of 1865, some weeks after the Civil War ended. While there is no record, it is likely that Alf Carney joined up with Quantrill's men about that time. He never talked about it. Anyone known to have ridden with Quantrill was still subject to arrest and trial by federal authorities.

Amelia and Alf Carney had only one child, Hattie, who was married at a young age to ne'er-do-well Algie Summers. Algie was killed in a grocery store fight that started over a dozen eggs. Later, Hattie married Hugh Tomlinson, a tenant farmer who lived on the Richardson place in Gum Flat. Hattie always called him "Mr. Hugh."

In the summer of 1977 I visited Hattie, then 87 and as bright and chipper as I remembered her when we all gathered to hear her mother's stories. At this meeting she recalled a story about Amelia's stepmother, Sally Ford, forcing little Amelia to carry heavy pails of water from the spring to the main house. Amelia would try to balance the half-filled pail on her head, as she saw the older slave children doing. She would spill the water, and old Sally Ford would beat her for not doing as well as the slave children.

At one point, Sally Ford decided that her husband, David Ford, had been fooling around with an attractive slave woman who was pregnant. Although she whipped the slave, the young woman refused to tell who was the father of her child. Dave Ford then tried to get the girl to talk, without success. He had his men dig a shallow ditch in the ground that would fit the pregnant body, and he forced the girl to lie face down, and threatened to have her lashed with a cat-o'nine tails. The girl decided to divulge the secret. The culprit, as it turned out, was Sally Ford's son by a previous marriage, and the apple of old Sally's eye.

Sally was so mean to Amelia that another member of the family, Aunt Puss, took Amelia into her home and raised her. Years later when Sally Ford died, Pa Ford came to tell his daughter—by then happily married to Eph Stanfield and living in Halls—of Sally's death: "The angels came last night and took her away." That infuriated Eph Stanfield, who told him: "Don't come telling us such a thing! The old Devil himself was right there waiting for old Sally Ford, and he snatched her away and carried her right down to Hell where she belongs."

World War I. Newspaper Boy

Besides the lynchings, I remember 1917 was the year my cousin Howard Young and I tried to enlist in the army to go fight the Kaiser and his horde of Huns. We went to a recruiting office in Ripley, Tennessee, where the officers asked us many questions, and then put us through a "Penis Inspection." Then we were told that we would soon get travel orders to report for training. The orders never came, and we both missed World War I.

Soon after the United States declared war on Germany and set out to make the world safe for Democracy, I became the town newspaper boy. I had the dealership for *Commercial Appeal, The News Scimitar,* and the *Memphis Press,* all published in Memphis. I did my part in the war effort by yelling the headlines, both morning and night. Sometimes, if I had some extra copies beyond what my subscribers required, and I needed some extra nickels, I made up headlines for the newspapers, such as "Yanks Break the Hindenburg Line," "War nearly over, says President Wilson." Anything to attract attention. On the evening of November 4, 1918, a report came over the telegraph that the Armistice had been signed. I wired for a hundred more copies of both afternoon papers. The *Memphis Press* carrying Roy Howard's "scoop" about the end of the war sent only a few extra copies, but *The News Scimitar* sent the full hundred extra copies. All the papers were sold or delivered to regular subscribers at the railway station. Men gave me quarters, half dollars, even dollars, and walked away without their change.

That false armistice report was a windfall to our family, now mainly dependent on my earnings from the newspaper route. Jim was away during most of the war, working in shipyards in Louisiana, attending a Bible training school, getting ordained as a Baptist preacher, becoming an evangelist, and abandoning tenant farming and his family at about the same time. He returned occasionally for short stays, usually long enough to get Maude pregnant again. It was around this time I began to understand what Maude meant about preachers being hypocrites. I started asking, "Where the hell is the *second* Baptist Church?" Every town seemed to have a First Baptist Church, and some churches called by other names, but I never heard of a *Second* Baptist Church.

The Mitchell family moved often, seeking lower rent, a better house or, in some cases, because we couldn't pay *any* rent. The longest stay was at Brown's Crossing, about one mile from the Halls business district, in a two-room cabin alongside the Illinois Central Railroad on the dirt road leading to Gum Flat. It was here that I added an extra room for my own use. It was built of lumber unloaded from railroad cars switched to the siding by the trainmen. Sometimes the railroad men and the hobos (as the itinerant laborers were called) assisted the Mitchell family by throwing off blocks of ice from refrigerated cars in the summer, and huge chunks of coal (to supplement the firewood that was bought to feed both the kitchen stove and the open fireplace) in winter. Both railroad workers and hobos knew that if the trains stopped at Brown's Crossing, there was a free meal to be had at the Mitchell house.

One day during the war, my cousin Howard and I joined a group going to nearby Dyersburg to visit the elaborate whorehouse near the railroad track. We got inside, saw all the pretty girls in colorful robes, and listened to the victrola playing the wartime songs. Drinks were passed around by the black waiter who noted that I was wearing short pants and, therefore, must be under age. I was summarily ejected by the Madam and told not to come back until I was grown. Howard, though a few months younger than I was allowed to remain.

In 1917–18 there was no such thing in Halls as a swimming pool, but we town boys had a swimming hole on a creek about two miles west of the town. There we spent most of the hot summer days in the water, and sliding down the side of the wet clay bank on what we called the "Slick Ass." One afternoon, we were visited by a black man whose cottonfield adjoined the swimming hole. He politely asked us to go home and stay away until his women folks got through chopping the cotton in the nearby field. We told him to go to hell, and to have his women folks go home if they didn't want to see naked boys swimming.

In an hour the constable arrived. Mr. Crittenden, a grim, silent middle-aged man, was almost smiling that afternoon. But he said that Judge Parker had ordered him to arrest the swimmers and bring them before him immediately. He said, "Judge Parker is a republican, and he is wrought up about you young men going in swimming before those colored women." He ordered everyone to get his clothing on, and follow him. Frightened, we boys taked about what we would tell the judge. Each one of us was trying to outdo the others in sheer bravado.

On arrival at Judge Parker's house, we were told to go around to the back yard. There, out near the barn, Squire Parker held court while feeding his pigs. He was a large man with long white whiskers; for the occasion he was dressed in overalls. The squire said he could not permit young men to run about the country naked, and he was therefore sentencing each and every one of us criminals to three months in the State Reformatory, near Nashville. Constable Crittenden pointed out that the last train to Nashville had already left Halls, and asked whether he should put the culprits in the town calaboose until the next morning at ten o'clock when the next train to Nashville would arrive. Mr. Parker decided to let us spend our last night at home since we were going to be locked up for three months.

We all promised to meet at the railway station at 9:00 A.M. with our clothes packed, ready to leave. I noticed Squire Parker's whiskers shaking with ill-concealed amusement, but I was frightened, nonetheless, and rushed home to tell my mother about having to go to reform school. Maude denounced Crittenden and Parker, called them a couple of old fools, and threatened to go downtown and give them a piece of her mind—scaring children like that.

The next morning, no one showed up at the assigned meeting place. Everyone had "escaped." I left home at 6:00 A.M. and before the dew was off the fields was out picking strawberries, for two cents a quart. I worked so hard that day that I earned more than a dollar in the strawberry patch. From the time I was eight years old until I was twenty, I worked as a field hand, picking cotton in the fall, strawberries in spring, and then chopping or weeding cotton in the summer. Wages ranged upwards from fifty cents for a day of "from can to can't." ("Can see" in the morning, to "can't see" at night—twelve to thirteen hours.) The highest wage I ever earned was two dollars a day, but that was while World War I was going on.

However, there were less strenuous ways of making money. Algie Hargett ran a small feed and seed store and on the side bought and sold frying sized chickens. Our gang soon learned that Algie never questioned anyone about where the chickens came from, so we boys would catch chickens wherever we found them on the streets of the town and go sell them to Algie. We would use the money to buy cigarettes, bowls of chili, ice cream, candy, etc. One day I went into Algie's store with a small-sized chicken under my arm and offered it for sale. Algie held the chicken on the scales, and looking down exclaimed: "Why, God damn it, boy! I done bought this chicken three times today already." The chicken was so small he would just get out of Algie's coop, and be caught again by another boy, and so on and on.

Sharecropping and $1 Cotton

In 1919, the family was back together again in Ruleville, Mississippi, where my father owned a barber shop. By that time there was Sarah, three years younger than I, and then another sister, Garnet, then Edwin. My third sister, Eris Kent, the last to arrive, was born in 1923.

I made my first sharecrop there, on four or five acres of land lying next to our rented house on the outskirts of the little town. The land was owned by Mr. Marshall, a large plantation owner who sent men to prepare the land for planting and provided a one-row cotton planter and a mule for my use to plant the seed. The mule and most of the plow tools were generally kept on the plantation. I would hitch a ride on a farm wagon out to the plantation and then ride a mule back into town. After a few days work, I would return the mule the same way. Once I was riding the mule back to the plantation when a rare automobile came down the dirt road. The mule got frightened, and I was thrown in the ditch.

In that year, the price of long staple cotton, grown only in the Mississippi Delta, was at an all-time high of 75 cents a pound, and everyone expected it would reach a dollar that fall. I picked out my first bale (1,500 pounds of seed and lint that were required to make a bale of about 500 pounds). Mr. Marshall said he was holding all his cotton and recommended that all his sharecroppers do the same. Before the second bale was picked out, the price of cotton went down—to less than 10 cents a pound. The big Delta planters went broke, and they carried down with them their sharecroppers and the few small business people in Ruleville.

The Eastland family, even then prosperous cotton planters, lived not far from the house we rented. Jim Eastland was later elected to the U.S. Senate, where he became chairman of the Agriculture and the Appropriations committees. He became very wealthy off New Deal government subsidy payments received for not producing cotton. When I first met him, Jim Eastland did not impress me, but there was a blonde Eastland girl who impressed me a lot. She may have been his sister. Anyway, she sat in front of me in the first year of high school, and I teased her by pulling her long hair, and threatening to put it in the inkwell on my desk.

The Mitchells were driven out of Mississippi by a tornado that destroyed the town of Doddsville where Jim had just opened a new barbershop. The night it struck, I was sleeping in my room, separated from the rest of the house by an open hallway called a dogtrot. I tried to join the family in the main house, but on opening my door I was struck by flying debris, and almost blown away. I remained in my room alone, expecting the house to be demolished at any moment. When morning came, the extent of the devastation was apparent even in Ruleville. The business section in nearby Doddsville, including Jim Mitchell's barber-shop, was completely destroyed.

How I Became a Socialist in Moscow—Tennessee, that is

Soon after the tornado, the Mitchell family moved to Moscow, Tennessee, a few miles east of Memphis. There my father tried to teach me the barber's trade, but without success. Other things interested me much more. It was in Moscow, during the presidential campaign of 1920 that I heard my first socialist speech. The elegantly dressed "horse doctor," John Morris, a veterinarian who followed horse racing from track to track, made a speech on the street in which he said: "I had rather be Eugene V. Debs in the federal penitentiary in Atlanta than Woodrow Wilson in his mansion in Washington." I've never forgotten those words.

I followed Dr. Morris around town, asking questions about this fellow Debs—why he was sent to prison, and how he came to be running for President from such a place. I was given books and pamphlets to read, and one by Upton Sinclair, called *The Cry for Justice*, an anthology of famous words by famous men, from Confucius to Debs. John Morris was my first teacher. Too young to vote for Debs, I spent my days telling men who came to the barber shop that they ought to do as Doctor Morris and vote for a man who stood for something good. Debs got more than a million votes that year, which was the all-time high for any presidential candidate ever on the Socialist Party ticket.

About the same time, the controversy over the teaching of evolution had begun to rage. Laws were enacted in several states outlawing the teaching of Darwin's theory of the evolution of man. One day I found a full page advertisement in the *Commercial Appeal*, saying, "If you want to oppose evolution, you should know what it is—send $1.00 and we will send you twenty books." I sent in a dollar to E. Haldeman-Julius of Girard, Kansas. Over the years, I kept buying the *Little Blue Books*, usually condensations of writings of philosophers such as Plato and Socrates, and of nearly all of those of the modern day, including Will Durant. It was in this series that I was first introduced to Karl Marx's *Das Capital*, Marx's and Frederick Engel's *Communist Manifesto*, and to the plays of Shakespeare.

About this time, I started dating girls. There were two favorites, Jessie and Ruby. Jessie was a slender brunette and Ruby a freckle-faced redhead. When smallpox broke out in the town, Ruby's family was quarantined. The affair with Jessie blossomed. One Sunday night we attended services at the Methodist Church just across the street from the Mitchell home in Moscow. We were sitting on the back seat. Feeling ill at ease, due both to being with the girl and to being in such an unaccustomed place as a church, I was twisting on the rough bench, got a nail in my new pants, and tore a big piece right out of the seat. Telling Jessie I had to step out for a minute, I backed out the door, ran home, changed pants, and was back in time to walk home with the young woman.

A few days later, the young principal of the school, Gerald Johnson, called me aside and asked if I would like to go with him to call on the Pruitt girls that evening. There was an older girl that the "professor" was interested in, and he probably thought he would take me along to entertain the little sister. Jerry and the older Miss Pruitt settled in the porch swing, and Ruby and I disappeared around the back of the house and remained out of sight so long that the others came looking for us. We were hugging and kissing. The next day I broke out in an ugly rash about my genitals, which really frightened me. While taking my smallpox vaccination two days later I fainted, and the doctor examining me found I had smallpox. It did not last long, but all the members of my family had to be vaccinated, and had sore arms for weeks. I had only three large bumps that showed, all on the end of my nose and was thereafter immune to smallpox or the vaccination for it.

I Become a Bootlegger

The Mitchells' next move was to Collierville, about fifteen miles from Moscow, where Jim worked in someone else's barbershop. I got a job at a grocery and meat market where I helped the butcher slaughter cows and hogs when there was no more experienced help around. I also worked as a clerk, kept the store swept out, polished the showcases, washed the windows, and twice a day made deliveries by pushcart around the town.

Every spring there arrived in Collierville a band of Irish horse traders whom some folks considered gypsies. The men would drink anything, so long as it was alcoholic. The store could not even keep lemon extract in stock. Soon a young entrepreneur from Moscow who made moonshine whisky heard about this ready-made market. Knowing that I was in a good spot, Sam Wheeler asked me if I would like to go partners. Sam offered to bring in the whisky, help bottle it, and stash it in places where no one could find it, if I would bootleg it to the horse traders.

Soon we were in business. Horse traders from far and near came to Collierville to buy their fifths of good Fayette County moonshine. The money rolled in. The supply of bottles became exhausted. Sam arrived with a small barrel of moonshine, but no bottles. I found a few, filled them, and started downtown with the whisky under my long trench coat, stashing bottles here and there. Unknown to me, the local policeman was on my trail, picking up the bottles right behind me. The law came to get me at the store. I denied everything. I had no whisky on me. The policeman claimed he had seen me walking along the street, stopping every now and then, just about where he found several bottles stored. I denied it. I was just going back to the store; I had been out delivering groceries for Mr. Strong. Mr. Strong allowed that was so. He had sent the boy over to Mrs. Brooks' home with a small order. The Irish horse traders came to my defense too and claimed that the only whisky they had, had been bought by others over in Memphis. The butcher, Mr. Leach, also lied for his young helper, but he called me aside, and said, "Look, boy, you go home right now, and empty that barrel Sam brought in last night, and don't go near a single other bottle you have stashed away." So that ended the bootleg business for me in Collierville, but not the excitement.

Soon after, word came that a bank had been held up in Memphis by Machine Gun Kelly, and that he and his band of desperadoes were heading toward Collierville in a big black Cadillac. All the men in town grabbed guns, and headed for the First Baptist churchyard up on the highway. Hidden by a high hedge, they awaited the arrival of the bandits. Soon a black Cadillac came down the street, going fast, and the men behind the hedge in the churchyard opened fire with shotguns, rifles, and pistols. One or two men were killed, and the others in the Cadillac were wounded. But the Cadillac that was supposed to be carrying the Kelly gang was loaded with Memphis policemen who also had a report that the gang was headed toward Collierville. I'm still trying to figure out what valuable lesson I might have learned from that debacle.

In Collierville, as usual, I had two girl friends: One a lovely redhead, Katherine, welcomed my attentions while she awaited the return of her fiance. Unknown to me, the wedding preparations were underway, and soon Katherine's young man returned to claim his bride. I then tried to drown my disappointment in Jamaica Ginger, but instead of making me drunk, it made me very ill. Lillie, to whom I had paid only slight attention before, came to visit me while I was still in bed, suffering from the effects of the Ginger. Lillie made her contribution to my recovery by coming to bed with me. Thereafter the strawberry blonde was forgotten.

Graduation from Halls High

The Mitchell family returned to Halls. Here I entered Halls High along with my former grade school classmates, among them Bell Irvin Wiley who became the Civil War historian. I had missed some schooling while away from Halls, and there were no records of any attendance. However, I was permitted to enter the eleventh grade. Halls High had some fine teachers then, and among them was W. S. New, the mathematics teacher. Though I sat through Mr. New's classes and pretended interest, I had little arithmetic, and found algebra and geometry (both required subjects) just impossible. When final examinations for Mr. New's classes were given, I didn't show up. Later I was permitted to take a special examination in both subjects. Mr. New wrote out the questions and answers, and then he erased the answers. Since the answers had been written with a hard lead pencil, the impressions were clearly visible, and I passed both exams with high grades.

My favorite teacher at Halls High was Elizabeth Batey, a young woman in her twenties who taught English and history. She soon discovered the budding radical in her classes and became fascinated with my ideas. I had returned to Halls as an atheist, an evolutionist, and a socialist. I campaigned in 1924 for Robert M. Lafollette, whom the Socialist Party had endorsed for the presidency. Much to the amusement of the others in Miss Batey's classes, most of the time was spent in arguments between the teacher and me. I would find a way to bring in my unorthodox beliefs, no matter what topic was before the class. Soon the young teacher was called in by the principal and ordered to end the classroom discussions with her star pupil. Miss Batey told me what had happened and suggested that I talk with her about the problems of the world after school or during recess. Sometimes we two walked together at the end of the day, engaged in profound discussions.

Professor R. L. Conley, the principal, also showed a special interest in me. I had become deeply involved in a class in commercial law. At that point, I was sure that I wanted to be a lawyer. After graduation from high school, for a summer I studied law with Frank, the town drunk. He proved to be of little help to the would-be lawyer, beyond lending me certain law books that were much too complicated to study alone. At that time, the Cumberland Law School, then in Lebanon, Tennessee, had a course in the practice of law that could be taken in nine months, and if the student could pass the bar examination, he would be licensed to practice law, regardless of his education. The Cumberland Law School turned out many of Tennessee's leading politicians and some with less knowledge than I had already acquired from reading my Little Blue Books. The Cumberland Law School was also widely known as the loser of a football game with Georgia Tech, 222 to 0.

By the time I graduated from high school, my father had left us again, and since I had to make most of the living for the family, I abandoned my efforts to become a lawyer or attend college. For a short time, I worked in a clothing store and later ran a one-pump gasoline station. Then I got a job as a rodman with an engineering survey party laying out U.S. Highway 51, then being built between Memphis and Paducah, Kentucky, parallel to the Illinois Central Railroad. On days when the weather was too bad for the survey party to work outdoors, we were each given long tables of figures concerning the length, depth and width of the highway. I learned to check the figures, but I never could understand why anyone was called upon to do such dull work. This survey job lasted nearly a year; then the crew was transferred to Eastern Tennessee. I did not want to leave home at that time and did not accompany them.

Among the reasons for giving up the survey job were two young women. One was Lois Starnes, who lived in Halls. Lois was a good singer and played the piano. The class of 1924-25 would gather many afternoons at the Starnes home to sing, to dance and to play games. Lois and I were making out. Lois had a rather prominent behind, and her mother made her wear a very tight girdle. One day we got everything else off that mattered, but we could not budge the rubber girdle. It is possible that Mrs. Starnes intended for the girdle to double as a chastity belt.

The second young woman was Lyndell Carmack, the oldest of a family of thirteen children. Her father was a rural mail carrier and prosperous farmer living near the community of Curve, Tennessee, seven miles from Halls. My pal, Thomas Simmons, whose family owned the Halls Hardware Store and undertaking establishment, also had a girlfriend who lived near the Carmacks. I met Dell on a double date with Thomas and Willie Sue. Tom Simmons' family allowed him to drive the 1924 Model T Ford to and from the two towns while engaged in courting. There were occasional trips to the larger town of Ripley, where once or twice a week a movie was shown. Every Wednesday, the Campbellite Church held a prayer meeting. Occasionally I was persuaded to attend, or to go hear some famed evangelist of the Church of Christ preach a sermon of hellfire and damnation. I would remember the preacher's points, and argue them with Lyndell on the way home — often quoting chapter and verse from the Bible to prove the minister wrong. The Carmack family was concerned that their oldest daughter had apparently chosen an unbeliever, but her father, Sam, thought I was a boy who with the right kind of wife and family life, would soon become a pillar of the church and community. No obstacles were placed in the way when plans were announced for the wedding to take place the day after Christmas in 1926. The only problem I had was what to do about Lois in Halls. I paid a final visit to the Starnes home on Christmas Day and told Lois that I was getting married to Dell on the next day. She cried and pleaded with me to run away with her that night.

Getting Married at Nineteen

Dell knew about Lois and was not sure that I would even show up on our wedding day. I might not have, had it not been that Tom Simmons came to my home, and remained there until it was time to drive to Curve to pick up the two girls. Willie Sue and Tom were the only witnesses to the ceremony performed in the home of the Church of Christ minister in Ripley. We newlyweds spent the first night together at the Carmack home, the marriage bed being the foldout living room couch where much of the courting had occurred. Dell was a picture of loveliness in her pink nightgown, while I didn't even know enough to have acquired a pair of pajamas. I was ready for bed in my long-handled underwear. The next day we went by train for a honeymoon in Memphis, spent with my parents, who were together again. We visited friends and relatives of both families in Memphis and returned early in January, so Dell could assume her duties as a country schoolteacher there in Curve. I was only twenty and very immature, but Dell was a year older and much better prepared to accept the responsibilities of marriage.

Two country schools had been consolidated and Dell kept school for eight hours a day, five days a week. There were 75 children in her classes. For this she was paid sixty dollars a month. Still, Dell saved her money and with her savings we were soon able to buy a few household items. We set up housekeeping in a large room upstairs in the Carmack farm home. I was offered a job as a schoolteacher at a school some miles away. While I had a teacher's license for the year 1925, I had not attended Normal School (now Memphis State University) for three months as had Lyndell. The valuable license was not renewed, and there were plenty of other newly graduated high school boys and girls waiting for every job in the County.

While unemployed I stayed home reading books available at the Carmack house. I would usually prepare dinner and have it ready when Lyndell came home from work. A man doing the housework created a sensation on the Carmack farm. I was considered peculiar anyway, and this was just further evidence of it. Actually, my mother, who was often ill when we were growing up, had taught me how to do housework and to cook simple meals.

We decided to make a sharecrop on the Carmack farm, and began to break land for the cotton crop before March 1st. Dell's school was let out in time for cotton chopping in mid-April, and even though she was already pregnant, she turned out to be a much better farm worker than I ever was. In the fall, school was let out again, and Dell came to the fields to help pick the cotton crop. She worked right up till the day before

Harry Leland, Jr., arrived. When the debts were all paid and the cotton sold, we had made a total of $185 for the year's work, and part of that was earned picking strawberries in May. The year 1927 was not a good crop year anywhere. One of the great floods came, and the levees along the Mississippi broke and millions of acres of Arkansas and Mississippi Delta lands were flooded.

2 Farming on Shares

Arkansas Plantation Country

In 1927 my folks were living in Tyronza, a small plantation town in northeast Arkansas. Jim Mitchell's Barber Shop was prospering. It was patronized by cotton planters, by riding bosses, and by the small business people of both the town and the surrounding trading area. My father wrote, urging that I come to Arkansas: "Here the land is rich. One can make two bales of cotton to the acre." Over in Curve, West Tennessee, where I had just harvested my crop, the best land with heavy fertilizer would scarcely grow a half a bale to the acre. So in December I made a trip to Memphis, changed trains, and rode across the Mississippi River into Tyronza, to see about making a sharecrop the following year.

I had been offered a place on the Brackenseik plantation about four miles north of town. One of the Brackenseik brothers had told my father that I could make a crop with them and also have a part-time job working in the plantation commissary, issuing rations to the other sharecroppers. I went out to look it over in my father's Model T Ford, although he had to find someone to drive me (I didn't learn until several years later). The gravel road ended at the company store. The Model T could go no further. The dry cotton stalks rattled in the wind as the driver and I took to the fields. Down the muddy road back of the plantation store were the sharecropper shacks. Each had two rooms, one for cooking and eating and the other for sleeping. There were a couple of cabins with lean-tos that some enterprising sharecropper had added at his own expense, but these were already occupied.

Cotton grew almost to the door of the shacks. There was no evidence of a vegetable garden anywhere. Most of the houses were occupied. Children, white and black, peered out through dirty window panes. Occasional puffs of white smoke rose from thin stove pipes that stood a foot or two higher than the tin roofs. I had been told to take my pick of three empty houses. The sagging doors were open. Inside, one could see daylight in every direction. The sharecropper houses were all made of green lumber, and the siding had warped in the hot delta sun. About twenty feet away was the water supply for two houses. This consisted of a three-inch steel pipe driven in the ground, with a hand pump attached. The pump brought the underground water to the surface from a depth of perhaps ten feet at most. I tried the pump, but the leather washer had dried out from lack of use. There was no water nearby to prime the pump. Across the narrow backyard stood the two-hole privy—still filled with the excrement left by the last tenant.

I decided to return to Tennessee where things were a little more civilized. The inducements of a twenty-acre cotton crop, free housing, even a part-time job in the plantation store were not enough. I had already heard the Arkansas sharecroppers' refrain: "Yes, the land is rich. You can make two bales of cotton to the acre—the landlord gets one and the boll weevil the other."

Actually, the Brackenseik houses were no worse than those on other plantations in the eastern Arkansas cotton country. Also, life for a sharecropper was usually better where the owner lived on and worked his own plantation. Most of the rich land in eastern Arkansas had been brought into cultivation after the swamps were drained during World War I. The timber companies had gotten possession of the land and cut down every tree that could be used for lumber. The new ground had been cleared of small trees and undergrowth, and had been burned over. The flat earth stretched as far as one could see. There were no hills, no trees, just row after row of dried cotton stalks rattling in the wind.

For a sharecropper the day started before dawn. The plantation bell was the first sound he heard upon awakening. His wife was soon getting a fire going in the cookstove. A cup of cheap strong coffee started the day off. She put biscuits in the oven to be eaten with molasses and fat back meat by the adults. There was cornmeal mush for the young ones. First the man would go to the plantation barn where the hostler assigned a mule to him. He harnessed it and was in the cotton field before sun was up. The day's work was well underway by sunrise, and it didn't end until after sundown. The plantation riding boss would be in the field supervising the croppers' work. Usually the riding boss was also a deputy sheriff. In eastern Arkansas in the 1930s, such men wore khaki hunting coats that barely concealed the Colt revolvers they carried. In addition to seeing to it that each sharecropper was in the field and plowing his rows straight, the rider represented the law to both black and white sharecroppers alike. He replaced the slave driver of pre-Civil War days. The emancipation of the slaves put both black and white poor landless people to sharecropping—a new form of slavery.

Normally the work on the cotton plantations was well underway by March 1st. The land was first broken, then harrowed, and the rows were laid out for planting the cottonseed by the time the frost was out of the ground. March 1st was "Furnish Day," when the company store opened its doors to the sharecroppers to trade on credit. Each family was entitled to draw its groceries and other supplies. There was a credit limit based on one dollar per month for each acre in cotton the cropper was to cultivate and harvest that year. The "furnish" was allowed only until the crops were laid by in July. Usually by about the 4th of July nearly all work was done in the cotton fields, until picking time in the fall.

Cotton planting started in April. A single-row cottonseed planter was driven down each row in the field, dropping the seeds and lightly covering them. In a couple of weeks, depending on the weather, the cotton plants pushed through the soft crust of soil. When the plants were firmly set and up to the right height, the sharecropper took a special plow to scrape the weeds and dirt away from his cotton. Great skill was required to scrape the cotton on each side of the row, leaving the plants still with a firm foundation. Then the sharecropper's wife and all children old enough to chop came to the fields with long-handled hoes to thin the cotton to a stand. As it was chopped and thinned, the sharecropper used another plow to gently cover the row without destroying the plant.

The weeding of the cotton continued along with the plowing for at least six weeks. Everyone who was old enough to swing a hoe was needed to keep the fields clean of weeds. The sharecropper kept his cultivator and his mule going from daybreak to dark. There would be a hurried meal in the middle of the day. Sometimes, if the work was going well, everyone had a short nap, resting on the shady side of the house; there was seldom a tree to be found to shelter either man or beast.

If a family was caught up with the work on its own piece of land, its members were often called upon to help other croppers who had fallen behind. Also, the owner might have a day-labor crop, where there was some extra work to be done. Usually there was a fixed wage for such work, 75 cents a day for grown folks, 40 cents for the young ones. I often worked chopping cotton back in Tennessee for 50 cents a day when I was growing up. By the time I was fifteen I was paid a man's wage. On the cotton plantations in Arkansas, however, wages were seldom ever paid in cash. The family was just given credit for its account at the company store. Sometimes payment was made by printed pieces of paper to exchange for goods at the company store. These slips showed that the bearer was due the amount set forth on the cover, and they came to be known as "doodlum books" or "due books." In some places they still used pieces of brass: 1¢, 5¢, 10¢, 25¢, 50¢ and $1 pieces, good only at the company store. This money was known as "brozeene." In 1935, brozeene was still in use on the Twist Brothers plantation near Earle, Arkansas.

The prices at the company store were always much higher than those charged by the few small grocery store operators who managed to survive in town. In addition to the higher prices that the sharecroppers had to pay for basics such as flour, meal, and the fat back meat also called sowbelly, they were charged interest on the "furnish" they received. Usually this was 10 percent per month, on each dollar. An interest rate of 40 percent annually was considered normal.

Covington Hall, organizer of the Louisiana-based Brotherhood of Timber Workers, also editor and poet of the Industrial Workers of the World, once wrote a poem that went something like this:

> Sloughfoot Sam and his gal, Lou,
> Rode up thar on a kangaroo.
> You've seen yore share of Hell on Earth
> Said old St. Pete,
> So come right in and rest a spell,
> Cause you paid more rent and interest too
> Than God in Heaven can count for you.

After the crop was laid by in July, there was no more work for the sharecropper and his family until the last of September when the cotton was ready to harvest. Naturally, credit was cut off at the commissary. It was a time for hunting, fishing, and going to "big meeting" where hellfire-and-damnation preachers held forth in the small churches of the black folks, and in hastily erected "brush arbors" for the white folks, which sheltered the sinners from the hot sun. All were there to repent their sins. Sometimes a white evangelist would come along who had his own tent. The plantation owners encouraged and often paid the preachers something extra to conduct the big meetings, so that field hands could hear their troubles blamed upon their sinful ways, rather than on the economic conditions under which they lived. Even in towns like Tyronza, the Methodist and Baptist churches held their revivals during the lay-by time. Few sharecroppers ever came to the town churches at any time. White or black sharecroppers were "looked down upon" by those who had a little more of the world's goods. Often, if a white family's daughter married someone who was held to be a worthless young man, it would be said, "Oh, she married some sharecropper." Of course, the black folks were completely beyond the "pale" as far as the whites were concerned.

For a sharecropper the plantation owners and riding bosses usually preferred the black—unless he was known to be an "uppity nigger," in which case he would be blackballed and would not find a place on any plantation. But a cantankerous white sharecropper was considered even worse than an "uppity nigger."

About the middle of September when the cotton started to open, the labor of every man, woman and child was needed in the harvest. Black and white, old and young were all in the fields. Schools, where they existed, always closed for "cotton picking time," usually in September, and did not open again until after Christmas. The same thing happened in the spring when schools were let out for "cotton chopping." Sometimes they would have a summer term of school for six weeks, starting in late July and ending in early September. Children didn't get much learning anyway. As soon as a boy became strong enough, he became a plowhand and a valuable addition to the family economic unit. Since plowing was considered man's work, girls as a rule did not plow, so they got a little more schooling than the boys. Some girls even learned to read and write quite well.

On some of the plantations, the sharecroppers were allowed to keep half of the money for which the seed was sold when their cotton was ginned. This was "cotton pickin' money." Sometimes black sharecroppers carrying their cotton to the gin to be baled were heard to say: "Git that white man's cotton off my seed."

Settlement Time—the Dee Ducks Got it All

After the crop was all about picked out, usually just before Christmas, "settlement time" came. Sharecroppers would gather hopefully at the plantation commissary and the owner or his agent would call each man into the office in turn. The verdict would be handed down something like this: "Well, you had a good year. You raised twenty bales of cotton. We sold it for seven cents a pound, that comes to $35 a bale, or a total of $700. Half of that is yours—$350. BUT you owe $200, plus interest of $80, on the furnish. You know we had to get the doctor when your wife was sick, and we deducted the doctor's calls and the medicines he gave, and then you bought some clothes for the children too. The amount due you is $49.50. At least you got some Christmas money." The sharecropper usually left the office grumbling to others waiting hopefully: "The Dee Ducks got it all." Few if any of the sharecroppers ever kept records of the purchases made at the company store. Even if they had, none would have dared to dispute the landlord's word. Stories were told, like the one about the sharecropper who came in for his settlement, and when the plantation owner had finished his calculations, the sharecropper would say, "What about those two bales that I picked but ain't ginned yet?" And the planter replied, "Oh hell, why didn't you tell me that to start with? Now I'll have to do this figuring all over again to bring you out in debt."

Often the crop was not too good, or the sharecropper's account was over the amount the cotton brought when sold, and the man would then start the next year still in debt. He could not leave the plantation owing a debt. If he found a way to get his things moved at night, the law—usually the deputy sheriff—would be sent to hunt the man down and force him and his family to return. Sometimes a man's debt would be bought by another plantation owner, and the sharecropper would start off in debt to the new owner. Sometimes a planter to whom a sharecropper owed money would just pass out the word that the sharecropper was unreliable, and no one would let him have a place where he could make a crop. When that happened, his only hope was to find part-time work as a wage laborer, but that was a downward step to an agricultural worker.

Small Business Man in a Plantation Town

After my visit to the Brackenseik plantation I told my father that I was returning to Tennessee to make another sharecrop on the Carmack place, where things were more civilized than on the large cotton plantations in Arkansas. Jim then proposed that I take over the pressing machine in the back of his barbershop. I agreed, and in a few weeks moved to Tyronza where Dell and I rented a three-room house for five dollars a month. There was electricity, a single cord and bulb hanging from the ceiling in each room. There was a well with a pump to draw water and a two-hole outdoor privy located some distance away.

I bought a Model T Ford, had it renovated into a panel truck and a sign painted on it: "Tyronza Cleaners, H. L. Mitchell, Prop." Then I went out scouring the back roads of the plantations, calling at the homes of plantation owners, riding bosses and more prosperous sharecroppers, seeking clothes to be cleaned and pressed and delivered back to their owner, all within a week. I soon had profitable routes built up. My truck stopped at the homes of blacks and whites alike.

At one point, some of the bigoted white women in Tyronza told me they were going to send their husbands' suits to Memphis, to prevent them from being cleaned together with clothing from those plantation "nigras." I assured them that while I had a few colored customers, their clothing was kept separate. I pretended that white people's clothing was always cleaned first, and that when the cleaning solution was ready to be dumped, the colored helper then did the colored folks' cleaning. Later, I got the idea of pointing out that there were two washing machines, on the continuous flow system, and said that one was for white, the other for black customers' clothing. There was no truth to any of this. All clothing was spotted, dumped in the machines and cleaned. The only way anyone could identify the clothing was by the tags affixed to each piece.

My business soon expanded and I rented a larger store in a building that adjoined the barber shop. I installed a Hoffman Klear Buck Press and purchased continuous flow cleaning equipment on credit. On the plate glass windows I had signs painted that announced "Tyronza Cleaners." Also I had two benches built and placed in front of my shop. There were no signs segregating my customers and friends, but usually the whites sat on the right and the blacks on the left.

Once when I had a young black boy, Johnny Butler, helping me, I told him to light the gas-fired boiler by priming the lighter with alcohol. He poured too much on the heating element and the place caught fire. My hair, eyebrows, and eyelashes were singed, and my face was slightly burned as I tried to extinguish the flames. Some customers' clothing was burned up. Soon after, I had a coal-fired boiler installed outdoors, and we had no more fires.

Each fall when the cotton was being picked and there was money in circulation, I sold made-to-measure suits and overcoats as the agent for mail-order tailoring firms located in Chicago and Cincinnati. I would take the measurements, have the customer select the material from a large sample book, and send in the order. My commission, amounting to one-third of the sales, was quite lucrative. Each fall the companies would send a special salesman to Tyronza, and notices would be mailed or handed out to all my customers, inviting them to come in and meet Mr. So-and-so from Chicago, and see the latest styles and materials in men's clothing.

The Man from Island No. 10

One day, a customer came to the barbershop for his annual haircut and shave. He was from Island No. 10, over in the Mississippi River. After being shaved and shorn in the barber shop, he came into the cleaning plant, and ordered a new suit and overcoat, and insisted on paying in full for both in advance. This was most unusual, and I asked the man if he was a farmer. "Hell no!" he replied. "We just make whisky on No. 10." He invited me to come over for a visit the following Sunday and to bring my samples. Some of the other boys wanted to order new clothes, and some would have cleaning to be done.

My helper Clifford, a young white man, and I drove over. We forded the old river bed, and just as we drove onto the island, a huge brown-skinned man stepped out of the canebrake with a highpowered rifle cradled in his arms: "Where you goin', white folks? If I wuz you, I'd jist turn round and go back the way I come!" I explained that Mr. Thomas had invited us over. Neither my samples nor the sign on my truck, TYRONZA CLEANERS, made any impression on this big fellow. After searching the truck for weapons or other evidence of "revenooers," the guard walked in front of the truck up the narrow dirt road to Guy Thomas' house.

There, Clifford and I were made welcome. A jug of the best oak-charred and aged whisky was set out and the neighbors soon gathered from all over the island. The whisky flowed, the men talked about the time they had served, about how they had escaped from the Cummings Prison Farm in Arkansas, or from the Parchman Prison Farm in Mississippi. One or two had served time as convicts in the coal mines in Tennessee. All were ex-convicts of one sort or another, living on the island with their families. I told them about my experience as a bootlegger of moonshine back in Collierville some years before. Clifford had also been in jail once for stealing an automobile and taking a joy ride. While neither of us had served time in the state penitentiary, we convinced them we were close to being convicts ourselves and so rapport was established with the men on Island No. 10.

Clifford and I were Guy Thomas' friends, so all talked freely, and a few were measured for suits. I told them they didn't need to pay but 25 percent down, but all said they would rather pay cash in full, and that I should just deliver the suits when they were ready. Late in the afternoon, the two cleaners from Tyronza, having made a real cleaning on No. 10 Island, headed home, but not before Guy Thomas went out to the smokehouse where his best whisky was stored, and drew a gallon to send back to Jim the barber and a half gallon for each of the mainland visitors. When I tried to pay for the refreshments, I was told that my money was counterfeit, but that I could just tell my friends that Old No. 10 Whisky was every bit as good as the Ike Williams brand from the Saint Francis River at Marked Tree. Thereafter the island in the Mississippi was a source of business and ready money, even up to the time the Southern Tenant Farmers Union started in 1934.

The community of moonshiners stayed on No. 10 Island until they were washed out by the big Mississippi flood in 1937. A year or so later at a union meeting in Oklahoma, a man came out of the crowd and asked, "Mitch, don't you remember me? I'm Guy Thomas you used to know on No. 10 back in Arkansas." Guy became a member of the Oklahoma Tenant Farmers Union Executive Committee, attended conventions regularly until he joined the trek of migrant farm workers to California. At a cotton pickers' strike meeting on the West Coast in 1949 he again appeared out of the crowd to identify himself.

Guy was a survivor, all right. He used to tell the story about how after he got out to Oklahoma and was making a sharecrop down on the Red River, he and some of the other boys were out dynamiting the stream to catch a load of fish. Guy tossed a stick of dynamite in the river, and his retriever, Old Fuzzy, jumped in, grabbed the stick and started towards his master with it. Guy lit out through the woods, yelling to his friends, "Call Old Fuzzy." Guy out-ran Old Fuzzy, and the poor dog was blown to pieces. Just about then the game and fish warden arrived. The men denied ever having done anything so illegal as to use dynamite to stun the fish. They claimed that Old Fuzzy found the dynamite and picked it up on his own. And Old Fuzzy was in no condition to dispute that he was the one killing the fish.

The life of those ex-convicts on Island No. 10 had been an eye-opener to me. There was a kind of community there. The families had no schools for their children, of course, but then there were no plantation preachers to rail about their sins and blame their poverty on their dissolute ways. These people who had escaped from prison were at least free of *some* of the evils that sharecroppers on cotton plantations knew.

I was beginning to learn more about Arkansas' rich delta country that had so many poor people. It was the great engineer, Arthur E. Morgan, who drained the swamps, never suspecting what would happen to the human beings. Morgan, who was also the first chairman and chief architect of the Tennessee Valley Authority, the showplace of Franklin D. Roosevelt's New Deal, later wrote to me: "When I was doing that drainage work, I was sure that rich land would become the site of many prosperous farms, but the timber companies got possession of it and turned it into tenant farms, whose operators made a meager income. You can imagine my surprise at seeing the result of my work in eastern Arkansas."*

Morgan was right. There were the Chapman-Dewey Lumber Company, the Chicago Mill and Lumber Company, and the feudal empire of R. Lee Wilson, which held thousands of acres of land. There were, of

*November 1972. Letter to H. L. Mitchell from A. E. Morgan, STFU papers.

course, other wealthy families, cotton factors, and bankers in Memphis and elsewhere who were absentee owners. Some from the Yazoo-Mississippi delta came to northeast Arkansas and bought up huge acreages and exploited the rich land as well as the black and white sharecropper families they employed. The land that averaged a bale of cotton per acre attracted the more venturesome little farmers from the Arkansas hills, as well as those from the less productive plantations elsewhere.

In those days, it was said that the way for a man to get ahead in farming was to start at the bottom and rise to the top. Only a few managed to climb that agricultural ladder to farm ownership, but it was said that the wealthy Lee Wilson started off as a sharecropper who squatted on government land, drained it, and eventually owned more than 50,000 acres. Lee Wilson's hired hand, Jim Crain, started at the bottom and ended up prosperous enough, too. But he and his wife were reported to be most unhappy in the mansion Wilson built for them. It was said they could find no use for more than three rooms in the big house. All they wanted was a room to sleep in, the kitchen to cook and eat in, and Mrs. Crain's sewing room, where Jim felt well enough at home to take off his shoes and prop up his feet.

There were rumors, fully believed by the sharecroppers, that there was a "blue hole" on Lee Wilson's plantation, where unruly workers were thrown in the quicksand, and were never heard of again. These rumors of the Lee Wilson "blue hole" were so persistent that in 1936 I reported them to the FBI. An investigation was made but no evidence was uncovered. Rumors always spread swiftly among the sharecroppers. One person told another—the news was passed along until an incident first reported in the early morning was known in a community 100 miles away by sundown. The rumor about the Lee Wilson "blue hole" may well have had its origin in a similar report of men killed and buried on the Cummings Farm. This was the Arkansas prison farm where forty years later, bones of prisoners were found by a reform prison warden under Governor Winthrop Rockefeller.

But I'm getting ahead of my story.

3　Two Young Men of Tyronza

On the corner, next door to my dry cleaning plant, at the far end of Tyronza's Main Street, near the railroad track, was a gasoline station operated by a young man named Henry Clay East. Clay was of medium height, sandy haired, athletic, and a year or two older than me. Like me, he had moved about from one place to another, although his family had been among the first settlers in eastern Arkansas. He had attended Blue Mountain Academy, then Gulf Coast Military School near Gulfport, Mississippi. Upon graduation, Clay East received orders to report to Officers' Training School, but the War ended and cancelled them. So he also missed World War I.

East and I, being next door neighbors, soon became fast friends. He once described me as a tall, lean, lanky guy who had little to say, but who read a lot, and was always bringing up some peculiar idea. For example, after the stock market crashed in 1929, and a severe drought in eastern Arkansas, we prosperous young businessmen found ourselves with little to do. The few sharecroppers who still owned an old Model T and a Sunday suit, bought less gasoline or none at all, and found they could do very well without my dry cleaning services.

One day Clay East came into my shop with a proposition. "Mitch, there are three filling stations in Tyronza. There is only enough business here for one. Why don't I talk to the other two fellows? If we would each take turns closing up for two days a week, and all stayed open on Saturday, we would get the same amount of business, with less waiting around and waste of time."

"That sounds all right," I acknowledged, "but that's kind of a socialist idea."

Clay protested that it was just common sense, and that he was a democrat. I offered to bring some of my Little Blue Books down so he could read them, and decide if he was a socialist or a democrat.

"Don't bring them if they are about socialism! Socialists are Reds! They are always dirty, they wear their hair long and have whiskers!"

Nevertheless, the next day I selected a few books and pamphlets, and brought them down for East to read. Among them was one by Upton

Sinclair entitled *Letters to Judd*. Sinclair's letters to a carpenter named Judd explained the operation of the capitalist system simply and set forth the principles of the Socialist Party in easily understood language. East would read the Blue Books when he was alone. If a customer drove into his station, he carefully placed the little book under the *Memphis Commercial Appeal*, so that it would appear that he was only reading the daily news. But soon Clay East became a convinced socialist, and was out in the street preaching socialism as the solution to all the problems of the world. Our end of Main Street then became known as Red Square.

Clay East became an avid reader of the *American Guardian* published in Oklahoma City by Oscar Ameringer. This newspaper was written in plain language, for the common man, and found a ready response all over the Southwest. East became a Minute Man for the *Guardian*, selling subscriptions to everyone who came by his service station. He would persuade his customers to take a year's subscription, and before he would give an order to a salesman, the salesman had to subscribe to the *American Guardian*. Then when the salesman returned, East would ask him if he had read that paper. If not, East would not give him an order until he had.

In Arkansas, Louisiana, Oklahoma, and Texas, there had long existed a socialist movement, drawn from the more radical elements of the Populist Party, the United Mine Workers in the coal fields, and the refugees from the Pullman Strike of 1894 led by Eugene V. Debs. They became the most militant of all American Socialist Party members. In fact, the state of Oklahoma had the most successful Socialist Party, at one point having a larger membership than New York. The party elected local and county officials and polled a large vote before the outbreak of World War I. In eastern Oklahoma, the Working Class Union (an anti-war movement led by socialists) sparked the Green Corn Rebellion, which occurred in the spring of 1917. Hundreds of sharecroppers started to march, first on the Oklahoma state capitol, where they expected other workers and farmers to join them in taking over the state government. After that they planned to march to Washington to take over the federal government, bring the European war to an end, and establish the Socialist Society. The movement got its name—the Green Corn Rebellion—from their plan to drive a herd of beef cattle on the march and supplement those rations by roasting ears of corn, then green in the fields. The Governor of Oklahoma nipped this sharecroppers' revolt in the bud by calling out the state militia and jailing the leaders of the movement. Later on, Renters' Unions were formed in both Oklahoma and Texas, likewise sponsored by socialists such as Oscar Ameringer.

One of their programs decreed that landlords must provide each tenant with a house of not less than three rooms and an outdoor toilet located in a southwesterly direction from the dwelling.

In Louisiana, the Brotherhood of Timber Workers, an interracial organization, had been formed in 1910. Later the Brotherhood joined the lumberjacks in the Pacific Northwest to form the lumber workers section of the Industrial Workers of the World (I.W.W.), the native American syndicalist movement that was smashed by the government during World War I.

Though not instigated by socialists, the race riots in Elaine, Arkansas, were a part of the ferment of that period. I was living in West Helena when they broke out in 1919. Clay East was also living near Elaine. Every such incident was firmly believed to have been communist inspired—at a time when the CP had just been organized and had few members even in the industrial centers. No evidence was ever found that communists were involved in the 1919 troubles. The Elaine race riots— also called the Elaine Massacre by the blacks—erupted after the formation of the Farmers and Laborers Association, set up to get a higher price for sharecroppers' cotton and to boost the wages of cotton pickers. Sixty-four black men met and hired an attorney, Mr. Bratton, to represent them. One night a drunken white man started shooting in the colored section of Elaine. Because of race riots in Chicago and elsewhere, the black people usually remained at home to avoid trouble, but one evening they met in the church house with their attorney. The county sheriff sent a posse out to investigate. The Sheriff's men opened fire on the sharecroppers. The men in the church house fired back. Some were wounded. The lawyer for the Farmers and Farm Laborers Association was arrested and jailed for 31 days. The leaders of the organization were hunted down and many were killed. Estimated deaths ranged from 20 to over 200. Many of the leaders fled for their lives. Among them was Isaac Shaw, who years later became one of the 18 founders of the Southern Tenant Farmers Union.

In Louisiana's Winn Parish, first the Populist and then the Socialist Party controlled the Parish government. The name of Huey Long's father, Pierce Long, was carried on the Socialist Party lists by Walter Dietz, the secretary of the Louisiana Socialist Party, far into the 1920s. It seems quite likely that Huey P. Long's ideas for a redistribution of wealth came from those early Socialist Party influences.

As the economic depression deepened all over the country and cotton planters as well as sharecroppers were seeking a solution to their economic plight, Long responded. In 1931, as governor of Louisiana, he called a meeting of governors of the cotton-producing states to discuss a plan developed by some of Louisiana's larger cotton planters. The plan would prohibit the growing of cotton for one year. Most of the southern governors were not at all interested, but the meeting was held, and Huey had the Louisiana State Legislature pass a law that would go into effect when other cotton states enacted such legislation. In this way, it was hoped that the year's carry-over of cotton would be exhausted and American mills would pay a high price for the next year's crop.

Clay East and I argued about this. I thought that the only people who would benefit under Huey Long's plan would be the cotton market speculators and a few large plantation owners who had been holding their own cotton. I argued that businessmen like East and myself would go broke and the cropless sharecroppers—with no one to furnish them rations while not making a crop—would simply starve. I predicted food riots in every town throughout the state. (One of the earliest food riots in the rural South had occurred earlier that year in England, Arkansas, where 300 sharecroppers swarmed into town, demanded food, and threatened to loot the stores if they didn't get it.) Clay afterwards said he just wanted to get my reaction to Huey Long's proposal, and that he didn't really think much of the plan either. Later, Senator Carter Glass of Virginia claimed that the New Deal program of plowing up every third row of cotton was basically the same as the proposal that was made by Huey Long.

In 1932 Hattie Carraway ran for the United States Senate seat for Arkansas that was once held by her husband. Mrs. Carraway wasn't given much of a chance to win out of a field of five candidates. However, no one expected the intervention of Huey P. Long, who came into the state during the last few weeks before the election, and won the election for Mrs. Carraway. Several days before the Kingfish's arrival, a sound truck blaring hillbilly music toured the small towns and back country roads of Poinsett County, urging everyone to come and hear Huey Long on why Arkansas should elect Hattie Carraway to a full term in the Senate. On the appointed day the great man arrived, with an entourage that included the hillbilly band. More than 5,000 people jammed the town square in Marked Tree. Long, with arms waving, orated for more than an hour, and even those like East and me who had come to scoff, went away convinced that Mrs. Carraway *should* be elected. This "pore widder woman," as Huey called her, got more votes than her four opponents combined.

Later on, when Gerald L. K. Smith, a Shreveport Baptist preacher turned political organizer, formed huge "Share the Wealth" clubs pledged to elect Huey P. Long for President, they flourished in the hill towns of Poinsett County. But there was not much activity in the big plantation country about Tyronza, and other eastern Arkansas towns. One reason was that Huey Long didn't want to get involved with those sharecroppers and their problems; besides, we socialists were there first.

Socialism in the Cotton Fields

The ferment from these rebellious movements first reached Tyronza in 1932 when I put up a red poster in the large plate glass window of my shop announcing the candidacy of Norman Thomas and Jim Maurer of the Socialist Party, for President and Vice President, respectively. We boosted the drive in which they won almost a million votes. Clay East and I had driven over to Memphis in September during the 1932 campaign to join 4,000 others to hear Norman Thomas speak at the Ellis Auditorium. Joe East, Clay's younger brother, recalled that it was at this time that he and I first talked about organizing the Socialist Party in Tyronza. Finally, we persuaded our wives to join, along with Alvin Nunnally and his wife, sharecroppers on John Emrick's plantation, and a carpenter named Coates. This added up to the seven required to get a charter for a Socialist Party local at Tyronza.

At first, Clay East wouldn't join because he had a better idea: He would run for township constable, as a Democrat. The township constable, elected by the people, was the chief peace officer for that area, and Clay thus proposed to provide legal protection for us socialists. Since the Baptist and Methodist ministers in town had formed a cabal to assure the election of "a dry," who would also stop gambling in the town, Clay was elected with the support of the community's moonshiners, bootleggers and gamblers. In addition to being township constable, he was named town marshall and deputy sheriff. He was "The Law" in Tyronza, at least until his two year term expired.

Soon after he was elected, he heard reports of communist meetings being held near Tyronza. When there was talk of forming a posse in town to stop them, Clay went out to investigate. Under a railroad bridge some miles distant, he found a group of white cotton-pickers talking of how they might get their wages raised. He told them a mob was coming, and they scattered.

East was quite an innovator. He was the first businessman in Tyronza to install one of the new-fangled flush toilets for his customers. Though he also provided toilet paper for his patrons, the sharecroppers persisted in clogging the water closet with corn cobs, or heavy brown paper, or with thick rags used by women during menstruation (sanitary napkins were as yet mostly unknown). East could be heard cussing sharecroppers as he had to clean up the big mess at his sanitary privy every

Monday morning, after the Saturday shoppers had come into Tyronza from the plantations. Clay said, "Comes the revolution," he was going to see to it that a bunch of inspectors was appointed to teach those damned sharecroppers to take care of an indoor toilet. Years later when I was in Vienna and heard about how one of the larger hotels had its plumbing destroyed by Red Army troops quartered there during the occupation, I thought of Clay and realized that Joe Stalin had failed to appoint a commissar to teach the Red Army the amenities—even thirty years after the revolution in the USSR.

Clay East and I began to take part in socialist politics after the 1932 election. Our Tyronza local selected us to be the delegates at a Continental Congress of Farmers and Workers, called by the Socialist Party of America, the Railway Labor Unions, and the Farmers Educational and Cooperative Union of America, to meet in Washington, D.C. soon after Roosevelt's inauguration on March 4, 1933. Shortly before we were to leave for the capital, we attended our first out-of-town party meeting in Memphis. Arriving at the city across the river late in the afternoon, we paid a call on the secretary of the Memphis socialist local. C. J. Braun lived right in the downtown section of Memphis, in the heart of what Clay East termed the red light district. Mr. Braun was away on his job when the budding young socialists knocked on the door of his home. A woman wearing very heavy makeup answered and invited us in to await the arrival of Comrade Braun. I was fascinated by his large library. It contained not only the works of all socialists I had ever heard of, but a great amount of theosophist literature. It appeared that Mr. Braun was not only a socialist, but a theosophist, as well. Braun soon arrived and described the trials and tribulations of a man who was secretary of the Tennessee Socialist Party, as well as of the Memphis local, during World War I. He told about sometimes being the only person to attend the state convention, and how he then acted as chairman, secretary, *and* delegate, and nominated the socialist candidates for Governor for the legislature, and for the United States Congress. Braun, with his long hair combed back, and with bushy eyebrows, reminded me of a picture I had once seen of John C. Calhoun of South Carolina.

Accompanying Braun, Clay and I attended the meeting of the Memphis Socialist local, which was held in Arbeiter Ring Hall (Workmen's Circle) a fraternal Jewish organization closely affiliated with the Socialist Party, especially in the larger cities such as New York, Chicago, Cincinnati, and Cleveland. The members, mostly elderly Jewish people, a few even wearing skullcaps, rapidly disillusioned Clay East with socialists. East called me aside, and said, "I'll make a little talk about the Tyronza local, and I'll say we can't send but one delegate to the Continental Congress in Washington, and that you are to be the one to go."

East was more favorably impressed with several other socialists who came in, among them Professor William R. Amberson from the University of Tennessee Medical College in Memphis. Dr. Amberson, investigating the relief situation in Memphis, had made a report documenting the poverty and the lack of resources to cope with it. This was the first indication to me of things to come, as the unemployed workers of Memphis came mainly from the plantations of Arkansas, Mississippi, and Tennessee. Amberson's report was in the hands of a Mrs. Tamm, who was welfare worker in charge of relief in the City.

The Memphis local chose as its delegate one of the young active members, Miss Willie Sue Blagden, a member of a prominent Memphis family.

At the meeting, and going to Washington, was J. C. Thompson, a seventy-year-old socialist who had been a party organizer, a labor union organizer, an editor of socialist and labor papers, as well as the Farm Labor Union of America lobbyist in both Texas and Arkansas. Thompson had often been a speaker on the same program with the incomparable Debs at the old-time camp meetings the Socialist Party held in the southwest. Thousands would gather, camp out, cook out, sing songs, and listen to a series of lectures by men such as Thompson and Debs, and by women such as Kate Richards O'Hare. These socialist encampments sometimes lasted a week or ten days, and the people returned home with an invigorated faith in socialism. J. C. Thompson later came to Tyronza as our first socialist organizer. He remained a week, speaking every night at a different meeting.

I traveled to the Washington convention with Willie Sue Blagden and J. C. Thompson in a brand new Model A Ford owned and driven by a couple from Smackover, Arkansas. At Nashville, where Howard Kester and his wife Alice joined the cavalcade, Willie Sue transferred to their car. This was my first meeting with Kester who was already a legend in the South. He had run for Congress as a socialist, investigated lynchings, and had taken part in a coal miners strike. We would become very closely associated over the next few years.

On our way to Washington, D.C., we stopped in Knoxville, Tennessee, and Roanoke, Virginia, to attend meetings set up for the delegates by the local socialists. At these meetings collections were taken up to assist the delegation with expenses. As I recall, the meetings were poorly attended. The collections would not have bought enough gasoline to get us to the next town. Perhaps they had inspirational value in getting men and women active in organizing the party in their cities. J. C. Thompson, I found, was not only an excellent speaker, but could tell tales of socialist activity by the hour. In Washington, Thompson and I were walking down Pennsylvania Avenue to the Capitol Building, where we met Benjamin C. Marsh, then the Executive Secretary of the Peoples' Lobby. Marsh was a graduate of Grinnell College in Iowa, had done studies in social problems for the Russell Sage Foundation, and had held other positions in the field of social work. He had also represented certain farm groups in Washington. Years before Ralph Nader, the Peoples' Lobby functioned as spokesman for the nation's consumers. Ben Marsh was a mine of information, and he was highly respected by even the most reactionary congressmen and senators. His work was supported largely by a wealthy woman, Mrs. Ethel Clyde, of the Clyde Steamship family. Mrs. Clyde is a book in herself. She lived long past her 90th birthday, and was a supporter of many causes.

Marsh told Thompson whom to see and exactly where to go to get a nice clean room on Capitol Hill. He asked Thompson to join him for lunch the next day. Thompson, tired after the long journey of more than 1,500 miles, told me he was going to take a nap, and suggested that I take a walk around the capitol and also take a look at the spacious Union Station nearby, which was even then one of the wonders of Washington. This was my first trip there so I was eager to see everything I could before the proceedings started.

In point of numbers attending, as well as representation of people from all over the country, the Continental Congress of Farmers and Workers was the nearest thing ever seen in America to the first All Union Congress of Soviets in Moscow, when the Bolsheviks launched the Communist Revolution. In the press there was a conspiracy of silence about the Continental Congress. Newspaper accounts were few. There were no radio broadcasts from the sessions. I suspected later that the old guard Social Democrats of New York were alarmed at the militancy displayed by the delegates. I heard a fiery speech made by John A. Simpson, then president of the National Farmers Union, who called for a takeover of the government by workers and farmers. Had John Simpson offered to lead a march on the White House or Capitol Hill, there would have been few delegates left in the meeting hall.

The program adopted by the Continental Congress called for the immediate enactment of the Socialist Party demands. Roosevelt was criticized for not having nationalized the nation's banks after he called the Bank Holiday; instead he insured deposits and handed the nation's banking system to the bankers as their private property. Soon after the adjournment of the Continental Congress, its entire program was proposed by Roosevelt and eventually incorporated into his New Deal. This included a minimum wage law, old age and survivors' insurance, public housing, farm relief, and a guarantee of the right of industrial workers to organize and bargain collectively. Roosevelt appropriated the socialist program to prop up the collapsing capitalist system.

Two things about the 1933 Washington meeting stand out in my memory. One was a resolution calling for the organization of the unemployed. The other was a demonstration—the first in which I was ever directly involved. Delegates from New York had confirmed reservations at the Cairo Hotel on 16th Street NW. When they arrived, however, they were denied rooms because they were black. Some 500 delegates, nearly all white, marched on the Cairo Hotel. Norman Thomas made a speech in front of the hotel, pointing out that black folks could prepare meals in the hotel, but could not be seated in the dining room. They could clean the rooms and make the beds, but they could never occupy one of those rooms. Thomas called segregation morally wrong, and said that socialists would never accept such a second class status for any American, no matter what his race, creed, or color. This was the first time it was brought home to me that segregation was wrong. Most of the time socialists avoided the issue, saying that such problems would be solved if there were a new economic system. Thomas was a different kind of socialist—a highly moral man in an immoral society.

Soon after I returned to Tyronza from the Washington trip, the first work relief program of the New Deal was launched. Men were hired for twenty hours a week, and paid 25 cents an hour, by the Civil Works Administration. The large plantation owners immediately placed their favorite sharecroppers on the CWA projects, which were mostly made-work cleaning out ditches, repairing the roads and bridges on the private plantations. But hundreds of unemployed white and black men were denied the five-dollar-a-week jobs on CWA. One day, several men came into my shop and asked that I go with them to Harrisburg to see why they were not being hired. I told them that I would not go with an unorganized mob, and besides, it was too far to walk. It was arranged that the group would call a meeting that night in the Odd Fellows Hall, where the Socialist Party had been holding its meetings. That evening the small hall that seated about 200 people was filled with more than 500 unemployed workers. They were standing on the stairway and spilled out on the street. I called the meeting to order. The group adopted proposed bylaws modeled on those distributed at the Continental Congress in Washington. The bylaws prohibited anyone but unemployed workers from being members of the organization, which they named the Tyronza Unemployed League. Temporary officers were elected. I was ineligible for membership.

That night, just after the organization of the Tyronza Unemployed League, the emergency relief director for Poinsett County arrived. She was Mrs. Alex East, wife of the manager of the Fairview Plantation and related by marriage to Clay East. Mrs. East was accompanied by the state director of Federal Emergency Relief from Little Rock, as well as by two other men who were never introduced. They were probably FBI agents. Mrs. East asked to speak, and called upon all of those present to join in repeating the "Pledge of Allegiance to the Flag," to show that they were good Americans. Mrs. East started to give the pledge, when she was rudely interrupted by a loud voice from the back of the hall: "That boy scout oath is all right, I guess, but this is not the time or place. We came about getting one of those relief jobs. If you have anything to tell us about the jobs, let's hear it. If not, you sit down, and let somebody talk who does have something to tell us that we want to hear."

Mrs. East slunk into her seat. Then the state relief director arose and promised that every man who showed up at the local office the next day would be hired by CWA and paid five dollars a week for his work. He also promised to see to it that no more work was done on privately owned plantations, or at the homes of rich folks in Tyronza by the men on relief.

The Tyronza Unemployed League lasted for a couple of months. Then, having served its purpose, it withered away. However, the leading plantation owners were reported to be buying machine guns to protect their property from the hordes of red agitators. The Women's Missionary Union of the Baptist Church voted to boycott the businesses of Clay East and H. L. Mitchell. As a result, I lost my cleaning business. Clay managed to survive longer, but finally sold his station and bought another near Memphis.

One effect of the Tyronza Unemployed League's success was an increased interest in the Socialist Party. Both blacks and whites became members. E. B. McKinney, a prominent tenant farmer and circuit riding minister became a volunteer organizer for the Socialist Party of America. Brit McKinney had once rented a farm from Clay East's family, and he was highly regarded as an upstanding citizen and black leader.

In the 1933 election, Clay East was named Socialist Party candidate for County Sheriff, and I was named candidate for representative in the Arkansas State Legislature. However, only a few days before the election; when the sample ballots were printed, we found that the socialists had been ruled off the ballot on a technicality: We had failed to file a pledge to abide by the Arkansas Anti-Corrupt Practices Law. We had never even heard of such a statute. In Tyronza, Truman, and Marked Tree, the Socialist Party called upon everyone to boycott the regular election, and instead to cast their ballots in a mock election. When the results were tabulated, it was found that more votes had been cast in the socialist election than in the general election, both in Tyronza and in Truman.

Truman, since 1912, had been a hotbed of socialism. The leaders of the group were Uncle Charlie McCoy, his wife, Miz Evelyn, and the J. H. Moody family. Uncle Charlie McCoy had been a millwright in the Singer Sewing Machine plant in Truman, and Moody was a carpenter. Both men had been blacklisted by the company following a strike led by the A.F. of L. soon after World War I. Moody made a precarious living at his trade, while Charlie McCoy, through political influence, had secured the right to clean the outdoor privies. McCoy collected a small fee from each householder. He made no charge to his socialist comrades, and he didn't press those who were without work to pay for his regular services. The McCoys had a nice comfortable house and about four acres of land. Charlie used as fertilizer the night soil he collected and had one of the largest and finest gardens in the entire area. He shared his abundance with the comrades of the Truman Local.

Miz Evelyn had been a country schoolteacher when she married the Irish Catholic immigrant, Charles McCoy, after he drifted into Truman early in the century. Charlie didn't know how to read or write, and he felt no particular need to learn until one day he heard a newspaper boy call out, "Read all about it, read all about the Haywood, Pettibone and Moyer frameup." These were the radicals accused of killing the Governor of Idaho. The paper being sold was the *Appeal to Reason*, published in Girard, Kansas, and edited by Eugene V. Debs. McCoy carried the paper home with him, and his wife taught him to read from it. Thereafter he became a socialist and bought every book advertised in socialist papers that he could afford. As a result, by the 1930s, McCoy had the largest socialist library in Arkansas. McCoy's home was always a stopping place for socialist lecturers and organizers. The McCoys always had a bed and three good meals to serve to all comers of the socialist faith.

Charlie, who had long since given up his Catholicism to become a freethinker, in the early twenties joined the Ku Klux Klan when it started organizing in Truman. McCoy and his handful of fellow socialists decided that they would break up the Klan from the inside. Soon the Ku Klux Klan represented a majority of voters in the Truman district. The KKK candidate for mayor exemplified that organization's bigotry toward Negroes, Catholics, and Jews, and but for McCoy and Moody he would have been elected. These two maneuvered so that they were both named as clerks to conduct the election, and while Moody cut off the electricity, Charlie switched the ballot box (which had been stuffed by the socialists). Later, there were accusations, but there was no proof. The winning mayor gratefully saw to it that Charlie got the night sanitation job.

Uncle Charlie McCoy suggested the name for our organization: Southern Tenant Farmers Union, and it was on his front porch that we held our first election of officers in 1934.

4   Revolt in the Cotton Fields

> We covet no man's freedom, no man's fields, no man's houses or barns; only our share of the Eternal's earth.*

Among the early visitors to the cotton plantation country of Eastern Arkansas were Edward and Martha Johnson, Socialist Party organizers. Martha had been a teacher in the public schools of High Point, North Carolina, and her husband had been involved in the bitter strike at Gastonia, North Carolina, in the early thirties. Both were to witness the slaughter of textile workers at Hones Path near Greenville, South Carolina. After spending a week in Tyronza, Martha wrote to Norman Thomas, urging that he take a day off from his forthcoming lecture trip to Memphis, to visit the sharecroppers. Wrote Martha on November 9, 1933:

"Here you will find the true proletariat; here you will find inarticulate men moving irresistably toward revolution and no less. Remember, these people are politically impotent. They can not vote out the poll tax, since they can't pay a poll tax to vote." She also sounded a warning in her letter:

*From *Ceremony of the Land*, written by Howard Kester and Evelyn Smith. This ceremony was first performed at the 3rd convention of the Southern Tenant Farmers Union in Muskogee, Oklahoma, on January 17, 1937.

"The communists, if they ever learn to use southern leaders, would sweep these bottom lands like wildfire. Here, people out on the plantations are political babes, but they know how to shoot, and are physically very brave."

She raised the question of whether the Socialist Party would recognize the plight of the sharecropper, and formulate a program that would be vital enough to attract and hold these people. Martha Johnson then described Clay East and me:

"Mitchell is a sharecropper's son who has a cleaning works in Tyronza. He is what we Southerners call a "Reading Fool." When you come into his shop, you will find the *New York Times,* the *New Republic,* the *Milwaukee Leader, The Nation,* the *American Guardian,* the *New Leader,* the Memphis papers, and some communist literature. He is local secretary [of the Socialist Party] and the intellectual behind the gun. Clay East, believe it or not, is constable and town marshall! That worries Mitchell, but Clay says he doesn't intend that socialist meetings encounter any opposition, so he conceives it his duty to keep the job. He is a native, and carries much insight with the town and country around. He is developing into a good and forceful speaker. Both boys (they are quite young) promise to tear this country up for you when you come. Also, they promise the finest publicity for your meeting, a bigger audience than the schoolhouse will hold, and the best care for yourself." And she added, "a day spent here will put the Socialist Party on a higher plane than ever in the past." The communication was signed: "Yours for the Revolution, Martha B. Johnson."

On February 18, 1934, East and I met Norman Thomas at the railway station in Memphis, and we spent the morning driving him around the cotton plantation country. We were greatly impressed with Thomas. He was then in his early fifties, over six feet tall, with silvery white hair. I, the small-town rebel who had read too many books, found much in common with the towering intellectual from New York City who had run for President in 1928 and 1932, and who was to be the Socialist Party presidential candidate four more times. East seemed reserved at first, maybe because I was monopolizing the conversation. Thomas had a delightful sense of humor and made witty remarks about Boss Crump taking better care of the animals in the zoo than of the residents of Memphis, and about the "Empty State Building," as he called the Empire State skyscraper, then one of the newer monuments to American capitalism in New York City.

Clay followed the back country roads so we could visit some sharecroppers. The Whites, a family of six, had just been evicted. We found them on the roadside huddled about a campfire in the midst of their household goods. Thomas asked White why they had been evicted. He replied, "The landlord said we were no longer needed after plowing up the cotton last spring." His wife added: "The children are too little to work yet, and the landlord wanted a family with larger children."

Thomas was impressed with the cleanliness of the two-room shacks we visited and with the native intelligence of the sharecroppers he talked with, the last being Mrs. Ed Boston. Thomas questioned us about the operation of the New Deal's Agricultural Adjustment Administration in the cotton country.

During lunch at Clay East's home, Norman Thomas told us that while he highly approved of our belonging to the Socialist Party, what was really needed was a sharecroppers' organization to fight for the rights of those being evicted and cast adrift, as well as for those being denied their share of the government payments for restricting cotton production. This was the real beginning of the Southern Tenant Farmers Union, which was formed some months later.

At the meeting held in the Tyronza High School auditorium, Clay East, acting as chairman, introduced Norman Thomas. I acted as usher. The audience was made up largely of plantation owners, their retainers, small businessmen and professional people from the nearby small towns. Possibly one-third of the crowd was composed of sharecroppers. One of these was Jim Reese, who came in just as Thomas started speaking. I offered him and his younger companion seats, but Jim allowed as how he didn't have time to stay. He had just been to the Tyronza Supply Store to pick up his rations and had a sack of flour on his shoulder and a piece of meat under his arm. Thomas launched into a slashing attack on the New Deal's Agricultural Adjustment Administration. Soon Reese became fascinated with the tall, silver-haired man on the platform, talking about problems that Reese had lived with all his life. He handed his rations to his companion and told him to stash them in a corner, then sat down and never moved his eyes from Thomas' face until the meeting ended. Jim Reese afterward joined the Union, and two years later was beaten nearly to death while leading a picket line with Frank Weems, a black sharecropper, near Earle, Arkansas.

The day after the meeting, the prominent citizens of Tyronza signed a letter and sent it to the Memphis papers protesting that Norman Thomas had abused their hospitality. Also, Oscar Johnston invited Clay and me to come to the Delta Pine and Land Company at Scott, Mississippi. Here, said the president of the South's largest cotton plantation (encompassing some 130,000 acres), we would not find any of the conditions that Norman Thomas had reported in Arkansas. This boast was later investigated and refuted. Also we learned that Oscar

Johnston had been one of the chief architects of the cotton section of the Agricultural Adjustment Act. Cully A. Cobb, the chief administrator of the Cotton Division of AAA, was also from Mississippi. Cobb, a former editor of a farm journal, had once been head of the Agricultural Extension Service in Mississippi and was also connected with the State Agricultural College at Starkville. Unknowingly, Norman Thomas had struck directly at the power structure of the cotton-growing South in his speech at the Tyronza High School that February day.

I wrote Thomas soon after that he had stirred up a hornet's nest. I also told him that he hd a new namesake, Norman Thomas White, born in an old truck where the homeless White family were still living. Later there was an exchange of letters between Thomas and the Whites, and Thomas and the Bostons.

The Agricultural Adjustment Act of 1933 was the New Deal's answer to the plight of the farmers in the midwest. In 1932, under the nominal leadership of 64-year-old Milo Reno, some of these farmers had formed the National Farm Holiday Association. These independent farmers were facing bankruptcy. Mortgages on their farms and livestock were being foreclosed by the banks and insurance companies. The protesting farmers tried to stop all production and sale of farm products. Milk was dumped on the ground; trucks were turned back at the market place. Hundreds of demonstrating farmers were jailed. Behind the scenes, directing the Farm Holiday movement was the Farmers National Action Committee, organized by members of the Communist Party, among them Lem Harris. Early in 1933, after declaring a moratorium on farm foreclosures, Roosevelt got through Congress the first Agricultural Adjustment Act. Under it, the producers of basic commodities—corn, cotton, and wheat—were required to destroy one-third of the crops produced that year, and to restrict production by 40 percent the following year. The theory was that prices were at rockbottom and agriculture was bankrupt because the farmers were producing more than could be sold in the market place. So, in 1933, southern sharecroppers and tenant farmers—over 8 million of them (5½ million white and 3 million black)—were ordered by the New Deal to plow up one-third of the cotton crop.

The sharecroppers of Eastern Arkansas sometimes said that the mules they used had more sense than some men. In 1933 when the cotton was plowed up, the mules balked at walking on the cotton rows. Every mule, from the time he was put to the plow, had been taught that the cotton plant was sacred. If he got too close to the plants, his head was jerked and he was hit with the plow-line. During the plow-up, the mules were reported to have let out vociferous brays of protest. Some people like

Norman Thomas pointed out that it didn't make sense to restrict cotton production when children lacked clothes, and families did not have enough bed sheets and pillow cases. Burning corn and wheat and killing little pigs made even less sense.

This program wrecked the already desperate lives of nearly a million sharecropper families who were no longer needed on the land; they were evicted and set adrift to roam the countryside, and crowd up with others in the small southern towns and cities. Under the terms of the AAA, the landlords were sent all of the money, and they were supposed to parcel it out among their tenants and sharecroppers. In "darned near half of the cases the sharecroppers didn't get a nickel of the money" said Gardner Jackson, who, along with Lee Pressman and Jerome Frank, was fired by the Department of Agriculture for their efforts to see that justice was given to sharecroppers.*

A section of AAA of 1933 provided that each producer should receive his share of the "parity" payment on all cotton plowed under that year, or not grown the following years. There was also an ambiguous Section 7 that provided protection for the rights of tenants:

The producer shall endeavor in good faith to bring about the reduction of acreage contemplated in this contract in such a manner as to cause the least possible amount of labor, economic and social disturbance, and to this end, insofar as possible, he shall effect the acreage reduction as nearly ratable as practicable among the tenants on this farm; shall, insofar as possible, maintain on this farm the normal number of tenants and other employees; shall permit all tenants to continue in the occupancy of their houses on this farm, rent free for the years 1934 and 1935 (unless any such tenant shall so conduct himself as to become a nuisance or a menace to the welfare of the producer); during such years shall afford such tenants or employees, without cost, access for fuel to such wood land belonging to this farm as he may designate; shall permit such tenants the use of an adequate portion of the rented acres to grow food and feed crops for home consumption and for pasturage of domestically used livestock; and for such of the rented acres shall permit the reasonable use of work animals and equipment in exchange for labor.

Howard Kester in *Revolt Among the Sharecroppers*, commented on Section 7:

It is clear that some thought was given to the protection of tenants and sharecroppers from displacement from the land. However, a close examination reveals the essential weakness of the document written in favor of the propertied interests throughout. "The producer will *endeavor . . .* to bring about reduction as to cause the *least possible* amount of labor, economic and social disturbance, and . . . *insofar as possible,* he shall effect the acreage reduction *as nearly ratable*

*March of Time, August 1936. "Land of Cotton" issue.

as practicable among tenants . . . shall *insofar as possible,* maintain . . . the *normal* number of tenants, shall permit all tenants to continue in the occupancy of their houses . . . free . . . (*unless any such tenant shall so conduct himself as to become a nuisance or menace to the welfare of the producer*)." It is readily seen that the contract placed the "producer" in complete control of the enforcement of all or any part of the contract. He was under obligation to no one save county agents who were in most cases incapable or unwilling to see that the contracts were strictly observed. He (the producer) himself, in most instances, was the interpreter of whether he had reasonably fulfilled the contract. Only in instances of the most flagrant violations were they ever cancelled.*

Socialist Activity

Soon after the Norman Thomas visit to Tyronza, the Socialist Party of Arkansas held its annual convention in Tyronza. There were about a dozen delegates from the central and western Arkansas locals. All of the others were from eastern Arkansas. At the convention, there was talk of organizing a union of sharecroppers about Tyronza. There were quite a number of both black and white members of the socialist locals at Tyronza and Truman in the audience.

Much to my surprise, I was elected State Secretary of the Arkansas Socialist Party. The nomination was made by the incumbent State Secretary, Billy Gilbert of Ink, Arkansas, and seconded by Clay Fulks, a delegate from Commonwealth College. Both were from across the state, near the Oklahoma line. The recognition was probably due to the fact that we had two or three hundred dues-paying members in the two Eastern Arkansas locals, and also that we had just been visited by Norman Thomas, the Socialist Party leader. We had more members in Poinsett County than in the rest of the entire Arkansas organization. I became a national organizer and was (sometimes) paid a $40-a-month salary promised by the national office in Chicago. The National Secretary was Clarence Senior. The state convention set a goal of a thousand members for the year 1934. We did not attain it, because we were busy making a survey of wages and working conditions of sharecroppers under the New Deal and laying the groundwork for the union.

Later in the year I was named as an Arkansas delegate to the 1934 National Convention of the Socialist Party of America held in Detroit. It was here that I first heard about the Reuthers. Walter and Victor were members of the Socialist Party, and were at that time in the Soviet Union working in an automobile plant near Moscow. I believe Roy Reuther was at the Detroit convention.

*Covici-Fiede, 1936, p. 30.

There was a bitter interparty fight that ended with most of the New York members—called the Old Guard—walking out and taking with them the party machinery: the newspaper, bank accounts, mailing lists, furniture, and so on. I was a member of the Militant Caucus, spearheaded by Andrew Biemiller, Paul Porter and Clarence Senior. Ward Rodgers, another Arkansas delegate, was a member of the Revolutionary Policy Committee, whose chief, Jay Lovestone, was former General Secretary of the Communist Party USA. We Militants and RPCers won a Pyrrhic victory, adopting a meaningless resolution to require all members to accept the principle of the Class Struggle in order to belong to the party. This interparty feud set the stage for the ultimate disappearance of the Socialist Party as an effective political instrument in the United States.

The basic differences between the factions were that most of us younger members believed the "Cooperative Commonwealth" of the future could not be attained through the ballot box. We believed that it could be brought about by organization of a class conscious labor movement and the use of general strike to topple the capitalist system. While we did not reject armed revolution in the event of repression by reactionary fascist dictatorships, we did not advocate it. Those who were in the Revolutionary Policy Committee believed that the socialist world could not be brought into being except by violent revolution. They were communists, but without the Russian dressing.

Then there were the Social Democrats, represented by the Old Guard of New York City, who were devoted to evolutionary methods, including building an alliance with the leadership of the conservative AFL, and working toward a welfare state to improve the conditions of workers. They rejected all approaches other than those of the ballot box. The Old Guard controlled the newspaper, *New Leader*, in New York City. It had ties with the immigrant and ethnic organizations. Led by David Dubinsky, President of the International Ladies Garment Workers Union, and others, they eventually set up the Labor Party which in time became the Liberal Party in New York State. They made deals with the Democratic Party bosses and often held the balance of power in New York elections. Today the remnants of the Old Guard are in a faction called the Social Democrats USA, derisively called "Seducers" by those in the other fragments of a once promising movement. Among these are the Democratic Socialist Organizing Committee led by Michael Harrington; the Socialist Party, USA (mainly Milwaukee Socialists like Frank Zeidler, the last socialist mayor); and the New America Movement. The last is in many respects like the RPC of the 1930s.

There is also the Communist Party of the USA, which always follows the party line of the USSR, but it too is fragmented into extremist groups, such as the followers of Chairman Mao; and there are some native American, mainly black, factions even more extreme. The CPUSA seems almost respectable these days. There are also the followers of Leon Trotsky, known as the Socialist Workers Party, who, because of their rhetoric, seem to attract more FBI agents than workers. All claim to follow in the footsteps of Eugene V. Debs.

While in Detroit, I attended a meeting with Dr. Harry W. Laidler, Miss Mary Fox, and Norman Thomas, at which time the League for Industrial Democracy of New York City, agreed to pay the cost of a sharecroppers' survey. Although it was a bit far afield from physiology, which he taught at the University of Tennessee Medical College, Dr. William R. Amberson had promised Norman Thomas to direct the project and to prepare a report. Soon after our return to Arkansas, the study of the effect on sharecroppers of the New Deal's Agricultural Adjustment Administration program was underway. Clay East and I were involved in the interviews which covered over 300 families. The report was prepared by Dr. Amberson and later published, with an introduction by Norman Thomas, as a pamphlet called *Plight of the Sharecropper*, which received widespread attention. The Department of Agriculture in Washington had enlisted the social scientists of North Carolina in making a similar survey in the cotton South. This survey, directed by Dr. Calvin B. Hoover, was released prior to ours. The "Amberson Report," as it was first known, was strengthened because it was the more conservative of the two studies. Dr. Hoover estimated that nearly a million sharecroppers had been displaced by the coming of the New Deal in the cotton fields. Our estimate was half a million.

We Socialists Invited to Investigate South's Largest Plantation

Soon after the visit of Norman Thomas to Arkansas, Clay East and I had some correspondence with Oscar Johnston, manager of the 130,000-acre Delta Pine and Land Company at Scott, Mississippi, in the heart of the Delta. The company was owned by English cotton manufacturers, and the royal family were among the shareholders. There were 1,000 families and 38,000 acres in cotton on the plantation. Johnston said that Norman Thomas had found an isolated case in eastern Arkansas, and that no sharecroppers had been displaced on his plantation as a result of the plow-up of every third row or the 1934 restriction of cotton acreage. He invited us down to see for ourselves. So Dr. Amberson planned to make an investigation in Mississippi. The survey party consisted of Amberson, Clay East, and Robert O'Brien, a professor at Lemoyne College for Negroes in Memphis.

They arrived in the Delta too late in the day to start their study of the huge cotton plantation, so they secured rooms for the night in a small hotel in a nearby town. The hotel was built around an open courtyard. The patrons on the second floor could look across and see into the rooms of occupants across the way. Soon East and O'Brien found some free entertainment—a couple across the courtyard from their room was busily engaged in love making and had not bothered to pull down the window shades. The dignified Professor Amberson's attention was called to the sight. Amberson was outraged at such unseemly conduct in a respectable hotel, and only against his better judgment was he finally persuaded not to go down and protest to the management of the hotel.

The next day the investigators got an early start out on the plantation where they talked to sharecroppers and others, and counted the empty houses. At lunchtime they stopped at a local restaurant, where they attracted considerable attention. After eating, Amberson, the dignified college professor, donned his black Homburg hat and went to pay the bill, whereupon the three were arrested by the County Sheriff on suspicion that they were members of the Dillinger Gang bent on robbing the nearest bank. Amberson protested. Fortunately, he had with him a copy of Oscar Johnston's invitation. A telephone call brought Johnston down to identify the suspects. Toward the end of his long life, William R. Amberson wrote the story of how he was mistaken for John Dillinger, the notorious bank robber of the 1930s.

The survey party found that conditions on Johnston's plantation in Mississippi were about the same as they were on plantations in eastern Arkansas. Because of the AAA acreage reduction program there were many wage workers who had once been sharecroppers, but even more had left to go to the large cities such as Detroit, Chicago, Gary, Memphis, and St. Louis, with stops in the small towns along the way. Nearly a hundred houses were vacant on the Delta Pine.

Unlike Johnston, Hiram Norcross, one of the larger planters in the Tyronza area, made no pretense about his position on payments to his sharecroppers: Since they had nothing invested in the crop but their labor and the labor of their wives and children, they should not share equally in the government payments for plowing up a third of their crop. Norcross said that perhaps they should be given a third of the government money. This was not acceptable to either his sharecroppers, or to the other plantation owners. One of the smaller planters, Jim Prestige of Tyronza, said the damned fool should have kept his mouth shut and padded the sharecroppers' accounts at the commissary. He could have gotten it all, and no one would ever have known the difference. That was in '33.

Then, in the spring of 1934, after crops had been planted, Hiram Norcross checked his books and found that he was allowing his sharecroppers an excess of credit at the Tyronza Supply Store. Usually, advances were made on the basis of a dollar each month for each acre being produced, starting March 1 and ending July 1. But Alex East (an uncle of Clay East), his plantation manager, being a humane man, had estimated the acreage of most of the sharecroppers on the basis of the family's actual need for groceries and other supplies. Perhaps a sharecropper had only 20 acres in cotton, and several children still too small to work in the fields. The manager just allowed that he had 30 acres, and could therefore draw up to 30 dollars a month on credit at the company store. Norcross hired a surveyor and measured each man's land. He then summarily evicted 23 of the nearly 150 sharecropper families. These people had no place to go. It was too late to find another place to farm. They tried to find a lawyer who would file a lawsuit against Norcross. The first rumblings of open revolt against the landowners in Arkansas were heard here. That anything was accomplished was due to the Socialist Party being organized, and to the Unemployed League being formed in Tyronza in early 1933, which brought jobs to those who could not get on the CWA relief program.

Revolt of the Sharecroppers: Founding the Southern Tenant Farmers Union

In July 1934, a meeting was held in the Sunnyside Schoolhouse adjoining the Fairview plantation owned by Hiram Norcross. Eleven white and seven black men met to form the Southern Tenant Farmers Union. Most of those attending made crops for Norcross, or had been evicted after starting work that year. Alvin Nunnally from the Emerich plantation near Tyronza was acting as chairman. When Clay East and I arrived, Nunnally was saying that what was needed was a legal organization like the FECU of A (Farmers Educational and Co-operative Union of America) and that it should be for all sharecroppers. Nunnally was also warning the group that if they did what some of those present advocated and lynched a few planters, they would all swing for it. Burt Williams, about 65 years old, asked whether every white man in the meeting did not agree with Nunnally that there should be only one union for all sharecroppers, both black and white. While some may have had reservations, no one took issue with Williams, who also told how his pappy had ridden with the Ku Klux Klan and had helped drive the last republican office holders from adjoining Crittenden County. Burt asked the black group what they thought about the subject of a joint, mixed union. Isaac Shaw then spoke for all and said that as long as they agreed that they would have a legal organization, with membership open to white and black sharecroppers, and stood by their principles, nothing could destroy the new movement. Shaw also told of being involved in the Farmers and Farm Laborers Association over in Philips County, which was all black, and was wiped out in the Elaine Massacre.

Clay East, in an interview in 1972* said he didn't remember how many were present, but estimated the racial mixture was about 50–50 and there wasn't any strong dissent against a mixed union. "We had to have an understanding among the union members, and there couldn't have been much understanding if we had two unions." East said he told the persons gathered in the schoolhouse that if they were going to have a union to start signing up. "We had some cards, and all there joined up." Clay continued: "Mitch sent out word to all socialists about the starting of the Union, and invited them to come and help. The first to arrive was Ward Rodgers, and the next was J. R. Butler."

Ward Rodgers was a young Methodist minister who had a circuit of churches near Paris in western Arkansas. One of the churches was at Pumpkin Center, across the mountains. Rodgers was about 23 years old, a slender young man, five feet eight inches tall, with a moustache like the one worn by Adolf Hitler. He had been born in the Big Thicket section of east Texas, but grew up in Alva, Oklahoma. He had attended Boston University, and then Vanderbilt Theological Seminary, where he had met Claude Williams and come under the influence of Howard Kester. Somewhere along the way he had joined the Socialist Party and become a member of its left wing extension, Jay Lovestone's Revolutionary Policy Committee. I had met him at the Arkansas convention in Tyronza, and at the national convention in Detroit. The members of Rodgers' churches were poverty-stricken coal miners and subsistence farmers. The young preacher's pay was small. He had to make his rounds by hitchhiking and on foot. It was an inside joke in the union that when Rodgers left his church at Pumpkin Center to answer the call to come help the sharecroppers organize, he didn't bring any of his parishioners' money with him. (They had none.)

Next to arrive was John Russell Butler (always called J. R.). A socialist most of his life, at various times Butler had been a tenant farmer, an oil field worker, a country schoolteacher and, when the union was organized, he was helping his brother run a sawmill at Pangburn, Arkansas. Although he had been a member of the Working Class Union—the rural antiwar movement sponsored by socialists in the

*Southern Exposure, op. cit.

southwestern states—as soon as the United States entered World War I, J. R. Butler joined the army and saw action in France. Butler was a self-styled Arkansas hillbilly, and he looked the part. He was nearly six feet tall, thin as a rail, and wore his hair straight. He was very reticent about his personal life. We knew he had been married, but it was a while before we found out he had two children. From time to time he would disappear, saying he was going to visit some folks in Oklahoma. He was a good speaker, and always made a favorable impression on visitors: He looked the way they thought a sharecropper ought to look. After Butler became president of the STFU they were even more impressed with him.

In an interview in 1975 Rodgers said, "As I remember, we started calling meetings. . . . Most meetings were held at black churches and schoolhouses. Right at the beginning, the whites and blacks came to the same meetings. In a number of areas it was all black. We ran into sections where they were all white as we got into the hill country."*

Butler: "None of us who were really interested in getting the work started would agree to having a separate union or separate meetings. We had threats, but nobody ever tried to break up a meeting. I think our effort at organizing was actually the beginning of the civil rights movement."† Butler remembered that for the first two years he never drew a salary for his work with the union, and very little money even for his expenses. He would come over to Tyronza from Pangburn, do what he could to help the union, and then return to work for his brother in the sawmill. Butler wrote the first union constitution, which was based on the bylaws of the Oklahoma Renters Union, sent by Oscar Ameringer, the editor of the *American Guardian* in Oklahoma City. Ward Rodgers recalled that Butler was made chief organizer, and he came up with the idea that the organizer should get a percentage of the dues. "We didn't go for it," Ward commented, "and probably a good thing, because it would not have amounted to much anyway."

I Tell Planter and Gunmen to Leave Union Meeting

East recalled an incident that occurred north of Tyronza in the Dubbs community in the early days of the union.

"Butler was there, and Mitch was there. We had a good turnout, possibly 100 to 150 people. Just before the meeting started, here came one of the big planters from over there, Mr. Sloan. He came in with a couple of big deputies, with their pistols buckled on them, and just came marching in there. He wanted to see what

*STFU supplement, "The Green Rising," (MCA).
†*Southern Exposure,* op. cit.

was going on. You don't know how a lot of those colored people must have felt when the boss-man came in and saw them at a union meeting. They were a little shaky, but I will say this, that the colored boys back then, if anything were more solid than the whites. They would go ahead, sacrifice, get killed or beat up, anything else, before they'd give up. I had a big six-shooter on, and a pretty bad reputation. They knew I wouldn't do to fool with. [Clay was still township constable.] So I got up and told them, if you folks are going to be scared because your boss walked in here, just quieten down, now this thing is perfectly legal. We have corporation papers, and we got our constitution.

Well he (Mr. Sloan) wanted a copy. Mitch said: "Well, if you got ten cents, you can have one," so he sold him a copy of the constitution. Then Mitch proceeded to tell him: "You folks are not eligible for membership in this [union] so we'll ask you to leave."

East said he had often wondered what I would have done if Sloan had refused to go, but as it happened, Sloan left. "He and his men trooped out of there, six-shooters and all. There were a raft of union members signed up that night. It did't take much. Those folks were in a bind, and were being mistreated. When these things were pointed out to them, there was no trouble in signing them up."

The Rust Cotton Picking Machine

Howard Kester paid a visit to Tyronza during the fall 1934 at the urgent invitation of Ward H. Rodgers, his former classmate at the Vanderbilt Theological Seminary. Another visitor to Tyronza around that time was the Director of Commonwealth College, Lucien Koch, a young man in his late twenties. Both were to have a role in the union. Koch, a graduate of the University of Wisconsin, had been persuaded by the sponsors of the college, located in the mountains near Mena, Arkansas, to make Commonwealth a resident college for workers. Commonwealth was an offshoot of the Llano Colony founded by Job Harriman, one-time Los Angeles labor lawyer and Socialist candidate for Vice President, and later for Mayor of Los Angeles. Harriman had an excellent chance of winning the mayoral election until he became involved in the defense of the McNamara brothers who had bombed the *Los Angeles Times.* When Clarence Darrow had the two McNamaras enter a guilty plea, Harriman's career as a politician and lawyer in Los Angeles came to an end. He organized a communal group of others like himself, who were ready to withdraw from life under capitalism and build a model socialist order. The colony was started in California and soon moved to southwest Louisiana, where it had existed for more than twenty years. The educators who set up Commonwealth in Louisiana broke away from the Llano Colony and relocated the college in western Arkansas.

Koch had led a delegation to "bloody" Harlan County, Kentucky, where the coal miners were trying to organize a union. There he and the students who had brought a truckload of food and clothing to the striking miners were beaten up by the coal company retainers and driven out of the state. Koch told me that if I ever got into trouble and needed help I should send a telegram to Commonwealth, and a delegation would come immediately. He asked me about the location of a plantation near Joyner, where the Rust brothers were operating a cotton-picking machine. He said the Rusts had spent some time both at Llano Colony and at Commonwealth while conducting their experiments with the machine. I had never seen a mechanical cotton harvester so I accompanied Koch on a visit to John and Mack Rust. John, the original inventor of the machine, was then about 40 years old, and Mack, a mechanical engineer, was several years younger.

John Rust had gotten the basic idea for the machine while walking through a Texas cotton field early one morning. The dew on the open cotton bolls made the cotton stick to his fingers. So Rust made a spindle, which when damped, lifted the cotton directly from the boll. This was the basic principle of the cotton-picking machine he invented. John had been a socialist for many years. In the 1920s he ran for Governor of Texas on the Farm Labor ticket, which was also supported by the Communist Party. Years later, Whittaker Chambers, the unsavory character in the Pumpkin Papers case that brought Richard Nixon to public notice, used this in an effort to discredit John Rust. John was concerned that his invention not be used to increase the misery of the southern sharecroppers. He offered to apply all profits to aid displaced people, and proposed to take only a modest salary for his efforts. He had tried to interest federal Emergency Relief Administration people like Harry Hopkins and Aubrey Williams and visionaries such as Rexford G. Tugwell and Henry Wallace of the U.S. Department of Agriculture, in government ownership and manufacture of his invention. He knew that it would revolutionize cotton production and that one machine would eliminate jobs for 40 field hands. Rust had gotten a contract to exhibit his machine in the Soviet Union, and had spent several months in the southern part of Russia demonstrating it. The government of the USSR purchased a single row model, and years later, John and I saw in a newsreel an improved version of the Rust machine operating in Russia.

Following that initial visit with Koch, the Rust brothers and I became close friends. Often, John Rust would attend STFU meetings, and he participated in some of our related activities, such as the operation of the cooperative farm in Mississippi.

In Search of a Lawyer to Free a Preacher

By the end of 1934 we had more than a thousand members and plans to start operation in other states. Considering that the majority of sharecroppers in Tyronza Township had already become members of the union, two ministers—Ward H. Rodgers (white) and C. H. Smith (black)—were dispatched to nearby Crittenden County as organizers. They were holding a meeting in a Negro church near Gilmore, an even small town than Tyronza, when a band of plantation riding bosses interrupted the proceedings. Deputy Sheriff Benton Moore, a long-time friend of Clay East, rescued Rodgers and drove him to the Poinsett County line. But Smith, the black minister, was beaten and carried to jail at Marion, the county seat.

Word spread rapidly that one of the charter members of the union, C. H. Smith, was being held in Crittenden County jail. There were threats among the members to storm the jail and rescue Smith. East was fearful of a race riot like the one he had witnessed in Elaine. I telegraphed the American Civil Liberties Union in New York City, asking for names of lawyers who might assist in freeing the union man. Director Roger N. Baldwin replied immediately with the names of three ACLU lawyers in Memphis. East and I hurried over there, and first thing we did was consult with Professor Amberson at the University of Tennessee Medical School. Amberson knew that the ACLU attorney, Robert Keebler, had just left to take a job with the National Recovery Administration in Washington; the second man on the list, Judge Pitmann, was ill, but the third, an assistant city attorney, Abe Waldauer, agreed to see us. After hearing about the problem, Waldauer said: "Boys, you are real diplomats. I admire your courage, but here is one Jewish lawyer who will not go to Crittenden County to get a Nigra preacher out of jail." Waldauer said that he had been in the Lost Battalion in Argonne Forest during World War I, and that he had left all his bravery over there in France. Waldauer was a Single Taxer, and presented both East and me with a copy of *Progress and Poverty* by Henry George. Waldauer was one of the few men in Memphis who were counted as liberals. He was on the list of lawyers of the American Civil Liberties Union. However, he was among those who made up the Ed Crump political machine that held Memphis in its iron grip for over forty years.

As we headed back across the Memphis bridge to Arkansas, East said that since we couldn't get a lawyer to get Smith out of jail, we might just as well fold up the union and call it quits. I refused even to consider such a thing, and said that we would find a way. East went on to say that if someone did something to him, he would stand and fight with his bare fists, with a knife, or a gun, and that I would probably run, rather than fight. But, he said, I had something he lacked, which was moral courage. I would not admit that I was defeated. Years later, a newspaperman told me he was going to write a profile of me, and title it "The Man Who Never Knew [when to quit]," perhaps meaning the same thing.

Clay East's remark about the difference in our approaches was proven true. In the first critical two years of the union's life, he was in and out of Arkansas. He always came in when the going was rough. He faced down two mobs of planters. Then, lacking my stubbornness, or knowledge of plantation life, he moved to Arizona and remained there from that time on, out of the controversy.

Seeing that I was determined to continue, East then remarked that he knew a lawyer in Marked Tree, C. T. Carpenter, who had come to Tyronza in the spring to hear Norman Thomas. Carpenter defended some strikers in Truman some years ago. Also, he had been run off a plantation where he had gone to see about a settlement for a share-cropper he represented. The next morning, East and I, and Alvin Nunnally, who was also a founder and was at the time Vice President of the STFU, went to Marked Tree. Carpenter had represented Nunnally in a lawsuit a few years before and Nunnally was sure that Carpenter would take the case. We climbed the stairs to Carpenter's office on the second floor over a store, and waited in his outer room until he was free to see us. Tall, distinguished, wearing a stiff high collar and a string tie, Carpenter looked like a gentleman of the Old South, which is exactly what he was. He listened carefully to why Smith had been arrested. The idea that a group of plantation riding bosses could storm any kind of a peaceable meeting was an outrage to his Jeffersonian beliefs. He set forth two things that we must do. The first was to retain him and promise to pay him a hundred dollars to represent the union in the Smith case. As East afterwards said, "Mitch hired C. T. Carpenter on the spot, though the union didn't have ten dollars in its treasury, and Mitchell probably had even less money of his own. But then, Mitch was a lot like Eugene V. Debs, who never knew the value of a dollar either." The second condition was that we should get fifteen or twenty of the union's white members and bring them to the courthouse in Marion on the day of the trial. Carpenter made a telephone call and arranged for a hearing to be held two days later. He told us: "Now, just have your white members come," he told us. "Don't bring a single Negro with you. Wait until you see me go into the courtroom. Then bring your men in, and quietly take seats. Don't let anyone say a word, or even talk among themselves."

White Union Members Rescue Black Organizer

On the appointed day, East's car and mine were loaded with white members, and a truck was rented and loaded with white men also. J. R. Butler, who was the chief organizer, rode with the truck and said he had never seen so many crippled men in any one group in his life. Nearly everyone had made or borrowed a walking cane to be used in case of attack. They all hobbled in, giving the impression that each man was physically handicapped. They took their seats without a word. C. H. Smith was brought in. Mr. Carpenter made his plea, and the prisoner was paroled in the custody of the union attorney. When the hearing was over, the white members filed out with C. H. Smith in their midst; and they returned to Tyronza and on down the road south to the Sunnyside School. Preacher Smith was the speaker of the day. He was greeted with shouts of welcome from the crowd of white and black members gathered in the schoolhouse yard. He told how he was beaten with a rubber hose to make him name those who belonged to the union in Crittenden County. He had refused. He had just prayed for the men who beat him, for he knew the union would get him out soon. Thereafter, the few holdouts among the black sharecroppers joined the union. Black and white unity had carried the day. There was never again any question that the union members would come to the aid of their brothers, black or white, in time of need.

Soon afterwards on the basis of Section 7 of the AAA, Mr. Carpenter filled a lawsuit for the union in behalf of the 23 members who had been evicted by Hiram Norcross. It was not until several months later that a ruling was handed down that since sharecroppers were not parties to the contract between the producer and the Secretary of Agriculture, they had no right under the act to sue in a court of law. The Supreme Court of Arkansas later upheld this decision. The Secretary of Agriculture, Henry A. Wallace, was urged by people within his department to intervene in the court test of AAA in behalf of the sharecroppers. Wallace, however, caved in under pressure of the planters, and ushered in "the century of the common man"—that he later proclaimed so enthusiastically—by allowing millions of farm people to be dispossessed from the land. Before it was settled we got to talk to Wallace about this question because of an invitation from another organization.

I had heard about a group called the Alabama Sharecroppers Union, and that the Communist Party was active in it, just as the socialists were in the forefront in Arkansas. I had read not only Karl Marx, but also the writings of Lenin, and I believed that there could be more than one road to socialism. Therefore, when letters and telegrams came from the Alabama Sharecroppers Union and from Donald Henderson, who then published a paper called the *Rural Worker*, I welcomed them and responded cordially. I remembered what Charlie McCoy had said when he reported voting for Earl Browder and James W. Ford, since the Socialist Party was not on the ballot. Ford was black, and McCoy was criticized by some of his friends for voting for a "nigger." McCoy replied that he would rather have a black friend in the White House than a white enemy. So when Donald Henderson invited the Southern Tenant Farmers Union to send a delegation to a Washington conference of rural workers, farmers, and sawmill workers, I proposed to the union executive board that our representatives not only attend the conference, but call on the Secretary of Agriculture as well.

Sharecroppers Go To Washington

Collections were taken up at every STFU meeting during the month of December 1934. Two white members, Alvin Nunnally and Walter Moskop, and two black members, E. B. McKinney and N. W. Webb, were chosen to go to Washington, D.C. I was also in the delegation since I had an old car and could drive them. Also having been there before, I presumably knew where it was. And so five of us set out on what in those days was a journey of nearly 1,000 miles. Not knowing where we could find a place to stay overnight with two blacks in the group, we decided to drive straight through to Washington. Late one night, in the Shenandoah Valley of Virginia, we became lost on an unmarked detour. I stopped at a well-lighted camp a mile or so off the main road. Assuming this was one of the new C.C.C. camps I had read about, Walter Moskop and I walked up to the gate. Finding it slightly ajar, we pushed it open and walked on into a building where I noticed that there were many young white men asleep in double bunkbeds, and wondered why they had gone to sleep with the electric lights on. There was an elderly man sitting next to a round, wood-burning stove. Apparently it was his duty to keep the fire going through the night. I approached him and asked if he could tell us the way to get to Roanoke. The old man replied that he just didn't know. I then asked: "Is this a C.C.C. camp?"

"No, son," said the keeper of the fire, "you are in a convict camp."

Moskop and I didn't wait for any further information. We didn't even go back to the gate, but jumped that fence just as fast as ever we could. Walter landed in a briar patch, and tore out through the vines without regard for the scratches on his face and hands. I landed in a clear spot. We arrived back at the car at about the same time though. "Let's get the hell out of here; that is a state convict camp." If the place had been better guarded, we might have been shot as escaping prisoners.

We lost no time in getting away from there, and we arrived at an early hour in Washington. We crossed the Potomac River bridge, and I recognized the Washington Monument, and the U.S. Department of Agriculture buildings. Exhausted by the long trip, we pulled up on a side street near the intersection of 14th and Constitution, and fell asleep. I had driven a thousand miles without any sleep at all. Guess I didn't trust anyone else to drive my 1926 Moon that I had bought for forty dollars that day in 1933 when President Roosevelt closed the banks.

About 7 A.M. we awoke. Traffic was beginning to move about the city. The delegation, thinking to get an early start on the Washington farmers, went promptly to the Administration Building. A night watchman, elderly and unarmed, came to the big front door and asked what we wanted so early in the morning. When told that we were there to see the Secretary of Agriculture, the watchman replied that we should return about 9 o'clock, as none of the top officials arrived before then.

We then looked for a place to get a hot meal—our first in 48 hours— but could find nothing open. Finally, we located a delicatessen and settled for some cheese, crackers, baloney, and cokes. After breakfasting in the car, we went to see the Washington Monument, but it too was closed. At 9 o'clock, we returned to the Department of Agriculture. By that time, a guard was stationed at the desk near the front door, and he directed us to the Secretary's office.

The First Sit-Down in the Department of Agriculture

Followed by the rest of the delegation, I was soon in the Secretary's outer office. I told the receptionist that we were a delegation from Arkansas representing the Southern Tenant Farmers Union, and that we wished to see Mr. Henry Wallace. The receptionist asked if we had an appointment to see the Secretary. When told that we did not, the receptionist informed us that Mr. Wallace was in conference that morning and could not be disturbed. I was at a loss to know what to do next, but black E. B. McKinney came to my rescue. Said McKinney in his most respectful manner: "Ma'am, if Mr. Wallace is busy, we will just sit down here and wait for him." With that, the entire group took seats. This was probably the first sit-down ever to occur in the Department of Agriculture. The young woman became flustered, and obviously did not know what to do about the strange group of people who refused to go away.

Then I recalled that C. T. Carpenter had written a letter of introduction to the Undersecretary of Agriculture, Paul H. Appleby. The receptionist accepted the letter and rushed it to Mr. Appleby who soon appeared, and when we told him we had driven day and night to Washington from Memphis and wanted to see Secretary Wallace, Appleby assured us that he would get the Secretary out to meet with the delegation. Mr. Wallace soon came to the outer office and listened to the group most sympathetically. I asked for a real investigation of the plight of the sharecroppers under the AAA program. I told Wallace that every time the sharecroppers complained, their complaints were turned over to the plantation owners, the very men whom they wanted investigated. McKinney added: "Mr. Wallace, we know you intend to do right by our folks in Arkansas, but we are getting a whitewash by the cotton people who are working for you."

I told Wallace that A. E. Miller, an AAA investigator, had said to me early in the fall of 1934, that sharecroppers were lazy, shiftless and no account, and he had advised me to leave them alone as the planters were all my friends. Wallace's face flushed with anger:

"I think I have a person who will make a thorough investigation."

The person he had in mind was Mrs. Mary Connor Myers, who had just joined his legal staff, after working on the Al Capone case for the Treasury Department. Wallace then told the delegation to go back and tell their fellow members that they had seen the Secretary of Agriculture and that he had promised a full investigation of their complaints. Wallace told us not to say who was coming to Arkansas, but just to assure everyone that steps were being taken. We promised to follow his instructions. We also discussed the lawsuit filed recently by the union's attorney, Mr. Carpenter, against Hiram Norcross for violation of the Section 7 of the AAA cotton contract. I urged that the Department of Agriculture intervene in the case and aid the sharecroppers in their efforts to uphold the letter of the AAA contracts. Wallace promised full consideration and suggested that the Undersecretary, Paul Appleby, arrange a meeting for us with the USDA's Consumer Counsel group.

Within minutes, the delegation was received at Jerome Frank's office. Frank and two young lawyers on his staff, Lee Pressman and Alger Hiss, were present. Both of these young men were destined to make their mark in public life. Pressman, a New York lawyer, was later fired by Wallace in the purge of the AAA, along with Gardner Jackson and Jerome Frank, for activity in behalf of the sharecroppers. Hiss escaped the AAA purge but in the 1940s he became the victim of the ambitious Richard Nixon, when he was convicted of perjury in the celebrated Pumpkin Papers trial. Pressman eventually became the chief counsel of the CIO. Jackson became the Washington representative of the Southern Tenant

Farmers Union and of other groups for whom there was no spokesman in the capitol.

Communists and Socialists in Washington

The delegation also met with Cully A. Cobb, head of the cotton section of the AAA, with whom we were able to establish no rapport at all. We then attended the Conference of Agricultural Workers that was getting underway in the Department of Labor auditorium. It took most of the morning to get clearance to use the auditorium. Red baiters on Capitol Hill had been informed that Donald Henderson was a member of the central committee of the Communist Party of the USA. Because of Henderson, congressmen were pressing Frances Perkins, Secretary of Labor, to deny the delegates the use of the hall. Some compromise was reached whereby a temporary chairman convened the conference, which then proceeded to elect Henderson as permanent chairman. Madame Perkins then welcomed the delegates to Washington. After these preliminaries, each delegation was asked to make a report on their activities. It was late in the afternoon when I was called upon to speak for the Southern Tenant Farmers Union. I stood up, got as far as "Ladies and gentlemen," and promptly fell asleep, standing on the rostrum. Again, E. B. McKinney saved the day for the STFU by making the report.

I had made contact with the Washington socialist local, so Val R. Lorwin and his wife, Madge, both employed at the Department of Labor, offered to share their small apartment with some of us share-cropper delegates. Years later, Val R. Lorwin, charged with having been a communist, was suspended from the State Department. After two years, Lorwin was given a hearing before the Loyalty Board. The charge, it was revealed, had been based on the word of a Cornell University classmate who had been living at the Lorwin's apartment while he looked for a job in the New Deal. This man, who apparently had absolutely no sense of humor, claimed that one night in early 1935, he had come home to find a group of strange-looking people in the living room. He had asked what was going on, and Val had replied, "Oh, we're having a Communist Party meeting." The so-called friend had accepted this at face value. Val Lorwin was the only person fingered by Senator Joe McCarthy in the 1950s ever to face loyalty charges in the Department of State. I made a personal appearance in that hearing, bringing with me a letter in which Lorwin warned me that the Alabama Sharecroppers Union was Communist-led and to be avoided. The letter is probably still in the Loyalty Board files.

Preacher Rodgers Calls a Meeting

Greatly elated by the results of the Washington trip, the sharecropper delegation left early the following morning for Arkansas. We sent a telegram asking Ward Rodgers to alert each local to have a representative in Marked Tree on January 15 to hear the delegates' report.

Back in Tyronza, Rodgers was having his own troubles. Since he had left his circuit-riding churches in western Arkansas to help the STFU, the union had helped him to get a job with the Federal Emergency Relief Adult Education Project, teaching black and white sharecroppers reading, writing, and arithmetic. After a six-week course of training in preparation for this work, Rodgers had returned to Arkansas and started to work. He had classes underway long before the delegation was sent to Washington. One of these classes, held in a Negro church near Tyronza, was disrupted one night by a band of planters, riding bosses, and deputy sheriffs, who claimed they had been sent by the school board to investigate charges that he was teaching communism and socialism to mixed groups, in violation of state segregation and criminal syndicalism laws. Rodgers was ordered to report the next morning to the principal of the Tyronza High School, R. A. Lynch. Lynch advised Rodgers to cease his activities and leave the county. He said that if Rodgers did not do so, he would likely be reported missing one day soon. Rodgers protested that this was a Ku Klux Klan threat. Lynch told him to call it what he liked, but if he valued his life, he had best leave.

That afternoon the delegation was scheduled to report in the Marked Tree lodge hall. When Rodgers arrived at the hall, there were so many people there that he decided to meet in the town square where there was a bandstand that was used in political rallies and by itinerant preachers. Rodgers called the meeting to order. Walter Moskop made a brief report. He was followed by Alvin Nunnally. E. B. McKinney and N. W. Webb were to appear, and then I was to make the final report. Rodgers asked if the Reverend Webb of Birdsong was present. Receiving no reply, he called for Mr. McKinney to come to the platform. I had arrived just in time to hear McKinney's name being called. As I walked through the crowd, I overheard Fred Stafford, the deputy prosecuting attorney, saying in a loud voice to a stenographer who was taking down in shorthand everything that was being said, "Did you hear that Yankee agitator calling that nigger 'Mister' McKinney?" An elderly white sharecropper standing nearby told Stafford: "I'd ruther call McKinney *mister* than you."

5 Terror in Arkansas

The voice of the young Methodist minister turned adult education teacher, who was acting as chairman of the meeting, boomed out across the town square: "I can lead a mob to lynch any planter in Poinsett County." The crowd of 1,500 sharecroppers threw their hats in the air and roared their approval. There were shouts of, "Come on, Rodgers! Let's go get them!"

When this threat of direct action was made, I took over the platform. I told of our meeting with the Secretary of Agriculture, the promised investigation, and the widespread interest that we found in the plight of the sharecroppers—in and out of government. I also described what had happened the night before when Rodgers' class had been disrupted by a band of planters, and of their threats to drive him out of Arkansas. I then gave what Ward Rodgers afterwards called the "Dan Hoan speech" on the Ku Klux Klan. Dan Hoan was the long time socialist mayor of Milwaukee who also defied the K.K.K. in the same terms I used. "Ward Rodgers is staying at my house," I said. "If any bunch of sons of bitches with their heads in pillow cases come to my house, they are going to get the hell shot out of them."

After making my own fiery blast at the planters, I turned over the platform to Rodgers and McKinney and left town immediately to see H. J. Panes, the secretary of the Fairview Community Council (as we called local unions). He had sent word that he had collected quite a bit of money to help cover the expenses of the Washington trip. I had given Donald Henderson a postdated check for 25 dollars and there was not enough money in the union's bank account to cover it. I found that Panes, like all of the other union members working on the huge Norcross plantation, had been evicted and was living near Wynne in Cross County, many miles from Marked Tree. It was dark by the time I returned home. Lyndell greeted me with the news that Rodgers was in jail, and that Alvin Nunnally had sent word by his son that the law was coming to arrest us both. Nunnally thought all union leaders were being rounded up. As I drove to Nunnally's home, I heard someone running through the fields, knocking down the dead cotton stalks as he ran. I called out for Nunnally at the house, and Ocie, the oldest son, came to the door. On learning that it was not the law, Ocie coaxed his father to come in from his hiding place in the field. We two then left on a trip, going first to find Mr. Carpenter, the union's lawyer. He was away from Marked Tree, so we continued on to Memphis. En route, we unknowingly passed Dr. Amberson heading the other way to see what had happened to Rodgers. The Amberson party was accompanied by a reporter from the *Memphis Press-Scimitar.* They found Rodgers had first been sent to jail in Harrisburg, but had later been transported for "safekeeping" to Jonesboro, 35 miles west of Tyronza. When attorney Carpenter returned to his office in Marked Tree, he prepared a writ of habeas corpus, and a hearing was set for a few days later. Meanwhile, Rodgers remained in jail. As Mr. Carpenter said, "They threw the law books at Rodgers." He was charged among other things with Anarchy, Blasphemy and Barratry.

All over the country, newspapers ran stories and the radio carried the news of the arrest of Ward Rodgers. Newspaper headlines blazed: "Minister Accused of Anarchy in Arkansas," "FERA Teacher in Jail," "Vanderbilt Graduate Incarcerated." The Scripps Howard paper, the *Memphis Press-Scimitar* ran an editorial entitled: "Free this Man," although the editor said he did not approve of Rodgers' ideas. One account reported that Rodgers had a copy of *The Southern Worker*, the Communist Party paper that was published in Birmingham. It also said he was a member of the Socialist Party. Both statements were true.

Some days after his arrest, Rodgers was given a trial in the local Marked Tree Justice-of-Peace Court. A jury made up mainly of planters was impanelled to hear the evidence as presented by the deputy prosecuting attorney, Fred Stafford. Rodgers was asked if he was a Negro, and if not, why was he calling niggers "mister." At one point, the prosecutor referred to Rodgers as an agitator from "that Yankee school, Vanderbilt University." He apparently did not know that Vanderbilt was in Nashville. Rodgers was sentenced to six months in jail and fined $500. Attorney Carpenter arranged bond for the "youthful anarchist," which was signed by K. K. Kreir, a store owner in Marked Tree, and by a small farmer who owned a place near Marked Tree.

Among those who sat in on the trial was a lovely redhaired woman lawyer from Washington, D.C., Mrs. Mary Connor Myers, who had been sent by the Secretary of Agriculture to investigate the union's complaints of AAA violations. Mrs. Myers sat spellbound through the trial. The Arkansas Justice-of-Peace Court was a far cry from the orderly procedures she had known in her legal career.

Mary Connor Myers set up an office in Marked Tree and interviewed hundreds of sharecroppers who had not received their payments for plowing up the cotton in 1933, and who had been evicted because of the production restrictions the next year. Mrs. Myers found a kindred soul in the dignified country lawyer, C. T. Carpenter, whose office was across the hall from hers. Besides interviewing sharecroppers who came to see her about their subsidy payments, Mrs. Myers rented cars and hired drivers to show her about the countryside. Sometimes members of the union were so employed. Since there was an absence of hotel accomodations in Arkansas towns such as Marked Tree, Mrs. Myers commuted 35 miles from Memphis every day.

One cold winter day in February 1935, I drove Mrs. Myers to the Twist Brothers' plantation eighteen miles south of Marked Tree. The union was well organized there, and once the community council secretary was located, one man after another came in to give Mrs. Myers a sworn statement. I assisted her, and we continued working until late in the afternoon. It was then too late for her to catch the train, so I drove her to Memphis. Rain had turned to sleet, and the road was covered with ice. Mrs. Myers insisted that I stay overnight, rather than drive all the way back to Tyronza. After a good steak dinner at Jim's Place, we turned in at the Peabody Hotel. The red-haired Irish woman insisted that I take a hot bath in a big bathtub—a luxury I experienced for the first time in my life. In those days, it was said that the Mississippi Delta started in the lobby of the Peabody Hotel and ended in Catfish Row in Vicksburg. The hotel was the center of life for the cotton planters of Arkansas, Mississippi, and Tennessee.

The Mary Connor Myers Report was suppressed by Chester C. Davis, who was in charge of administering the AAA. After the Arkansas Supreme Court decision dismissed the union's lawsuit against Hiram Norcross, Davis said the report was "too hot to print." A member of Congress read it, however, and Mrs. Myers made an oral summary at a staff meeting within the Department of Agriculture in which she confirmed the STFU's complaints in nearly every detail.

About this time, a delegation from Commonwealth College arrived in Tyronza. The director, Lucien Koch, who had visited us early in the fall, was accompanied by two students. One was Atley Delaney, a young socialist from Boston, a large bear-like youngster who was a member of the Young Peoples' Socialist League. The other was Robert Reed, a Young Communist League member, originally from Texas. Reed was about 18 years old, but looked even younger. I gave him assignments that were least likely to bring him into conflict with the planters. Lucien Koch had volunteered to drive another organizer into adjoining Crittenden County. A meeting was being held at a Negro church on the outskirts of the town of Gilmore. At the last minute the local man who was to accompany Koch couldn't go, and Reed joined the Commonwealth College Director on the trip.

Reed and Koch went to Gilmore, about 10 miles east of Marked Tree. There was no local organization; they were in virgin territory. Some members from Marked Tree had helped set up the meeting, but were not there that night. There was a crowd of 40 or 50 sharecroppers, all black. The meeting started with the singing of the union song, "We Shall Not Be Moved." Lucien Koch was introduced, and almost immediately, four white men broke in with guns in their hands. They started shouting at the blacks to get out of there, telling them that the next time they were caught at a union meeting, they were going to be lynched. Said Reed:

They started clubbing Lucien, and covered me with guns. They were drunk. Those guys were really plastered. At least one of them was a deputy sheriff. He was driving an official car, and a couple of others were riding bosses. They slugged us around pretty bad, with threats of killing us. Those guns were boring into us, and could have gone off any minute. They had a rope with them which they dropped on the steps of the church. The rope was tied in a hangman's knot. We picked it up later. They took us to the cars—there were more than one. There were three in the front seat, and we were in the back, with another guy, who was slugging us both. The driver was warning us not to get blood all over his car. They took us to the county seat. Nope, they didn't put us in jail. They took us downstairs to the washroom, and told us to clean up. I was beginning to feel a little bit safer there. They are not so likely to shoot you in the county courthouse. Then they took us into the office of the county judge. I don't know his name. He was a kindly faced old gentleman, and as much of a racist as anyone I ever saw. They wanted to know our background, where we came from, and why we were in their county, and what were white men doing involved in dealing with blacks, though they didn't call them that—they called them "niggers" but that's a word that I find difficult to use. The old judge questioned us. He told us about how they had a lot of black politicians in Arkansas up until about the turn of the century, and hundreds had been driven into the Mississippi River, and that a lot of lives were lost then, and the whole thing was likely to occur over again if we persisted in the sort of activities we were in. The judge finally said that they were going to escort us back to the Poinsett County line, and that if we came back again, we would be lucky to get off next time with our lives. Then a couple of deputies loaded us in the back of a car, and took us first to the church where we got out of their car and into ours. We picked up the rope tied in the hangman's knot. Then they followed us on toward Marked Tree, and when we got to the county line they dropped off. Then, right after that, we met a truck coming from the direction of Marked Tree, and it was loaded with members of the union. They were all white men, and they had guns. Someone had gotten word back to Marked Tree, where there was a meeting going on. The meeting was adjourned, and they met again under the river bridge near the town. They all had guns. They had only one truck, and they loaded that with white members, as many as could get on. They had a lot of other people there, but no means of transportation. They set out to rescue us. We didn't know what was going to happen when we reached the county line. They [the union men] scared hell out of us, until they recognized Lucien's old car. The men from Marked Tree wanted to go right on into Crittenden County and get the ones who had beaten us up, and settle the score then and there. Lucien and I were tempted to go along with them, but we recognized that it would result in a lot of people getting killed.

Benton Moore, a deputy sheriff who had saved Ward Rodgers some weeks before, when he and preacher C. H. Smith had been caught in the same county, was also involved in this incident. The other deputies were sure they had caught Ward Rodgers again and were going to lynch him, but Moore told them that Koch was not the man they wanted. Atley Delaney, organizer of the Young Peoples Socialist League (YPSL), was attending the Marked Tree meeting and had led the party of armed men going to rescue Reed, the Young Communist League (YCL) organizer. Those were the United Front days.

It was in the middle of this trouble that the union got help from a brave and unusual man. Howard Kester came to work for us full time. In November 1934 Kester had stopped by Tyronza to visit with me. He had just returned from Marianna, Florida, where he had made an investigation of the brutal lynching of a young black man, Claude Neal. Kester was wearing a pellet of cyanide on a chain around his neck. He explained that he had stopped overnight in Tuskegee, Alabama, on the way to Florida, and his friend Dr. George Washington Carver had given him the cyanide pellet and fashioned the chain for it. The famed black scientist had advised Kester, should he be captured and threatened with torture, to take the pill and end his life quickly.

Kester's report to the National Association for the Advancement of Colored People contained a photograph of Claude Neal with his fingers, toes and genitals cut off. The mutilated body was shown swinging from a tree limb. This report led to renewed demands on the Roosevelt Administration for the enactment of a federal anti-lynching law.

Kester had met Dr. Carver some years before at a YMCA-YWCA summer institute at Blue Ridge Assembly in North Carolina, near Asheville. Though Dr. Carver had been invited to speak to the students, no arrangements had been made for his overnight accommodation or for his meals. Kester invited Dr. Carver to share his cabin, and he arranged for a special dining room to be set up where those students who wished to do so could share their meals with the black scientist. Later, Kester spent the summer at Tuskegee Institute, and he was disinherited by his father for doing so. Howard was an embarrassment to his father, William Kester, a small businessman active in the Presbyterian Church and in politics. Whether or not he belonged to the Ku Klux Klan, the elder Kester was sympathetic to its philosophy of keeping blacks and poor whites in their respective places.

Howard was born in Martinsville, Virginia, but the family moved to Beckley, a coal mining company-owned town in West Virginia, when Howard was 11 years old. At 17, he entered Lynchburg College and graduated with honors in 1925. In the summer of 1923 he traveled with other students on an American Pilgrimage of Friendship to European Students. Two years later he entered Princeton Theological Seminary. He came into conflict with the establishment back home in West Virginia as well as in Princeton. The West Virginia miners were on strike. His father was among those who brought in Billy Sunday, the anti-labor evangelist, to persuade the miners to break up their union and end the strike. Howard now learned that while family upheld segregation, one of its members had practiced miscegenation and that he had a distant relative who was half black. These two things seriously affected the young would-be minister who was about to be ordained in the Presbyterian Church. He preached a sermon on labor relations and racial hypocrisy and, needless to say, never became a minister in his family's church. Soon after, at Princeton, he preached a sermon to the student body denouncing a prominent professor for supporting the National Association of Manufacturers in opposition to the National Child Labor Amendment. Kester also advocated the admission of black students to the Princeton Theological Seminary. The budding radical was not asked to return for a second year to Princeton, which was then in many ways as racist as its counterparts below the Mason-Dixon line.

Howard Kester entered the Vanderbilt University School of Religion in the fall 1926. There he became secretary of the YMCA, led a protest movement against imperialism in China, and was promptly fired from his job. Then for several years he was employed as Southern Secretary for the Fellowship of Reconciliation. He and his wife Alice became involved in relief work among striking coal miners. In 1932 he saw his friend Barney Graham, the strike leader, shot down on the streets of Wilder, Tennessee, by coal company gunmen. In the same year he ran unsuccessfully for Congress on the Socialist Party ticket; still he received more votes than his republican opponent. He became a close friend of Norman Thomas, and for some years was a member of the National Executive Council of the Socialist Party of America. At one time he was seriously considered as a socialist candidate for Vice President of the United States but he declined the honor. In addition to investigating lynchings for the NAACP, he worked for the American Civil Liberties Union and later for the Workers Defense League.

Howard Kester came to work with the Southern Tenant Farmers

Union early in 1935. He arrived just in time to help get Ward Rodgers, Lucien Koch, Atley Delaney, and Robert Baker released from jail in the town of Lepanto, a few miles north of Tyronza. The men had held a union meeting on an open lot in town. They were arrested for trespassing and blocking traffic, and had spent that cold weekend in the township calaboose. When Kester and I arrived in the small town of Lepanto, we were greeted by a reporter from the *Memphis Commercial Appeal*, "Mitchell, when are you going to start the riot?" He evidently had a deadline to make. About a dozen riding bosses were there and listening. I loudly assured the reporter that we were there only to meet our attorney, C. T. Carpenter, and to attend the trial of Ward Rodgers and the others. Before the trial got underway, the Justice of the Peace announced that he was going to convict the men on charges of Barratry. The prosecuting attorney, who apparently knew the meaning of the word, declined to prosecute on that charge, but convicted the men instead of blocking traffic and disturbing the peace. Since Rodgers was already under $1,000 bond as a result of his conviction for threatening to lynch the planters, he was remanded to the county jail.

While in jail, the four men were all probably guilty of disturbing the peace of Lepanto. For two nights, the quartet kept the townspeople awake by singing union songs, almost continuously. Among the favorites was the "Internationale": "Arise, ye prisoners of starvation, Arise ye wretched of the earth, for a better world's in birth. . . ." Local union supporters brought them food, and there was some talk among the sharecroppers of breaking down the jail doors and releasing the prisoners. Attorney Carpenter, hearing the "Internationale," and not knowing that it was the socialist anthem, informed me that it was the most stirring song he had ever heard.

Kester, Carpenter, and I were almost continuously engaged thereafter in getting union workers out of jail. In nearby Cross County, four volunteer organizers for the STFU—William H. Stultz and L. M. Mills, whites, and A. B. Brookins and R. T. Butler, blacks—were jailed and charged with disturbing labor and collecting union dues. They were convicted in the Circuit Court on the disturbing labor charge. They were held in jail for several days before the union could arrange bond for them. Rev. A. B. Brookins, a self-styled "cotton patch preacher" and later the "singing leader" for the STFU, claimed to have converted all the prisoners and their jailers to the union cause while he was incarcerated. Following the release of the four organizers in Cross County, a large meeting was held in the town of Parkin. It was attended by hundreds of white and black sharecroppers. Ward H. Rodgers again presided. After hearing from the recently freed prisoners, Lucien Koch and Atley Delaney both made brief speeches. A local plantation owner, Vernon Paul, asked to address the gathering. He was introduced by Ward Rodgers. Mr. Paul advised the sharecroppers that their complaints would be heard by government officials, and he ʳged that they abandon efforts, then and there, to form an interracial orgaˑization. According to the newpaper account, plantation owner Paul ol. ʳred to shake hands with Lucien Koch, who refused.

Soon after his arrival early in February, Howard Kester, with ᵗ ucien Koch and about fifty white union members from the Marked T ᵉe and Tyronza locals, held a second meeting on a Saturday afternoon in the New Prosperity Church yard at Gilmore, where Koch and Reed had been pistol-whipped a few nights before. Only a few brave men from the Negro community turned out, but the plantation riders were there, and pistol shots were fired over the heads of the speakers. They did not try to break up the meeting, or arrest the speakers that afternoon, as there were too many white men present, and they didn't dare risk an open attack when they were so greatly outnumbered. They always assumed that the union men had weapons too, and sometimes they were right.

Three Women from Across the Sea

In mid-February, 1935, two young women from the British Isles arrived in Arkansas. They were Naomi Mitchison and Zita Baker. Mrs. Mitchison was a well-known author of historical novels and of the then best seller *Vienna Diary,* an eyewitness account of the destruction by gunfire of the socialist movement in the Austrian capital. Her moving description of what happened to men, women, and children in the bombardment of the Karl Marx housing project shocked the liberal world. Chancellor Dollfuss, the predecessor of Adolf Hitler, was responsible for the suppression of the socialist movement, and he paved the way for Hitler to take over Austria.

Naomi was the daughter of John Scott Haldane, the physiologist and her uncle was the Viscount of Cloan, Lord Chancellor in the first British Labor Party Cabinet in 1924. Naomi's brother, J. B. S. Haldane was a famous biologist and writer on social subjects. Naomi Haldane married Richard Mitchison, a Labour member of Parliament who was later elevated to the peerage. Mrs. Mitchison's traveling companion in Arkansas was Zita Baker, who became the first wife of Richard Crossman, one of the leaders of the British Labour Party. Dr. William R. Amberson must have known of all these people since he too was a scientist, a famous physiologist conducting experiments in blood transfusion, but neither Kester nor I knew much about our two guests who were making many field trips in the Marked Tree area. The Rev. A. B. Brookins gave us a vivid account of how the two women rolled their dresses up to their waists and waded through ice-cold water to carry relief to a beleaguered sharecropper family who had sought refuge from plantation terror in the swamps and were cut off when the river overflowed. As long as A. B. Brookins lived, he and Mrs. Mitchison kept up a correspondence. From time to time, she would enclose a pound note. Brookins would bring his "funny money" to the union office to get it exchanged for dollars. When Brookins was over 80, he proposed to move to Scotland to work on the Mitchison estate in Argyle. I advised him against it.

While Naomi Mitchison and Zita Baker were in Arkansas, they were joined by fiery Jennie Lee, who was then a member of the House of Commons, representing the Independent Labour Party, at that time the most radical wing of the labor movement in Britain. Jennie Lee later became the wife of British Labour Party leader, Aneurin Bevan. She was then on a lecture tour of the United States for the League for Industrial Democracy and was booked for an appearance in Memphis. Having an extra day, she decided to spend it with the sharecroppers in Arkansas.

The union announced that Jennie Lee would speak in Marked Tree's town square on a Saturday afternoon. Hundreds of sharecroppers gathered to hear the young woman from across the sea. Half an hour before the rally was to take place, we were told that Mayor Fox and his city council had passed an ordinance the night before, prohibiting union meetings or speakers unless they first obtained a special permit. Religious, political, and patriotic groups were exempted.

Instead of defying the new law and incurring wholesale arrests, including those of a member of Parliament and our other guests, I suggested a march through town to the outskirts of Marked Tree. A half mile outside the city limits, a "lorry" as Jennie Lee called a truck, was driven onto the railway right-of-way, to serve as a platform. The crowd of over 500 people remained for three hours to listen to the speakers. As I had anticipated, there were few customers in the stores that Saturday afternoon, and the merchants fumed at the city fathers for being so stupid as to drive away their trade. Jennie Lee, a true daughter of a Welsh coal mining family, eloquently denounced the inhumanity of the Arkansas cotton planters. Then the women from the British Isles led the crowd of sharecroppers—singing "The Union is a Marching, We Shall Not be Moved"—back through the streets of Marked Tree, across the railway tracks to the Negro Lodge Hall, where the march disbanded.

Years later, I was invited to stop in for an hour at a party being held in the Gramercy Park area in New York to raise money for the International Rescue Committee. I was not told who the guest of honor was to be. When I walked in and the hostess announced: "Here is H. L. Mitchell, Secretary of the Southern Tenant Farmers Union," a dark-haired woman rushed across the room to greet me, with open arms. It was Jennie Lee, still fiery though not so slender as she was that Saturday afternoon long ago when she had led the sharecropper march in Marked Tree, Arkansas.

Norman Thomas at Birdsong

In March 1935, Norman Thomas returned to Arkansas to speak at a series of mass meetings arranged by the union. He had also paid a call on Arkansas' tobacco-chewing Governor J. Marion Futrell, and he had spoken to the Planters Club of Pulaski County in Little Rock. After a full day, Thomas was returning to Memphis with me in my car. As soon as we reached eastern Arkansas, I left the main highway and stuck to the back country roads. I wasn't about to risk an ambush by Arkansas planters, and possible injury to the union's most distinguished friend and spokesman. On one of these backroads my old car stopped running, and I had to rouse a friendly sharecropper to get a pair of mules to pull us into an all-night service station on the highway a few miles away. The car required only minor repairs, and we were soon on our way again. Norman Thomas decided then and there that I should have a new car, and he promised to raise the necessary money to get one. This was the first of the "getaway cars" acquired by the union leaders, J. R. Butler, Howard Kester, E. B. McKinney, and F. R. Betton (after the latter succeeded McKinney as vice president of the STFU). We often owed our lives to these cars, which enabled us to get away from the mobs.

Norman Thomas was in Arkansas several days that trip. He spoke to hundreds of sharecroppers, attending as many as four meetings a day. All went well until Thomas and his party, including a newspaperman, arrived in Birdsong, in Mississippi County. The crowd was too large to hold the meeting indoors so it was decided to have Mr. Thomas speak from the front doorsteps of the small church. On the outskirts of the crows were numerous riding bosses in their familiar garb of khaki hunting coats that only partially concealed their guns. All wore deputy sheriff badges. Howard Kester started to introduce the speaker. He got only as far as "Ladies and gentlemen" when a rough voice yelled: "They ain't no ladies in the crowd, and there ain't no gentlemen on the platform. That God damned white-headed Yankee son-of-a-bitch can go back up North where he come from."

The dignified Norman Thomas protested that his right to speak was guaranteed by the Constitution of the United States and that the Constitution of Arkansas was even more explicit in guaranteeing free speech. The mobsters pulled Thomas from the platform; he was told that they "didn't give a damn about such things as the Constitution, and that this was the best God damned county, and the best God damned state in the whole United States, and that they would take care of their labor, and weren't gonna have no outside interference from any white haired Yankee son-of-a-bitch."

One of Thomas' assistants, John Herling, was hit over the head and, according to a sharecropper, "it sounded just like when you thump a green watermelon." At this point, I drove up with a reporter from Little Rock, and as we stopped the car, it was surrounded by riding bosses. The reporter put out his hand to those nearest him, saying, "My name is Baumgartner, and I'm from the Associated Press." They told him they didn't care who he was or where he was from, but to get the hell out of Mississippi County. I got out of the car on the other side, and there stood a one-time friend and customer from Tyronza. I greeted him: "Why Bob Frazier!" Frazier's face was trembling with fear and anger; he had his gun in his hand, ready to kill me. I got back in the car with the newspaperman and followed the half dozen cars escorting Kester and Thomas to the Memphis River bridge. In Memphis, Thomas had someone call the city desks of the two newspapers. The United Press sent a man to the hotel. Kester recalled that the angry Norman Thomas, striding around the small hotel room, kept repeating what the plantation mob had called him. Thomas had never been known to utter such rough language before.

Soon after the Birdsong episode, Mary Hillyer, a Socialist Party activist from New York, arrived on a lecture tour. Clay East insisted on accompanying her to Marked Tree, even though he had been warned by two of that town's citizens, "If you hold this meeting with that woman, it's going to be bad." Mayor Fox and Chief of Police Shinaberry also came to warn East not to hold the meeting in Marked Tree. Clay East told Shinaberry, with whom he had once played baseball: "You are the officer of the law here. You know there will be no violence from us. If you want some men to keep the peace, I have a bunch of guys inside. If you will deputize them, we'll stop any trouble. If you fear there is going to be bloodshed, you must do something to stop it." Shinaberry and the mayor gave up and drove off.

In the union hall at Marked Tree, East noticed that there were a number of tough-looking white and black men, wearing overalls and jumpers, lined up against the walls. He thought at first that they were sent to break up the meeting, but he learned afterwards that they were union men with Winchester rifles and shotguns down the legs of their overalls, which they would have used to stop any attempt to break up that meeting. Fortunately, nothing untoward happened. Said East: "Mary Hillyer made her talk, then we left with a man and his wife. Driving out the plantation road, our way was blocked by a car with six men in it, most of whom I knew. I pretended I was going to stop, slowed down, and then stepped on the gas and drove around to lawyer Carpenter's office. As I stopped the car, I reached in the glove compartment to get my automatic pistol, but the guy with me cautioned me that if I got the gun out some innocent people might get killed, so I left it in the car, and Mary and I went on up the stairs to Carpenter's office."

East told Carpenter there were at least 50 men in the mob outside, ganging up about his car. Mr. Carpenter called the mayor to come to his office. Carpenter was nervous, but Mayor Fox was ashen. His face was jumping with red blotches of fear on it. Carpenter finally persuaded the mayor to go talk to the mob and find out what they wanted. Fox came back with the answer: "They want Clay East."

Clay, very angry, exclaimed, "They can shore as hell get me!" With that, he stormed down the stairs and right into the gang. Fred Bradsher, with whom Clay used to go to dances, was the spokesman and led East around to the back of the building. Clay thought, "If they start something, I am going to knock the shit out of them. If Mitchell and Kester were here, they would have took them on." The fact that East was a native and knew most of the mob saved him. The spokesman told East: "We are not going to put up with any more of these mixed meetings. We are telling you now not to come back over here." East told them that Mary Hillyer was on her way to New Orleans and would probably never return to Arkansas again, but that he would make them no promises at all about what he would do. Then East and the woman from New York were allowed to get in his car. The mob followed them, but East was driving a Terraplane, the fastest automobile around in those days, so he just ran off and left them far behind. Clay afterwards reported that Mary Hillyer was so frightened that she lost control and ruined the front seat cover of the getaway car.

Soon afterwards, the second STFU Convention was held in Marked Tree. Clay East, who had left Tyronza, refused to serve any longer as president, and insisted that a sharecropper be elected to serve in that position. William H. Stultz was chosen president to replace East. Stultz had once been a country schoolteacher and later, as a sharecropper in Arkansas, was evicted because of the New Deal program. E. B. (Britt)

McKinney was chosen vice president of the STFU, and other Negro members were elected to the executive board. By resolution, the STFU convention adopted its previously unstated policy of nonviolence. Howard Kester was responsible for the wording of the resolution. Thus the union officially became an interracial organization with nonviolence as one of its basic precepts, and it was probably the first such organization in the rural South. This interracial unity was soon tested by opposing an organization that originated at this time. The planters organized the Marked Tree Co-operative Association, which offered to place unemployed workers on jobs in the community. The cooperative was led by the Methodist minister, J. Abner Sage, who had become an unofficial spokesman for the plantation owners' interests. He had previously appeared before a legislative committee in Little Rock to denounce both the STFU and the Commonwealth College as communist operations. Sage relied on *The Red Network*, a book by Elizabeth Dilling that named Mrs. Roosevelt, Norman Thomas, and other liberal Americans as agents of a world communist conspiracy. From time to time, Sage had spotted individuals who visited the area as persons named in *The Red Network*.

Sage made a fatal mistake for his association when he publicly announced that only "white unemployed were to be considered for jobs." The two Marked Tree branches of the union, meeting together, adopted a resolution calling on all union members who had signed up with Sage "to crawfish out." The resolution, written on tablet paper in pencil, is in the STFU papers. This concrete action on interracial affairs bound the two groups together more than ever before. They saw the folly of having two community councils, or local unions, in Marked Tree, with one set of officers for white and another for black units meeting in the same lodge hall, and they merged into a single unit.

Sage and his cronies were routed one night when the union was meeting and the outer guards rushed in to report that planters were in a box car on the railroad siding behind the Union Hall, listening in on the meeting. Men started to leave for home to get weapons. I urged them to stay: "Let's stand our ground. We can use the tops of these benches to whup hell out of all the planters that could get in that boxcar." Then, accompanied by the guards, we went to investigate. As our group approached the boxcar, over on the dark side, Preacher Sage—all alone—jumped out the door and lit out toward town.

The Reverend J. Abner Sage stepped up his tactics of violent repression. He told a New York Times reporter that his group had just decided to form the Nightriders, since the Ku Klux Klan had a bad reputation. The Nightriders unleashed a reign of terror against the union and its officers. Union meetings were broken up, churches were burned, attacks were made on groups of blacks going to church. The home of A. B. Brookins in Marked Tree was shot up, and his terrified teenage daughter, seeking to hide, received a head wound from a ricocheting bullet. The house of vice president E. B. McKinney was machine-gunned, and one of his sons was injured. As usual, the blacks bore the brunt of the violence. Still, the whites came in for their fair share. The president of the STFU, W. H. Stultz, was threatened with death. Walter Moskop and Ed Pickering were framed and jailed on charges of stealing coal. They had picked up a half sack of coal on the railroad track. Many others had to flee for their lives. Howard Kester and I were sought by bands of armed planters. Round-the-clock road blocks were placed on the main highways as the planter mobs sought out the union leaders. The lights were shot out in attorney Carpenter's home. He met the nightriders, gun in hand, and blasted away at the intruders in his front yard. Mrs. Carpenter had a nervous breakdown and her husband had to call a halt to further defense of the union. The violence continued through 1936, with sporadic outbursts thereafter.

In his column for the *Socialist Call* entitled "Up Front," in March 1935, soon after his visit to Arkansas, Norman Thomas reported another incident:

Near Marked Tree, about four miles out, we came across a family, a mother with five children, a couple of young hogs, six chickens, two puppies in the children's arms, and a few scraps of furniture. They had just been dumped on the side of the road by a deputy sheriff. The father came walking down the road a little later. He had been beaten up a few days before, arrested and jailed on the nominally untrue charge of stealing a couple of eggs. This white man had joined the Union, and he and his wife had sought to get "the law" on a riding boss who had kidnapped their 14-year-old daughter, and held her for some two or three weeks. The plantation owner, the family said, had "fixed the law," and there they were by the roadside.

The family was the Vernons. The names of all participants in this despicable affair were made public in 1937 through Howard Kester's book *Revolt Among the Sharecroppers*, but first in the STFU pamphlet, *Acts of Tyranny and Terror*. This superb document, put together by Kester, listed the names of individuals involved in 27 incidents of violence against the union and its supporters. We put out a thousand mimeographed copies and mobilized local union leaders to distribute them.

Kester and I ran the gauntlet of planter bands roving the main highways as we made the rounds of local leaders. Copies of *Acts of Tyranny and Terror* were all delivered in one night and appeared on the porches of the planters, local businesses, and professional people in Marked Tree, Tyronza, Lepanto, as well as out on the plantations the next morning. So thorough was the documentation that not a single charge was ever challenged.

With Norman Thomas' help, and that of other socialists and sympathizers around the country, money was raised in 1935 to rent a small farm near Memphis for a year. This became the place of refuge for the sharecropper leaders and their families. The union was forced underground. All open meetings were suspended.

Alfred Baker Lewis, a Boston socialist leader, later national Treasurer for the NAACP, started a campaign to raise money to provide the union leadership with an armored car. Such a car would have cost several thousand dollars. Howard Kester received a personal letter from Lewis saying that he thought he could swing the deal, and that Powers Hapgood was ready to bring the armored vehicle down for use in the "Sharecroppers' war." Hapgood was a veteran of the coal mine wars. He was the campaign manager for John Brophy in the late 1920s in a bitter contest against John L. Lewis for the presidency of the United Mine Workers of America.

Kester informed me about the offer, and he recalled that I said, "Tell Alfred Lewis to just send the money, and damn the armored car. If we get in that thing and go to Arkansas, the planters will dynamite it and blow us all to hell and back."

Powers Hapgood eventually arrived, without the car.

6   A Time of Trial

In all movements, there is a time of trial or testing of those who make up the leadership as well as the membership. For the Southern Tenant Farmers Union, this period came in early 1935. During the reign of terror unleashed by the plantation owners, families of union leaders had to leave their homes on the plantations and in the small towns. I was one of the refugees, being among the first to leave Arkansas, just ahead of the lynch mob. I left the union records, correspondence, and also my library—mainly Little Blue Books—in the back room of my shop where I had also stored my cleaning plant fixtures. These were to be picked up by a truck the next day. The sheriff of Poinsett County sent a deputy to Tyronza and confiscated the union records and my books, which were never returned. My family and I settled in Memphis. By this time I was getting used to the Nightriders' tactics, but I was not prepared for the series of rifts in the union which followed.

A Green Swastika in the Cotton

In mid-January of 1935, J. O. Green, one of our first white organizers, an effective speaker, came to me with some proposals to place before the union. J. O. Green claimed to be an old time socialist. He had also been a member and organizer of Huey Long's "Share the Wealth" clubs, in the hill country along the edge of the delta plantation area. Green's proposals were to reorganize the STFU under a new name; to place the Negro members in separate locals; and to have all members wear green shirts. A green-shirt brigade would protect the meetings. Green had a constitution and bylaws drafted for what he called The Arkansas Farmers and Tenants Association, having as its emblem a hooked cross similar to the one used by Adolf Hilter, but it was also to be colored green, on a white background. I reported J. O. Green's proposal to other leaders of the union. Green was expelled from the STFU.

Later in February, at a meeting in Truman, one of Green's followers attempted to assassinate me. I was standing on a raised platform in the town square, speaking to about a hundred people. Suddenly there was a sharp explosion at my back. Thinking it was a firecracker tossed by a planter stooge, I kept on talking. After the meeting, I learned that one of Green's men had pulled a pistol and aimed it at my back. An elderly union man, W. W. Lee, grabbed the man's arm and wrested the gun away from the younger man. Only a few persons actually observed what had happened. Most of the crowd, like me, thought it was just a prank, that someone had thrown a firecracker.

On the small farm near Memphis, leased by Howard Kester, which became a refuge for blacks and whites who had to leave Arkansas, lived the family of William H. Stultz, Clay East's successor as union president, and Myrtle and Walter Moskop. Both Stultz and Moskop had been jailed, and they had been warned by the Nightriders that they would be killed if they remained in Arkansas.

With nothing else to do, the refugees from the sharecropper war plotted among themselves. The plantation owners who had taken up J. O. Green after he was expelled from the union made overtures to Bill Stultz. They urged him to return the headquarters of the union to Arkansas. They promised that if he would lead a rank-and-file membership revolt against me, he and his family would be well taken care of. Stultz was not much of a leader. He was well meaning, but he was dominated by his wife who was most ambitious to advance his position as union president. Also, about this time, there arrived in Memphis, a well-to-do young socialist from Nashville, Jack Fies. He was a spastic, with an attendant who moved him from wheelchair to automobile, wrote letters for him, and in general did everything Fies could not do for himself. With Fies providing the know-how, W. H. Stultz and Walter Moskop filed a series of charges against me that ranged from misusing union funds to cussing sharecroppers. I was then put on trial before the STFU executive council. Since Stultz was a party to the charges, J. R. Butler was selected as temporary chairman.

Some of the charges were so far fetched, that even Stultz refused to support them. On the charge of cussing sharecroppers, I admitted that I was guilty of having cussed out the "National Songster" of the STFU, A. B. Brookins, one of my best friends and most loyal supporters. Brookins had been opening boxes of used clothing sent to the union for distribution, and without telling anyone, he appropriated several of the best men's suits for his own use. I discovered what he was doing and raised hell with him. Moskop, bitter at me, voted to sustain every charge. Howard Kester recalled that during the proceedings I made some caustic remark directed at Moskop. At one point I reached for my briefcase lying between us. Moskop thought that I was going for a gun because he ran to his room and grabbed a shotgun. Howard Kester and Bill Stultz took the gun away from Moskop, and I opened the briefcase on top of the long table to demonstrate that I had no weapon in it. Relative peace, if not exactly harmony, was finally restored in the meeting.

After the trial, Norman Thomas wrote expressing his confidence in me. On May 8, 1935, Thomas sent a letter to the STFU urging that there be no more divisions among us. He repeated that he had confidence in Mitchell: "The fact that there is a union at all is largely due to him."

Dr. William R. Amberson, in a letter to Thomas' assistant John Herling was more realistic: "There has been criticism of Mitchell for a long time. It is my judgment that he is by all odds the biggest man in the outfit. He has grown tremendously in the last year. He will never entirely overcome his educational and cultural lack, but he has determination that commands my admiration. I have supported him, and will continue to do so." Amberson showed a thorough knowledge of our strengths as well as our weaknesses: "We must not idealize these people. Many are incapable and incompetent. Yet there is a stirring of thought and idealism among them. They fight on, not for what they may gain for themselves, but for their children."

Amberson was right on both scores. I never entirely overcame my lack of formal education, but Amberson, Kester, Norman Thomas, and the several women in my life were my teachers, and to some extent they remedied the cultural lack. The factionalism was not to end until after World War II was underway.

At another executive council meeting, while the refugees were still occupying the union-rented farmhouse, the Oklahoma member of the council, Odis L. Sweeden, proposed a plan to blow up the Mississippi River levees and flood eastern Arkansas plantations in retaliation for the mistreatment of union members. The executive council came close to approving that scheme.

Sweeden was a Cherokee with full rights in the tribe. He had been a member of the STFU since early 1934, having joined through the mail. One day, while sitting in his outhouse, he was looking over some newspapers (the last year's Sears Roebuck catalogue having long since been used up). He found an article in the *American Guardian*, calling upon persons interested in helping the STFU to organize in their communities to write to H. L. Mitchell, Box 207, Tyronza, Arkansas. Sweeden wrote and he was sent a volunteer organizer's credentials. In less than a year, the Oklahoma branch of the STFU had more than 7,500 members in nearly 100 community councils. Sweeden was a fiery, imaginative person who aligned blacks, whites, and American Indians in a fight for land redistribution in Oklahoma, where banks and insurance companies held title to much of the productive cotton land in the eastern part of the state.

At the union farm, Sweeden held forth throughout the night advocating the destruction of the Mississippi River levees, while Kester, the advocate of non-violence, kept voluminous notes on who said what. When the meeting finally broke up, just before daylight on a Monday morning, Howard Kester, too exhausted to return to the Memphis office, went to sleep on the floor. He was aroused about 8 A.M. by a pounding on the door. The county sheriff was there. He said the neighbors had been disturbed by out-of-state automobiles coming and going at all hours of the night, and the loud talk of men on the rented farm. Kester, ever the diplomat, invited the sheriff in, put the coffee pot on, then explained that they had a meeting there the day before and had continued far into the night. He apologized for having disturbed the neighbors and said he wanted to assure them, and the sheriff, that he would personally see to it that it never happened again. Kester's two fears were that the sheriff would search the place and find the incriminating notes that were casually lying on a shelf; or that a fifteen-year-old union partisan in the house, who had a violent dislike of sheriffs or any other representatives of the law, might make some uncalled for and perhaps damaging remark. Fortunately for peace-maker Kester, neither happened. The sheriff knew that the union had rented the place, and for what purpose. Also, the political boss, Edward H. Crump of Memphis, had passed the word to leave the union alone, as long as no law was violated.

Edward H. Crump had run Memphis with a hand of steel for more than 20 years by then, and he was to continue as the benevolent dictator for another 20. It was known that I had become friendly with Abe Waldauer, the follower of Henry George, after our first efforts to secure legal help. I later paid a visit to the City attorney to inform him that the union was moving its headquarters to Memphis and wanted to operate without interference from the Memphis police. Waldauer said, "I suppose you want me to tell the 'Fair Haired Boy' [E. H. Crump] that if he will not organize sharecroppers, you will not take any part in his political affairs." I agreed that something like that was what I had in mind. For all the years that the STFU maintained its offices in Memphis, there was seldom any deviation from the agreement by either party.

Will D. Lee was Crump's chief of police. His best qualification for the office was that he was a big man and looked like a policeman. Dr. Amberson reported attending a civic meeting once when Chief Lee was speaking on the dangers of communism. According to Amberson, Chief Lee sounded something like this: "Them there communionists believe in the dictatorship of the prolaterate." The chief was also reported to look under his bed each night to see if there were any "Reds" hiding in his bedroom. The joke around STFU headquarters was that the Chief was really checking to see if he could find H. L. Mitchell hiding there.

After I bought a new Chevrolet, partially paid for by Norman Thomas, Chief Lee had me picked up and brought to Police Head-quarters on the premise that they had to check the car's ownership to see if it was stolen. I was left in an office and told to wait there. After about an hour, Chief Lee came to the door, looked at me, and then walked away. When the Union lawyer, Newell Fowler, arrived along with a newspaperman, the police chief denied ever having arrested me and pointed out that I had not even been booked. They gave no explanation as to why I was at the Police Station.

Following my trial before the executive council, I attempted to resign as secretary of the Southern Tenant Farmers Union. Instead of accepting my resignation, the council sent me on an organizing mission to Texas and Oklahoma, with Norman Thomas' blessing. With my wife, Lyndell, and our children Harry and Joyce in the new "getaway car," we were off. It was a very pleasant interlude, with picnic stops in the piney woods and on the banks of streams along the way. Both Dell and I forgot the worries of the past. We were closer than we were ever to be again. This was a real escape into a different world.

In Denison, Texas, we stopped to visit a socialist correspondent interested in organizing for the STFU. We remained several days in the lowlands dividing Oklahoma and Texas while waiting for a river at flood stage to go down. We were on our way to Muskogee, Oklahoma, as soon as the roads were dried out and bridges were reported to be safe for passage. In Oklahoma we were provided with both board and room by hospitable union members. Among these was Henry Pippin, from near Okmulgee. It was here that we visited the Creek Nation's Council House, and learned that the Indians had a House of Warriors, and a House of Chiefs, which corresponded to the United States Congress. We also learned that the Indian Nation had the equivalent of a Supreme Court.

We also visited with Mr. and Mrs. John Berryhill. Berryhill was a leader of the union and also a leading member of the Creek Nation. John Berryhill's father, Captain J. H. Berryhill of the Creek Indian Dragoons, had been in charge of the firing squad that executed the last Indian convicted of a capital crime under tribal law. The man was tried early one spring, but was permitted to return to his home and make his crop for the year. He gave his promise to return after the harvest in the fall. Upon the day set, the Creek Indian who had violated a tribal law, drove into town in his wagon, sitting on his coffin, and was thereupon shot to death by Captain Berryhill's firing squad. The bronze marker on the Council House grounds commemorating the event was made more vivid by the presence of the son of the executioner.

Odis L. Sweeden and I were also invited to meet with the Tribal Council of the Choctaw Nation, near Durant, in southeastern Oklahoma. I was called upon to speak, and Sweeden, who was also fluent in the Choctaw language, gave a long translation of my brief talk. The members of the council sat cross-legged on the ground, their faces expressionless, although very serious as the two speeches were made. For some time, they remained still, exchanging a few words now and then. Finally the chief, a magnificent elderly man, arose, and in a glowing oration with gestures, made his reply. It appeared to me that a great decision had been made, and that perhaps all of the Choctaws, most of whom were tenant farmers, were going to join the STFU. At the end of the chief's talk, the council adjourned. As Sweeden and I drove away, I asked Sweeden what the chief had really said.

"He said: 'The white man talks well. Our brother from Muskogee talks well. When the white man, and the black man get ready to take back the land—just let the Indians know. We will get our guns, and we will come too. We do not need a union. We are already organized.'"

In attending meetings, especially among the Creeks, I noticed that there were always a few Negroes—really very black—but they were grim and silent men like the Indians. These men were descendants of the slaves owned by the Creeks and had taken on all of the characteristics of the Indian. They were also full members of the tribe, and if there was any discrimination against them, it was not apparent to outsiders like me.

While in Oklahoma, I also made contact with the Socialist Party, and met with Oscar Ameringer, editor of *The American Guardian*, the famed socialist paper.

Too soon our western tour ended. Suddenly recalled to Memphis, I found all the old problems waiting for me.

The Union in Trouble

J. R. Butler, who had been named acting secretary of the STFU, realizing his lack of ability to carry on the administrative and public relations work, had dumped the job on Kester's hands. Kester, with agreement of a special committee, reinstated me to my former job.

By that time, William H. Stultz, the elected president, was in a complete fog. He moved back to Arkansas and set up headquarters in Truman. With the guidance of "Green Shirt" advocate J. O. Green, he tried to reorganize the union along racial lines. This group employed as their attorney Fred H. Stafford of Marked Tree, the man who had prosecuted Ward Rodgers for anarchy earlier in the year. Stafford, acting for Stultz, filed legal action in the Shelby County, Tennessee, courts and seized the office equipment and records, including the great seal of the STFU which showed white and black hands clasped across its base. A hearing was held on Stafford's writ of replevin. The day before the date set, W. H. Stultz, the disaffected president of STFU, came to our attorney, Herman Goldberger, and admitted that he had been misled by anti-union and racist agents of the Arkansas cotton planters. Goldberger prepared an affidavit to this effect which Stultz signed, and when this affidavit was presented to the court, the case was dismissed. However, the books, records, and the great seal of the STFU were never returned to the rightful owners. (Many years later, some of the correspondence turned up on microfilm in a library.) A humorous editorial appeared in the *Memphis Press Scimitar* suggesting that now that the great issues had been settled as to which was the real STFU, now all the sharecroppers need do was to collect hickory nuts and use their union seal to crack them during the winter months.

The union was now in shambles. Its members were confused and unsure as to who were the leaders. The highways were being patrolled by bands of plantation men seeking Buck Kester and me. We traveled only back roads and had many close calls. McKinney, the black vice-president, while he was on a fund-raising tour in the East, was warned by his wife Lula and her friends never to return to Arkansas. In his absence, his home, halfway between Marked Tree and Tyronza, was machine-gunned by Nightriders, who had a report that Kester and I were meeting McKinney there. C. T. Carpenter had been forced to end his association with the union. The court cases filed by him had been lost. To Kester and me, it was the darkest hour, but we refused to call it quits.

Cotton Pickers Strike (1935)

Then early in the fall, the large planters announced that the wages paid cotton pickers of 60 cents per 100 pounds the year before would be reduced to 40 cents for the season. This was a reduction from about $1.20 per day to 80 cents per day, since an average picker could gather about 200 pounds in a day. I had an idea. Why not call a wage conference and set a union scale? So Kester and I went riding the highways and byways at night, always watching out for the Nightriders, as we spread the word calling a union wage conference in Memphis. The day came and a representative number of members gathered at the farmhouse near Memphis for the union's first wage conference. I thought that everyone should stay out of the fields until the rate was paid. I was overruled. It was decided that the people would go to work for whatever the planters offered and earn enough money to lay in supplies for their families. Then, when the peak of the cotton harvest was near, they would all stay at home on strike. Wage committees were formed with a key man named for each county. These men kept in touch, and when the harvest was at its peak, they came to Memphis to pick up bundles of printed circulars that had the union label on them. The leaflets read: "Demand $1.00 per 100 lbs. for picking cotton." The operation went off smoothly. The circulars appeared one morning on every plantation and in every town. They were tacked to barn doors and telephone poles. Every plantation riding boss found one on his front door. The colored circulars covered Crittenden, Cross, and Poinsett counties, like dew on a cool September morning. The plantation bosses asked sharecroppers, "Where did these things come from?"

"Why," they were answered, "that feller Mitchell came over last night, and dropped them from a plane." The cotton pickers did not explain how Mitchell had put them on barn doors and front porches of the planters.

At the first Wage Committee meeting, Walter Moskop said that when the strike was called, he and his pal, Ed Pickering, would start rumors going that some scab pickers in another county had got killed for picking cotton while the regular pickers were out on strike. Those and similar rumors provoked some concern all over the area. In Cross County, the sheriff and his deputies were out day and night searching for the dead men killed by the strikers. Of course none were found, but the tactic was effective. The Arkansas Deputy Labor Commissioner, H. C. Malcolm, toured the strike scene. He reported that he could find no pickers anywhere, but that he saw a lot of people fishing. He said in all three counties, only five people were observed picking cotton.

The news of the strike spread. George Stith, living in Howell, Arkansas, on a small plantation nearly a hundred miles away from the strike scene, said someone came in the night and spread the strike handbills all over the plantation where he lived. The owner never got up early in the morning. He had a rope tied to his bed, and as soon as it became daylight, he rang the plantation bell, calling his laborers to go to the fields. That morning they did not go, and the boss was furious when he roused himself about noon, to find that no cotton picking had been done. In 10 days, wages rose everywhere. It had been agreed that whenever the rate reached 75 cents per hundred pounds, the workers could decide if they would accept that. In most places they did accept the 75 cents rate, but in others, the pickers held out longer and won the dollar.

Confidence in the union returned. New areas were opened to organization in Arkansas, Missouri, Mississippi, Tennessee, and Texas. Soon I was claiming 25,000 members in the Southern Tenant Farmers Union. If one member of a family signed up, I counted three more also as members. Sometimes, when talking to some government official or a news reporter, I was inclined to stretch even this number. When reproached by Clay East for exaggerating, I protested: "Hell, Clay, they don't know how many members we have. I sure as hell don't know, and you don't either, so when I say we have 25,000 that's it, until the next idiot comes along and asks the same fool question."

The truth was that the STFU never had many dues paying members, but there were perhaps a hundred involved for every ten that got their names enrolled. Said Deacy Real, the wife of a sharecropper in St. Francis County, Arkansas: "I joined the union. I never did get no card, but I was really active in it. I attended the meetings. We were meeting in churches and places like that. On Sundays we would sometimes go away back in the woods and hold a union meeting."

Often there was no organizer to attend the meetings. Sometimes a man or a woman who had just been visiting some distance away and attended a meeting would tell friends. Sometimes one would attend church services, or a prayer meeting, and be asked to tell about the union. Often such people didn't even know the address of the office in Memphis. Usually they knew there was a white man named Mitchell in it, a Reverend McKinney, or a Reverend Brookins, or a Reverend Blackstone; and that some were white and some were colored. Often the church members would decide to join the union then and there. Sometimes the minister would take the leadership in the union, but sometimes the preacher would be a stooge of the plantation owner and would tell on his flock. If union feeling ran high, sometimes the preacher lost his church for refusing to go along with the union.

I recall that once when I appeared unannounced at a local union meeting, some older man came up to me and asked: "Who be ye, young feller?" On being told that I was H. L. Mitchell, the secretary of the union, the man protested: "You can't be *that* H. L. Mitchell—you must be his son." Until I was forty, although tall, I weighed less than 130 pounds and was often told I looked like a teenager.

Early in May of 1935 we sent a second delegation to Washington— this time to picket the Department of Agriculture—demanding the release of the Mary Connor Myers Report, suppressed by an assistant of Henry Wallace as "too hot to print."

GARDNER JACKSON:
The Man Led Around on a Leash by an Underdog

Someone had informed the government workers lined up on the grass watching the picketing of the Department of Agriculture, that the STFU had its singing leader in the delegation. They started calling out asking to hear the union songs. A. B. Brookins stopped the picket line and started to sing: "The Union is a Marching," "We Shall Not be Moved," "Like a tree planted by the water," and so on. Then a policeman who had earlier threatened me came up and grabbed Brookins: "Old man, stop that singing, or I'll run you in." There were catcalls and protests from the crowd of watchers. Out of the crowd rushed a very important looking man, who asked in a commanding voice: "What right do you have to interfere with this man?"

The policeman said Brookins was violating the District of Columbia ordinance against singing on the street. Pat Jackson roared with indignation: "You know very well there is no such District ordinance against people singing on the street." There were cheers by the crowd. The policeman gave up. Pat Jackson told me afterwards that he didn't know whether or not there was such an ordinance, but he felt sure the policeman didn't either. A lifelong relationship between the two of us was begun on the spot. As long as Jackson lived, he was the Washington representative of sharecroppers and farm workers, no matter whether he was employed by some government agency, or by a newspaper as a reporter, or by CIO or finally by AFL-CIO. He was my advisor and guide, and aid to the nation's farm workers from 1935 through 1960.

Gardner Jackson first got involved with sharecroppers when he was working in the Department of Agriculture. He was one of the group in the AAA who protested when the Mary Connor Myers Report was suppressed. Soon after, Jerome Frank, consumer counsel of the AAA, and his assistants—Gardner Jackson and Lee Pressman—were fired by Henry Wallace. They had tried, among other things, to involve the Secretary in the union's suit again the Arkansas planters. It was partly to protest this "purge of the liberals" at the AAA that the union sent a delegation of nine members to picket the Department of Agriculture in the spring of 1935. We carried signs demanding the release of the Myers report. One of the charges against Jackson was that he had had a secretary make a copy of it. The charge was not true. He had not seen the report, although he and others had talked to Mrs. Myers upon her return from Arkansas. Pat Jackson never hesitated to follow his convictions even if it meant losing his job.

Gardner (Pat) Jackson was the son of William Sharpless Jackson, and his second wife, Helen Banfield. The name "Pat" came about from the remark of his father upon seeing his prematurely born son for the first time: "He looks just like a little Irishman." Although given the name Gardner, he was thereafter called "Pat" by all.

Pat's father was a wealthy Colorado Springs banker, silver-mine and railway owner, whose first wife was Helen Hunt Jackson, American novelist and poet. Legend has it that Helen Hunt Jackson, dying of cancer at age 55, asked her husband to marry her favorite niece, also named Helen, which he did. Helen Hunt's great book *Century of Dishonor* was most critical of our government's policy toward the American Indian. When her documented study received little attention, she wrote a popular novel, *Ramona*. Since his mother was so close to Helen Hunt, it is possible that Gardner Jackson acquired some of his social conscience from that early fighter for the human rights of American Indians.

Jackson was sent to exclusive schools and was finally expelled from Amherst College in a controversy involving the president, Dr. Alexander H. Mieklejohn. Set to work as a bond salesman for a New York brokerage house, Jackson quit and became a reporter for the *Boston Globe*. It was soon after the arrest of the Italian anarchists Sacco and Vanzetti, that Gardner's wife Dorothy called his attention to the case.

He investigated, and found that the two men were being tried, not for the commission of a crime, but because of their political beliefs. Jackson became the secretary of the Sacco-Vanzetti Defense Committee, which carried on a worldwide protest against the obvious frameup of the two anarchists. Many lasting relationships were formed by Jackson as a result of the seven-year legal battle. Among these was one with Harvard law professor Felix Frankfurter, later named by FDR as an associate justice of the United States Supreme Court. Justice Frankfurter was often enlisted in fund-raising campaigns by Jackson and became one of the group of Washingtonians who from time to time supported the Southern Tenant Farmers Union. After Gardner Jackson had spent seven years and thousands of dollars in the defense of Sacco and Vanzetti, he was partially disinherited by his father. Trust funds were set up so that "Pat" could have money on which to live, feed, clothe, shelter and educate his three children, but little to waste on "causes." However, Jackson's home in the exclusive section of Chevy Chase, Maryland, became a gathering place for those "do gooders" engaged in unknown, unpopular, and often highly significant movements for defense of the rights of poor people such as sharecroppers, farm laborers, American Indians and striking tin miners in Bolivia.

The Jacksons were occasionally invited to the White House by President and Mrs. Roosevelt (as the formally courteous Pat Jackson always referred to them). Roosevelt apparently considered Gardner Jackson a necessary part of the New Deal. He had him assigned to work with several agencies in the Department of Agriculture, and may have persuaded John L. Lewis to hire Jackson in 1938 to work in Lewis' political action committee known as Labor's Non-Partisan League.

A great trial to those who knew and loved Pat Jackson was the fact that he was an alcoholic. He would go for weeks without a drink. When others had highballs, Pat would indulge in cranberry juice. Then suddenly, without warning, he would be off on a "bat," as his wife Dode called his periodic drunks. He would start drinking, usually with the "guys" at the National Press Club, of which he was a member. When he reached the point of no return, a certain employee of Washington's favorite men's club would see that he got safely across 14th Street into the nearby Willard Hotel. There the desk clerk and the bellboys would take over, often locking Pat in his room while he slept off his "bat." If the hotel failed to shut off the telephone, Jackson would proceed to telephone his friends all over the country, at all hours of the day or night. While his words sometimes became slurred, what he had to say made sense—drunk or sober. Once, while on one of these binges, he was among the guests at the country home of Drew Pearson, the newspaperman. Pat pushed some New Dealer whom he considered a phony (and probably was) into the Pearson's swimming pool. Normally the epitome of courtesy, when in his cups he often sought out people and dressed them down for their failings. Once he tackled the distinguished Senator William Borah of Idaho, telling him: "Bill Borah, you are the worst phony ever in Washington," and as usual, Pat was right. FDR was known to have reveled in the exploits of his friend Pat Jackson.

One time in Washington, Jackson invited me to lunch with him at the National Press Club. He introduced me to a number of well-known newspapermen, top government officials, and to various hangers-on. Suddenly another drunk approached us, and after having been introduced to me, put his arm around Jackson's shoulders and said: "Gardner Jackson, the only man alive ever led around on a leash by an underdog."

After Pat had come to the rescue of A. B. Brookin on the picket line, we named him Washington representative of the Southern Tenant Farmers Union.

7   Strike of '36 and Its Aftermath

Roll the Union On

We're gonna roll, we're gonna roll,
We're gonna roll the Union on;
We're gonna roll, we're gonna roll,
We're gonna roll the Union on.

If the planter's in the way
We're gonna roll it over him,
We're gonna roll it over him,
We're gonna roll it over him,
We're gonna roll the Union on.

—John L. Handcox

The Union had won a signal victory in the strike of 1935 when the cotton pickers demanded $1.00 per hundred pounds for picking the crop, and had accepted 75 cents or the equivalent of $1.50 per day, winning a wage increase of 50 percent. The union membership grew to 25,000. The organizers in the field, the local secretaries, and above all, the newly liberated women leaders, were determined to win a wage increase for the six weeks work in the spring of 1936 and force the planters to sign contracts with the union. The day to stop work was set for those who were chopping cotton in the green fields. Circulars were printed; meetings were held; and on the morning of May 18, pieces of union literature were found everywhere.

The Marches

A new kind of picketing started spontaneously. There were long lines of men, women, and children marching down the roads. A working cotton chopper would look up and see what appeared to be thousands coming his way and he would join them. All the people in the line were eight or ten feet apart, and the number increased as hoes were thrown down and all work on the plantations ceased. The planters also took to the roads, riding in cars day and night. Bands of men with guns and baseball bats began to attack the peaceful marchers. Near Earle, Arkansas, Paul D. Peacher and Everett Hood led a mob in an attack on black and white marchers. Among those almost beaten to death was one of the eighteen men who had founded the movement two years before, Jim Reese, the white sharecropper who was so amazed when Norman Thomas first came to Arkansas in early 1934 and spoke at the Tyronza High School auditorium. A black woman, Eliza Nolden, was so badly beaten that she died of her injuries. Frank Weems, a black man, was beaten to the ground. Weems disappeared. Everyone in the union believed him dead. Accompanied by Evelyn Smith, the office secretary, I search the back country roads for two nights, calling on union members for news of him. All reported having seen both Weems and Reese left for dead on the side of the road. A few days later, there was a report that Reese was alive, and that Frank Weems' body was at the home of a Baptist minister in the country.

A National Human Interest Story

Kester had participated in a union funeral service for Barney Graham, striking coal miner shot down on the streets of Wilder, Tennessee, but he was away, so I sent a telegram to Reverend Claude C. Williams, who then lived in Little Rock and was conducting something he called "New Era Schools." Williams, who had once been a Presbyterian minister, preaching hellfire and damnation on Sundays, had boasted that he had married many couples and conducted hundreds of funerals and while some of the marriages didn't last, he never had a funeral go back on him. I asked Williams to go to Earle and conduct Frank Weems' funeral.

The next day Claude Williams arrived in Memphis to get information as to the persons to contact. While waiting in the outer office to see me, Williams was joined by Willie Sue Blagden who, hearing of his mission in Arkansas, asked to join him on the trip. I told Williams how to get to the leading union members in Earle, and he asked if he should allow Willie Sue to accompany him. He felt that the presence of a white woman might be some protection; southern chivalry was still presumably alive even in Arkansas. I reluctantly agreed that Willie Sue could go, but warned Williams that she was young and impetuous. Williams and Blagden then started for Earle, first stopping at Clay East's service station over on Poplar Avenue, not far from Union headquarters. While East filled the gas tank, Williams told him of his mission to preach a union funeral, and Willie Sue called her home to inform her parents where she was going. East later said he hadn't said anything, but he thought that the idea of a white minister going to preach a Negro's funeral in Arkansas was just plain crazy and was probably one of Mitchell's weird ideas. Apparently someone in Willie Sue's family called her brother, who was a sports writer on the *Memphis Commercial Appeal*, the voice of the Arkansas planters. Anyway, word of the Williams-Blagden expedition reached Earle before the pair arrived there. Stopping at a drugstore in town for a Coca Cola, they were apprehended by a band of planters and taken out to a woods. Williams was roughly handled, called a Yankee agitator, and severely beaten with harness straps. Willie Sue was given only two or three hard licks. About sundown, she arrived back at the railway station in Memphis and called me. She was hysterical. She said that Williams had been killed and that she was so badly beaten she could hardly walk. I sent a telegram to the Attorney General of the United States demanding an immediate investigation by the FBI, and then called the Memphis newspapers, and all of the wire services. I was asked to bring Willie Sue to the office of the *Memphis Press Scimitar* for an interview and pictures. Pictures of the black and blue welts on Willie Sue's prominent thighs appeared in newspapers all over the country.

I also asked Benton Stong, Associated Press bureau chief, to have Little Rock reporters contact Williams' home. Williams had arrived home, having been escorted halfway to Little Rock by the planters. He reported that he had been beaten, but refused to say anything further. He would not be interviewed or have pictures made of his injuries.

The beating of a white woman and a white minister became a nationwide human interest story. No attention was paid to Eliza Nolden, a black woman soon to die from the effects of a severe beating, nor to the serious condition of white sharecropper Jim Reese, injured for life, or to the fact that Frank Weems, a black sharecropper, had presumably been beaten to death. After all, these three people were just sharecroppers. Willie Sue Blagden belonged to a prominent Memphis family, and Williams, though recently ousted from his church, was still a minister. As it turned out, we were lucky about one thing, anyway. Some months later, Frank Weems was found alive, in Alton, Illinois.

Dave Benson—Jailed

Shortly before the Blagden-Williams affair occurred, and while we were on strike, the WPA in Memphis had cut off relief recipients by the thousands and instructed them to go chop cotton in Arkansas. The union replied to this strike-breaking activity by the Federal government with protests to Washington and by picketing at both ends of Harahan Bridge across the Mississippi that joined Tennessee and eastern Arkansas. The Workers Alliance, a national organization of the unemployed relief workers sent one of its top organizers to aid the STFU. His name was Dave Benson. He arrived in Memphis driving a car with Washington, D.C. license plates, accompanied by a young woman said to be his fiancée. After setting up picket lines and helping to stop thousands of laid-off reliefers from going into the fields, Benson offered to go to Arkansas to aid the marchers, crisscrossing the plantation roads over several counties. I told Benson not to become active in the marches; to remain an observer only. Nevertheless, Benson started following the marchers in St. Francis County, driving behind them in his car, along with his girlfriend. They had been in the field only two days when Benson was arrested and charged with "interfering with labor," having an automobile with "foreign" license plates, and not having a valid driver's license. Dozens of strikers were being arrested and jailed at this time. Benson's fiancée, who was not arrested, returned to Memphis to report what had happened to him.

Clay East Faces a Mob

Clay East volunteered to take a Little Rock lawyer, D. M. Moody, over to Forrest City to defend Benson. Moody was the son of the lawyer assigned by the court to defend the Scottsboro Boys in their first trial in 1931. As Clay East recalls:

I brought the lawyer from Little Rock to Memphis. He stayed overnight at the William Len Hotel. Then we went to Forrest City the next day. I had a .38 automatic that I used to wear on a rubber band tied on my leg. Nobody could tell I had a gun. I had this gun with me. Moody told me that if I was going to take the gun, he would not go with me—that it would not be fair to him if I went armed, and got both of us killed. That's what would have happened. I didn't take it. When we first got there (Forrest City) we went to see Benson in jail. I am telling you, he was scared to death. He told the lawyer not to defend him, or they would both be taken out of there—not to say a damned word. The lawyer didn't make a defense, he only arranged for a continuance of the case. The trial was conducted in the St. Francis county courthouse. The lawyer just said "continued" and Benson went back to jail. Moody passed me in the courthouse and was out by my car. It was lunch time. The sheriff and all his people were taking off for lunch. My car was parked right in front of the courthouse. There was a mob all around the lawyer, and I thought, "Oh Hell, I've got to go down there." It took everything I had to walk down those steps to the car. Then E. F. Bunch, whom I had known back in Tyronza, pointed me out as "the damned guy who started this thing down on his uncle's farm." The mob took out after me and left the lawyer alone. I don't see how the hell he could eat, but Moody went on down town to a cafe and had his lunch. Bunch led the mob on. They were hollering, "Kill the son of a bitch," and all kinds of stuff like that. There must have been 50 or more of them. I was backing up. I backed into a hedge, and there was a ditch. I fell into it, and the mob, hollering "Kill him" was trying to get to me. I was lying on my hips, and every time one of those guys would get close to me, I'd kick hell out of him. Then some nice, great big guy, six foot or more tall, got astraddle of me in the ditch, and said, "Get off this man, and let him get up." I never did know why he did it. Anyway, when he got the mob off me, I said that if I had done anything, they should put me in jail. Bunch was a deputy sheriff. The mob didn't have any plans right then, so they put me in jail. Even after I was locked up, the mob was trying to get at me. I backed off into a corner so they couldn't get at me. The jail was in a separate building back of the courthouse. Then the sheriff, Mr. Campbell, came and ordered the mob to get back from me. He carried me to another part of the jail. Dave Benson was there and he said that he had been there 72 hours, but felt he would never live to see another 72 hours. The mobsters told me they would string me up that night. "Your body will bust your neck." I was there about an hour. In the meantime, a classmate who had been to Blue Mountain College with me came in and just looked at me. He didn't say a word—just looked as if he wanted to say: "What's a nice guy like you doing in this mess?" Then the sheriff came in and asked if I would like to get out of there, and I told him: "HELL YES, I haven't done anything!" They had searched my car, and found a list of customers who had bought inner tubes from me. They thought it was names of people who would "take their places" (union men). The sheriff said he was going to get the state rangers (highway patrol) to take me out. Benson was pleading with me that it was a trap and not to go, but I told him I would rather take my chances outside than stay in jail. The sheriff and I started out. I started to straighten my car seats. A big ranger sitting in my car told me, "Let's get out of here *fast*."

So with a patrol car in front and another behind him, Clay East and escorts headed for Memphis. A front page news story in the *Press*

Scimitar read: "Memphis merchant drives 95 miles an hour in getaway from Forrest City Mob." Clay later learned of a planned rescue attempt by a former policeman in Memphis, and a young black man, both friends of his, who heard over the radio about his being jailed and threatened by a lynch mob. The ex-policeman mounted a machine gun on the back seat of his Ford, and the black had a 30-30 rifle. They were en route to Forrest City when the three cars passed them going to Memphis.

Clay East did not know that day who called the state rangers. I discovered later that it was a small and courageous man, John F. Hynds, who had paid no attention to the union, until he saw the mobbing of East. He got angry and called the ranger captain, and demanded that he get there to rescue East who was fighting off a mob of fifty men. Hynds then joined the union. He became an organizer, and along with his black partner, Jim Sisk, organized St. Francis County solidly. They had 4,500 members before the year ended. Hynds was jailed along with others for calling a strike of WPA workers and picketing the courthouse where only a few months earlier East had been mobbed.

Hynds also had a run-in with E. F. Bunch, the deputy sheriff who led the mob that day the cotton choppers quit. Bunch pulled a gun on Hynds and threatened to shoot him. Hynds pulled his knife out, grabbed Bunch about the neck and said, "Go ahead and shoot, you S.O.B. I'll cut your throat as I fall." Bunch dropped his gun and ran. Incidentally, Hynds was a good republican who voted for Alf Landon that year and for Wendell Wilkie in the 1940 presidential race.

In the meantime, despite mob attacks and jailings, the marches kept rolling every day. Here is an extract from a news bulletin issued June 9, 1936 by the Southern Tenant Farmers Union:

Black terror closes down over Eastern Arkansas as the Southern Tenant Farmers Union battles for its life. The strike of cotton choppers goes on with Union members hunted down with dogs, beaten, jailed and driven from the state. Bands of armed planters patrol the roads and highways turning back all workers who attempt to leave the plantations. Men arrive in Memphis singly, only to be arrested on charges of vagrancy. Five members of the Union, Robert Brunson, John Riley, Gus Bentley, Simon Walters and Willie Wilson were sentenced yesterday in a Memphis court. They are being sent to the County Workhouse today. The men were arrested at the home of E. B. McKinney, Vice President of the STFU. His home was raided yesterday. McKinney is now in Washington on a speaking tour for the Union.

Chief of Police Will D. Lee says Mitchell and McKinney are responsible for the strike in Arkansas. Asked by a local newspaper reporter if he intended to have H. L. Mitchell picked up, Lee replied, "Not Yet" intimating that they would get him later. Herman I. Goldberger, STFU attorney, had to ask for protection from police to get back to his office [after appearing at the trial of the five men, and being surrounded by a group of plantation owners from Arkansas after the trial was over].

A raid on the Union headquarters on Broad Street, or H. L. Mitchell's home, is being expected momentarily. Threats have been made by planter gangs to kidnap Mitchell, take him into Arkansas to be lynched after torture by the mob, while Memphis police stand by and refuse protection for the Sharecropper Union Leader.

The above press release was written by a student volunteer, probably Prentice Thomas, a black from Howard University. Whether it was ever published is unknown, but it expresses the terror that affected everyone in the union in those days. Readers were called upon to send letters and telegrams of protest to Mayor Watkins Overton of Memphis, and Chief Will D. Lee of the Memphis police.

The governor ordered in the National Guard to eastern Arkansas in an effort to break the strike. *The Arkansas Gazette,* the state's largest and oldest newspaper, sent its war correspondent to cover the share-cropper conflict. However, it was not the governor or the National Guard that ended the strike. It was the weather. For nearly six weeks no rain fell. Most of the cotton had been thinned for the first time before the strike started. Without rain the grass and weeds didn't grow, and the workers weren't even needed. The men and women grew tired of marching and singing. So the union called off the strike. No material gains were made. Wages offered for plowing and hoeing remained at near $1.00 instead of the $1.50 a day demanded. No contracts were signed, but some interesting things happened in the strike's aftermath.

The Arkansas Peonage Case

Not long after the end of the cotton choppers' strike, a crew of cameramen from *March of Time* came to the area and reenacted events of the preceding month. A movie called *Land of Cotton* was produced and released in August 1936. It was shown in 6,000 movie theaters throughout the United States. The governor of Arkansas, when he appeared in the *March of Time* film, said there was "no peonage in Arkansas." However, we created such a stir throughout the country that after an FBI investigation in the early fall, Paul D. Peacher, deputy sheriff and city marshall of Earle, Arkansas, was tried and found guilty of holding 13 union members in slavery. His plantation-owning friends, for whom he had been acting in breaking up union meetings and jailing our members, did not come to his aid. He had to raise the money to pay his $3,500 fine and to pay his own lawyer's fees and expenses. Peacher sent a letter to the editor of the *Memphis Commercial Appeal* telling who was responsible for his anti-union activity, giving names, dates and places. The editor called in the union's attorney, Newell N. Fowler. Fowler agreed with the editor that much of the letter was libelous, and it was not published. "Mr. Peaches" as the union folks called him, finally sold out and left Arkansas.

The conviction of Paul Peacher, with the intervention of the federal government, was a great victory for the union. Men and women were no longer so afraid. In one county we now had 4,500 members where there had been none before. Volunteer organizers, many of them unable to read or write, carried the message throughout the big plantation country. Word spread about how the union was going to take over the plantations, and how the sharecroppers were all going to become farmers on their own land. While some estimated the union membership at 31,000, I am sure that no fewer than 200,000 men and women came into the union during the years 1936 to 1938.

New Union Rituals

Some of the established locals in the area near Earle, Arkansas, worked out a special initiation ceremony. When the people who had held back during the strike applied for membership in the Edmondson local, they were required to run a "gantlet." Since they had escaped getting whipped by the planters, the original members formed a line, and with leather straps, they took a whack at every new member as he or she ran through the line.

John Alford Gammill, president of the Roundpond local, with some assistance from Butler, prepared an *STFU Manual and Ritual*. Every member had to subscribe to an oath never to reveal the secrets of the union. When a new member applied, he or she was blindfolded and, hands tied with a rope, led to a chair. Underneath the tin seat was a lighted candle. As the seat grew warmer, the new member began to squirm until, finally, unable to bear the heat, he would rise from the chair. The new member was then told that he had learned not only to obey the union rules, but had learned to get up and go and was no longer shiftless and no-account, as the plantation owners always claimed every sharecropper to be. There were also special handshakes, so members would recognize each other. The distress call was: "I'm K.O." and when another member heard the call, he was pledged to go to the aid of his fellow member, even at the risk of his life.

Every three months, the executive council would send to each local secretary a "password" written in code. The local president was the only one who had the code book. He translated the new password and then would whisper the word to each member as he came to meeting. When a member visited another local union, or met another member, he would ask: "What is the time?" The proper reply was "It's not too late," and after the correct handshake, the two members would exchange the password. All of this sounded to me like a lot of rigamarole, but it seemed to hold the members together, and it created between the races a very strong fraternal bond. One couldn't take an oath and refuse to live up to it, just because the other member happened to be of a different color.

Gunfire at Commonwealth College

But there was still internal dissension in the STFU as I found out through an incident that occurred shortly after the end of the strike. On July 2, 1936, en route to Oklahoma, I arrived at Commonwealth College in the mountains of western Arkansas. I was accompanied by two young friends, Sidney Hertzberg and Tony Peterson. Sidney was a New York socialist and a former reporter for *The New York Times*, and Tony was an ex-coal miner. We were too late for a free lunch in the dining room. We were met and assigned to rooms in the guesthouse near the commons, by Charlotte "Chucky" Moskowitz, secretary-treasurer of the college. There were perhaps a dozen students playing volleyball, or just lounging about. I thought it strange that no one showed any interest in our arrival. Other times when I had visited there, students and faculty had turned out to welcome me and shower me with questions about the activities of the union.

We had stopped by mainly to see Walter and Myrtle Moskop. Myrtle was a new member of the executive council, having been elected along with a black woman, Marie Pierce, as a result of a women's movement at the STFU convention in early January of 1936. I went into the kitchen to see Ed Pickering, another STFU member. I asked where Walter Moskop lived and if Ed could show me the way to his cabin up the mountain. There were separate dormitories for men and women, a few two-room cabins for married couples and for youngsters who in today's parlance would be considered special friends who shacked up together. But Pickering said he had to finish cleaning up and to start preparing for the evening meal, and he couldn't get away. Then Richard Babb Whitten, the director of the college came by. He said he'd go with me to see the Moskops. Dick, Tony, and I started up the mountain path. I urged Tony to stay behind. "This is one place in the world where I don't need a bodyguard."

Tony, whose family had been in the Herrin, Illinois, coal fields when the miners massacred dozen of Pinkerton detectives and other scabs during a strike, had attached himself to me for the duration of the strike of '36. Every morning, when I would get ready to leave my home in Memphis, where I had been living since the previous year, there would be Tony, sitting on the front porch. He would get in the car, go to the office, stay within ten feet of me the entire day. Tony carried not one but two guns: one in a holster on his hip; another in a shoulder holster under a coat he wore all the time. He was never without his weapons, and I was never without Tony. Howard Kester, fearful that I would be assassinated by planters, even in Memphis, was largely responsible for my bodyguard. This day, at my request, Tony stayed behind.

Soon Whitten and I were at the Moskop cabin, sitting in the front room, talking. Whitten and I were seated on a day bed. Moskop and his wife were across the room in chairs. The talk was friendly, all about the conditions of the union and how the Moskops should get ready to go to Muskogee the next morning to attend the executive council meeting. After about fifteen minutes, Walter Moskop rose, and in a calm voice said, "Mitch, I have something I want to show you." He went into the back room where he remained for at least five minutes. Whitten, Mrs. Moskop, and I continued talking. Suddenly Walter Moskop was standing in the doorway, a pistol in hand, shooting at me. Whitten, who was in the line of fire, jumped up and ran outside. I was standing sideways to the gunman. Moskop's face was deathly gray and aquiver. All of the shots—five or six of them—missed, although I was less than twelve feet away. Mrs. Moskop took the gun away from her husband, and Walter yelled: "I will get my shotgun! I shore as hell can hit you with that!" He made a dive for the back room, and Myrtle Moskop told me: "He has a loaded shotgun in there, and you had better run for your life!"

I tore out down the mountain, soon overtaking Whitten, shouting: "Tony! Tony! Moskop is trying to kill me!" Tony Peterson and Sidney Hertzberg were at the guesthouse, and they reached the commons about the time Whitten and I arrived. We decided not to stay overnight after all, and we quickly loaded the car with our belongings and drove out. Whitten was riding on the running board of our car, talking earnestly about how this must not get into the newspapers, and that the attempted assassination must be handled by a peoples' court, in line with working-class justice. He was fearful that both the college and the union would be hurt if it became known that a union member had tried to kill the secretary of the STFU at Commonwealth. Sidney Hertzberg later described his reaction: "I heard the shooting. The incident seemed unreal. I didn't see it, but the whole idea that someone was shooting at Mitch within earshot of me, was unbelievable. I had never in my life heard gunfire, and the idea that a friend of mine was involved, was something I couldn't absorb."*

Leaving Commonwealth, we met Howard Kester in his car, accompanied by Evelyn Smith, office secretary of the union, and E. B. McKinney and A. B. Brookins, both blacks. It was Kester's idea to test the sincerity of the Commonwealth administrators by having two black men remain there overnight. The College was located in a lily-white county, and no Negro had even been allowed to visit there, let alone stay overnight. This was just one of the incidents in which Kester tried to force people to live up to their professed beliefs. It didn't work that time, because of the gunfire at Commonwealth. The two cars went on to Muskogee that night. The next day the executive council met, and after considering the Commonwealth incident, agreed that the latter must not be publicized. Myrtle Moskop did not attend the meeting.

Saturday was July 4th, and the council had its final session at an all-day picnic at Taft, a town entirely owned by sons and daughters of ex-slaves who had staked their claims when Oklahoma was opened for settlement. Here they had built a community, and for a long time there was a sign on the highway as one entered the town: "WHITE MAN, DON'T LET THE SUN GO DOWN ON YOUR HEAD IN THIS TOWN." (At one time, there were signs in towns all over the South warning blacks not to stop after dark.) During the Fourth of July celebration, I was given special consideration. Two heavily armed black deputy sheriffs stayed near me throughout the day. (There is a picture in the STFU files showing the two lawmen and me). For the first time in my life, I felt comfortable with the law on my side.

Moskop had been one of the first whites to join the union in Marked Tree. He had been a sharecropper, but was evicted prior to the coming of the plow-up under the New Deal. He had made his living as a bootlegger and had served time for this. He was also a small-time gambler, and got a job now and then in "public" work, when he could find one. He had some education, and had obvious leadership ability. He had been sent out on the first sharecropper money-raising expedition to the East. A drawing of Moskop by a revolutionary artist, Joe Jones appeared in the *New Masses* in 1935. Moskop could tell stories that greatly affected his hearers up North. One was about the kind of clothing little children had to wear. Their clothes were made by their mothers from worn out cotton sacks, and all of them used the soft sacks in which flour came for the underclothing. According to Moskop, any little girl among the share-cropper children, if turned upside down, would show on her panties the label: "Mother's Best," a self-rising flour.

*Interview, *Green Rising* (MCA Microfilm).

When the second convention was held in Marked Tree early in 1935, Moskop had conducted a campaign to be elected president of the STFU, but William H. Stultz was chosen instead. Then he ran against E. B. McKinney for vice-president. I openly supported the black McKinney, and Moskop was defeated for that place. He was chosen as a member of the executive council and served one term only to be replaced by his wife, Myrtle. Someone pointed out that it might not look right for both a husband and a wife to be on the executive council at the same time. I agreed. These things rankled. Moskop had brought charges against me in the trial of 1935. There was also the incident of the shotgun being taken away from him at a council meeting, when he had once before threatened to shoot me. While there was no reason for it, Moskop also may have been jealous of me; Myrtle was a nice looking woman, and no doubt there may have been a glance passed between us, but nothing more.

After the gunfire at Commonwealth, there was some talk of sending the Moskops to California, where Ward H. Rodgers was working as an organizer for the Socialist Party. He had gotten involved in the Salinas lettuce strike, as well as one among the citrus fruit pickers in Ventura County. Rodgers offered to help find Moskop a job as a field worker, but in view of his record back in Arkansas, Rodgers wanted no part of getting the Moskops involved in union organizing. While Rodgers didn't always agree with me, he did agree in the choice of McKinney over Moskop.

While the story of the attempted assassination never got into the newspapers, word spread from person to person, and many in the movement knew of it. A few months later, I met Donald Henderson, the Communist Party's gift to the nation's agricultural workers. Henderson told me that he wanted me to know he had nothing to do with Moskop attempting to kill me. This protest caused me to wonder whether the party might possibly have aroused Moskop's hatred of me. It was unusual for the students to have ignored me at Commonwealth on July 2nd. I had been involved in the cotton choppers' strike since May 18th. There were stories going about Commonwealth that I had sold out the strike to the planters. Putting everything together, I was almost convinced that party rivalry had a part in the incident. This was the beginning of my anti-communist paranoia. Prior to that time, I had welcomed communists and socialists alike, considering them to have the same ideals. However, assassination of political rivals had never been a part of the Socialist Party program in America or elsewhere in the world. The purges by Joe Stalin were already underway in the USSR. I never really disliked any communist except Don Henderson, and I had a great deal of admiration for men like Leif Dahl, Lem Harris and Clyde

Johnson. The strike of 1936 was just about over. The weather was dry and the cotton was high and few hoe hands were needed in the fields and then came some news from Washington.

Early in June 1936, the day before the Democratic National Convention met in Philadelphia, Gardner Jackson telephoned me, saying he had arranged an appointment with Senator Joe T. Robinson of Arkansas, chairman of the Convention Resolutions Committee. We were to speak to him about including sharecroppers and farm workers in the projected New Deal labor legislation. I was told to come to Washington at once and go with Jackson to Philadelphia to meet the Senator. I protested that there was no way to get from Memphis to Washington so quickly. Jackson asked if I had ever heard of airplanes. I said I had, but I knew nothing about possible connections to Washington. Jackson told me to stand by; he would work out a schedule and wire money for the trip. Late that afternoon, I boarded my first plane. I left Memphis at dusk in a small twelve-passenger plane for St. Louis. Flying over the Arkansas delta, I wished it had been daylight, so that I could see from the air the small towns and back roads I knew so well. I changed planes in St. Louis for Indianapolis, and flew to Pittsburgh, where I made another change. I arrived in Washington just as the sun was coming up. Pat Jackson and John P. Davis, of the National Negro Congress, were awaiting my arrival. We took the next train to Philadelphia, arriving before noon, and checked into the Bellevue Stratford Hotel.

At three o'clock, Davis, Jackson and I, accompanied by Assistant Secretary of Labor Ed McGrady, a former AFL man turned government agent, called on the senator. Upon our arrival, almost the first words to come from the senator, the politician whom I had dubbed "Greasy Joe" in a column of the *Sharecroppers Voice*, were, "So you are Mitchell! They say you are a foreign agitator." Joe T. Robinson, the majority leader in the Senate was one of the most powerful political figures in the country, but he did not scare me. I was not much of a diplomat in those days. My temper flared. "Let me tell you something, Senator! I lived in Arkansas for seven years till your God damned friends in Poinsett County decided to lynch me. I left just ahead of a mob, but let me tell you, I have just as much right in Arkansas as you or any other man!"

Jackson and Davis were stunned by this outburst from one usually so mild and soft-spoken. McGrady's eyes were dancing with excitement, and he could hardly contain his laughter at the idea of this important Senator being told off. The Senator too was taken aback, and began to apologize, saying that he was just repeating what some of his friends had told him. But he agreed that I had every right to come and go in Arkansas. Thereafter, the Senator was most cooperative. He was willing to see that the resolution on rights of labor was changed to cover all agricultural workers, including sharecroppers, under the National Labor Relations Act. Then McGrady, who had not intended that the resolution go so far as to name agricultural workers, much less sharecroppers, proposed that Robinson's promise be couched in broader terms, such as that the Democratic Party should pledge itself to protect the rights of "all" workers to organize and bargain collectively. I insisted that the Senator was right—sharecroppers should be specifically named. The meeting broke up with an agreement that Jackson and I were to appear before the Resolutions Committee at ten o'clock the next morning, and that our presentation would follow that of AFL President William Green. Jackson was sure that he had it all arranged so that we STFU spokesmen would be on all three national radio networks—NBC, CBS, and Mutual.

Jackson and I were sharing a room, but he disappeared soon after dinner. When he did not return by the following morning in time for the Resolutions Committee meeting, I went in alone. Ed McGrady called me out and said: "Mitchell, you have double-crossed us." I wanted to know what he meant. McGrady went on: "We arranged the meeting for you yesterday with Senator Robinson on the premise that there would be no picketing of the convention. "Well," I said, "no one from our union is picketing." McGrady replied that a group of students from New York, and the Philadelphia Teachers Union, had a picket line on Governor Futrell's hotel, and they were expected to start picketing the Convention Hall soon. I later learned that a report had spread in Washington that hundreds of sharecroppers from Arkansas were to be in Philadelphia to picket the convention and that it was to stop this that Robinson had met with us.

When John L. Lewis had been called upon to stop the STFU members from coming to Phladelphia to disrupt the convention, he is said to have responded: "If the Congress doesn't pass the Guffey Coal Bill now, I will send 10,000 miners to Philadelphia to help the sharecroppers picket your convention." Lewis got his legislation; the STFU got an interview with Robinson.

It was near noon when Gardner Jackson, unshaven and disheveled, arrived. He said, "I am ashamed of myself, but last night I was out with Heywood Broun, Dorothy Thompson and some of the other newspaper people, and I had too much to drink. I woke up about a half hour ago on a park bench three miles away."

We then had our say before the Resolutions Committee, but by that time the radio networks had shut off their live coverage and were over at Convention Hall broadcasting the start of the proceedings. The picketing by the teachers and students attracted little attention. The convention adopted a vague resolution pledging the party to support the right of workers to organize and bargain collectively, and to defend civil liberties to the full extent of the law. Sharecroppers were not mentioned. The outcome would no doubt have been the same had Pat Jackson remained sober and arrived on time. But at least I had had my first airplane ride and the pleasure of telling off "Greasy Joe" Robinson.

Farm Tenancy Commission Named

Soon after the cotton strike of 1936 ended, a delegation from the STFU was in Washington, and Gardner Jackson arranged a meeting with Mrs. Roosevelt, who proved to be most interested and sympathetic. J. R. Butler, the Union's President, E. B. McKinney, Vice President, and W. L. Blackstone were in the group conferring with the first lady, who relayed her concern to her husband.

After his landslide victory for a second term in office, President Roosevelt agreed to see Norman Thomas on the sharecropper problem. It was at such a meeting that F.D.R. welcomed the socialist leader with the remark: "Norman, I am a damn sight better politician than you are." Came Thomas' quick reply: "You are right, Mr. President. You are on that side of the desk, and I am your visitor." Roosevelt counseled Thomas to be patient, that in time the problems of the sharecropper would be solved along with the other problems of the South.

During the 1936 campaign, the President had made a trip to Arkansas, speaking at a mass meeting in Little Rock, on behalf of his majority leader in the Senate, Joe T. Robinson. Presidential assistant Marvin McIntyre had been designated to meet with a group from the STFU, when the President found it impossible to do so. In any event, McIntyre also avoided the scheduled meeting with the union people. As a result of some of the conferences, pressures, and public outrage, however, the President announced the appointment of a President's Committee on Farm Tenancy. As usual, every farm group had a representative on it. The president of the Farm Bureau, the master of the Grange, and the president of the National Farmers Union were among those named. But there was no representative of the tenant farmers. As soon as the President's Committee was announced, Gardner Jackson, by then our official Washington representative, called on L. C. Gray, the director named by Henry A. Wallace to do the administrative work of the Committee. Jackson told Gray, "You can't name a President's

The Mitchell family's home around 1916, a typical two-room sharecropper shack, at Browns Crossing, near Halls, Tennessee.

H. L. Mitchell, age 18 (Halls High School)

A lynching

Clay East

Early STFU leaders. Left to right: Mrs. W. H. Stultz; H. L. Mitchell, Secretary (in rear); Bill Stultz, President, M. L. Mills, organizer.

Otis L. Sweeden (right), Cherokee Indian, STFU organizer in Oklahoma, 1934–39, with fellow tribesman.

Rev. E. B. "Britt" McKinney, STFU Vice-President.

Norman Thomas speaks at a sharecropper meeting.

Below: Rev. Ward A. Rodgers (right) and H. L. Mitchell at Ward's 1935 trial at Marked Tree, Arkansas, for "anarchy, blasphemy and barratry." (Wide World photo)

Rev. Ward A. Rodgers, tried and convicted of "anarchy and blasphemy," speaking to sharecroppers. (Wide World photo)

Top: Howard A. "Buck" Kester, union adviser. (Wide World photo) *Above:* Gardner "Pat" Jackson.

Arkansas farm workers at a union meeting. (photo by Louise Boyle)

Top left: H. L. Mitchell. *Top right:* Rev. W. L. Blackstone, STFU organizer, and member of the President's Farm Tenancy Commission, 1937. *Center left:* Mrs. Myrtle Lawrence, sharecropper, an STFU leader, 1936–37. (photos by Louise Boyle) *Center right:* Evelyn Smith, first STFU office secretary. *Right:* Rev. A. B. Brookins, Union Chaplain and Song Leader (left), and Farish R. Betton, STFU Vice-President from 1938 onwards. (photo by Howard Kester, 1950).

Committee and have representation from every other organization in the country, and leave out the tenant farmers." Replied Gray, "Pat, you wouldn't tell us we had put a chicken on a poultry board would you?"

To Jackson, a long-time newspaperman, starting as a reporter on the *Boston Globe* and, until he joined the New Deal, Washington correspondent for the *Toronto Star*, this was the most callous treatment he had ever encountered. He threatened to call a press conference and quote the director, unless a member of the Southern Tenant Farmers Union was chosen within 24 hours. After a hurried conference within the Department of Agriculture, Jackson was asked to submit three names from which list the President would appoint one delegate. Jackson gave the name of Howard Kester, the STFU's most forceful speaker; the name of H. L. Mitchell, the union's executive secretary; and recalling a recent visitor who had been an overnight guest in his home, he named the Reverend William L. Blackstone, of Wynne, Arkansas. Later, Jackson got the word from within the Department that the decision was made on the following basis: "Kester was too articulate, Mitchell knew too much." Therefore, as the least of three evils, they decided to appoint Blackstone. Thus William L. Blackstone became the STFU's representative on the President's Committee on Farm Tenancy.

Blackstone proved to be both knowledgeable and articulate. He attended every hearing held by the committee, and when the official report was made, Blackstone filed a minority report on behalf of the union, advocating such things as a guarantee of the right to organize for all farm workers, including tenants and sharecroppers, housing for working farm families, a massive rehabilitation loan program, and the abolition of farm tenancy and its replacement by a system of cooperative farm ownership and operation. The recommendations of the minority report later became the basic program of the Farm Security Administration, headed by Dr. Will W. Alexander, who proved to be one of the union's best friends.

Gardner Jackson, rich man's son, sometime newspaperman, and government official, always a crusader, continued to be a liaison with political and labor leaders, without considering cost or consequences.

"The Land of Cotton"

Partial transcript of *March of Time* film, August 1936:

In all the United States, there is no parallel to the economic bondage in which cotton holds the South. Victims of this one-crop system are the five and one half million white folk, 3 million Negroes, tenant farmers, sharecroppers, laborers who own no land themselves, but farm 60 percent of the South's 27 million acres of cotton. Victims too, and completely dependent on the cotton belt's one source of income, are the planter-landlords. (Landlord to share-cropper:) "I know times are hard, and I know the pickin's are far from plenty, but it's the system that is all wrong. It has been handed down to us through generations. It can't be corrected over night. You don't think I'm getting rich, do you? (Sharecropper:) "No sir." (Commentator:) "A surplus of 13 million bales, a whole year's production, piled up in southern warehouses. Then the New Deal stepped in, ordered every third row of the new crop plowed under. The next year increasing the program to cut 40 percent of all cotton acreage. 900,000 men and women were let off the land. Vast sums were paid out in benefits, but some of the sharecroppers failed to receive their part of the government's benefit checks, and their protest reverberated in Washington's Department of Agriculture where three officials were fired, among them, Counselor Gardner Jackson of the AAA. (Jackson to newspapermen:) "Well, one of the reasons we were fired is because Jerome Frank, Lee Pressman, and some of the rest of us tried to see to it that these sharecroppers got something approaching a square deal." (Newspaperman:) "What percentage of the share-croppers do you figure got jipped?" (Jackson:) "In darn near half the cases, the sharecroppers didn't get a nickel of the benefit payments. The landlords pocketed it all, but actually politics is in back of it. It would be political suicide to go against the planters. They are the Democrats who have the real power in the South." (Commentator:) Echoing across Arkansas are the first rumblings of revolt in the Southland." (Young sharecropper) "You have been share-cropping all your life and you ain't got a thing to show for it." (Speaker:) "We can't live on 75¢ a day, and I defy any planter to show me how a man can live on that wage. (Applause) Singing: Blackstone: "Let's build the Southern Tenant Farmers Union and make our country work while to live in." (Commentator:) "The headquarters of the Southern Tenant Farmers Union is set up in Memphis, just across the Mississippi River from the troubled region. As membership swelled to 10,000 to 25,000, the cotton farmers demanded that the planters sign written contracts to pay wages of $1.50 for a ten hour day, and recognize their right to organize. Soon many a country road was peopled with families wondering aimlessly, some homeless because of curtailed production, others evicted by planters for joining in Union activities. Then the Union called its members to unite for the cotton fields' first strike. (Sharecropper organizer:) "Let them jail us if they want to. We'll fill every jail in Arkansas, but get out of the fields, and stay out until the bosses give in." (Singing of "We Shall Not Be

Moved") (Commentator:) Faced with the prospect of ruined profits, the Arkansas planters closed ranks. (Planter:) "If they haven't got sense enough to know that this Union business is going to make things worse, we've got to teach them." (Cars of men driving down the road.) (Claude Williams and Willie Sue Blagden are stopped on road.) "News of the investigating expedition from Tennessee had already reached planters in the little Arkansas town of Earle." (Williams:) "What do you men want?" "All right, (planters) now get going down that highway." Williams led by men, one remarks, "We have had enough of you Yankee agitators coming down here stirring up trouble." (Then having beaten Williams, the men came for Willie Sue). "Allright, come on out. You're next sister." The next day the violence in the Blagden-Williams investigation came into sharp focus for the entire nation. Newspaper headlines—"Eastern Arkansas Planters Flog Woman and Man." From Arkansas' Capitol at Little Rock, Governor J. Marion Futrell speaks out in defense of the planters. (Governor:) "I deny that there is any peonage in Arkansas, and I defy any one of these outside agitators to prove that there is." (Commentator:) "According to the Arkansas Governor, it is not the planter who is at fault in the Southland, but the one-crop system which has both planter and sharecropper in peonage. Gone are the days when U.S. cotton dominated the world's supply. Foreign countries stepped up production and took U.S. markets while U.S. planters were being forced to curtail their production. Gone too are King Cotton's traditional boundaries where southern wealth was born. Today one-third of all U.S. cotton grows in the new fertile stretches of Texas and Oklahoma, where large scale industrialized farming can produce cotton 40 percent cheaper than in the old South." (Church scene—singing of Holy, Holy, Holy). (Commentator:) "It is plain today that planter and sharecropper alike are the economic slaves of the South's one-crop system that only basic change can restore the one time peace and prosperity of the Kingdom of Cotton." Time Marches On.

8 Voices of the Disinherited

> Hungry, hungry are we
> Just as hungry as hungry can be
> We don't get nothin for our labor
> So hungry, hungry are we.
>
> —John L. Handcox

There are thousands of letters in the STFU collection at the University of North Carolina, Chapel Hill, and also on microfilm in most of the nation's important academic and public libraries. Here are a few samples.

Marked Tree, Ark
April 1, 1935

Mr. Norman Thomas
  Kind Sir.

We have appealed to every forse we no and now we are coming to you to no if its posible for us to get some help. My husband and I belong to the Suthern Turnent Farmers Union. And my husband is an Organizer, and the nite Riders is making it plenty Tuff for him. And we have been ordered to vacate and denied any Garden at all. So we haft to move and haven't got any money at all and it seems to bad to Walk of and leave our House hold stuff, for it means more to us than it would to them. And if we could get twenty five or thirty dollars it would mean so much to us. We tried to get in tuch with Mr. H. L. Mitchell but it seems he can't be found. So this is the only thing we no to do now. We guarded our House and been on the Scout until we are wore out. And hasn't any Law to look to. They and the Land lords have all turned to nite Riding and Mr. Dubard the Sheriff was ask to stop it and he replide I cant stop it. They shot up some houses and have beat up several and have Threaten our Union and won't let us meet at the Hall no more. We are going to haft to have some releif from some source, so trusting it will be possible that you may help us to get away from this place. Hoping to here from you by return mail, I'll close and oblige

Mrs. L.P. Martin,
Marked Tree, Ark.

The following extracts are from undated letters received about the same time:

104

Lisen Mr. mitchell, ant we suppose to get some money for sickeness in case by your land low forced you out in the bad Weather in it make you sick" so Mr. a.g. sweet forced us out an it maid my wife sick, an I ant non the best of my selft, and we had a hod time tring to fine a place to move but we got one at last, so this is all from your truly,

Jessie Townsend

Now mr. Mitchell in our meating we discussed the lesson you sent us tell me how many time are we supposed to discust one lesson and we discusted the defience committie and their work in our past meating now; tomorrow we will hafter to discust the same lesson because i didn't know how many times we had to discust one lesson and i hadent ordered another lesson now the women disided in our past meatting to put on a big progrom at the church in the behafs of the union.

Dear Sir I take great plasure in Writeing you a few Linds to let you no that thro a Long Stougle We was Bless With 21 Men in our organizing Monday night, May the 4th, 1936, by MC Bass. We Pray Gods Blessings for Success.
Please Sen Me a full Line of instructions, the obglation Sheat.
hopeing to obtain Early Reply. We no in union there is Strainth first & last.

Oblige,
C.C. Latcher.

One of the sharecroppers who wrote to the Union Office likened his condition to the fate that awaited the convicted kidnapper of the Lindberg baby:

Kind Sir   I am on the Twist farm, the Place I Suppose Huptmann will be Sint Provided they don't Kill him in the Electric Chair.*

Many of the local unions had colorful names. There was the Blue Woman's local of Wabbasecka, Arkansas, whose secretary wrote as follows:

Mr. H. L. Mitchell
Memphis, Tenn

Dear Secretary:
The Defense Committee of this Local give a box supper for the purpose of rasing money to defend our cases, in which we rased $2.25. The price of boxes was 15¢. You will fine enclose a money order for $2.13 in full payment of our account today. I am use 2¢ to by a stamp and 10 sents to by a M.O.

Yours very truly
Mrs. M. L. Hendricks.

*These letters were first published in a pamphlet *The Disinherited Speak* (New York: Workers Defense League, 1938).

This group of women was most active in the strike of 1936. All were black.

Early in 1936, a member of the Southern Tenant Farmers Union wrote the Memphis office that his landlord's plan to end the labor troubles in East Arkansas was to "Hang old Mitchell on a tall cypress tree." I was then thirty years old.

Madison, Ark.
4/5/36

H.L. Mitchell
Box 5215
Memphis, Tenn.

Dear Sir:

I am a widow woman and trys to live peaceful always. I have been here since 1934 and paid rent. This man is so unjust its the same as a slave farm. He aint got enough mules, nor food stuff, neather a wagon and he is trying to run a big plantation with day labor. They works us from sun to sun at a dollar. Conditions are pitiful with we pore folks. We get nothing scarcely. Wesley Jackson the landlord fights the Southern Tenant Farmers Union. I wants only a chance to make my own living and not have and other get the profit on my labor. I am tired of being denied the chance to live. I only want the potion that due me.

Fraternally yours
Lula Parchman, Sec.
St Johns Local No. 2

Mrs. Parchman was black. She remained in the union for several years and often attended the annual conventions of the STFU.

Mena, Ark.
April 13, 1936

H. L. Mitchell
National Secretary
Box 5215
Memphis, Tenn.

Dear Comrade:

We are building a local here and it consists of revolutionary socialists. Some arrived in these woods during the time of the War (WWI, 1917–18). Some of them hid out here during the war. They are men that own their little tracts of land. Some of it is under mortgage. We want to get a Charter for the Local, but they are so they cannot pay just now, but they will pay in 30 days (their joining fees 25¢ and dues 10¢). We are working as unit now. There is 9 of us and I am Secretary

Yours, Truly
Mrs. Rosie Lee Morelock

They got the charter. Mrs. Morelock, wife of Roy Morelock, came from Poinsett County, near Truman. They were members of the socialist local whose leader was "Uncle" Charlie McCoy. The Morelocks were whites and had attended Commonwealth College, but they settled in a rural community east of Mena known as Ink. W. A. "Billy" Gilbert who became secretary of the Arkansas Socialist Party, was among the leaders of this group of anti-war protesters. He came from New Llano Colony in Louisana, as no doubt did some of the other revolutionary socialists Mrs. Morelock wrote about.

> Edmondson, Ark
> April 13, 1936

Mr. H. L. Mitchell, Sec'y

Please send me 14 dues stamps at 7 cents each. Also send me *The Voice* at 2¢ each (The STFU Newspaper). 14 x 2¢ + 16¢. Send me statement of our account. Now we have 2 men we all know. One owns his farm—George Austin, Edmondson, Ark. He works in the field, but he haves one tenant on his little farm. Shall we take him in? And there is A. Norris who is buying back his home which was lost to the Federal Land Bank. His address is the same. Now these men are leaders in this community and have been for 30 years and they want to join our Union. Shall we take them in? Let me hear from you at once,

> Brotherly yours,
> C. A. Withers Sec'y
> Edmondson Local 32

Brother Withers got an early reply:

C. A. Withers, Sec'y
Edmondson, Ark.

Dear Secretary Withers:

In answer to your question. The Constitution of the Union provides that only workers who receive wages or part of the crop as wages, may be members of the Union. In such cases as you cited, where small landowners who are in the same shape as croppers want to join the Union, the Local might decide to admit them. That is a question which may be decided by your Local.

> Fraternally,
> H. L. Mitchell
> Executive Secretary

HLM/ES ENCL

The Edmondson Local was made up of residents of the all-black community founded originally by former republican officeholders who were driven out of Crittenden County about 1900. Their story is told elsewhere. The issue about which Brother Withers was writing had come up many times. The executive council had ruled that people who were similarly situated to sharecroppers and/or were sympathetic to them could be admitted by the local unions.

April 11, 1936

Mr. H. L. Mitchell

Dear Sir:

Listen one of our members house burned down and he have no where to stay. He wants a tent. Please let us know about it as soon as you can.

Yours very truly
Anderson Wade President
Rt 1 Box 259 Proctor, Ark.

P.S. Don't forget the tent.

Since I didn't have a tent, I sent a volunteer organizer to see about the member. Other members took his family in, and he eventually found another home. The union sent clothing for the family and a little money to tide them over.

April 18, 1936

H. L. Mitchell Executive Secretary
Box 5215
Memphis

Please congratulate a man named Mr. Pete who owns a little store on the St. Francis River. Mr. Pete sent word by one of our members that if we have to strike, don't worry about suffering because as long as he has anything in his store, we are welcome. We are on the road ahead.

Nathan Wiley
Rt 2, Box 55
Widener, Ark.

On April 21, I replied to Nathan Wiley, saying that we knew Mr. Peterson and was pleased to know that he would help members of the STFU if help was needed in the upcoming strike. Peterson was a former coal miner and owned a small store. His customers were mainly people from the plantations. It was his son Tony who became my bodyguard during the 1936 strike.

Nathan Wiley was then secretary of the Widener Local. He became an organizer, was a member of the Executive Council, and remained active in the STFU until his death in the early 1940s. Wiley was the man who wrote to me earlier asking me what to do about some white men who wanted to join his local. My reply was, take them. "There are no niggers in the union, and there is no white trash either; just people joining together to get a better deal for all."

Des Arc, Ark
April 27, 1936

Mr. H. L. Mitchell

I am ritting you a few lines for informas [information] as of crop I made in 1935, in St. Francis County for Mr. Ackin. I made a crop he furnish me $15 a month for five months. He has us sign some papers and he told it was to get tags for our cotton. [Note: Each bale had to have a tag with a number before it could be sold.] We didn't get no tags and we didn't no no better until a governor man from Little Rock come and told me I sign to work for day labor (wages) of $15 a month and I went to Little Rock the state capital. They told me they was going to see about me getting my money. They started to rite Mr. Ackin and told me to give it to him. I told them that I was scared of that man, and I wasn't going there untell some of them go with me. They mail the letter I guess but I don't git no anscer. In the Fall we all picked cotton by the 100 pounds—50¢ a 100. He would not let us go to gin (with our own cotton) wouldn't give no ticket [cotton weighing receipts or tags for bales]. i had 13 bales picketed out and some more in the field. I would a stayed there and pick the rest. Mr. Ackin started to resting [arresting] us and shooting at us. The people all got scared and all run off. If you can get my money I'll pay what you charge. Rite soon and let me heare from you.

From Willie North, Rt 3, Box 76, Des Arc, Ark.

On April 30, I wrote H. C. Malcom, Deputy Labor Commissioner, and sent a copy of Willie North's letter to Mr. Malcom. I also wrote Willie North the same date saying, "The case against Atkins is now in court." The Arkansas Labor Commissioner could and often did file suits against landlords under the Arkansas "laborer's lien" law that required them to make settlements with sharecroppers like Willie North. I also told North to get in touch with Mr. Malcom, the Deputy Labor Commissioner and assured him that there would be no charge for anything the union could do for him.

Mr. Malcom was a railway labor union member and had represented the railway brotherhoods in Little Rock. His superior was a printer, Ed I. McKinley from Pargould, the home town of Arkansas Governor J. Marion Futrell. Both men were kept on as commissioners in spite of their going after plantation owners for defrauding their tenants of their earnings. Malcom, who was quite outspoken, once made a public report on the cotton pickers' strike of 1935, saying he had traveled all over three East Arkansas counties and saw only three people picking cotton.

Meanwhile, as preparations got underway for the cotton choppers' strike of May 1936, letters arrived at the Memphis office. Here's one from Leon Turner, secretary of the Jefferson County Council of the STFU.

H. L. Mitchell
Executive Secretary

We have some traitors in our ranks, and we want to know what we shall do about them. We know about who they are. Some of our Comrades have suggested we throw them, hands chained behind them, in the Wabbasecka Bayou.

Leon Turner

There is no record of my reply to this one. Perhaps I considered it just a local matter. Turner was a young and forceful leader. He had been a country schoolteacher, and had attended the Agricultural and Mechanical College for Negroes (now Arkansas University, Pine Bluff). Turner was elected to the STFU executive council, and in 1938 he was chosen assistant to the executive secretary. He was corrupted by Claude Williams (see Chapter 12) in his effort to break our racial solidarity. Turner left Arkansas in the late 30s and we heard nothing more from him.

There was evidence that the cotton chopper's strike of 1936 spread even into the Mississippi delta. A friend of Howard Kester's believed to have been an industrial secretary of the YWCA of Fall River, Massachusetts, wrote as follows:

Boyle, Miss.
May 22, 1936

Dear Mr. Mitchell:

Tenants quit on Mr. Knotts place near Boyle today. My brother-in-law is the manager of this plantation. All Negroes, 14 families. He had been paying them $1.00 per day for chopping cotton. He started cutting off a quarter (25¢) from their daily pay. He said this was because they were "slow workers" according to his books. They all quit this morning. He now threatens to pile their beds on the gravel road. I wrote you from Fall River last. I may be seeing you soon. Has a general strike been called? Please let me know at once. I am lying low until I hear what the other croppers intend doing. If this strike spreads, send help. Please write. Do not use Union stationery. I am afraid my mail is being tampered with.

Sincerely yours
Eleanor K. Flavell

Box 234
Turrel Ark
May 23, 1936

Dear Sir:

Every landowner around here working day labor. The Golightly Brothers, Daniel Sanders plantations all have signed up for that "Southern Liberator" paper put out by H. S. Barbour, who with another fellow in a car is going about telling every farm hand not to join the Southern Tenant Farmers Union. Oliver Sanders is going from house to house looking for STFU membership cards and taken them up. He is a little law [a deputy sheriff]. So you can see how low down this place is.

Mary Lee Moore

It is possible that mail sent to both these women was tampered with. On May 28, 1936, I found time to reply to letters from Eleanor K. Flavell, and Mary Lee Moore. I wrote Miss Flavell that there wasn't much organization in the Mississippi delta as yet, but if the strike spread to let me know and I would send an organizer. (There were always volunteers to undertake any kind of mission for the STFU. Often one white and one black man would go together into a new area.) Two such organizers once visited the Delta Pine and Land Company plantation at Scott Mississippi. Word spread that the union was going to take over the British-owned 130,000-acre plantation and that we intended to distribute the land to the sharecroppers. More than 500 signed up. J. R. Butler, president, and F. R. Betton, vice-president, attended a meeting at Scott, Mississippi, and when they told the people that as much as the union would like the government to take over the plantations it wasn't going to happen right now, the crowd in the church melted away until there were only thirty or forty persons left who were willing to stay in the union.

To Mrs. Mary Lee Moore, I wrote advising all members to hide their union cards and buttons. Mrs. Moore was soon evicted from her home, and the union helped her to get to St. Louis where she had relatives.

The Sharecropper Troubador

One of the great voices of the disinherited was that of John L. Handcox, the Sharecropper Troubador. The Folk Song Collection at the Library of Congress has recordings made by John Handcox of many of his songs. They were recorded by Charles H. Seeger, Pete Seeger's father.

One day in 1935 John Handcox appeared at the office of the union in Memphis and said to me, "Mitch, I got a piece I want you to print in our paper" (*The Sharecropper's Voice*). Written with pencil on ruled tablet paper, it read:

> When a sharecropper dies
> he is buried in a box
> without any necktie,
> and without any sox.

John L. Handcox was born and reared on one of the big plantations in St. Francis County, Arkansas. He had about a fourth grade education. I encouraged him to write more poems and songs, and he began singing his songs at our union meetings. His best one—"We're Gonna Roll the Union On"—became very popular and is still being sung on picket lines, in union halls, and wherever workers strike to gain their rights. It's a stirring song that appears to have been based on a spiritual, but I am not sure where the melody originated. The "governor" referred to in the original version was of course J. Marion Futrell of Arkansas, who ordered out the National Guard during the 1936 strike. Another of Handcox' songs was "Hungry, Hungry Are We." (See "Songs and Verses," at the end of this book for these and other songs by John L. Handcox.)

9   Women of the STFU

Union Wives

The first women to become involved in both the Socialist Party in Tyronza and in the Southern Tenant Farmers Union were Clay East's wife Maxine and my wife Lyndell. Neither of them appeared to have much interest in such things, but they went along because their husbands were involved.

Lyndell was a devout member of the Church of Christ, as were the rest of the Carmack family. She had attended an occasional union meeting before we left Tyronza early in 1935, before the night riders began to prowl. She had made both J. R. Butler and Ward Rodgers welcome to our small home in Tyronza. She was fond of "Buck" Kester who stayed with us after we moved to Memphis. She prepared meals for all comers and made pallets on the floor for those who came to spend the night. All were welcome regardless of race, creed or color.

The year the union started, our oldest son, Harry Leland Jr., was in the first grade and was being taught by the wife of one of our most bitter opponents, R. A. Lynch, the school principal in Tyronza. Early in the fall I wrote to Norman Thomas about this and the fact that my family was being ostracized by the townspeople. Dell went with me on several dangerous missions. We made several trips on union business, taking Harry and our daughter Joyce who was two years younger. In 1935 Dell accompanied me to Texas and Oklahoma. The following year we went to Alton, Illinois, where we found Frank Weems, who we thought had been killed. We were also in Springfield together, and attended an extradition hearing held by the governor of Illinois for one of our members who had escaped jail in Arkansas and fled to Chicago. The governor refused to allow the Arkansas officers to take Sam Bennett, Jr. back to their state to serve out his term for taking part in a union strike. Bennett had been sentenced to six months on a charge of "disturbing labor."

When our youngest son was born in 1936, I suggested that we name him Samuel for his grandfather Carmack, and Howard after my friend and co-worker, Howard Kester.

The Girl Friday of the STFU

The Women's Liberation Movement of the Southern Tenant Farmers Union first manifested itself at the union's 1936 convention. It was sparked by Evelyn Smith, the dynamic young woman who had been our office secretary for a few months. Evelyn saw to it that black Marie Pierce and white Myrtle Moskop were elected as the token representatives of the sharecropper women on the union's executive council.

When the women first demanded equality in the Southern Tenant Farmers union, including the right to set up separate organizations, none of us males knew just what to do. I first suggested that the woman problem be referred to the incoming all-male executive council. Like all men, I thought I could use my not inconsiderable powers of persuasion with the opposite sex to forestall any further action. The women would have nothing to do with my proposal, however, and they won all their demands.

Evelyn had already been asked to attend executive council meetings to take down the minutes of the proceedings. Thereafter, she was always present with her notebook, and though ineligible for membership in the union—being only a hired hand who had never seen a cotton plantation until she came to work for us—she was there to back up Marie Pierce and Myrtle Moskop on every issue that arose.

Evelyn Smith came from New Orleans in October 1935, to work in the office of the STFU for a grand wage of fifteen dollars a month, plus board and room provided by Professor William R. Amberson. Promised a job for one month only, she stayed for five years. Evelyn had been recommended by Richard Babb Whitten, a young revolutionary socialist who tried unsuccessfully to seduce her, but only succeeded in persuading her to join the Socialist Party. En route through Memphis to become Director of Commonwealth College, Whitten had told me of this young woman, then employed as a typist and file clerk in the business office of the newspaper, *The New Orleans Item*. Anxious to bring order to the Broad Street office on the outskirts of Memphis, I wrote Miss Smith. She replied promptly, saying she would accept the job but that she would need five dollars to pay her rail fare. I sent ten dollars and wrote that I would be away for about a week, attending some meetings in East Tennessee.

Evelyn Smith knew nothing of life on a cotton plantation, but she had heard of sharecroppers. As a new member of the Socialist Party, she wanted to help. She had never been away from home before. It was cold and raining the night she arrived in Memphis, and she looked in vain for someone fitting Dr. Amberson's description. There was no one there to meet her. She telephoned the Amberson home and was told by Mrs. Amberson that her husband was out of town. She invited Evelyn to take a taxicab to their home. The next day Evelyn reported to her new job. For a week she read correspondence from sharecroppers and organizers in the field, and she began setting up a filing system for our Union's records. She felt privileged to be living in the home of a University of Tennessee professor, which was an education in itself. Evelyn and Amberson often washed the dinner dishes together, and she stated that she learned a great deal from him.

Jonathan Daniels, in his book *A Southerner Discovers the South*, described the union offices at 2527 Broad Street, which he visited one day in 1937. He told of sitting on a hard chair talking to J. R. Butler, the STFU President, while rain dripped through the leaking roof into a tub between them. He also noticed Evelyn Smith, whom he described as a pretty, dark-eyed, young woman, more suited for riding a cotton carnival float in a parade than for working in such a grimy two-room office in a slum building.

Long after, Evelyn wrote:

I sometimes dream about the office of the Southern Tenant Farmers Union, where I spent much of my time for five years, rather than the month H. L. Mitchell's letter had suggested. I ride with Mitch in search of union member Frank Weems, reported killed by planters, but whose body can't be found for the union funeral. Great material for dreams was there, terror and nightmare, adventure and romance, heroes and villains, and always the long rows of cotton, with men, women and children dragging behind them long sacks to hold the cotton they picked. . . . To reach the office, one climbed an always dark, narrow stairway that permanently smelled of over-cooked cabbage. I never met or talked to any of the other tenants, whom I sometimes passed on the stairs.

The union rented two rooms for ten dollars a month from an elderly Jewish gentleman, who lived with his wife in the back apartment on the second floor above the hardware store. There were several other front rooms that were rented for light housekeeping by young families, usually with one or more small children. Always on Saturday, Mr. Hanover could be heard saying his prayers, while children cried, their mothers fussed, and somewhere a radio blared out hillbilly music. The union office doors were always closed, but the front windows were open and looked out over the streetcar tracks. Trolleys ran day and night. Rides cost a nickel, but Evelyn usually walked through the Overton Park from her room at the Ambersons, two miles away. I usually drove her home when the day's work was done, sometimes late at night. Evelyn, who soon named herself "the Girl Friday of the STFU," had this to say about me:

Harry Leland Mitchell, always thereafter to be known as "Mitch," returned to the office the second week after my arrival, and made me welcome in a casual, simple, accepting way. Although not the type to set my heart aflutter, it was easy to see how he attracted many of the visiting females who came to learn about the sharecroppers, and found him their most fascinating and educational study. He was young, with a charming unselfconscious boyishness and naiveté which he had learned to make the most of for his admirers. He was also the Man with the Hoe, Billy the Kid, Abraham Lincoln, with a little of Jesse James thrown in. His drawl was authentic if his simplicity was not. He took his work seriously, and his unhurried contemplative examinations of situations, which matched my own tempo, could be transformed into passionate bursts of activity that might keep us working until dawn, or send us off on a non-stop trip to Washington, D.C. . . . He once gave me a two-hour notice to get ready for a trip to New York City.*

There was nothing in the world that Evelyn loved better than to get into a car, and go anywhere, at any time. We were a pair of different

*Evelyn Smith Mungo, unpublished Ms.

individuals devoted to the same cause. We remained the best of friends after our years together. Our relationship was platonic, without a hint of scandal.

Evelyn wrote further:

Mitchell's imagination and a sort of ambition (though not for personal wealth or honors) always kept him one idea ahead of the rest of the union leadership. He had a natural-born knack for publicity. His letters to the Department of Agriculture got attention when he wrote: 'We are on the edge of bloodshed, and these people (the croppers) will defend themselves if attacked. When the blood flows, it will drip down over your Department, from the Secretary (Henry Wallace) to the cotton section at the bottom'. [This letter does not appear in the STFU Papers, so it is possible that while it was written, it was never mailed.]

When he called Senator Joe T. Robinson [Majority Leader of the United States Senate in the New Deal Days] "Greasey Joe" in an issue of *The Sharecropper's Voice,* the name stuck. Mitch couldn't spell, and his grammar wasn't anything to write home about, but he knew what would make people respond—whether to a Union handbill, an appeal for funds, or an exposé of government ineptitude. Someone was around most of the time, usually me, to edit and smooth out the copy. His work, his recreation, and his consuming interest was the Union and the Socialist Party. A combination of innocence and sophistication, he was extremely smart, and got to the core of a problem quickly. He used his country boy mannerisms to enlist and disarm others, whether consciously or unconsciously. He looked less like a sharecropper leader, and more like a news reporter, a rather romantic one with a lock of hair falling over one blue eye. Later, others in the organization would criticise him for driving a good car, a Chevrolet that he turned in on a new model every year, but Mitch could justify this practice on various counts.

On her own initiative, together with Maxine East, Clay's wife, Evelyn went to Earle, Arkansas, to get evidence in the Paul Peacher peonage case. Evelyn and Maxine, pretending they were on a picnic, took a camera and went to the Peacher Plantation, from which they were summarily ejected—their camera confiscated in the process—but not before they had located a stockade where Peacher, a deputy sheriff, held thirteen union members in slavery on his own plantation. Peacher had taken part in an attack on a "union march" as the sharecropper picket lines were called. He had arrested some of the men, had taken them before a justice of the peace, and had them sentenced to jail. Then he set them to work in his own fields. This occurred in the summer of 1936, during the cotton choppers strike.

Earlier that year, Evelyn was present when a sharecroppers' meeting was raided by a mob of plantation riding bosses and deputy sheriffs. Kester and attorney Goldberger were dragged from the church near Earle and threatened with lynching, and only some fast thinking by

Kester, who threatened the mobsters with the FBI and trial in a federal court, saved their lives.

In those days it seemed that every time Evelyn went out on an expedition without me she would get into some dangerous situation. I discouraged these field trips as much as I could. When she went with me, we kept to back country roads and outran the nightriders on the prowl.

Evelyn developed a knack for writing. About 1940 she became the education director for the STFU and prepared a series of mimeographed booklets and hundreds of leaflets containing study courses on subjects ranging from reading, writing, and arithmetic, to manuals of procedure for use in our locals. She collected the songs and poems written by members, and other things that she thought appropriate, arranging them and having some of the pieces set to music. The *STFU Song Book* is hers.

Finally, after being with the STFU for over five years, she joined the staff of the International Ladies Garment Workers Union, and was assigned to work in Knoxville, four hundred miles away from STFU headquarters in Memphis. There she organized two large garment factories. Later she directed a campaign for electoral reform that centered in Virginia, co-ordinated with the work of National Committee to Abolish the Poll Tax. For a while, Evelyn Smith was assistant secretary of the Workers Defense League.

Sharecroppers on the Platform

Women became active in the union during the strikes. There was Henrietta McGhee, a black woman who was jailed for calling a strike on the plantation where she worked. Henrietta was farmed out by the court and set to work out her fine on a privately owned plantation. The Union's lawyer went to Forrest City and posted bond, and she was released. There was great rejoicing when she came back to Mr. Belshias's plantation (the members called him Mr. Belcher).

One of the white women who became active following the 1936 strike was Myrtle Lawrence. She said that when she first heard about the union, she thought it was another church getting started. The following year, these two women, Henrietta McGhee and Myrtle Lawrence, were sent to New York City to help raise funds for the union during National Sharecroppers Week. Two college girls who had been working with us offered to pay the railway fare of the union's vice-president, E. B. McKinney, if they could ride up in the car with the sharecroppers. Janet Frazier of Bennington College and Hazel Whitman, later at the

University of Chicago, traveled with Henrietta McGhee and Myrtle Lawrence. Also with the group was D. A. Griffin, one of the outstanding leaders of the STFU. I drove the party of six the 1,200 miles to New York. En route, we stopped overnight at a tourist court. Since there was only one black person in the group, I had no trouble explaining to the owner of the cabins that we needed two rooms for the ladies and their maid, and one room for Dave Griffin and me. The two college girls who had been living together while working in the union office, naturally appropriated one bedroom, leaving the two sharecropper women to occupy the other. Myrtle, the white woman, dipped snuff, and while attending as one of the STFU students, the Southern Summer School for Workers, located near Asheville, N.C. the year before, had learned to carry a paper-covered tin can about with her and to stop spitting on the floor or ground. For this and other reasons, Henrietta didn't approve of her companion. About the only thing the two sharecropper women had in common was the union. Just before the group arrived in New York City, we stopped at a service station to buy gasoline; it was always cheaper in New Jersey than in New York. Henrietta was the last to go to the restroom. Growing impatient, I asked one of the college girls to go see if she could hurry her up. Just as Henrietta got back in the car, she handed me a note scrawled on a paper towel. It read: "Mitch, don't make me stay with that ole white woman, she have fits." Apparently, Myrtle had nightmares, and had kept Henrietta awake the night before, and Henrietta wanted no more of it. I arranged with the secretary of the Sharecroppers Week to separate the two for their stay in New York City.

Before the group left New York City, we were invited to attend a large mass meeting being held at Mecca Temple. Senators Robert M. LaFollette, Jr., of Wisconsin, and Robert Wagner of New York, and Norman Thomas were the speakers. Since the sharecroppers' plight had been well publicized, our delegation was invited to sit on the platform. As always, I preferred to avoid the limelight and occupied myself with finding a place to park my car until the meeting was well underway; then quietly I entered the back. Upon the platform sat Henrietta, Myrtle, and Griffin. Myrtle was the center of attraction. She had her "spit can" covered with bright pink paper, and was busily engaged in using it. The people down front who had the best view of Myrtle's performance were amused, laughing at the sharecropper woman, and paying no attention whatever to the speakers. Henrietta afterwards told me she was never so embarrassed in her life as by that old white woman making everyone think the union folks were all just like those Tobacco Road people they had heard about.

Myrtle remained in New York for a while. Henrietta, Griffin, E. B. McKinney and I, en route to Arkansas, made a final stop in Washington. Henrietta put on her best performance of the trip at the Friends Meetinghouse on Massachusetts Avenue the last night. She told her story of the cotton choppers strike, and of how she had been jailed and sentenced to work on a privately owned plantation. To her first audiences, Henrietta had told of being set to work burning brush in new ground being cleared for cultivation. By that last night in Washington, she had added to the story, so that she was also toting heavy logs. She told how bad her back ached and then limped off the stage at the end of her talk. Several women rushed up to take her to the ladies' lounge to rest. I, thinking that Henrietta, who was about forty, was really ill, also went over to inquire if I could do anything. She just smiled and said, "Don't you bother, I'll be all right." That night, after all had left except the ones with whom the delegation was stopping overnight, Henrietta started down the steps, laughing, "Ho, Ho, I even fooled Mitch this time." Henrietta was a natural leader, an actress who could amuse as well as inspire people.

Three years later, just before the United States became involved in World War II, there was a large "Keep America Out of War Congress" held in Washington. Henrietta was among those from the STFU who attended the meeting. She was asked to speak at the opening session, and she made a very brief talk, just saying how hard it was on women left behind when husbands and sons were called into the armed services. At noon, Henrietta, in search of a place where she could get some food, wandered into what she thought was a little store, but it turned out to be a combination delicatessen and dining room. She was standing, waiting to be served, when a waiter told her "We are sorry, but we don't serve colored people here." She turned to leave, mumbling something about "Where can I go," when some ladies who had heard her speak that morning rushed to her aid, and invited her to come and sit with them. The proprietor of the establishment then came to the table and apologized: "Mrs. McGhee, the waiter just didn't know you were a visitor from a foreign land." It seems that there was a law in the otherwise rigidly segregated District of Columbia that prohibited discrimination against foreigners with dark skins who were likely to be from some foreign embassy. Said Henrietta later: "That was the first I ever heard that Arkansas was not in the United States."

Women Organizers

Besides those women mentioned above and elsewhere in these pages, there were many other strong personalities who played vital roles in the Southern Tenant Farmers Union and its successor organizations. Among these were Carrie L. Dilworth, who joined the STFU in the late

1930s. Carrie traveled to New Jersey and to California, representing union workers in the wartime migration program. She continued her activities all through the turbulent 1960s. Her house became the headquarters for the Students Nonviolent Coordinating Committee, and it was burned down one night when all the black and white civil rights workers were away on assignments. Among the SNCC workers living with Carrie Dilworth in Gould, Arkansas, was Laura Foner, related to historians Phil and Eric Foner.

One evening, in 1975, while speaking at the University of Washington, Seattle, I gradually realized that I had an Arkansas woman in my audience. She kept remarking: "Say on, brother, tell it like it was!" and "Amen, brother." It was Deacy Real, with her friend Booker T. Clark (one of the leaders of 1939 Missouri Highway Sitdown), neither of whom I had met before that evening. Later I sought them out and arranged for them to come and spend all day Saturday with me, and I tape recorded their stories.

Deacy Real

Mrs. Moore walked into the kitchen, and said to me: "Deacy, the next time you go out of here and don't leave dry wood in this kitchen, I am going to slap your face." Then, I ran to the water bucket and got a mouthful of water to keep me from saying anything, because if I had said anything then, I would have said too much. I was still mad, even after I had served supper. I was too stubborn to walk out, because I really wanted to get her told. Then, when she came back in the kitchen, I had kind of cooled down, but I was still mad. I said: "Mrs. Moore, let me talk with you." She said "Yes," real snappy like. Then I spoke up. "I want to tell you one thing. I am a full grown woman and the mother of five children. The last one that slapped me was my mother, when I was twelve years old. I love my husband better than I do you. I ain't going to take no slaps off him either."

I shook my finger in her face, and told her: "The day you slap me, that's the day I am going to slap you until I get tired. Then when I get through slapping you, I am going to choke you to death. I know they will hang a colored woman for slapping a white woman, but I am damn sure going to take you with me." I worked for that woman six months longer after that, and she respected me. I never had no more trouble. After she found I would speak up she let me alone. I was one of the *crazy* niggers. The white folks called us crazy if we stood up for our rights back there in the 1930s.

Deacy Real said she and her husband were making a crop on the Shellhouse Plantation, not far from Forrest City in St. Francis County, Arkansas. The government was sending everyone a parity check for taking part in the AAA.

My husband got a small check, and the landlord just took it. My husband couldn't read or write. I tried to teach him, but he just couldn't learn. When the next check was due, I told him: "If you put your X on the next parity check, I am going to leave you, because that's our money." Then when the checks came, he went up to the County Agent's office, to pick up his check. All the riding bosses were there. Edward was handed his check, and this fellow snatched it out of his hand, and he told Edward to sign it and give it to Mr. Shellhouse. Edward said: "No, I won't sign it," but they took the check away from him. When he came home, I asked: "You didn't put your X on it did you?" and he said he hadn't. I told him, "There is a bank there in Forrest City." We went to the bank and told them not to cash our check.

We didn't have any money the rest of the year, and that was when Mr. J. F. Hynds came in. I don't remember how we got in touch with the union organizer. Somebody must have told us about him. Mr. Hynds took up our claim. He wrote to all sorts of government agents about Edward Real's check that had been taken from him by a plantation owner. He must have even sent a letter to the White House. The checks were made out and mailed from Dallas, Texas. By that time, I had another job cooking for a man who was Justice of Peace, Mr. Crutchfield. I was making $2.50 a week. I was laying down across the bed one day resting, before I had to go back to the Crutchfield house to cook dinner that night. It was about four o'clock. Two big robust, portly looking white men came to our house. They showed me their identification cards from the government. First, they had gone to Mr. Shellhouse and asked him what he had done with our parity check, and what had become of it. They got the check out of the post office. It had been there all the time. We had been to that post office many times asking for it, but it hadn't been given to us. Shellhouse's daughter worked in the post office. Anyway, the government man gave Edward the check and told him: "Next time they take your government check, get a club and beat hell out of them." We had some close calls. My husband had to watch his P's and Q's thereafter. We attended some union meetings down there in St. Francis County, but I never did get a union card. We moved to Albert Bird's plantation. They called him A. Bird. We were going to union meetings in churches and places like that picture you have of the people. I think I was there under that St. Francis river bridge when the picture was made. Some places we had to go way back in woods to hold our union meetings. Sometimes the speakers would use a flatbed truck. I remember one Sunday we were waiting for someone to come to speak when I began my singing career. I used to be a soloist. I got my training singing the union songs.

Then I really did work for the union. I even taught night school. Mr. Hynds would pick me up in his car at night, and he'd take me to these little one-room school houses where these old people were trying to learn how to read and write. I don't think I ever got paid anything for the work I did. I was interested in trying to do something to better the lives of poor people, and I was right in that category too. I was in the union for over three years, but I never did get a union card. After we left the A. Bird farm, we first moved to Kansas City. We stayed there until 1944 when we came to Seattle. My husband left me after selling our farm. I live here now, and I draw social security, and so does Mr. Booker T. Clark. [Mr. Clark and Mrs. Real were married November 17, 1976.]

Alberta Hynds Richburg

For about two years, Alberta, the daughter of STFU organizer, John F. Hynds worked in the STFU office in Memphis. She had lived all of her life and gone to school in Forrest City, Arkansas. She was about fourteen years old when she first started going to union meetings with her father and mother. Said Alberta:

The mass meetings are the ones I remember best. Several of them were held under the St. Francis River bridge on the highway going to Memphis. [See picture of interracial group, made by Louise Boyle of such a meeting in 1937.] We had speech-making and singing, and dinner on the ground, and they were always attended by both whites and blacks. There was no division on account of race. We just ate where we wanted to and with whom. There were no separate tables for whites and blacks that I can recall. Of course, the younger generation doesn't really understand the relationship that the whites and blacks had in the Southern Tenant Farmers Union. My father bought a 1932 Chevrolet, and he and Jim Sisk, a black STFU organizer would go almost every night to a meeting. The mass meetings were usually held on Sundays or holidays like the 4th of July.

After I finished high school in Forrest City, I went to business school in Memphis. Before that, though, I went to Hudson Shore Labor School in New York State, up on the Hudson River, not far from President Roosevelt's home at Hyde Park. H. L. Mitchell told me that I needed to know something about the labor movement before I went to work in the STFU office.

Alberta recalled that I arranged for a free scholarship at the Hudson Shore Labor College, and gave her a round trip bus ticket, and five dollars for expenses en route. And with that the eighteen-year-old, who had seldom been away from home overnight, was off on the great adventure of her life. She recalled also that Miss Hilda W. Smith, one of the leaders of the workers' education movement in the United States, was director of the Hudson Shore Labor School. They had the best teachers, men and women from the eastern colleges like Smith, Vassar, Wellesley, Harvard, and Yale. Hudson Shore Labor College was for women only. Said Alberta:

A lot of the girls were job stewards and officers in their local unions, such as garment, clothing and leather workers. I remember one girl who worked in the Bulova watch factory. Then there were college students and teachers too who had a special interest in the labor movement.

I came to work in Memphis in September of 1941 after returning from Hudson Shore. I went to Memphis Business College a half day, and then worked in the STFU office for half a day. The union paid me six dollars a week, and that paid for my room and board. My father sent me a five dollar bill each week. Eleven dollars a week was all I had, but I made it.

Mrs. Ramona Wood was the office secretary for the STFU. Cleo Butler had been working in the office with J. R. Butler, and had left Silas Butler, his nephew, and married another man. Mrs. Wood was working full time for the STFU. Mr. Butler had hired her. She was an experienced office worker. She remained for nearly two years, and then left to take a job at the army depot at a much larger salary than the union could pay. It was then that I took on the job full time, and ran the office when Mr. Butler and Mr. Mitchell were away. I remember Mrs. Wood saying her husband was always calling H. L. Mitchell "Superman," because like the comic character, he was always flying about here and there over the country.

One of the funniest things I remember was when H. L. Mitchell took a group of people to work in the tomato harvest in New Jersey. They got off the train in Washington, or Philadelphia, and they had escalators in the station. The workers had to ride from the train level to the station level. None of them had ever seen an escalator before. Some old man was in front, and he had a big suitcase, and the minute he got off the escalator, he just set the suitcase down. There was a big fat woman right behind him, and she fell over the suitcase, and everyone else fell that came up the escalator. They were all piled up in the station. No one was hurt, fortunately, but all were laughing and having fun about riding the escalator.

I remember going to Colt, Arkansas, attending a meeting there. The members were nearly all white at Colt. I remember Madison, Roundpond, and Widener best. There, most all the people were black. We also had a mass meeting at Brinkley where Norman Thomas was the speaker. The first time I came to Sheffield, Alabama, was when a convention was being held by the STFU. Mrs. Woods was still working for the union. She came, and we stayed at the old Sheffield Hotel. I remember Miss Lillian Smith, and I think two other women from Georgia came with her. They attended the convention. Miss Smith wrote the book about a lynching called *Strange Fruit*.

W. M. Tanner was there. I remember he always ate such big meals that he had to take Tums afterwards. At the Sheffield convention he was after Mr. Butler's job as president, but the convention elected Roy Raley. Raley may have had some racial prejudice, but he never let it interfere with his representing black as well as white workers. The Laborers local that he worked for at that time was all white, but when he became business agent for the Teamsters, that local was integrated. As far as I know, the Teamster locals in the South were never divided on a black and white basis, but the Laborers locals were separate, with separate charters for black and white workers. I guess this is where some of the people these days got the idea that the STFU had become segregated because of Raley's being in the Laborers, and then becoming president of the STFU for a year or two.

I went to work for the Teamsters after Raley left the STFU, and became their business agent. I was office manager in Sheffield for 25 years. I saw many other business agents come and go, and there were none better than Mr. Raley. He was not too well educated, but he took care of the members, and represented them well.

10 We Had a Dream

> We face the future with all those who earn their bread by the sweat of
> their brow, who hate tyranny and oppression and who love justice,
> truth and freedom.
>
> From *Ceremony of the Land,* written by
> Howard Kester and Evelyn Smith.

The most revolutionary idea ever advanced in American agriculture was
the proposal of the Southern Tenant Farmers Union for collectivization
of cotton production on the huge plantations of eastern Arkansas. Prior
to this there had been the agrarian movement sponsored by a group of
intellectuals centered in Nashville, led by writers and teachers such as
Donald Davidson, Allen Tate, John Crowe Ransom, Robert Penn
Warren, Stark Young and others who were becoming well known in the
late 1920s. In a collection of writings called *I'll Take My Stand,** by
southerners, the agrarians called for a return to the simple life of a small
family-owned farm as the basic unit in both agricultural and industrial
production. Professor William R. Amberson was disturbed by the
thinking behind the agrarian movement. We started talking about this
early in 1933, before Amberson was asked by the League for Industrial
Democracy to undertake the study of the economic and social effects of
the New Deal agricultural program on the sharecropper and tenant
farmer in the Delta plantation area bordering the Mississippi River.
Amberson's report was based on a survey by socialists, including Clay
East and me. This became the basis of the pamphlet issued by the LID,
called *The Plight of The Sharecropper,†* by Norman Thomas.

Before the Southern Tenant Farmers Union was formed, there had
been proposals for establishing in Arkansas a cooperative farming
project and a socialist educational center not in opposition to, but
parallel to the Commonwealth College at Mena in western Arkansas
and Highlander Folk School in east Tennessee. Correspondence about

---

*I'll Take My Stand: The South and the Agrarian Tradition by Twelve Southerners
(New York): Harper & Brothers, 1930).
†The League for Industrial Democracy, 1934, New York.

this project between Amberson, Norman Thomas, Ward H. Rodgers, Howard Kester and me focused on the acquisition of a farm owned by an elderly socialist near Hot Springs, Arkansas. I recall visiting the farm and staying overnight with this farmer, who had a large herd of goats. However, once the union got started in Poinsett County, the project at Hot Springs was abandoned, but not forgotten.

During the first years of union operation, Professor Amberson and I discussed a project for cooperative farming as a model to replace sharecropping. After I moved to Memphis, we made a practice of telephoning each other once a day. Amberson was an M.D., and during World War I had been attached to a field hospital in France. He had apparently been slightly deafened by concussion caused by a field artillery shell. He would always say to me: "Speak up! Speak directly into the phone! Mitchell, speak more distinctly!" As a result of those talks, I eventually learned to speak well on the telephone and, incidentally, elsewhere.

Amberson, a physiologist, conducted experiments in blood transfusion. Many times he believed he was on the verge of a breakthrough in finding a blood substitute. Guinea pigs and other animals often lived for days and weeks during such experiments. Undoubtedly, Amberson made significant contributions to medicine. He ended his career at the University of Maryland Medical College in Baltimore and continued work at the Woods Hole Marine Laboratory in Massachusetts until he was past ninety.

By the end of 1934, the Southern Tenant Farmers Union had a membership of about 2,000 men and women, mainly in its home county. Before we made any move on the cooperative farming project, at the insistence of Dr. Amberson we made a survey to determine whether such a project had the approval of the members of the union. With the assistance of our local leaders in each community, questionnaires were distributed among all members, who were asked to list their first and second choices of the following:

1. Small farm ownership with government loans to purchase a farm at low interest rates to be repaid over a period of forty years.

2. Farming with a long term lease on land owned by the federal government.

3. Cooperative farming on larger acreages with teams, tools and the land to be owned by groups of farmers and all profits made to be divided at the end of the year.

4. To continue farming on the plantations as sharecroppers, but with a union contract.

A total of 478 questionnaires were returned, and tabulated as follows:

	1	2	3	4
First Choice	284	94	72	28
Second Choice	42	118	318	

In view of the fact that 318 selected collectivized farm operation as their second choice, and considering that few, if any, sharecroppers had ever even heard of collectivized farming, this was considered by the union leaders as a mandate to replace the plantation system with a new type of farm operation.

I prepared a memorandum setting forth my ideas, and Dr. Amberson drafted a bill calling for legislation to nationalize all large-scale farm operations. He called it "A New Homestead Act." It was proposed to redistribute all the land not worked by an individual owner. There was correspondence between Amberson and Norman Thomas on this matter. Then the proposal was submitted to the second annual convention of the STFU held in Little Rock, early in January 1936, where it was ratified.

Norman Thomas and others had been consulted on the STFU plan from its beginning. However, when a story appeared in the *Socialist Call* some days before the STFU convention acted, calling it "a Socialist Party proposal," it created consternation within the party. Most socialists were devoted to the idea of small farm operation, and many owned such farms in the midwest. Caught in the middle between the STFU revolutionaries and the middle class farm owners, Thomas stood his ground, pointing out that the rising tide of fascism in Europe found its strongest supporters among the peasantry. Furthermore, Thomas had been to Arkansas and had seen the poverty and degradation growing out of the plantation system which the union now proposed to abolish. Legislation was drafted with assistance from a group of young New Deal lawyers in Washington. It was proposed to establish a National Land Authority modeled on the Tennessee Valley Authority set up by the Roosevelt Administration as its showpiece of advanced social planning. Eventually, the bill was introduced in the House of Representatives by Congressman Tom Amlie of Wisconsin. It was sponsored in the Senate by Lynn Frazier, the Non-Partisan League Senator from North Dakota, after changes based on the old populist slogan of "Use and occupancy to be the title to land," were written into the proposal. The bill never reached the hearing stage in Congress. However, the mere introduction of legislation to confiscate large landholdings raised a spectre to haunt the planters in eastern Arkansas, as well as the banks and insurance companies in every state where farm tenancy existed. They were concerned that this fundamental proposal of the scarcely noticed movement of black and white sharecroppers could become the wave of the future in American agriculture. While the Communist Party sponsored the Alabama Sharecroppers Union, and greatly influenced the Farm Holiday movement in the midwest, the party never considered such a radical departure as a new farm system. As soon as the STFU's land program became known, nightriders responded with a reign of terror unequalled in the South until the civil rights confrontations of the 1960s.

The Southern Tenant Farmers Union, composed as it was of people at the bottom of the economic heap, was striking at the heart of the power structure. In a sense, we presented a greater threat than did the civil rights movement nearly thirty years later. The land collectivization proposal may have been the most significant contribution of the Southern Tenant Farmers Union.

At a meeting of the Southern Policy Committee in a hotel on top of Lookout Mountain near Chattanoga in the spring of 1936, there was an open clash between spokesmen for the Southern Agrarians and the Southern Tenant Farmers Union. Allen Tate, an English professor, poet, and writer, and one of the twelve southern intellectuals who composed *I'll Take My Stand,* charged that the union was communistic and seeking to impose Russian collectivism on sharecroppers. William R. Amberson defended the STFU and said that the large plantations along the Mississippi River were already established in a form of collective farming, and that the union was seeking to give to the men who worked the land the profits now being pocketed by absentee landlords, banks, insurance companies, and corporations. Amberson also said that in 1932 Allen Tate drove James Rorty, a known communist and once editor of *New Masses,* to Marked Tree, and both were run out of town by the planters because they asked too many questions. This ideological clash ended Southern Agrarianism, which had sought to turn back the clock to pre-Civil War days of moonlight and magnolias.

It should be recalled that in the 1930s, more than 60 percent of the South was agricultural. The New Deal of Franklin D. Roosevelt, devoted to propping up the capitalist system, was just getting underway. There were some people in the government with unorthodox views, like Harry L. Hopkins, Aubrey Williams, and Rexford G. Tugwell. Along with Eleanor Roosevelt, they were considered dangerous revolutionists by the Bourbon politicians and economic royalists of the South.

Following the STFU's convention in Little Rock, Howard Kester and I set out for Washington again, to begin knocking on doors of liberal members of Congress and friendly representatives of the Roosevelt Administration. We had sessions with relief administration people. Among those most receptive to our revolutionary land policy program was Aubrey Williams, a native of Birmingham, Alabama, who had been a relief administrator in Texas before coming to Washington as an assistant to Harry L. Hopkins of the Works Progress Administration (WPA). Another person interested in our ideas was Colonel Lawrence Westbrook, a career army man, originally from Texas, married to a liberal wife from Hot Springs, Arkansas. Westbrook was then head of the Rural Rehabilitation Program, which operated as a separate agency at that time.

On a late Friday afternoon, just at the end of the week for government workers, Kester and I reached Dr. Rexford G. Tugwell's office. Tugwell had been a professor of economics at Columbia University and was one of the original members of the "Brain Trust" that Roosevelt had brought down from New York in 1933. At the time, Tugwell was undersecretary of agriculture as well as the person in charge of rural resettlement projects. I did most of the talking and proposed that the government provide enough money to make a down payment on about 2,000 acres of rich cutover land near Harrisburg Corners, in Poinsett County, Arkansas. There I proposed to set up a cooperative farming project with about fifty selected families and to employ a good farm manager. As I visualized it, the men would need loans while they cleared the land and planted a cotton crop. They would build log cabins to live in. Kester and I had worked out a budget requiring about $50,000 overall. Tugwell and two assistants listened carefully. Then Tugwell told us to meet him on the following morning, and he would give us an answer. Kester and I left the Department of Agriculture with high hopes that things were going to start moving immediately.

At the appointed hour, Kester and I were at Tugwell's office. We were told that a preliminary investigation had been made, that the land was available, and all reports indicated it could become a productive farming operation. Tugwell liked the idea of a project started by both black and white sharecroppers who were willing to experiment in collectivized farming. However, he thought our carefully prepared budget was much too small. Said Tugwell: "The government doesn't operate the way you propose. No less than $250,000 will be required." When asked how long it would take to get the project underway, Tugwell said it would take at least two years. I pressed him to start it sooner, in view of the evictions that had already occurred and others in the offing. Tugwell said he would try to get it launched within a year, but it would more likely take eighteen months. Kester and I left for home, overwhelmed by the slowness of government. Since I was an incurable optimist, I would not give up the dream.

There had been many cooperative or communal projects in this country. One of those still in operation during the thirties was located near Leesville, in southwest Louisiana. I knew of the Llano Colony, and had met some people who had visited there and a few who had lived in that project that had been founded by socialists. While we were idealists too, we hoped to make our project one that was based on economic reality and one that could be beneficial to sharecroppers who participated, as well as set a pattern for the South as a whole. We visualized cooperative farming as the first step on a thousand mile journey to freedom. It was Howard Kester who said, "Mitchell *had a dream*," and that was long before an eloquent young black minister echoed these words before thousands gathered at the Lincoln Memorial in Washington.

I returned from my trip with Kester to find a disaster had occurred, for which I was partly responsible. In a fiery speech to delegates at the Little Rock Convention, I, as union secretary, had thrown down the gauntlet to plantation owner, C. H. Dibble of Cross County. I said: "Sign a contract with the union, or a picket line will go on your plantation." When this threat was duly reported by both Little Rock and Memphis newspapers, C. H. Dibble proceeded to give eviction notices to every family on his place. He had been meeting with Herman Goldberger, the union attorney, and had indicated that he was agreeable to making a deal with the union. However, my ill-timed threat brought down the wrath of the local power structure upon the head of this friendly plantation owner. Mr. Dibble had been called in by the local banker and told in no uncertain terms to fire all his union sharecroppers, or face foreclosure on his mortgage. He was told that the ginner would not even gin his cotton the next fall if he signed a contract with the union.

This was the news that greeted me when I returned from Washington, where Howard Kester and I had gone immediately after the close of the Little Rock Convention. Twenty-one families, men, women, and children, working on Dibble's plantation had been suddenly evicted from their homes by the Cross County sheriff and his deputies. It was January, and the families were camping on the roadside. Kester was at his home in Nashville, Butler had accepted a job as teacher at Commonwealth Labor College, three hundred miles away. Evelyn Smith, our "Girl Friday," was the only staff member in Memphis. I telephoned her, and she told me the bad news. I picked her up, and we went to the office. We waited until midnight to leave Memphis, thinking that any nightrider patrols would probably have given up and returned home—or holed up in some all-night joint where it was warm. About 2 A.M. we arrived at the forlorn roadside camp. The evicted families were hovering around campfires. Some of the younger children had been taken in by nearby families. The adults, however, were just waiting for someone from the union. The leader of the group said: "We know you were sent in answer to our prayers."

They had been camping out for two days. Some of the white union members, led by Reverend William L. Blackstone from nearby Wynne, had been out to see them and had brought extra quilts and food. I proposed visiting planter Dibble, but was told that it would do no good. Mr. Dibble was a good man; he had been out to see them and was crying because he had been forced by the big folks in town to let the sheriff throw them out of their houses. Someone mentioned that there was a church in nearby Parkin, to which some of the folks on the roadside belonged. The minister, Reverend Bennett, had been a union member for a long time. Evelyn and I, with a carload of men drove to see Mr. Bennett. He agreed that the people could camp inside the church until the union could get tents to house them. We then made several trips between the roadside camp and the church. Two tenants with wagons and teams were hired to help with the moving. It was a full night's work. The sun was rising as Evelyn and I drove back across the Mississippi River bridge into the comparative safety of Memphis.

Soon the Emergency Committee of the National Council of Churches, led by Reverend James Myers, made a grant of $500.00 for the dispossessed sharecroppers. The money was sent by telegraph to the union. Tents were bought to house each of the families, and a camp was established in the churchyard. It was not long before sticks of dynamite were thrown into the camp, but they landed in soft mud and failed to explode. The Nightriders left messages threatening to kill the campers if they didn't leave at once. The Governor of Arkansas, J. Marion Futrell, paid a visit to Parkin, and reported to the newspapermen that the whole affair was "much ado about nothing." The Governor said it was a publicity stunt by that damned Mitchell, hiding in his big office over in Memphis, misleading a bunch of "pore white trash and shiftless niggers." Soon Howard Kester returned to the Memphis office and paid a visit to Arkansas to see what could be done for the Dibble families.

The Near Lynching of Howard Kester

Howard Kester, attorney Herman I. Goldberger, and office secretary Evelyn Smith set out to see what could be done. A meeting scheduled to be held by union members at the New Hope Baptist Church between the towns of Earle and Parkin, was already in progress. Kester was asked to speak and had just begun when a band of deputy sheriffs and plantation riding bosses broke into the church. They were armed with axe handles and guns. As they moved into the church, it became apparent to Kester that the mob was led by a cotton buyer from Earle. They started to whack people over the head with the axe handles. Terrified, some of the people jumped through windows, taking glass and sash with them. Others sat still as a rock, and Kester kept on talking. The mob moved to the front of the church, and the leader said to Kester, "Are you coming peacefully, or will we have to take you?" Kester replied, "I am breaking no law, and if you want me, you will have to take me." They thereupon seized Kester and Goldberger and forced them into Kester's car, where Evelyn Smith sat waiting. With the mob leader holding a pistol to Kester's head, they were taken to a wooded section west of Earle. Kester said later, "I decided it was time to talk, and I began talking directly to the cotton buyer. I told him that I had harmed no one, and had no intention of doing so; that I was not from Arkansas, and that if they harmed me, the case would be tried in a federal court, and that there were scores of people who could identify them as our kidnappers. The leader called the others aside, and I heard him say, 'the man is right, we can get into a peck of trouble.'" He came back and tried to make Kester promise never to come back to Arkansas. Kester replied, "I cannot predict the future, and cannot promise what I will or will not do." The leader then told him, "We will escort you to the Tennessee line, and if you ever come back, we will shoot you on sight." Fearfully, the three drove across the Memphis bridge, to safety.

Meanwhile, W. L. Blackstone, a STFU leader who was at the church, telephoned me to report that Kester, Goldberger, and Smith had been kidnapped and were likely to be lynched. I telephoned the Associated Press Bureau, and they sent the news to New York. Norman Thomas was handed a copy of the news bulletin, and read it to an assembled meeting. Word spread that Kester had been lynched. Before he could telephone his wife Alice at home in Nashville that he was safe, she had received numerous calls of condolence on the loss of her husband.

Dibble had trouble finding replacements for his evicted sharecroppers, but eventually found some willing to take the place of the union members. The families evicted from the Dibble plantation formed the basis for the cooperative farm started that summer in Mississippi.

Professor Amberson played a part in this too. He had met a young man, Sam H. Franklin, who had come to Memphis to lecture at one of the churches on problems in the Far East. A native of east Tennessee, Franklin had been a Presbyterian missionary in Japan and had been

working with Kagawa, the founder of the peoples' cooperative movement in that country. Because of the growing tension and war preparations, Franklin had returned home and was considering becoming
involved with those in deepest need in his own country. He and
Amberson began a correspondence. Franklin, who had participated in
the work of Dr. Sherwood Eddy, an educator who had once been an
officer in the World Council of the YMCA, enlisted Eddy in the cause of
the sharecroppers. Soon Eddy and Franklin came to Memphis. Accompanied by Dr. Amberson, they paid a visit to the Dibble families camped
in the churchyard in Parkin, Arkansas. Upon arrival in Cross County,
the trio was arrested and held for several hours until Eddy hired a young
man to send a telegram to his college classmate now in Washington, the
Attorney General of the United States, Homer S. Cummings. Upon
hearing about this telegram, the Cross County sheriff decided to release
these men.

On the return trip to Memphis, Amberson told Eddy of the union's
proposal to purchase a large tract of land to house the people evicted
from the Dibble plantation, as well as others. Eddy recalled that he still
had some money in a fund used for relief work he did in Germany after
World War I. He said he would provide up to $20,000 to purchase land. I
urged Eddy to buy the land we had found in Poinsett County, on which
we had tried to persuade Rex Tugwell to finance a government project.
Eddy had been through enough that day in Arkansas to veto the idea of
a project anywhere in that state. Later, a real estate agent in Memphis
whom Amberson knew, located a 2,130-acre plantation in Mississippi,
near Hillhouse. It was here, some weeks later, that the Delta Cooperative Farm was founded. To Eddy's statement that he "would not put
money in that Arkansas tornado," I replied quietly that he was putting
money in a Mississippi Vesuvius that would blow sky-high one day.

Sam H. Franklin became a missionary among the poor whites and
blacks in the South while managing the cooperative project, later named
Rochdale for the town where pioneer Englishmen had blazed the path
for the first successful consumer cooperative.

The cooperative plan was fine, but the land was poor. I asked Clay
East to go down and make some inquiries. East reported that there were
only about 500 acres of good cotton land on the place. There was
however, a fine stand of cypress timber.

We Southerners Discover the South

Jonathan Daniels a year later visited the Delta Cooperative and wrote in
his book *A Southerner Discovers the South* that the best crop harvested
on the farm was the money given by visitors from the North, who were

persuaded to contribute to sustain the production. With such resources, the Co-op farm flourished for a while. Here was a refuge for 30 sharecropper families—18 black, 12 white, including many of those evicted from the C. H. Dibble plantation. A cooperative store was set up, and a fine young doctor from Texas, David Minter, came to establish a health clinic that served all comers. Dr. Minter recalled that among his many patients there was one who had not been able to hear for several years. The doctor found that the man's ears were stopped up with solidified wax. After some skillful picking and oiling, the man's ears were cleaned, and thereafter he sang the praises far and wide of that doctor who had restored his hearing.

New houses were built for some of the cooperative farm members with timber from the land made into lumber at the cooperative's saw mill. O. C. Morgan was the mill operator, J. H. Moody the head carpenter. Both were from Truman, Arkansas, and for many years they had been members of the Socialist Party, along with Uncle Charlie McCoy. Nearly all the full-time residents of the new cooperative were southerners. Like the union, the project was interracial from the start. However, the founders, Dr. Amberson, Dr. Eddy, Sam Franklin, and those of us from the STFU were determined that the Delta Cooperative should not be destroyed by coming into open conflict with local segregation laws and customs. For instance, the houses for blacks were on one side of the road, and those for whites were on the opposite side of the road. The community facilities were open to all. All meetings that involved decision-making were interracial, as were economic units such as the cooperative store, the clinic, and later, the credit union. Church services were open to both races, as were union meetings of the local branch of the STFU. The children attended separate schools because this was the law in Mississippi. However, since the children of the black members were not receiving equal educational opportunities at the public schools, as one of its first projects the cooperative farm set up a school to supplement their inadequate education. There was no overt social mingling of the races, but when visitors like Dr. Charles S. Johnson of Fisk University, who was black, and his white friend and co-worker, rural sociologist Arthur Raper, came to visit, both were housed, entertained, and dined at the home of the Franklins or some other family of the management staff. In the beginning, the union was in constant communication with both management and the members. Evelyn Smith, the STFU office secretary, was a frequent visitor to "The Farm." At one point there was a report that planters were hearing that every black man and woman was being given a courtesy title by those on the farm. I wrote a letter to Sam Franklin urging caution, suggesting that the people on the Delta Cooperative Farming Project use "brother, sister, or comrade" instead of "Mister and Missus," as the union did. Apparently they adopted a policy of insisting on all but the older people being called by the first name, regardless of race. Prentice Thomas, the black student volunteer organizer for the STFU, reported having seen white and black people mingling together, in every phase of life. While this may have been true to some extent, certainly none of the resident members of the project was willing at that stage to defy the laws of Mississippi or, for that matter, of the nation itself, which upheld segregation of the races. The project, like the STFU, paved the way for the ultimate abolition of segregation. If it had not been for patterns of interracial activity established by people like us in the 1930s, the civil rights leaders would have found the going even harder in the 1960s, when they too laid their lives on the line.

Patterns of segregation varied from place to place within a county and in every state. For instance, when F. R. Betton, vice president of the STFU, in the early 1940s went on a mission to the newly established Providence Co-op Farm, he was met at the bus station in nearby Tchula, Mississippi. He and his driver were slowly following an old truck on a dirt road out to Providence. When they came to a wider place in the road, Betton suggested that his driver speed up and pass the slow poke in front. The black driver said, "No sir, that man in that old truck is a white man, and it's against the law for a Negro to pass a white man, because the black man might stir up dust that would get on the white folks." Mr. Betton had never heard of such a thing before.

Among those who also came to help run the farm was A. E. (Gene) Cox, a young man who was a student at Texas Christian University in Fort Worth. As Cox told it, he had seen some letters in the sky— G.P.C.—that he interpreted as "Go Preach Christ." And so he was going to college to become a minister. But along came Dr. Sherwood Eddy, who convinced the young Cox that the letters really meant "Go Plant Cotton" down in Mississippi. And so here he was. Gene managed the store, kept the books, and saw to it that the others didn't wander too far from reality. The most successful part of his life on the Delta Co-op Farm began with the arrival of Lindsey Hail, a registered nurse from Boston General Hospital, whom Gene married soon after. They continued on, working, living in Mississippi, and saw three daughters grow into fine young women.

Another person who spent time down on the farm was Blaine Treadway, a union man and printer on the Memphis *Commercial Appeal*. Blaine was a socialist and probably an agnostic, as were Amberson and I.

After W. B. Bankhead, a union leader at Edmondson, Arkansas, was evicted for his activities in the 1936 strike, I asked him if he was interested in moving to the farm. Bankhead agreed to look it over, but soon returned to report to me that there were too many preachers down there. Bankhead said the only people he met there that he liked were Mr. Cox, who ran the store, and Mr. Treadway, and that Mr. Treadway was an infidel. Bankhead decided he would remain in Arkansas and do battle with the big planters.

The cooperative farms continued for about twenty years. A second farm had been purchased in Holmes County, Mississippi, where the Cox and Minter families tried to fit into the ordinary life of the community. They quietly went their way, but never compromised with their deeply held beliefs. Then came the school desegregation order of 1954.

KKK in Business Suits

Within a few days, U.S. Senator James Eastland, of Mississippi, made a speech back home, calling upon the white citizens to organize and fight the Supreme Court decision. The Senator, who had grown wealthy by collecting subsidy payments for not planting cotton, set the stage for the formation of White Citizens' Councils throughout the South. Among those who were first victimized by the councils were Dave Minter, the doctor who ran the health clinic, and Gene Cox, by then the manager of Providence Cooperative Farm, who also had a hand in running the cooperative store and credit union.

One day a truck carrying a group of teenage black boys en route to work in the fields, passed the farm. A white teenage girl was waiting for the school bus. As the truckload of youngsters passed, they made some remarks to her which she thought were offensive. She told the school bus driver about the incident. He repeated it. The sheriff had the boys arrested and put through a third degree interrogation. He recorded their answers. Did black and white children swim together on the farm? Did the doctor get a lot of communist papers among his medical supplies from the North? Were credit union meetings attended by both blacks and whites? A mass meeting was called by the Citizens' Council, and more than a thousand people turned out. They listened to the edited recording of the boys saying "Yessir" to every question asked. Then the Council leaders called for a vote on a resolution condemning the Minters and Coxes as undesirables and recommending that they leave Holmes County.

Out of the large crowd of men and women, only two people dared speak in defense of the Minter and Cox families. One was a plantation owner whose plantation adjoined Providence Farm. He said he could call any black boy on his farm and by threats make him say anything he wanted him to say, and that he for one would have nothing to do with such proceedings. The other person to speak out was a bank teller who urged the group to go home and pray about the matter before they acted. The resolution of condemnation was adopted. For several months the Minter and Cox families held out. But the doctor's practice was disrupted. He was followed while making house calls. A guard was placed on the road to the clinic to turn back his patients. Finally the two families had to leave Mississippi. Minter went to Tucson, Arizona, and Cox to Memphis.

Thus ended a dream of a new way of life for sharecroppers down South. Cooperative farming operations ended on Providence Farm soon after World War II began. The younger people had left for wartime jobs and never returned, but there were several dozen families, mainly older folks living near by, so the project became a community center; the health clinic was its most important feature. The store and credit union survived too. The land, some 1600 acres, was owned by the Delta Foundation in the late 1970s. The trustees included Sam Franklin, Dave Minter and Gene Cox. While the objectives were never realized, this experiment in cooperative farming in Mississippi, like the STFU, left a significant heritage of interracial cooperation that has yet to be fully appreciated.

11 Raising Money to Help Poor Folks

In the late 1930s it was difficult to collect union dues from people who only had a little money and that only in the fall, when the cotton was picked and sharecrop settlements were made. When the union was first started, it was decided to set dues at 10¢ a month, or $1.00 a year if paid in advance. Later the rate went up to 25¢ a month, or $3.00 a year. Each local kept some of it, the county council had a part, and the STFU office had a share. Divided three ways, it amounted to very little. Soon the union discovered that there were better means of raising funds. As the years passed, I became an expert at enlisting the sympathies and financial support of well-to-do folks up North. My friend Margaret Valiant, introducing me as a speaker at the Unitarian Church in Memphis many years later, told it this way:

I was called in one day by my superior, Aubrey Williams, the administrator of the National Youth Administration, and asked what did I think of the idea of hiring Mitchell to work for the NYA. Never having heard of H. L. Mitchell at that point, I asked "Just what does Mitchell do?" The administrator looked out the window, and down at his feet, and finally answered: "The best thing H. L. Mitchell does is to get money out of rich widows up North, to help poor folks down South." Then Mitchell wound up getting $100 out of this poor widow who came from Mississippi.

There were also very welcome unsolicited small donations. Dorothy Day, then editor of the *Catholic Worker*, wrote:

June 15, 1936

Dear Mitchell:
   Enclosed is a check for $10 which comes from St. Josephs College, Hays, Kansas. They wish it to be used only for food for those in need. I enjoyed meeting you when I was down in Memphis. Will you drop a line to Father Carney, O.M. Cap., 215 W. 13th St. in Hays, Kansas, and let him know that the Tenant Farmers Union got the money.

Yours for the Christian Revolution
Dorothy Day

PS: Telegraphed Futrell [Arkansas Governor] and Mrs. Roosevelt, about the flogging of Rogers [Claude Williams] and Miss Blagden. I am afraid I'll be liable for libel, as I told Mrs. R. that Futrell was a "Criminal Anarchist."

   The last time I met Dorothy Day was in 1971 at the headquarters of the United Farm Workers at Keene, California. We were both there to meet with Cesar Chavez. Dorothy Day remained an extra day for a visit with me. In 1973 she was jailed during a United Farm Workers strike in the San Joaquin Valley of California, along with many others including priests, ministers, nuns, and Anne Loftis, a writer and one of the editors of this book.
   In the early days of the Southern Tenant Farmers Union, funds to assist us came mainly from the Strikers' Emergency Relief Committee set up in New York City by the League for Industrial Democracy. SERC was formed in 1929 to raise money to help striking cotton mill workers in the South. John Herling, later to become a national labor news reporter and editor of *John Herling's Labor News-Letter*, was the secretary of the Strikers' Committee. Early in 1935 Herling was in

Birdsong, Arkansas, when an STFU meeting where Norman Thomas was speaking was broken up by planters. There was also a Socialist and Labor Defense Committee that aided the STFU in some of its legal cases. In 1936 this committee became the Workers Defense League, which in turn became the authorized defense agency for the STFU members.

Norman Thomas and other directors of the American Fund for Public Service (more often called the Garland Fund after its founder, Barney Garland) also voted a special grant for the Southern Tenant Farmers Union. Thomas wrote me concerning an unexpected windfall that made the grant possible. The Fund had unexpectedly received repayment of a loan made in the 1920s to the Reconstruction Farms of Russia. This was soon blown up into a story—completely false—that had the Russians subsidizing radicalism in America by funneling Russian gold through the Garland Fund.

During the first strike of cotton pickers, I appealed to President William Green of the American Federation of Labor for strike relief. A resolution of endorsement had been passed by the AFL annual convention that year, so Green sent out letters to all international unions, state and city central labor bodies in the AFL. Many responded with small donations that totaled more than $1,000.

The year 1936 started with a convention in Little Rock. With money left over from the AFL strike donations, and the first of the Garland Fund donations, we made arrangements for the use of a large hall in the Little Rock Temple on Markham Street. Several blocks away, near the railway station was the Lincoln Hotel. The STFU rented the hotel for the use of its delegates for two nights, at the rate of $1.00 per room, with two to four occupants in a room. Arrangements were made that the back entrance and the rooms near it were to be occupied by Negro delegates. There was a hall door in the center, with heavy wooden bars to separate the races. Once the delegates were assigned to their respective rooms, someone threw away the bars. Across the street from the hotel was a small restaurant which, for 75¢ per person, agreed to serve three meals a day to the delegates. Here too there was a dividing wall to segregate the customers according to race. I noticed that this barrier also fell quickly. At noon the next day, men and women, black and white, from the same community, were sitting and enjoying their meals together, and no one interfered. It must be remembered that this was still in the dark days of the Depression; owners of small businesses, including hotels and restaurants, were interested in making money, and not so worried about whence it came. So with good AFL dollars and money from the Russian loan repayment, the Southern Tenant Farmers Union desegregated two establishments in Little Rock about 20 years before President Eisenhower sent in the 92nd Airborne Division to enforce the desegregation order in public schools there.

The Founding of Sharecroppers' Week

Soon after the 1936 cotton choppers strike, Sidney Hertzberg came to work for the STFU and remained several weeks. Sidney was a young socialist who had been a copy boy on *The New York Times*. He edited the *Sharecroppers' Voice* while in Memphis. Later he was to become editor of several national magazines. For a time he was labor editor for *Time* magazine. He spent some time in the Far East as a representative of the United Nations and afterwards served as United States correspondent for the *Hindustani Times*. He was an assistant to Vice-President Hubert Humphrey and remained with Humphrey through the 1968 campaign for the Presidency of the United States. Most of his life Sidney Hertzberg was a freelance writer doing special jobs for newspapers and magazines on subjects of which he had a special knowledge and interest. Among his life-long interests were the southern sharecropper and the nation's farmworker. To me, he was a guide and consultant on every issue that arose. It was Sidney Hertzberg who conceived the idea for an annual sharecroppers' week. In 1937 he organized the first National Sharecroppers' Week, which was celebrated in many large cities and proclaimed by many mayors and several governors. During this week, there were meetings, luncheons, dinners, at which prominent citizens as well as STFU delegations appeared. Fund-raising events were sponsored by nationally known artists, politicians, actors, playwrights, novelists, and poets. Among those who became involved in National Sharecroppers' Week was Tallulah Bankhead; she was finally forced to drop out because her connection with a radical movement was a source of embarrassment to her father, Speaker of the United States House of Representatives, William Bankhead, and her uncle, John Bankhead, United States Senator from Alabama.

In New York, National Sharecropers' Week was proclaimed each year by Mayor LaGuardia. Among the young socialists who appeared in Times Square to collect money for the STFU was a youngster named Jerry Wurf, destined to become president of the American Federation of State, County and Municipal Employees, one of the larger unions in the AFL-CIO. Harriet M. Young was one of the volunteer workers involved in the first National Sharecroppers' Week. In both 1938 and 1939 Harriet was the executive secretary of the NSW. In 1939 she arranged for a benefit performance at Carnegie Hall to be given by Richard

Tauber. This bid fair to be a great success, but it occurred at a time when the STFU was in a life-and-death struggle with the communist-led Agricultural and Cannery Union of the CIO. The Carnegie Hall performance became a near disaster when the Communist Party passed out word to its members and friends to cancel ticket orders and to demand a return of the money for all tickets paid for. Afterwards, Harriet Young personally made a gift of $2,000 to the STFU that compensated for the Carnegie Hall losses.

Harriet Young

Harriet was a lovely person. She was handicapped by poor vision, and she had suffered through several painful eye operations that were only partially successful. Nevertheless, she graduated with highest honors from Vassar College. Afterward, she lived in Germany for a year, witnessing the rise of Adolf Hitler and his storm troopers. On her return to America she joined the Socialist Party and worked with Norman Thomas.

She came from a well-to-do family. Her father was a leather goods manufacturer, and her mother, Marjorie, was then married to the founder of a New York corporate law firm. Harriet's stepfather's family had a country home near Huntingdon, Long Island, not far from one owned by Norman Thomas' wife, the former Violet Stewart, of the New York investment banking family.

In 1937 Harriet was working as the unpaid assistant to Sidney Hertzberg. Never having seen a sharecropper, and knowing nothing of how such people lived and worked, she decided to pay us a visit. Early one morning, she appeared in Washington, D.C., and called me at my hotel near the railway station. I invited her to come on over to my room and have a hot toddy. Harriet had never even heard of hot toddy (bourbon and hot water), much less been in a man's room. Nevertheless, if that was the way sharecropper leaders started the day, she was game to try it, at least once. After downing the drinks, we had breakfast. She ordered an egg and bacon, and not being able to see too well, asked me, "What is this white stuff on my plate? It looks like worms." Though I assured her that grits was a southern delicacy, she never could learn to eat them and thereafter told waiters to eliminate the grits. Soon after breakfast we left for Memphis by car, accompanied by Dave Griffin and E. B. McKinney.

Harriet spent several days with Evelyn Smith, who by that time had a small apartment not far from the union office, on Broad Street. One night they attended a large union meeting held by the Cotton Plant local. Sam James, the dignified president of the local, introduced me in rather pompous terms. Said Jones: "J. R. Butler and H. L. Mitchell are the kind of men we all look up to. Why, they wear Stetson hats and ten-dollar shoes!" To Harriet, this was hilarious. Butler had never worn a hat on his closely cropped hair, which stood straight up, and so far I had never owned a ten-dollar pair of shoes, although I once had a Texas cowboy hat made by Stetson.

I was scheduled for a trip to Muskogee, Oklahoma, where the Cherokee Odis L. Sweeden had returned home after a stint in the West as a migratory farm worker. As usual, Sweeden was raising hell about money for organizing purposes. Harriet asked if she could accompany me, saying that she would also like to visit Commonwealth College in western Arkansas. While I had a distinct distaste for the place where I had been shot at only a year before, I agreed to an overnight stop. Arriving in the late afternoon we were shown about the place by Charlotte Moskowitz, the school secretary, and were assigned rooms in the guesthouse. After sessions with students and faculty members lasting until near midnight, we retired to our respective rooms on opposite sides of the common living room. I was almost asleep when Harriet called out: "Mitch, there is a big bug in my room, please come and catch it." Sleepily, I replied: "Kill it yourself, you are bigger than any bug that could get in your room."

The next evening, after checking in at the New Huber Hotel in Muskogee, we had dinner at my favorite steakhouse. I had bought a bottle of bourbon before we left Arkansas since Oklahoma was officially a dry state. I had also arranged for adjoining rooms with connecting door. That evening we sat talking, Harriet in a chair and I propped up on my bed, telling each other of our most recent love affairs. Harriet talked about Sidney back in New York. Sidney was one of my best friends, and I had no intention of becoming involved with his girlfriend, but she soon joined me on the bed, saying that I was the only one in the world who could make her forget Sidney. It developed that her "affair" with Sidney had been nothing more than an infatuation on her part.

We remained in Oklahoma for several days, then drove through Kansas and Missouri to St. Louis. There Harriet caught a plane for New York, writing me later that she had slept all the way home. Once when Harriet asked me, "Why do you love me?" I replied: "Dorothy Parker says 'Men seldom make passes at girls who wear glasses,' but I think that girls who wear glasses have just as good asses." Harriet, who always loved a bawdy joke, appreciated this.

She had a beautiful voice and loved to sing and to play the piano. She had a fine collection of classical music which she taught me to appreciate. She took me to concerts at Carnegie Hall, and to plays on and off Broadway. When I first visited her, she lived with her friend Gretchen in a small basement apartment in Greenwich Village, but soon the girls moved to a larger apartment on Charles Street. Here there were two bedrooms, affording privacy, a huge living room, and a kitchenette. Gretchen was the secretary to Lewis Gannett, book review editor of the *New York Herald Tribune*. Gannett, a long-time supporter of the STFU, was in the socialist caucus of the American Newspaper Guild. Through his secretary, he kept up with the love life of the STFU secretary. Another interested spectator was Norman Thomas, who got a kick out of the spicier side of the lives of his associates. Harriet would often meet Norman on the Long Island train, and he would question her about their mutual friend Mitch. When I would stop in at Thomas' office for a visit, he wanted to know where I was staying, how long I would be in the city, and how I could be reached by telephone. While I never told him that I was staying with Harriet, he always knew, and over the years, he would often ask me what she was doing.

Harriet ran National Sharecroppers' Week in 1938 and 1939 and was also designated by the STFU as its eastern representative. She would meet me in Washington, and we would spend weekends in Virginia, often driving to Williamsburg, to the seashore or the mountains. We were at the founding convention of the CIO, and often she went with me to call on government people in Washington, meeting Senators and Congressmen and sometimes appearing at hearings in behalf of the union when I could not be present. She was with me once when we called upon John L. Lewis, whom she considered a phony and a ham actor.

Once while Harriet was living on Charles Street, and Gretchen was away, Howard Kester came to New York and was persuaded to stay overnight with us. While we were having drinks, Harriet asked jokingly: "Buck, when Mitch and I are ready, will you marry us?" Later that night, Harriet thought she heard Howard talking in his sleep, and she got up and went to the door of his bedroom, which was slightly open. There was Buck Kester, down on his knees, praying for his sinful friends, Harriet and Mitch. She was touched, but I laughed—"That's not the first time Buck has been heard praying for me."

Harriet had a comfortable income of about $10,000 a year. She was most generous, lending money to her friends and contributing to causes. Often she gave me money for travel expenses when the union was low on funds. She once lent me money for a new car.

Harriet supported her maid, Gladys, whose family in Harlem increased once a year. Gladys in turn worried about Miss Harriet neglecting to pay her own utility bills. Sometimes Gladys would show up for work, only to find gas, lights, and telephone services disconnected. Harriet seldom even looked at her mail except the personal and handwritten part. The rest, including bills, would be consigned to the wastebasket. She could not be bothered with bills, credit ratings, and other accoutrements of capitalism.

A Visit to Hyde Park

Once when I was in New York for a meeting of officials of the National Youth Administration, the entire group was invited to spend a day at Hyde Park, with President Roosevelt. On my return to Harriet's apartment, I found both Harriet and Gladys waiting to hear about the trip. My first remark was, "I almost missed the last bus, and as I rushed out the back door, my coat got caught on a broken screen—just look what a hole I tore in it! Gladys, do you have time to fix it for me? It's all I've got with me to wear."

This was too much for Gladys. She didn't believe that Miss Harriet's "boyfriend" really had visited the President of the United States, anyway. Said Gladys: "Here he comes, been visiting the President, and all he can tell us is he tore his coat on the President's backdoor."

The bus trip to Hyde Park took a couple of hours each way. When we reached the estate, we met the President driving his specially equipped Ford runabout. He had to pull off on the side of the narrow road to let the two buses loaded with his guests through. F.D.R. had two attendants—or maybe they were secret service men—with him. The meeting actually took place at Mrs. Roosevelt's cottage. The President's mother didn't want the manorhouse cluttered with "petty government clerks." The group lined up to shake hands with President Roosevelt. Each person was introduced by Aubrey Williams, the NYA Administrator. I was introduced as the Executive Secretary of the Southern Tenant Farmers Union, now on leave to work for the NYA. Mr. Roosevelt, never at a loss for words, and politician that he was, said: "Oh yes, I know all about Mitchell."

An American Black Man

Harriet and I made a memorable trip to Mexico in the fall of 1939. The union had been invited to send a delegation to Torreón, about 200 miles west of Monterrey. STFU Vice President F. R. Betton and I were named to go. Harriet and her stepbrother Gino joined us for the trip, which was uneventful until we reached the Mexican border. From there on, at every stop, Georgia-born Farish R. Betton was the center of attention.

He was a powerfully built man of about five feet ten inches; his skin was a deep black and glistened in the sun. His hair was white and his eyes dark blue. He was then in his late fifties and was a striking personality. Once, at a "Night of Stars" benefit at Carnegie Hall, arranged for the union during Sharecroppers' Week, the STFU president, J. R. Butler, was called to appear briefly just before the program was to end. The tall, gaunt white man looked the part of a sharecropper until he spoke his few words in clear clipped English, sounding like a college professor. Then the spotlight was switched to Vice President Betton, as he came bounding onto the stage. Here was the representative of all the power of the black people enslaved in America for 300 years! The audience got to their feet shouting. F. R. Betton was really the star of that "Night of Stars."

At Torreón, the union delegation found 40 young Americans at a Quaker work camp. They were helping construct public buildings on the nearby *ejido*, made up of land formerly owned by William Randolph Hearst, whose estate had been expropriated by the President of Mexico, Lazaro Cardenas, under the constitution adopted after the Revolution of 1911. The thousands of acres were presented to the village, to be held and farmed on a cooperative basis. Hearst was left with the huge ranchhouse and about 250 acres for his own personal use. Soon F. R. Betton, who spoke not a word of Spanish, was out in the fields with the farmers of the *ejido*, who knew no English, helping to harvest hay or driving mules behind the plow. Betton was all over the place, up on the roof of the Escuela Eugene V. Debs with the work campers, or dropping into a class at Escuela Karl Marx to hear the children recite their lessons.

The union delegation had been invited at the suggestion of Clarence Senior, former secretary of the Socialist Party of America, whom we met at the Quaker camp. Senior, with his wife Ruth, was living in Mexico City, while trying to recover his health after years of toil and deprivation in Chicago. One evening the delegation went up to the town plaza to observe the young people's ritual promenade around the square, boys going one way, the girls the other, looking each other over as they passed, sometimes selecting a partner and dropping out of the parade. That evening, all eyes were on the union delegation. Senior and I assumed that the señoritas were interested in the group as a whole, but we soon realized that they were looking only at F. R. Betton. All had seen pale-faced gringoes before, but none of them had ever seen such a dark and handsome man as Betton.

After about a week on the *ejido*, Harriet, Gino and I left for a trip to Mexico City. Betton decided to remain in Torreón and get a ride back to the U.S. a few days later. Afterward he said that the only time he was ever treated like a man was during those days in Mexico. After the return to Memphis, he and I prepared a report on our trip called "Land and Liberty for Mexican Farmers."

Through a friend, we were able to rent a suite near the center of Mexico City, consisting of two bedrooms, a sitting room, and a kitchen, for a week at the equivalent of twenty-five dollars, breakfast included. Other friends suggested things to do while we were there—trips to Xochimilco, the pyramids, the bull fights, the president's palace, and other sights both in the city and nearby places like Cuernavaca. Harriet and I skipped the bullfight, and Gino scaled the pyramids alone. We remained in the hotel most of the morning, then went shopping for leather and silver gifts to take back with us. We also laid in a supply of tequila to see us back.

Harriet returned to the New York School of Social Work and later became a social worker holding top jobs in New York City, at the Henry Street Settlement and up in Harlem, too. For a time she was an educational director for the International Ladies Garment Workers Union out in Ohio. She taught at Hudson Shore Labor School, an outgrowth of the Bryn Mawr summer school for women workers, just across the river from Mrs. Roosevelt's cottage on the Hudson. Her main interest throughout her life remained the union, and perhaps H. L. Mitchell too. The warm friendship remained over the years, but the romance faded. It was a sad time for me when I learned of her illness.

When Harriet died of cancer in November of 1972, her family and her close friend Laurel Boligiano had a notice inserted in *The New York Times*, requesting that donations be made in her name to the Association of Members and Friends of the Historic Southern Tenant Farmers Union, in lieu of flowers. Donations to the Harriet Young Memorial Fund were afterwards used to aid old-time members of the STFU. She would have liked that.

Sharecropper Fund Organized

In 1940 and 1941, the National Sharecroppers' Week was directed by Pauli Murray, a remarkable woman from North Carolina, who became its executive secretary. Pauli Murray was one of the few black women lawyers involved in the civil rights movement of the 1960s, and after attending seminary, was the first black woman priest ordained by the Episcopal Church in the United States.

Then in 1942, a man who was to become an outstanding fund-raiser for worthwhile causes accepted the STFU as his first client. The fund-raiser was Harold L. Oram, a reporter who had been induced to leave his newspaper and become a public relations assistant to the North American Committee for Spanish Relief during the war in Spain. He put on the "Night of Stars" with a galaxie of stage and screen personalities giving benefit performances during National Sharecroppers' Week in New York and other cities across the land. Harold Oram also arranged for the incorporation of the National Sharecroppers' Fund in 1943.

The incorporators of the National Sharecroppers' Fund were Eduard C. Lindeman, head of the New York School of Social Work, who became the first chairman of NSF; James Loeb, Jr., an educator who became editor of a small town newspaper and, under the Kennedy Administration, ambassador to Peru, as well as a White House staff member; Sidney Hertzberg, founder of National Sharecroppers' Week and freelance writer; and Harriet M. Young, co-founder, National Sharecroppers' Week.

Among the individuals making up the first National Board of the National Sharecroppers' Fund were Mary McCleod Bethune, founder of Bethune Cookman College for Negroes, director of negro affairs for the National Youth Administration, and a member of President Roosevelt's unofficial black cabinet; Albert Sprague Coolidge of Harvard University, socialist and friend of Norman Thomas; Malcolm Boyde Dana, president of Piedmont College, Georgia; Frank P. Graham, former president of the University of North Carolina, and later United States senator and United Nations mediator; Sidney Hertzberg and Harriet Young; Charles S. Johnson, famed sociologist of Fiske University; Alfred Baker Lewis, later treasurer of NSF and also treasurer of the NAACP and a long-time socialist; Bishop Francis J. McConnell (Methodist); Bishop Edward L. Parsons (Episcopal); Jennings Perry, editor of *Nashville Tennessean;* Mrs. Gifford Pinchot, wife of the former governor of Pennsylvania; Arthur Raper, sociologist and author of *Preface to Peasantry*; Ira De Reid, professor and co-author with Raper of *Sharecroppers All*; Norman Thomas, socialist leader and America's greatest platform speaker, six times candidate for President of the United States and godfather of the STFU; John H. Tolan, member of Congress from California and chairman of the House Committee on Interstate Migration; Charles S. Zimmerman, vice-president and official representative of the International Ladies Garment Workers Union on NSF's Board; Mrs. Raymond V. Ingersoll, wife of the Brooklyn Borough president and a long-time contributor to the STFU.

The incorporators were listed on a Certificate of Incorporation dated June 18, 1943 (in the STFU papers, at the University of North Carolina

Library, Chapel Hill). Also originally listed was Mrs. Twila Lytton Cavert, the wife of the then president of the Federal Council of Churches, who asked to be removed from the list. Mrs. Raymond V. Ingersoll took her place.

Among the STFU papers is a copy of a letter dated October 7, 1943 sent by Dr. Lindeman to Mrs. Gifford Pinchot, Dr. Frank Graham, Dr. Arthur Raper, Dr. Ira De Reid and Dr. Will Alexander, requesting that each of them agree to serve as members of the National Board of NSF. There is a note saying similar letters were sent to others. The files also contain a letter dated November 13, 1943 from Chairman Lindeman, requesting that I write him a letter stating that STFU agreed to turn over to NSF all rights to NSW lists, etc., in return for NSF agreeing to make STFU its first priority, and to see to the STFU receiving not less than $12,000 a year for carrying on its work.

Harold L. Oram, after getting the NSF firmly established, turned over the work to people elected by the committee. Oram helped establish the International Rescue Committee that sent daring men and women to risk their lives in German-occupied Europe to rescue anti-Nazis. Later Oram helped form the Committee for the Marshall Plan and also the Legal Defense Fund of the NAACP. Oram's suite of offices on Madison Avenue was always open to anyone representing the National Sharecroppers' Fund or the Southern Tenant Farmers Union.

One of the early executive secretaries of the National Sharecroppers' Fund was Hazel Whitman, whose chief contribution to the success of the Fund was a multi-paged official-looking annual report on sharecroppers and farm workers. This kind of direct mail appeal was contrary to all past practices among fund raisers. However, Hazel knew that NSF lists were made up of people who cared about social problems. The annual report brought in contributions, and was itself so impressive that often contributors returned their copy, requesting that it be sent on to someone else. *The Annual NSF Report on Conditions Among Farm Workers and Small Farmers* was issued for many years thereafter.

Hazel Whitman was succeeded as executive secretary of NSF by lovely Beth Biderman, who once edited the *Bulletin of the Atomic Scientists*, the publication of a group created by Albert Einstein and others who, like him, were concerned that their work in atomic physics would be used to destroy all creation. Beth Biderman had also worked with Harold L. Oram and was recommended by him. With encouragement from her successful advertising public relations husband, George Biderman, and an occasional assist from me, she kept working during the difficult Cold War days and the time of the DiGiorgio strike.

The next person to undertake the often thankless task of operating the

National Sharecroppers' Fund carried it for nearly 20 years. Fay Bennett had been a socialist and an educational director for the International Ladies Garment Workers Union in the Maryland-Virginia District. There she met and married conscientious objector Rowland Watts, an attorney who became legal director for the American Civil Liberties Union and was to serve for many years as president of the Workers Defense League.

Fay Bennett was an innovator who started new programs and got special grants from government, private foundations, and wealthy individuals with which to finance them. Fay loyally supported the efforts of the National Farm Labor Union to survive the merger of the AFL and the CIO. She was the executive secretary of the National Advisory Committee on Farm Labor, which held public hearings and brought pressure to bear on the AFL-CIO that resulted in its first organizing campaign among farm workers.

Sparking all the efforts of the National Sharecroppers' Fund, and the agencies created to raise money to help the sharecroppers and farm workers, was Norman Thomas. In later years, he was joined by that great man of the South Frank P. Graham, for many years president of the University of North Carolina, and for a short term the United States Senator from North Carolina. After making an impressive record as mediator while a member of the National War Labor Board, Frank Graham was appointed to a similar post in the United Nations. These two men, Graham working behind the scenes in behalf of the nation's farm workers, and Thomas openly applying pressure on the powerful in the labor movement, together kept AFL-CIO officials on the ball. They never permitted the organized labor movement to shirk its responsibilities to the least of its brothers, the farm workers.

While both Fay Bennett and Rowland Watts maintained their connection with the National Sharecroppers' Fund, in 1970 a new man was brought in as executive director. He was James M. Pierce, an American Indian born in Oklahoma. Pierce had been an organizer for the CIO Electrical Workers; then as southern director for AFL-CIO Industrial Union Department, he had led an abortive effort to organize migrant farm workers in Florida.

Pierce had also been the organizer for the American Federation of State, County and Municipal Employees that led the sanitation workers' strike in Memphis during which Martin Luther King was assassinated. After having organized maintenance employees at the University of North Carolina, Chapel Hill, Pierce resigned as a representative of AFSCME. In early 1970 he had just been named as a board member of NSF, and Fay Bennett announced her intention to leave. Pierce was persuaded by me and several others to take the executive director's position. Pierce, like some others, thought that a black man should head the organization. There were two other candidates, both black. One I considered to be a "clock watcher," interested mainly in quitting time and payday. The other man, who had ability, was a Black Muslim. Pierce was finally persuaded that after all, as an American Indian whose ancestors were here first, no one had a better right to the job than he. Pierce served for seven years and raised large sums of money for the development of the Frank P. Graham Experimental Farm and Training Center near Charlotte, North Carolina. I had hoped that Jim Pierce with his background as an organizer would make the National Share-croppers' Fund into what it was originally, a committee of citizens concerned with helping develop grass roots organizations of, by, and for all poor people. Too much money, like too much power, often causes an organization to lose sight of its basic goals.

The National Sharecroppers' Fund continues as the Rural Advancement Fund. In 1979, Kathryn Waller was appointed executive director.

Postscript: Muriel and Me

One of my close associates in the early days of the STFU wrote many years afterward:

Among the visiting females who came to work with the Union and found H. L. Mitchell a fascinating subject, was a pretty, romantic young woman, the wife of a socialist comrade from Chicago. Whether Mitch had been involved with other women I never knew. He was then married to a pleasant and attractive young woman who had been a country school teacher. They had three young children. But Mitchell was never cut out to be a conventional husband or father although he was fond of his family. Perhaps this marriage was really over and neither he nor Lyndell knew it. In any event, his tempestuous affair with Muriel almost wrecked the Southern Tenant Farmers Union, and had repercussions in the Socialist Party as well.

Herbert Walters (not his real name) was a brilliant writer and a coming figure in the Socialist Party of America. He told me about his beautiful wife and how lonely she was left behind in Chicago while he worked with the union in Memphis. Muriel was a good stenographer, he said, and she could also keep books. Thinking solely of acquiring another office worker, I arranged for her to be employed by the union.

One day in December, Muriel arrived. She was dressed in what may have been the hand-me-down clothing of her several elder sisters. The Jewish families I had known were all well-to-do, usually owned stores, or they were in one of the professions. Not until the union was organized did I learn about the thousands of American Jews who lived in the ghettos of New York and Chicago and worked long hours for low pay, especially in the garment industry. Nearly every person of Jewish descent who came to work for the STFU had parents working in the garment industries. In other fields, they were the last hired and the first fired. That had happened to Muriel, who had held a job for over a year in an insurance office and had been laid off to make way for some other (non-Jewish) young woman.

I was delighted when I found that she could indeed take down my letters, transcribe them correctly, and type them beautifully. She took over the chore of keeping the books, and thus freed Evelyn Smith for other work, such as helping women organizers and setting up an educational program. Muriel was very beautiful, with the features and smile of a Mona Lisa. Sometimes, as I was dictating letters in my slow southern drawl, I would notice Muriel looking at me attentively, and, I even imagined, admiringly.

On many mornings, after getting the office work underway, I would have occasion to drive downtown on one errand or another—sometimes to meet our lawyer, Newell Fowler. One morning as I was leaving, Herb, who had been hard at work for two hours, asked me to stop at his hotel and bring Muriel back with me. He said she was not feeling too well and had decided not to come in until mid-morning. I first called on Fowler who was busy with a paying client. At the hotel I called the Walters's room, and Muriel asked me to come up. I knocked on the door and she called me to come on in. To my astonishment, she was waiting for me, but not dressed to go out. She held out her arms. Her robe dropped from her soft shoulders. One hour, two hours passed. For us, time stood still. Suddenly the door opened, and there stood Herb. His first words were: "This is all my fault."

Herb told us that before Muriel had arrived he had visited a whorehouse on Beale Street, and come down with a dose of gonorrhea. For this reason he had avoided sex with his wife all that time and had been too ashamed to tell her the reason. He was still taking treatments, but hoped soon to be well. Muriel assured him of her forgiveness and understanding, and Muriel and I made solemn promises to see no more of each other except at the office in the presence of others.

But it didn't work. The attraction was too great. Herb's work often took him out of town for a day or two, and on any evening when Herb was away, there would be excursions on back country roads. Sometimes we rented a "tourist cabin" maintained exclusively for the "couple trade." Then came the union's convention in Muskogee. Most of the delegates from Arkansas were transported by train, but about 25 white sharecropper delegates drove across the state in a canvas-top truck and almost lost their lives. Charcoal heaters, suggested by me for use against the cold, exhausted the oxygen. The passengers were saved only because the driver and his two companions in the front seat stopped on the roadside to investigate and found them all unconscious. There was so little oxygen that even the coals had died out; the men and women were limp. Fresh air revived them, and though many were very ill, they all made it to the convention.

Our office group drove in from Memphis. Kester and I occupied a double room at the New Huber Hotel, and when the convention adjourned for lunch the first day, Kester came to the hotel room looking for me. He found Muriel as well. Kester, the minister without a church, was more shocked than Muriel's husband had been when he found us in similar circumstances back in Memphis a month or two before.

In early February, Frank and Elaine Blodgett proposed to go to New Orleans to see the Mardi Gras celebration. They invited Muriel and Herb to go with them, but Herb had to attend an important Socialist Party meeting in New York. Muriel decided to go with the Blodgetts and perhaps return within a few days with Evelyn Smith, who was at her home near New Orleans.

I found then that I also had to make a trip—to south Texas to visit the leader of a Mexican Agricultural Workers Union in Laredo. Instead of continuing to New Orleans with the Blodgetts, Muriel left them in Clarksdale, Mississippi, where we had arranged to meet. We two lovers took the long way to the Mardi Gras, riding through the moss-covered Natchez Trace road into the oldest town in Mississippi. Muriel used to call me her "riding boss" or sometimes just "Boss", or "RGB." So that evening when we arrived at Natchez and checked in at the Eola Hotel, I signed the register, "Mr. and Mrs. R. G. Boss." After a dinner by candlelight, we had the first of many romantic evenings. The next day, after visiting one of the ante-bellum homes that was open to the public, we drove to New Orleans and found a room in an old-fashioned hotel in the French Quarter.

At the office of the Louisiana Farmers Union, we made the acquaintance of Gordon McIntyre and Peggy Dallet, with whom we watched the carnival parades from a choice spot overlooking Royal Street, where Gordon had an apartment. We explored the French Quarter and tried out the many small restaurants where food was cheap and good. We splurged and bought Muriel a whole new outfit—dress, a lovely suit, shoes, stockings, underclothing, and a cute blue-grey hat with a red feather in it. She was as proud as a peacock, and to me she looked like a million dollars.

I had left Memphis with more than a hundred dollars, in those days a great sum of money. Colonel Lawrence Westbrook, head of the Rural Rehabilitation Program in Washington, had the idea that if I would contact the leaders of the Mexican farm workers and prepare for a strike as soon as the cotton crop came in, in July or August, Westbrook would buy cotton futures. Then, when the strike hit, the cotton market would go sky high, Westbrook would cash in and thus we would finance the union operation, including the strike. Westbrook had given me one hundred dollars expense money. I was sure that more would be waiting upon arrival in Texas. By the time we reached Houston, we were almost broke. I registered under my own name and sent a wire to Colonel Westbrook in Washington. Hearing nothing after three days, I had Western Union trace the message. A report came back that the colonel was away for two weeks and could not be reached.

There was one faithful friend to whom I could turn. I telephoned Gardner Jackson in Washington, explained my plight, and said we needed at least a hundred dollars. Jackson had already heard of our disappearance, and my phone call brought the true situation to light. Instead of condemning me, Jackson sounded positively pleased. He said he would wire me what I needed within an hour. He sent two hundred dollars. Elated, we threw caution and precaution to the winds. We stopped in small towns in the Rio Grande Valley on our way to Laredo and crossed over into Old Mexico at several border points, having a wonderful time as tourists. We bought a cheap camera and took pictures of each other standing in the citrus groves.

Getting down to the business of visiting the leader of the Mexican Agricultural Workers Union, I learned that he had led an abortive strike of cotton pickers only the year before. He and his members were still too frightened to undertake another strike in 1937, so Colonel Westbrook's idea was not practical, as I reported to him on my return to Memphis.

Meanwhile, back in Memphis, Herb had returned. He found two or three letters from New Orleans, and nothing more. Muriel had written letters in advance for each day she was to be away, stamped them, and arranged for a friend to mail them, one at a time. The arrangement had failed, as the friend forgot to mail the letters. Kester, Evelyn, and Fowler kept the heartbroken Herb company, persuading him not to set out for New Orleans to look for his missing bride. By that time the others knew where Muriel was. As Evelyn wrote Pat Jackson: "Young Lochinvar is still out in the West," and Kester said: "Yes, the Bishop of Tyronza ran off with the Rabbi's wife." What lawyer Fowler had to say was never recorded.

En route home, we discussed the possible repercussions of our adventure, naturally with some trepidation. I was to pay my personal price. On her part, Muriel seemed confident that Herb would forgive her again, and he did. They moved back to Chicago and started a family there. Many years later I learned that Muriel had named her first daughter "Eola"—for the inn at the end of the Natchez Trail.

This affair caused a stir in Socialist Party circles, and even more so in the union. Efforts were made to replace me as secretary. Said one opponent, "The character of an officer of the union should be, like Caesar's wife, above reproach." There was an attempt by Claude Williams and his followers to use this incident at the annual convention of 1938 to oust me as an officer of the union. Unsuccessful in this endeavor, they elected Leon Turner, a black, as assistant secretary, a post not provided for by the union's constitution.

12   The Strange Case of Claude C. Williams

On August 22, 1938, an amazing document was found by J. R. Butler, president of the Southern Tenant Farmers Union, on the dining room table in his home in Memphis. Addressed to The Central Committee of the Communist Party, USA, it read in part as follows:

A situation has now arisen which offers an extraordinary opportunity to move into the most important organization in the agricultural South. H. L. Mitchell, who has always opposed the Party, is away on leave. J. R. Butler, who is friendly to our line, is in charge.*

A request was made to the "Center" for five hundred dollars to take over the Southern Tenant Farmers Union. The document also related how the "Center" had arranged entry for the Director of Commonwealth College, Claude C. Williams, to go to Hollywood to solicit funds from party members and sympathizers in the movie industry. The

*The original document as corrected by Williams is in STFU Papers, as well as a mimeographed copy sent out by Butler dated Aug 22, 1938, Reel 8, STFU Papers.

document ended with: "Another like opportunity is hardly likely to occur."

This paper, bearing notations in Claude Williams' handwriting, was found by J. R. Butler when he returned from an overnight trip to Arkansas. Butler's nephew, Silas, who lived with him, had come in during the early evening, and found a nice black coat belonging to Claude Williams on the back of a dining room chair. Silas decided to wear the coat on a date that night. Finding a lot of papers in the inside coat pocket, he piled them all on top of the table. When J. R. Butler arrived the next morning, he found them. The straight-laced union president first hit the ceiling, then rushed to the newspapers with the news that an appeal was being made to the Communist Party for money to take over the Southern Tenant Farmers Union.

I was working for the National Youth Administration as a consultant on rural problems and was in Georgia when the article appeared in the newspapers. I did not see the story until I arrived in Columbia, South Carolina, the next morning. There was a front page story in the paper with a headline saying, "Reds in take-over of Sharecroppers Union." After reading it, I telephoned Butler. Cleo, Butler's niece and private secretary, told me that Claude Williams was with the STFU president in the other room. Cleo knew that Williams was most persuasive and that J. R. Butler was weak. She said Claude had just about convinced J. R. to go to the newspapers again and say that his charges against Williams the day before were untrue. When Butler came to the phone, I told him: "If you go back to the newspapers and withdraw the statements you made previously, you are going to look like a damned fool." I also told Butler that if I had found the papers, I would have handled the matter differently, but now that he had already gone to the newspapers and made the matter public, the entire union should stand behind him.

Butler told me that he had just promised Williams to withdraw the charges he had made, for personal reasons, but said there was no reason another member of the Union could not file similar charges with the Executive Council of the STFU. David Griffin, ex-sharecropper turned union organizer and one of the most loyal STFU men, filed charges against Williams, and some days later Howard Kester joined Griffin in filing the charges.

Ever since Williams and Willie Sue Blagden had been beaten by planters in June 1936, he had used that incident to influence the unsophisticated sharecroppers to follow his lead in all issues arising in the union. Williams had also capitalized on real and fancied grievances of individuals. He appealed to Negro members of the STFU and in some cases succeeded in driving a wedge between blacks and whites in the interracial movement that had done so much for both. Williams had tried every way possible to get on the executive council of the STFU. The ability to organize and to represent sharecroppers in their home area was the usual requirement for membership on the council. Williams later admitted that he had never organized a local or enlisted a single member.

When the STFU convention met in Muskogee, Oklahoma, in January, 1937, Williams was there, accompanied by a large delegation from Commonwealth College. The college spokesman, Mr. Freeberg, held press conferences and expounded to the rabidly conservative local press. He was quoted as denying that the college was a center of communist activity, but admitted that there were party members on the campus. Freeberg also strenuously denied that the college taught and practiced free love. As a result of this kind of publicity and the presence of Claude Williams, the district president of the United Mine Workers, David Fowler, refused to speak to the convention. Kester, Gardner Jackson, and I went to see Dave Fowler and assuaged the ruffled CIO spokesman. When Fowler appeared on the platform, Williams left in high dudgeon, after first breaking his promise to Kester to refuse a nomination to the executive council. Kester and Butler had, however, promised to support Williams at a future meeting of the executive council, if there was a vacancy to be filled. Later in the year 1937 Williams was elected to the executive council.

It was afterwards revealed that the Communist Party District Organizer Wagenknecht from St. Louis was lodged in the best hotel in Muskogee and was directing the Communist Party caucus on the floor of the STFU convention. There were perhaps a half dozen delegates out of 150 present who followed the party line in the convention. Nevertheless, they tied up the proceedings for two days. First, they proposed to have the STFU dissolve. Its tenant and sharecropper members would then join the National Farmers Union, and the farm laborer members would join in forming AFL chartered federal labor unions. This move was soundly defeated. Then the party members embarked on another course, in which the STFU would include small farmers, tenants and sharecroppers only, and would exclude all farm laborers from its ranks. Such proposals would have required a change in the STFU constitution. The constitution said all working farmers, tenants, sharecroppers, and farm workers who shared in the proceeds of the sale of crops were eligible for membership. The deeply religious delegates held the STFU constitution in just about the same reverence as the Holy Bible. They didn't like the idea of strangers coming among them and tampering with such a basic document. After a full debate in which Williams attempted to confuse the issue and was given a tongue lashing by Howard Kester, these moves were defeated. Thereafter, both Williams and the communist contingent left the convention, possibly to meet with Wagenknecht to plan future strategy.

The strange case of Claude C. Williams was heard by the STFU executive council at the regular quarterly meeting in September 1938. The council was composed of rank and file union members elected by the annual convention in January. The members of the executive council who held the hearing in Williams' case represented each area where the STFU had organized locals. They came from the states of Arkansas, Missouri, Oklahoma, and Texas.

J. R. Butler, as presiding officer of the council, had no vote except in the case of a tie. I, as the STFU's only regular hired hand, had only a voice, but no vote in executive council sessions. A year before, the convention had voted to pay me a salary of $25 a week, provided I could raise the money. Prior to this action, I had not been paid a salary by the STFU; only my expenses were paid, and then only when funds were available. Butler and others had worked on the same basis until the STFU joined the CIO; then, as vice-president of the International UCAPAWA for a brief time, Butler had been paid $200 a month, plus mileage and per diem when out of town. Butler was thus the only capitalist in the ranks of the STFU. Howard Kester, who held no other position, served as a member of the STFU executive council and acted as adviser to its members. Kester's salary and expenses were paid by the Committee for Economic and Social Justice. Kester had partially replaced Professor William R. Amberson of the University of Tennessee, who had been the union's adviser in the first two years of its existence and a one-term member of the Executive Council.

In the hearing before the Executive Council, Williams was given every possible consideration. He was allowed to remain in the meeting and was permitted to bring a parade of witnesses before the council. Each witness, incidentally, told a different story. Some claimed that the document addressed to the central committee of the Communist Party, was an exercise which each student and faculty member at Commonwealth College had been assigned to write. Ralph Fields, a hanger-on at Commonwealth claimed that he was the author. Winifred Chappel, a functionary in the Methodist Social Action Committee, claimed that she too had written a similar appeal for funds to help the STFU and sent it to the Methodist Church. However, she did not present the council with a copy of the alleged letter. Williams did not claim that the document was a forgery. He admitted that he made corrections on the paper in his own handwriting. Speaking in his own behalf, he also admitted that he had been in contact with "Old Wag" (Wagenknecht) and that with Wagenknecht's help, he had secured entry to Hollywood, through V. J. Jerome, the leading theoretician of the Communist Party. Williams said he had tried to raise $3,000 for Commonwealth College in the movie industry, but had only collected $1,300. He also claimed to have resigned from both Socialist and Communist parties when he assumed the post of director of Commonwealth College. Claude Williams did not deny that he had held membership in both parties at the same time. He was openly a socialist and secretly a communist. (I had seen Claude Williams' Communist Party card made out in the name of John Galey, while I was at the founding convention of UCAPAWA-CIO at Denver in 1937.*) In 1936, Williams had been nominated by the Arkansas Socialist Party as its candidate for governor. When he was unable to qualify, J. R. Butler, a resident of White County, was nominated to run in his place.

I was secretary of the Arkansas Socialist Party in 1935, but when I had to leave the state just ahead of a lynch mob, I resigned that post. Later, Donald Kobler, a student at Commonwealth, and a Williams follower, became secretary, and Williams became chairman of the Arkansas Socialist Party.

Cedric Belfrage, an English writer who said he first met Williams in Hollywood, wrote a book about the college director-preacher, which was first published in 1939 in England under the title *South of God*, and in 1944 in the United States under the title *A Faith to Free the People*. Most references to Claude Williams' activity in the STFU were absent from the later edition. However, things that had happened to Howard Kester during his investigations of lynchings for the NAACP were reported as incidents in the life of Claude Williams. Belfrage also reported on a visit Claude Williams made to Earl Browder, the general secretary of the Communist Party, which resulted in his becoming a party member. A similar visit to Browder, made by Howard Kester earlier in the 1930s, convinced Kester that he wanted no part of the Communist Party. Kester said: "It was Earl Browder himself who convinced me—his duplicity, his disregard for morality and ethics. He was very frank about it. 'This is the goal, and it doesn't matter what you do to achieve it.'" It was quite apparent that Williams had none of his friend Kester's scruples. In his last years, Williams claimed that Belfrage had written the document found by Butler, but no mention was made of

---

* The practice of having a party alias was perhaps started in Tsarist Russia when the early revolutionists were seeking to escape the secret police. The general secretary of the Communist Party USA operated under the assumed name of Eugene Dennis as late as the 1950s.

Belfrage during the hearings, or at any time during the convention proceedings.

During the executive council hearing in the Williams matter, there were a number of interruptions. Once when members were considering an insurance program, W. B. Moore, president of the STFU local at Blytheville, Arkansas, showed the other council members a tattoo on his right arm—STFU-CIO, remarking, "I don't even know what a communist is, but I wouldn't believe Claude Williams on a stack of Bibles as high as the ceiling of this room." Blaine Treadway and Odis L. Sweeden said nothing, as they had been sworn to silence, but they had also seen the Communist Party card issued to Williams in the name of John Galey, when he showed it to all of us in Denver, back in July 1937 at UCAPAWA's first convention. While I refused to take such an oath of silence, I had made no big issue of the matter. However, I had told socialists that Williams was a communist agent in the socialist movement and many, including J. R. Butler, STFU President, had refused to believe me.

Williams' hearing ended with the council voting unanimously to expel him from the Southern Tenant Farmers Union. Two other formerly active, but now inactive members, were also removed.

One of these was William L. Blackstone, who had served with distinction as the STFU's representative on the President's Committee on Farm Tenancy. Blackstone's greatest problem was his huge family—sons, daughters, their wives, husbands, and children. All these Blackstones simply could not live on the allowance made by the STFU to its organizers from its meager funds. Apparently his family considered that Blackstone should have a living for his tribe forever on the basis of his past services to the union.

The other member to be expelled was E. B. McKinney, one of the early officers of the STFU. He was a minister and an evangelist serving several churches. McKinney had been termed by Howard Kester in his book *Revolt Among the Sharecroppers* as "A rock in a weary land." At one time, McKinney had been a follower of Marcus Garvey, who wanted all blacks to go back to Africa. Later he had been a labor recruiter for the steel mills in Illinois and Ohio. By the late twenties he had settled down to farming and preaching. White members of the STFU often said, "McKinney makes more sense than any white man we ever heard." But McKinney now had problems. One night during the strike of 1936, the Associated Press bureau chief called me to say that there had been a report in New York City that the union's vice-president had been shot by planters. McKinney did not have a telephone at his home on a farm near Memphis, so I rushed out to see my friend. Mrs.

McKinney was quite disturbed. A doctor had come and dressed McKinney's head wounds, and had said he would be all right soon. The oldest of the McKinney boys followed me out to my car, and revealed what had happened. McKinney had not been shot by a planter, but by another black man over a personal matter. I called the AP bureau chief, who wired New York headquarters and reported that nothing had happened. My knowledge of this incident was evidently a source of embarrassment to McKinney, however. Afterward, though he had always been close to me, McKinney stayed away from the office in Memphis and started sending letters claiming he was being discriminated against because he was a Negro. This was due in part to his dislike for J. R. Butler. After Butler became international Vice President of UCAPAWA, and remained president of the STFU, it was more than McKinney could bear. He then tried to start a rival movement among Negroes within the STFU. Perhaps he was encouraged in this initially by Claude Williams, but we never knew for sure.

After his expulsion from the STFU, Williams formed an alliance with McKinney and Blackstone and served notice of appeal to the annual convention originally scheduled to be held in Memphis in late December. Williams worked out a program attacking the union, claiming it was run by a bureaucratic clique based in Memphis. He demanded equal rights for Negroes, with representation on the executive board in accordance with racial composition. He made little headway with the local unions. They had always elected their delegates to the conventions and had freely chosen their officers and executive council members. Sometimes Negroes outnumbered whites, and sometimes whites were in the majority.

With convention time approaching, J. R. Butler called members of the Convention Arrangements Committee together and explained that they could not hold the next annual convention at the Memphis Labor Temple on Beale Street. This hall was owned by AFL unions, and the STFU was now a part of the CIO, so the arrangements formerly made with the custodian were no longer valid. F. R. Betton and other members of the union arranged for the annual convention of the STFU to meet at the Presbyterian Academy for Negroes in Cotton Plant, Arkansas. The Academy, its meeting hall, dormitory and dining room were made available to all delegates on a nondiscriminatory basis, at a low cost.

F. R. Betton, who had joined the STFU during the strike of 1936, was working behind the scenes in Cotton Plant to make his home area an all-union stronghold. He was almost successful. Betton was an upstanding citizen. For over twenty years he had served as justice of the peace in his township. Kester, Butler, and I had often spent the night, and had wonderful meals, at the home of Mr. and Mrs. Betton. They owned a small farm near town and rented additional land which they also farmed. There were thirteen children in the Betton family, and it was the father's boast that every one of his children was sent to college. All but one graduated.

As justice of the peace, Betton was a member of the county court, which was composed of all the elected justices in a county. Under Arkansas law, they are the administrative body for each county. The people had held on to the rights gained under reconstruction laws and practices. Black men, and a few women, paid their poll taxes and regularly voted in Monroe County, once a stronghold of the Populist Party. It was in nearby Desha that the Agricultural Wheel, a forerunner of the National Farmers Alliance, was organized. The Colored Farmers Alliance had been strong in this area too.

Williams and his few followers spread rumors that it would be unwise for delegates to attend the convention in Cotton Plant, alleging that they would be attacked by planters. However, Cotton Plant was the one place in Arkansas where the membership was so strong that no vigilante incident ever occurred.

Roy Wilkins, assistant secretary of the NAACP, was to be the principal guest speaker of the convention. Wilkins arrived in Memphis on the morning of the Williams hearing. I met Wilkins at Union Station. When the distinguished, trim young black man stepped off the Pullman car from Chicago, I picked up his largest bag and started through the station. The nearest exit to the parking lot was through the white waiting room. Wilkins held back for a minute, and insisted that I exchange bags with him, saying: "If you are carrying my briefcase, and I am carrying my heavy bag, they will think I am just a redcap, even it I don't have on a uniform." I rejoined, "Come on, let's go! It's over a hundred miles to Cotton Plant, Arkansas." There was no reaction, and the visitor was not embarrassed. The people in the STFU continually got away with violations of the rigid segregation laws just by acting natural. We never made an open issue of it. We were only behaving normally.

There had been correspondence and several meetings with NAACP leaders in New York. The NAACP was concerned that the only inter-racial movement in the rural South not be destroyed. Two years before, Walter White, the national secretary of NAACP had attended the STFU convention in Muskogee and had witnessed the efforts being made by the tiny communist minority to take over the sharecropper movement.

Another visitor to the Cotton Plant convention of the STFU was

Donald Henderson, president of UCAPAWA, and a top-ranking member of the CPUSA. I told Henderson that the convention would probably uphold the expulsion of Williams. Said Henderson: "The Center has never trusted Claude Williams. We don't give a damn if you hang, draw and quarter him."

On the first day of the Fifth Annual Convention of the Southern Tenant Farmers Union held in Cotton Plant, Arkansas, on December 29, 1938, J. R. Butler, the union president, announced that a special order of business would be conducted. This involved the appeals made to the convention on an executive council decision to expel E. B. McKinney and Claude C. Williams from the union. (W. L. Blackstone had sent word that he would not attend the convention, so no action was taken on his appeal.)

E. B. McKinney was called first and asked to state his case to the delegates. McKinney asked for his hearing to be postponed. Then, President Butler reviewed the charges and the action of the executive council in the case of Claude C. Williams and called upon Williams to present his appeal. One of the delegates asked that the charges against Williams and the action of the executive council be read. This was done. Williams was then given complete freedom to make his appeal to the convention. He made an impassioned plea to the delegates, using every oratorical trick in the book to influence the delegates. Following Williams's half-hour oration, a delegate made a motion to uphold the decision of the executive council in his expulsion. The motion was seconded, and a vote by show of hands was taken. The vote was 58 for expulsion and 7 against.

The following day the McKinney appeal was heard. I had spoken privately to nearly all the delegates, urging that McKinney be restored to membership. McKinney spoke of his record as a leader of his race and denied that he had any intention of separating the Negro union members from the white. He had been charged with seeking to establish a dual union made up solely of black people. After his appeal, I asked McKinney whether he, if restored to membership, would stand by the constitution and the program adopted by the convention. McKinney refused to answer the question. Several delegates spoke, saying that if McKinney would answer the question they would vote for his reinstatement. McKinney stubbornly remained silent. I then suggested that perhaps McKinney felt he should not be asked to make this statement, because he had made the pledge to abide by the constitution when it was adopted three years before. McKinney replied to this by saying emphatically, "That's right." A motion was made to restore him to union membership as vice-president. A substitute motion was offered that

"McKinney be restored to membership in the union." This was adopted 53 to 8.*

After expelling Claude Williams, and reinstating McKinney as a member only, the convention delegates elected officers for the following year. McKinney was not nominated for office. F. R. Betton was named first vice-president, and Owen H. Whitfield of Missouri became second vice-president. J. R. Butler was named again as president, and I continued as secretary. Of the eleven members of the executive council, five black and six white members were elected. F. R. Betton remained with the union until his death at the age of 88. McKinney's family moved away in 1940 and he was never heard from again. In 1951, W. L. Blackstone appeared at the convention in Fresno, California. He was a migrant farm worker living in a farm worker camp near Indio, and he assisted Hank Hasiwar in organizing in the Coachello Valley.

Williams continued for a brief time as director of Commonwealth College, but he soon turned the college and its assets over to some New York group who permitted it to fall into the hands of the local and state authorities. He moved to Evansville, Indiana, and then to Detroit.

A former sharecropper and union member working in the automobile industry during World War II reported that the "Reverend" Claude was going around with his collar on backwards. Apparently, for a time, he was readmitted to the councils of the Presbyterians. Later, there was a report that Williams had been defrocked by his fellow Presbyterians for heresy. Some enterprising reporter also dug up the story of how Claude Williams had been expelled by the Southern Tenant Farmers Union nearly ten years before for trying to sell the union to the Communist Party.

Williams always made an impression on impressionable religious fundamentalists with his Institute for Applied Religion, in which he showed the relationship of old Jewish Prophets and early Christians to organized labor and communism. While Williams again became a minister, being licensed to preach by an obscure black church, he never again held a pastorate. He once applied for admittance to the Fellowship of Southern Churchmen, but was not accepted by the believers in the Social Gospel. Apparently, he continued to live precariously on funds raised from wealthy people on whom he was able to make a good impression.

Claude C. Williams was born on a small farm near Martin, Tennessee,

*The above is from copy of *The Proceedings of the Fifth Annual Convention of the STFU,* filed by the union with the New York City Public Library, directly following the convention. For some reason, full proceedings of the convention are missing from the STFU files.

in 1895, not many miles from my home town Halls. His mother's name was Galey. Both his father and mother claimed to be Cherokee Indians who never migrated to Oklahoma. His family's farm was apparently too small, and the land was so poor that they rented additional acres from a larger farmer. Claude left home when he was about fifteen; he lived with relatives, worked on farms and at any other jobs available. In 1916 he joined the army and became a drill sergeant for recruits in World War I. He was selected as a candidate for officer training, but the war ended before he completed his course. He remained in the army for a year or so afterwards and specialized in poker playing and other forms of gambling. When he returned home, he joined the Cumberland Presbyterian Church and was sent to Bethel College for training as a minister in this denomination. There he met Joyce King who was also attending college and intended to be a missionary. They were married, and Claude became pastor of several small churches near Nashville. in the early 1930s, he took a few courses at Vanderbilt Theological School, where he came under the influence of Howard Kester, and became involved in Kester's activities in unions and interracial affairs. Williams soon transferred to a more liberal branch of the Presbyterian Church and was assigned a pastorate in París, Arkansas.

In the mid 1970s I tried to bring the aged Claude Williams back into the fold of friendship with those with whom he had been associated forty years before. For my pains as a peacemaker, I was roundly denounced in pages of vitriolic diatribe. Williams seemed to think that every person with whom he had disagreed in the past must now admit his error and accept Williams's version of what really happened so many years ago, regardless of the record. Claude Williams was a pathetic figure living out his life, never again in the mainstream of movements whirling about him, always preaching to all comers about how important his contribution was to the sharecroppers from 1936 to 1938. He admitted he followed the Communist Party line all the days of his life, because he knew of no other line to follow.

13 The CIO in the Cotton

Gardner Jackson, the free-wheeling, New-Dealing man-about-town in Washington, dropped into the office of the president of United Mine Workers one morning in early 1937. There, waiting in the outer office to see John L. Lewis, was Harry Bridges, head of the Pacific Coast Longshoremen and the CIO's regional director in the far West. Along with him was Donald H. Henderson, sometime editor of *The Rural Worker* and the Communist Party's specialist on the nation's farm worker. Jackson asked: "What are you fellows up to?" Replied Henderson: "We are here to get a CIO charter for a national agricultural and cannery workers' union." Jackson then asked: "Are you going to include the Southern Tenant Farmers Union?"

Henderson said that the STFU was neither fish nor fowl, and "We are not planning to do anything about that crappy outfit." Bridges did not know who Jackson was and for the moment remained silent. Jackson told the two that as the Washington representative of the STFU, he had been talking to John L. Lewis about a CIO charter for the Southern Tenant Farmers Union. Bridges allowed that the CIO would be unlikely to issue two charters in the same field, and that this was one of the problems the old AFL had with too many unions claiming the same jurisdiction.

Later, Jackson met Don Henderson at Webb Powell's office. Powell edited a news bulletin called *Facts for Farmers*. Henderson told Jackson that Lewis had insisted that the STFU be included in the new international union of agricultural and cannery workers. A convention was to be held as soon as possible, probably in Denver where the AFL had several locals of sugar beet and refinery workers. Henderson claimed to have contacts among these workers and many others organized in the AFL and was sure they would affiliate with the new international soon to be set up by the CIO. Henderson made it clear that he expected to become the new international's president. Jackson pointed out that if the STFU affiliated, then its leadership would have to be given consideration, in view of the fact that the union claimed over 30,000 members and was known nationwide.

Jackson suggested that I be considered for the number two spot of secretary-treasurer. Henderson replied that Mitchell was not too easy to control but that the suggestion would be given consideration. Jackson telephoned me late that evening, talking for nearly an hour. He found I had reservations about Henderson, too. I thought the STFU should be given a separate charter by the CIO, and be allowed to work in rural areas on both economic and political issues where the CIO was organized or planned organizing drives. Kester and I had fully discussed the possibility many times with the rest of the STFU leadership, though nothing had been done officially.

At the 1935 convention of the American Federation of Labor there was a clash between the leaders of the industrial-type unions, organized on an industry-wide basis, and the leadership of the trade or craft unions. The conflict came to a head in Atlantic City when a fist fight broke out between John L. Lewis of the United Mine Workers and William "Big Bill" Hutcheson, president of the Brotherhood of Carpenters. Kester witnessed that fight. The industrial unions then set up a Committee of Industrial Organizations. Ordered in 1936 by the executive council of AFL to dissolve and cease its activities, the industrial unions united to form the Congress of Industrial Organizations. The first constitutional convention of the CIO was held early in 1938 in Pittsburg.   I was there accompanied by my friend Harriet Young.

Because it seemed to be the logical wave of the future, Kester and I then agreed to go along with the new agricultural and cannery setup of the CIO. I knew that John L. Lewis would see no profit in organizing the nation's farm workers. Contracts with dues check-offs were not within the realm of possibility. Therefore, in Lewis' order of priorities, the farm workers were about on a level with domestic household workers. Representing the largest organized bloc of farm workers, the STFU could only raise enough money to send nine delegates to Denver in July, when the CIO founding convention met.

Gardner Jackson and John L. Lewis had a meeting before the convention opened. Since Jackson and his wife Dode had the ear of the President, they were important to John L. Lewis and his daughter Katherine. They had met socially over the years, sometimes at the Lewis home on King Street in the old port town of Alexandria, Virginia, or in the Jackson home on Kirke Street in Chevy Chase. Jackson, and perhaps Lewis too, had serious questions about Donald Henderson's qualifications to represent farm workers. He was known to be domineering and generally hard to get along with. Lewis had told Jackson that he not only had confidence in Harry Bridges, but that Bridges was the best organizer in the country. Bridges had convinced Lewis that the

CIO could organize everything in California, from docks to fields, in a march inland. Lewis was going along with his West Coast director. Nevertheless he agreed that Gardner Jackson should go to Denver early and be on hand for all of the proceedings. Lewis would send someone else to Denver to present the charter officially, but Jackson was to report everything, assist with publicity, and be otherwise helpful.

Before he left Washington, Jackson arranged with his friends in the House and Senate to send letters and telegrams of greeting to the founding convention, as he had when the STFU convention met in Muskogee, Oklahoma. On arrival in Denver, he encountered some unexpected tactics. His mail had been sent in care of the convention headquarters and included a personal letter from Lewis indicating that H. L. Mitchell should be chosen as the international secretary-treasurer. This letter was opened but not delivered to him. Instead, it was read to the convention minus, of course, the personal recommendation from John L. Lewis.

Late one evening, just before the slate of officers was to be submitted to the delegates, I was called aside by Donald Henderson. He offered to support me for the post of secretary-treasurer, if I would secretly join the Communist Party. I replied that if I were going to join the Communist Party, I would want to announce it publicly, but that I had no intention whatever of doing such a thing. I said I was a socialist, that Norman Thomas was my friend, and I did not want the damned CIO post at the cost of betraying my friends and associates. Henderson then sounded me out as to my opinion of Butler as vice-president of the international. Disgusted with such proposals, I warned Don Henderson: "You better never make such a proposition to J. R. Butler as you did to me for he will beat hell out of you."

This was the beginning of a two-year wrangle with Donald Henderson. Butler *was* elected vice-president. He was put on the CIO payroll at $200 per month, plus five dollars a day while out of town, and five cents a mile for his car. This sudden wealth went to Butler's head. He had been holding his bonus for service in World War I, and he now splurged and bought a new Oldsmobile with the first-ever automatic transmission. The Oldsmobile was very expensive and was held to be the next thing to a Cadillac. Later, when STFU organizer Dave Griffin saw a double-decker bus on Fifth Avenue in New York City, he said, "We better not let J. R. know about that bus, or he will want to buy the damn thing."

I and three others from the STFU were named to the executive board of UCAPAWA (United Cannery, Agricultural, Packing and Allied Workers of America), consisting of 29 members. An Alabama coal miner, N. W. Martin, was named to represent farm laborers in the federal labor union affiliated with the AFL. Then James Sager from Texas was also chosen from the STFU District IV. Neither of these men had ever been heard of before and they were never heard of again. Few of the delegates to the founding convention of UCAPAWA in Denver were elected by votes of members in the organizations they purported to represent. They were, with a few exceptions, selected by the Communist Party faction in local unions, and in some instances, the Communist unit in a nearby town or city from whence they came.

Outnumbered and out-maneuvered, and forced into an affiliation with Henderson's International Union, the nine STFU delegates went home. Howard Kester was so unenthusiastic that he had refused to go to the Denver meeting and allowed Claude Williams to go as his alternate.

A special convention was held in September for the STFU to vote on affiliation with the CIO. Howard Kester, Gardner Jackson, and I then made a final effort to secure a special charter from the CIO for the Southern Tenant Farmers Union. Jackson in Washington met John L. Lewis at his office and early on the morning of our first session got an agreement that if the convention requested a special charter for the STFU, it would be granted. Jackson telephoned Butler, Kester, and me soon after his meeting with Lewis. Butler appeared willing to go along with a peitition for a separate charter, but Henderson was present and told the delegates that the only way they could be a part of the CIO was through affiliation with UCAPAWA. He promised that the STFU would remain just as it was, with its own officers, functioning through the central office in Memphis, and that every cent paid in dues to the international union would be returned with extra matching funds from the national CIO to help organize the unorganized. This promise sounded good to the delegates. Then Claude Williams, supporting Henderson in full, made an impassioned speech calling for immediate affiliation with UCAPAWA. Butler stalled the proceedings. He had never liked Jackson. Also, Jackson had promised to get Lewis to speak to Butler as soon as the CIO chieftain returned from a luncheon engagement. Butler wanted confirmation of what Lewis had told Jackson earlier in the day about a separate charter for the STFU. Kester and I kept telephoning Lewis' office. Mr. Lewis was not in, but was expected soon. Negro delegates came to me, saying, "We have always gone along with you because you are the one white man we know we can trust, but our members sent us here, and we can't go home unless we are in the CIO."

The hours passed and still no call from John L. Lewis. Butler stood by the phone, turning over the gavel to Vice-President McKinney. Finally, at 2 P.M. Memphis time, Butler gave up, and put the motion before the house. When the votes were counted, Henderson had won, but only by a narrow majority. Soon after the decision had been ratified, Butler was called to the phone. John L. Lewis had returned, and was ready to talk. Butler, who had refused to accept Jackson's word, heard directly from the CIO chieftain himself what he had relayed to Jackson earlier in the day. Butler had to tell Mr. Lewis that the delegates had already voted to affiliate with the Henderson Union. Butler may have been influenced by the $200-a-month salary and lucrative expense account he was receiving as the vice-president of UCAPAWA. Soon afterwards, he got his comeuppance. The CIO checks were cut off by Don Henderson, and thereafter Butler was Henderson's most vociferous denunciator.

The year 1938 started off with the annual convention of the Southern Tenant Farmers Union being held again in Little Rock. Since the union was now a part of the CIO, the Labor Temple and other facilities of the Arkansas Federation of Labor were not available. On a trip to Little Rock, Butler and Kester found a nice hall owned by a Mr. Manning who afterwards revealed that he was an East Texas plantation owner. We rented it for three days. About a hundred delegates assembled and were issued green and red badges bearing the STFU-CIO labels. The convention got underway with the national songster of the STFU, A. B. Brookins, leading the singing of "We Shall Not be Moved." We must have been good, or we must have been loud because we were soon evicted. Mr. Manning claimed that Butler and Kester had not told him that the union was interracial, and belonged to that radical CIO. The real reason behind the eviction, we suspect, was that the "Four Square Gospel" members made regular use of the hall as a meeting place for their church. And their church was headed by Amy Semple McPherson, out in California. Her performances rivaled the best Hollywood productions and often were as profitable. The lady "Billy Sunday" just packed them in. Her followers in Little Rock wanted no part of a union, much less one whose membership was half black. Bradley Smith, later to become a famous photographer, was learning his trade at this time. He snapped pictures of the eviction of the STFU and its delegates moving out of Mr. Manning's Hall into a Negro fraternal order meeting place in the segregated black section of the city. The newspapers gave full coverage to these unusual proceedings.

After the STFU joined UCAPAWA, union affairs were totally confusing. Over half of the local unions in the STFU refused to affiliate. Local union secretaries, most of whom could just barely read and write, received large packages containing ledgers, receipt books, and minute books, plus almost daily letters from Henderson's office, making appeals for funds to assist strikers in faraway places. I then remarked that though I had a high school education, it would have been impossible for me to have kept the accounts each local union secretary was now called upon to handle.

Every commitment made by the International (UCAPAWA) to the STFU was broken by Henderson. There were many meetings with top officials of the CIO and appeals to John L. Lewis himself to require Don Henderson to live up to his promises to the STFU. At a meeting, I told Lewis that I believed our problems with Henderson stemmed from the fact that Henderson was a member of the central committee of the Communist Party. Lewis bristled, his eyes flashed fire, his black eyebrows stood straight out, and he roared at me: "By what authority do you make such a charge? What evidence do you have to substantiate such an accusation."

I stood my ground. Just recently *The Communist*, the theoretical journal of the CPUSA, carried an article on farm labor by Donald Henderson who was identified as a member of the central committee and the party's farm specialist. Lewis knew very well that Henderson was a party member, and was simply putting on an act. Perhaps he did not like to be reminded of his use of communist and socialist organizers to build unions in basic industries such as auto, steel, rubber, and textiles. Lewis hired a hundred radical organizers at one time in the early days of the CIO. When questioned by newspapermen as to whether or not the reds might not take his members, Lewis asked disdainfully, "Who gets the bird, the hunter or the dog?"

Years later, Lee Pressman, who was close to the Communist Party if not an actual member, when questioned by an interviewer for the Columbia University Oral History Program about the communist policy-making influence in the CIO, said that there was none. Pressman said that organizers for the CP built business trade unions, just as John L. Lewis ordered. In certain unions like UCAPAWA, later known as the Food, Tobacco and Allied Workers (FTA), the CP leaders ran the unions with an iron hand, but there is little evidence that Marxist doctrine ever seeped down to the rank and file. In 1949, Philip Murray, Lewis's successor in the CIO, had some ten unions expelled as communist dominated. Henderson's FTA was among them.

We were advised by Lewis to take our problems to the executive board of UCAPAWA, and if not satisfied there, then to the International Union convention, and finally, said Lewis: "If you don't get a fair settlement of your grievances, come to me again, and I will see that justice is done." The STFU followed Lewis' direction to the letter. At an International executive board meeting in Washington, Butler and I, along with the other two STFU members, asked official approval of promises made by Henderson to the STFU convention. Howard Kester, the STFU's best spokesman, was ordered out of the meeting when the STFU problems were to be discussed. No objections had been raised to his sitting in during the preliminaries. The sharecropper delegates were infuriated at this treatment of one of their people who was universally loved by all members of the STFU. I had difficulty persuading my fellow members to refrain from walking out of the meeting.

At still another meeting convened by John Brophy, the CIO's organization director, we recounted how Henderson had made specific promises to the STFU convention and then reneged on them. Henderson coldly said: "I will have to call Mr. Mitchell a liar." I picked up a chair and swung it at Henderson, who ducked. The chair went out the window, four floors up. John Brophy and Howard Kester forcibly restrained me, and then Henderson made a halfhearted apology.

The Second International Convention of UCAPAWA was called to meet in San Francisco in early December of 1938. This time, the STFU could raise only enough money to send one auto-load of delegates. Butler, who knew he would not be re-elected vice-president of UCAPAWA, remained in Memphis. David Griffin, a white STFU organizer from Arkansas, two blacks, Owen H. Whitfield of Missouri and W. S. Simmons of Oklahoma, and I made up the delegation. We attended the convention preliminaries and heard Harry Bridges of the International Longshoremen Union and CIO director for the West Coast make a speech. The STFU folks were greatly impressed by Bridges. I told the others it was too bad that UCAPAWA didn't have a man like that as its president. The STFU delegation was given a hearing in executive session. When we presented our bill of grievances, we were booed, and told to shut up. We warned that the STFU was going to insist that Henderson's promises, which he made in writing, be honored. Then the four of us walked out. We left San Francisco for the long trip home.

At the next STFU convention in Cotton Plant, Arkansas, the following month, the union made it plain to Donald Henderson and company that the agreement made by UCAPAWA had to be lived up to. No more dues from the sharecroppers would be sent to the international's headquarters in the Rust Building in Washington, until this happened.

Almost immediately Henderson made his countermove by calling conventions in Missouri, Oklahoma, and Memphis to reorganize the Southern Tenant Farmers Union in accordance with his ideas.

14 The Missouri Highway Sit-down

The most spectacular event to occur in the sharecropper movement was the highway demonstration in January 1939. In a protest against the planters, 1,700 sharecropper families, who had been ordered to vacate their cabins by January 10th, moved out on the highways of southeast Missouri. For nearly a week these black and white families camped on the roadside in bitter cold weather. Pictures of men, women, and children, huddled about open campfires in the snow, appeared in newspapers throughout the country. Their only shelter was makeshift tents made of household blankets and quilts.

During 1938, the Southern Tenant Farmers Union had finally secured a ruling from the Department of Agriculture that henceforth all cotton producers, landowners, tenants, or sharecroppers should receive their government checks from the Agricultural Adjustment Administration, direct in their own names. In this way, the plantation owners would be stopped from appropriating the subsidies for reducing cotton acreage. But the victory was short-lived. In the rich delta of southeast Missouri, the landowners made plans to change over from sharecropping to wage labor, so they would not have to share the government subsidies. They gave their sharecropper families eviction notices, requiring them to move out by January 10th. For weeks, STFU locals had been meeting and talking of what they could do.

Owen H. Whitfield, a charismatic black leader and vice-president of the STFU, wrote me a letter on December 4th that plans were being made to stage a protest by moving out on the highways when the people had to vacate their homes. Whitfield's brief note never reached me. In my absence from the office, President J. R. Butler had written "File" across the top of this note. If Butler had read it, he had failed to grasp its significance. Forty years later the message was found when the STFU papers were being microfilmed at the University of North Carolina Library. Had I known of this letter, I would not have told Mrs. Roosevelt, and through her, the President of the United States, and J. Edgar Hoover, Director of the FBI, that the Missouri highway demonstration was a spontaneous movement by evicted sharecroppers. Another letter found in the STFU files showed that the Communist

Party in St. Louis had a hand in staging the demonstration. This second letter was from Al Murphy, also known as Albert Jackson, who was the first secretary and one of the original organizers of the Alabama Sharecroppers Union. Murphy was then living in St. Louis and had been in touch with Owen H. Whitfield about plans for the demonstration.

On Sunday, January 8, final meetings were held by STFU local unions all over southeast Missouri. According to Booker T. Clark, who was one of the secondary leaders of the protest movement, there were more than a hundred at the meeting held near New Madrid. He and Whitfield attended meetings in seven counties that day. Clark said:

A lot of people at the meetings weren't even members of the union, but when they saw others moving, they moved too. Before morning there were more than 1,500 out on the highways from Charleston and Wyatt, and between New Madrid and Lilbourn. The snow was deep when we started. We made rag tents, and quilt tents, all makeshifts. The newspapers sent men to take pictures. They took my mother's picture trying to cook with snow on the stove out on the roadside. It was a pitiful looking sight.

On Wednesday, January 11, 1939, I was in New York City. I picked up a copy of *The New York Times,* and there were pictures of the members of the STFU camping on the highways of southeast Missouri. News reporters and photographers had been tipped off in St. Louis of the impending demonstration, and they were at several meetings where the sharecroppers mobilized to stage the protest.

The highway sit-down was an interracial event. White families had also been given eviction notices, and they followed the lead of Owen Whitfield, the black preacher, who called for everyone "to move out on the U.S. highways, and watch the rest of the world go by." South of Sikeston, at Lilbourn, and near Carruthersville, the majority of the protesters were whites, but the black families, for once, got most of the attention from the newspapers, radio, and newsreel cameramen. Once the Memphis papers found out about the demonstration, they covered the southmost area, while their colleagues from St. Louis played up the story of the blacks around Charleston and north of Sikeston.

The family of Owen H. Whitfield, the leader of the sit-down, was not directly involved. The Whitfields were tenants on the LaFarge farms, a project of the Farm Security Administration. Leaders of the STFU and the friendly planter, Thad Snow, had seen to it that Whitfield was accepted as an FSA client the year before. As soon as the highway demonstration got underway, Whitfield, fearing for his life at the hands of the planters whom he had defied, headed for St. Louis. Whitfield

Above: Meeting with New York Mayor Fiorello LaGuardia. Left to right: Beatrice Johnson, who had been jailed on a charge of "nightriding" (for distributing strike circulars); J. R. Butler, STFU President; Mayor LaGuardia; Harriet M. Young, Secretary, National Sharecroppers' Week, 1937–38.

Missouri highway sitdown of January 1939. Center: Evicted sharecroppers camping by roadside, their camps being broken up by state police. About 100 families were taken from the highway to the New Madrid County Spillway (*bottom*) and held under armed guard without access to food or water. (photos by Arthur Rothstein, FSA. Courtesy Library of Congress).

The Delta Cooperative Farm near Hillhouse, Miss. Building started in 1936.

Upper left: Dorothy Dowe (1948), Secretary-Treasurer, National Farm Labor Union, AFL. *Upper right:* Rev. David S. Burgess speaks at the STFU Convention, 1945. *Lower left:* Isaac Shaw (1948), one of the 18 founders of STFU. *Center:* George Stith (1948), STFU organizer in Arkansas, California, Florida, Louisiana, and New Jersey. *Lower right:* Rev. Arthur C. Churchill, with STFU-NFLU 1946–54.

had sent a telegram to Butler, telling him that he and Mitchell must stay out of southeast Missouri. The mystifying telegram had been read to Butler over the telephone upon his arrival at the STFU office on Broad Street. Butler had not even had time to work the crossword puzzle in the *Memphis Commercial Appeal,* as was his custom each day. He had not read even the brief account in the paper about the Missouri exodus when I telephoned from New York to tell him what was going on among the STFU members. At my urging, Butler left immediately for where the action was. I got the next train to Washington where I first called on Aubrey W. Williams, head of the National Youth Administration, to enlist his help for the evicted sharecroppers. Having completed a temporary assignment with NYA in the summer of 1938, I had been scheduled to go to work for Williams again as a consultant on rural problems.

Upon meeting with Aubrey Williams in the late afternoon of January 11th, I was advised to first see Dr. Will W. Alexander of the Farm Security Administration. An appointment was made, and Dr. Alexander, who had been in touch with the FSA people in the Missouri area, told me frankly that the wheels of government moved so slowly that those people sitting out on the roadside would freeze and starve before anything could be done. Alexander advised me to call on the Red Cross for assistance. I telephoned Mr. Delano, chairman of the American Red Cross and a relative of President Roosevelt. He said, "Mr. Mitchell, we know about the southeast Missouri situation. Our committee on disaster relief is meeting in the morning, and if you will call me again about fifteen minutes to twelve tomorrow, I will then tell you what the Red Cross is prepared to do."

Promptly at the time suggested, I called Mr. Delano and was told: "Mr. Mitchell, I am very sorry, but the American Red Cross considers the southeast Missouri situation to be a man-made disaster, and therefore we cannot act."

Disgusted and disappointed, I returned to the NYA office and telephoned Dr. Alexander about Mr. Delano's reply. There were consultations throughout the afternoon with other New Dealers, and finally Aubrey Williams suggested an appointment with Mrs. Roosevelt to enlist her help. Miss Thompson, the First Lady's secretary, was sure Mrs. Roosevelt would want to see me about the plight of the sharecroppers, but she was out of town and would not return until the late afternoon. When she returned, the First Lady agreed to see "the young man from Missouri" (as she ever afterward identified H. L. Mitchell, even though he was not from Missouri) at six o'clock, at the White House (January 12, 1939).

I arrived about five minutes before six, and drove right up to the front door of the White House in a taxicab. The fare was then twenty cents, and I generously gave the driver a nickel tip. While there were, no doubt, guards about, the gates were open, and the taxicab was not stopped. At the door was a middle-aged black man, the White House Usher. The Usher said Mrs. Roosevelt was expecting me. I was shown into a large room with red wallpaper, that had apparently been cleared for an official reception that evening. There was only a single chair and a small sofa in the room, and a large picture of Grover Cleveland on the wall. I sat first in the chair, and then on the sofa, while waiting for ten, twenty, and thirty minutes, growing more frightened as the minutes passed. If I had known how to get out of the President's house, I might have left, but since I didn't, I just waited for Mrs. Roosevelt. Suddenly a tall, stately woman arrived. She was dressed for an evening social affair, in a gown all covered with sparkling spangles. I thought her the most attractive woman I had ever met anywhere. She apologized for keeping me waiting. "Mr. Mitchell, you know how it is with us ladies. It always takes us longer to dress than we think. Sit down and tell me about the Missouri people, and what I can do to be helpful."

I was immediately put at my ease. I described the sharecropper exodus as a spontaneous protest movement of people who were ordered to vacate their homes, and who were offered at best, temporary work in the spring and fall as farm laborers. The plantation owners had decided to employ wage labor, to avoid having to share their government subsidy payments with the sharecroppers. I asked if Mrs. Roosevelt would request the President to order the National Guard to send field kitchens and tents to take care of the hundreds of men, women and children camping on the roadside in the Missouri boot-heel. Mrs. Roosevelt said: "I'll place a memorandum on the President's bedside table tonight, so it will be the first thing he reads. In the morning, I will talk to him about it, and I am sure he will act. Then," said Mrs. Roosevelt, whose column "My Day" appeared in nearly 500 newspapers throughout the country, "I am going to write a column about this unfortunate situation. What shall I ask my readers to do?"

This was not on the program, but I rose to the occasion and said: "Please ask everyone who can to send food, clothing, and money." Then Mrs. Roosevelt asked where it should be sent. I feared to have it sent into Southeast Missouri where the charismatic Whitfield was already on the run, so I said: "Have them send everything in care of Miss Joyce Crawford in Blytheville, Arkansas; she has been helping members of the union run a cooperative store." Mrs. Roosevelt recalled knowing of Miss Crawford's family in Kansas City. They had been among the founders of the Consumer Cooperative Association in that area.

The following morning I left Washington by train for Memphis, after first telephoning Butler about what I had done. Butler reported that he had been up to Missouri, and that members of the union in Arkansas were getting together carloads of food from their own meager resources. The next day, accompanied by Vice-President F. R. Betton and organizers W. M. Tanner and David A. Griffin, Butler drove to Missouri with a food caravan. They were stopped by Missouri State Police, and Butler was held for several hours and questioned. In the meantime, President Roosevelt called Governor Lloyd Stark and instructed him to mobilize a detachment of National Guardsmen to proceed with field kitchens and tents to house and feed the weary people on the roadside. However, the troops never got there, for word reached the plantation owners, and the highway demonstration was declared a menace to public health. The sheriff and the state highway patrol broke it up.

Booker T. Clark, a local union officer and close associate of Whitfield, recounted what happened in the camp near New Madrid: "One evening, the state police patrol captain told them that a mob was forming in seven counties. The state patrol wasn't in a position to protect us. At night things can happen. 'There will be a massacre. We can't do you no good, because when we get there its done happened.'"

The spokesman for the group, R. A. MacAdory, thanked the patrolman, and then told him, "We are just like a tree planted by the waters, and we will not be moved. Since you say you can't protect us, there will be a few sharecroppers laying around here, but there will be some of the mob lying here too. We both will be here."

The crowd was yelling: "You talk to him! Tell him about it! We are not going! Let the mob come, we will take care of that bunch!" The patrolman and his partner left. MacAdory was a sergeant in World War I. That evening they had a meeting. MacAdory told everybody: "If there is anyone who has rabbit hair on him, go now." The women, children, and the very old were to leave and go to friends and relatives in nearby places. The men would stay and fight. One man said he wanted to go. MacAdory told him to go at once, because if he stayed longer and then left when things got hot, he would be treated like any other enemy. The man walked off with some of the women.

Booker Clark:

When the sun went down, and it began to get dark out there on U.S. Highway 61, MacAdory placed men in positions to guard the camp. He placed them so that if they had to fire they would not crossfire on each other. The guards stayed out all night. There was no one in the camp. We left kerosene lamps burning so it looked like people were there. Then about eight o'clock the next morning, just as the sun rose, they played a trick on us. A truck came up. A lady and several men got out. They claimed they were from the Farm Security Administration office in Sikeston. One man made a long talk to us. He said:

"You people have put up a noble fight here in this cold weather, and we have a place where we want to move you people off the highway. We have a place where we can put you in tents, give you food and medical care, and things like that, until FSA can appraise your land." The woman showed us a list of things she said the Farm Security was going to do. She had a typewriter, a table and chair, and advised all the heads of families to get over on the lefthand side of the highway. A truck was over there. I was ready to follow those people because I thought they were from the FSA office. I was young in the cause those days. It was government paper. My mother and me, we signed up to get forty acres. We were going to get resettled.

The lady talked so nice. She said, "I don't know just how it will be, but in two or three days the government will move you off this highway and end this living in this cruel way. The Farm Security Administration is going to furnish you with real tents to live in." So she said to us.

Just as she was making out the last application, the state troopers moved in. They had about twenty trucks waiting. They were following the trucks with fixed bayonets. They was scared to death. They began saying: "Hold it, hold it, don't cross the road!" Then another bunch goes and knocks down the old makeshift tents we had. They searched us for our guns, and they checked even women for a weapon. They felt their bosoms to make sure. They found no weapons, of course. Then they moved the trucks in and told the people: "Get in the trucks, we are going to carry you where you have long wanted to go." The county sheriff was there with the state highway patrol, too. He said: "We just can't have this hazard out here on the highway. Load up your things on the trucks. We are going to take you where you will be out of the way."

There was no problem. They took us eighteen miles back in the woods on the Spillway. That was the New Madrid Spillway, between the Mississippi River and the levee. They took us out there and dumped us. We didn't have nothing. There was a few white families out there with us, but most was colored. There was a school nearby for white children, but the guards wouldn't let us go there to get water to drink. We had to drink water out of the ditches. MacAdory said we had best send someone to St. Louis to get some help down here, and someone to help straighten this out. We remembered some men from the Socialist Party had been down to see us on the highway, and they had given us a key as to where to come for help.

Two of our fellows volunteered that night to go to St. Louis for help. They had us hemmed in, nobody was allowed to go out, and nobody could get in. They just planned to starve us to death. MacAdory told the two fellows: "You can't go together. One of you go into the woods in one direction, and the other go in another direction. If one has the misfortune to get caught, maybe the other will get through." A few of us out there had some change. We all put in nickels, dimes and quarters. We gave them enough for bus fares, and a little something to buy some food on the way. They left about 12:00 o'clock that night.

We waited all the next day, and the next night. Then on the second morning, here came a small airplane circling the area. Everybody rushed out to look, all excited. Some of us wondered if the landlords were fixing to start something else. Again MacAdory took charge. He said, "Take it easy, everybody. Just scatter out. Let everyone lay down on his stomach. Then if a bomb is dropped, it won't kill everyone." So we all scattered out, laying flat on the ground. Then the plane went up high and circled about some more. Finally, something dropped, and a white parachute opened. I wondered what was going on. MacAdory said, "Everyone hold it—stay where you are. Give it a few minutes. There might be an explosion. Just wait for thirty minutes."

The plane had gone away, and finally MacAdory and another man went to see what had dropped. Guess what it was! It was a big lot of bread for us! Also there was a note in it, which said, "Your friends arrived. Help is on the way." It was from Sam Hill and Martin Lechner who were socialists. They lived in the university section in St. Louis. They had set things in motion. Some people came the next day. The sheriff had a pump driven in the ground for us so we had water to drink. They opened up the roads again, and we could come and go freely once more. (From a taped interview with Booker T. Clark, April 6, 1974).

What happened in southeast Missouri was also reported by one of the famed photographers of the Farm Security Administration, Arthur Rothstein, who made some photos of the highway sit-down. In a letter dated January 16, 1939, Rothstein wrote, "The situation was created when the planters gave the croppers an alternative of getting off the land or remaining as day laborers, paying rent in cash and existing just as the miners exist in company towns. The move to the highways was a public protest against this kind of economic slavery." Rothstein also said that the local officials had systematically weeded out the leaders of the protest movement, leaving the remainder lost and bewildered. He said: "They are much worse off now than they were before. While they were along the roads, people brought them food and clothing, although the Red Cross refused to do anything under threats from local planters —but the State Troopers moved them from the highway. Most of them are now in the open fields or barns, well away from the public eye."

Rothstein was right. Whitfield was the first of the leaders to flee. But there were people like R. A. MacAdory and Booker T. Clark who remained. Clark said they had considered Whitfield a sellout for a long time.

The Southern Tenant Farmers Union, with Howard Kester and F. R. Betton in charge, set up union relief headquarters in Blytheville, Arkansas. They sought out the displaced persons on the backroads of the Missouri cotton section. They transported tons of food and clothing, setting up stations where those in need could get relief. Admittedly, they did more to help people who were south of Sikeston than they did in the northern part of the area—which was closer to St. Louis. The Negro Elks Club in that city sent two huge trucks loaded with food and clothing to Charleston, Missouri, in the northern area. The truck drivers could not find leaders of the union in the area, so they turned everything over to an ad hoc committee set up by the black ministers in the town. The committee proceeded to give the relief to members of the churches, most of whom didn't know anyone on the highways.

Kester and Betton made a complete report on everything received— food, clothing and money, and its distribution. When the Communist *Daily Worker* in New York City accused Butler and me of stealing relief funds, a suit was filed against the paper. The editors agreed to a settlement out of court, and offered an apology, claiming that one of the correspondents had received false information.

In the meantime, the Farm Security Administration began making weekly grants to the evicted sharecroppers, applications for which had to be renewed every seven days. The union organizers' time was taken up in helping the sharecroppers get new forms filled out every week.

Later in February, F. R. Betton and I with a delegation from Missouri were back in Washington. There we called upon Dr. Will W. Alexander and first proposed the building of what later became known as the Delmo Labor Homes Project. While working on the NYA the past summer, I had visited the migratory labor camp built by FSA in Texas. I proposed a similar kind of permanent development, but thought the homes should have some land provided for subsistence farming. Apparently FSA people had already been considering such a project, but they had not visualized it as I had, as a village of fifty to a hundred families, each having access to land for growing food products, while working on nearby cotton plantations, or in industries—if and when such were established in southeast Missouri.

As it was eventually constructed, each community, averaging sixty houses, was built around common facilities such as laundry, meeting hall, etc. There was land for gardens at each project. Four of the Delmo Labor Homes Projects were for Negroes, and six for white families. While separate but equal housing was provided by the Farm Security Administration, the Delmo Labor Homes were close together in several localities. In some cases, union meetings held in the Delmo Labor Homes were attended by members of both races, as were other functions. The tenants were charged a nominal rental. Lights, water, and community laundry facilities were provided. An effort was made by the union to get those who were once on the roadside selected as tenants at Delmo Labor Homes. The FSA officials also cooperated in this endeavor. However, some who had no part in the roadside demonstration also benefited.

In the midst of this constructive work, the STFU officers and members had to contend with the break of UCAPAWA. Don Henderson, having finally secured the complete loyalty of Owen Whitfield, moved to take over the STFU and oust its leadership. He called a convention in Memphis to reorganize the STFU. Several of us from the union were in New York for the observance of National Sharecroppers Week. Our delegation returned to Memphis, driving 1,200 miles without a break. We arrived three days before Henderson's rump convention was scheduled to be held. It was determined that the STFU would pack the hall Henderson had rented down on Beale Street with our own delegates, and vote down any proposal that he placed before the convention. Trucks, cars, and buses were dispatched into Arkansas, Missouri, Tennessee, and Mississippi. They picked up delegates who had been in attendance at the Cotton Plant convention in December. It was decided that neither Butler nor I would attend Henderson's meeting. Loyal leaders F. R. Betton, George Stith, David Griffin and famed STFU singer Reverend A. B. Brookins were there. Frank McAllister, who had considerable experience in Florida and Georgia battling the Ku Klux Klan and the communists seeking to infiltrate unions and other organizations, was on hand as a reporter. McAllister had worked behind the scenes with the union for a long time, investigating meetings being broken up and freeing blacks and whites from peonage. He was the southern secretary for the Workers Defense League, and he helped organize the packing of Henderson's meeting.

The union leaders did not foresee that Henderson would come to his meeting with a set of actions already approved by his executive board to remove all STFU officers and appoint a new slate who would be subservient to UCAPAWA and the Communist Party. Henderson had been speaking for two hours when McAllister called the STFU office, urging that Butler and I come down. He said the STFU people were so furious that they were on the verge of attacking Henderson. Henderson had only ten of his people present, and the STFU delegation numbered more than 75. But, McAllister warned, at least three of Henderson's "delegates" were Beale Street thugs, who had been spotted by police as dangerous men. He said the Memphis police were outside the hall in full force, and threatened to jail everyone present if a riot broke out. Reluctantly, Butler and I went into the convention. Butler, a bit taller than I, was bristling right to the top of his close-cropped head, where the hair was standing stiffer than usual. As he walked into the hall, Henderson spotted him, and said, "If Mr. Butler doesn't leave this hall, I am going to have the Sergeant at Arms throw him out." There was yelling throughout the hall: "You had better not try. We will tear you apart!" The loudest shouts against Henderson came from Flotine

Hodge, a rather large white woman organizer and secretary of the Woodruff County STFU council. While Henderson's attention was centered on Butler at the entrance, I came through an anteroom, and walked up to within ten feet of the podium where Henderson stood. I said: "I hear this man has been telling lies about me and every one of you. I demand the right to answer him." Henderson turned pale and glared, shouting, "I have the floor, and will not yield it to you, you fascist louse!"

The crowd, led by Flotine Hodge and A. B. Brookins, surged forward, surrounding Butler and me. Knowing the danger everyone there faced from the Beale Street gunmen and knife wielders, I had visions of bloodshed. The police would crash the meeting, we'd all be jailed, and then the STFU would have to bail us out. I called out, "Everyone who wants to stay in the real union, follow me." Even some of Henderson's own people arose and followed me down the stairs and on to the Labor Temple, three blocks away. There, a proposal was made by A. B. Brookins to appoint a committee to go seize Don Henderson, take him to the foot of Beale Street, where he, Brookins, a Baptist minister, would baptise Henderson in the Mississippi River, and make a Christian of the UCAPAWA president. Brookins' offer was not acted upon.

Later, Henderson called similar meetings to set up statewide unions made up of STFU locals in both Missouri and Oklahoma. Booker T. Clark said that there was a lot of confusion between the Southern Tenant Farmers Union and the United Cannery, Agricultural, Packing, and Allied Workers. Clark said they paid their per capita tax of fifty cents per month on each member to UCAPAWA. Clark was secretary-treasurer to one of the local unions. He said he was responsible for keeping in contact with the socialists Martin Lechner and Sam Hill in St. Louis, who aided his group by furnishing them with a typewriter and a mimeograph machine. Clark said Henderson didn't like him because he "dealt with that bunch of socialists in St. Louis."

Sometime later, Whitfield got people in St. Louis to buy a piece of land at Harviell, Missouri, near Poplar Bluffs in the hills. The people called it "Homeless Junction." Families who had been on the roadside near New Madrid, Charleston and Wyatt moved over to this colony. Clark said the women went fishing in a stream while the men stood guard. Clark described the citizens of Harviell as a radical bunch. He said there were threats to poison the well used by the colonists. There were two prowlers killed by guards one night. The colonists were getting relief from the Farm Security Administration in Poplar Bluff and Jefferson City. Clark told of a meeting he attended with Governor Stark at the state capitol. Apparently, this had been arranged by Whitfield. Clark said that Whitfield never came to the camp at Harviell, and that the people there didn't even hear from Whitfield. "It seemed like Whitfield just went out of the picture for some time," said Clark. "Whenever we would hear of Whitfield, he was off somewhere with Don Henderson. It seemed to me that Don Henderson was mostly out for what he could get for Don Henderson."

They were having a meeting near Charleston one time. Clark was acting as chairman since Whitfield was not there. Katherine Lewis, John L.'s daughter, was to be there, along with a black man named Boyd from the United Mine Workers District 50. As Clark remembers it, "A boy came in with a telegram. It was from Miss Lewis saying she was not coming. There were newspapermen there from St. Louis, *The Post Dispatch,* and *The Globe Democrat,* the Sikeston and Charleston newspapers, too. Photographers were taking my picture. They wanted to know about the agenda. I didn't know what that was at the time. When the St. Louis papers came out the next day, my picture was on the front page, and the whole proceedings of the meeting was printed. Thereafter I had to dodge the Sheriff and his men. I moved first to Portageville, and then to Lilbourn when the Delmo homes for Negroes were built and opened." "Homeless Junction" broke up about the time the United States entered World War II. Apparently Clark continued until 1941 as an organizer and a local union secretary for UCAPAWA.

The ex-sharecroppers—many of whom were by that time living in the Delmo Labor Homes Project—went on strike for higher wages in the cotton fields. It was labeled a wildcat strike, and Henderson removed the charters of the remaining UCAPAWA locals in the area, for striking in wartime. Thus Henderson became a strike breaker, and the Southern Tenant Farmers Union was left alone. Every now and then, one would hear about UCAPAWA, which soon became known as FTA (Food, Tobacco and Allied Workers), contesting a National Labor Relations Board election in a tobacco plant in North Carolina or Virginia. Sometimes one would hear of Owen Whitfield being involved in such non-agricultural activities. However, after the Second World War ended, such activity ceased. In 1949 Henderson's FTA was among the ten communist-dominated unions to be expelled by the CIO convention under Philip Murray, a move that cleared the way for the merger of the CIO with AFL seven years later. Remnants of the FTA, such as the Fruit Tramps Local 78 in California, were absorbed by the United Packing House Workers of America, which had narrowly escaped the CIO purge. Years later, that local, greatly reduced in numbers, became a part of the Amalgamated Meat Cutters and Butcher Workmen AFL-CIO.

15 Rebuilding After the CIO Debacle

Even the new left historians, who seldom see anything wrong in whatever the Communist Party USA did as it followed the foreign policy twists of the USSR under Joe Stalin, found that there was justification for the withdrawal of the STFU from the UCAPAWA–CIO. Mark Naison, a radical SDSer (Students for a Democratic Society) of the 1960s, endorsed our move after reading the correspondence of the period. Naison also found that the sharecropper, deprived of education and burdened by debt, was in no position to pay dues, much less carry on the paper work the CIO demanded of industrial workers.

Naison summarized a letter I wrote to Donald Henderson after the merger and the flood of forms began: "Mitchell was convinced that the STFU did not have ten secretaries among its 200 local unions who could handle the paper work. One of the STFU organizers suggested that the CIO materials be kept for fifty years, during which time sharecroppers might be educated enough to handle such work."

Said Naison: "Mitchell chose to challenge Henderson's drive to re-organize the Union. Rounding up whatever loyal members he could find, Mitchell crashed the dual convention [called by Henderson in Memphis], took it over, and led his supporters out. Henderson was left with a handful of croppers, most of them followers of Whitfield and McKinney. With no basis for an interracial movement, Henderson was never to make a serious effort to re-organize in cotton." Naison also called the STFU one of the most radical mass forces for change in American society, and blamed both the Communist Party and the CIO for its failure, as both had stood aside from its real strivings, smothered it with forms, and crushed it with obligations. As Naison also said, "The STFU was almost devastated."

By the end of 1939, there were only 40 local unions left functioning in the several states (down from a peak of 200 locals and 31,000 members in 1938). However, there were the loyal organizers, F. R. Betton, vice-president, and George Stith, the able young black man who had joined the union at the age of 18, and because no one else in his local could write, was elected secretary. In four years, Stith had become the outstanding organizer of farm workers, ready to accept any call to go anywhere. These two were soon joined by Mrs. Carrie L. Dilworth of Gould, Arkansas, another capable organizer and leader, who came to the forefront and remained through the years. These three blacks were also assisted full time by Reverend Joseph E. Clayton, who had helped organize in Texas, where he was principal of the Littig High School, some miles east of Austin.

I had found Clayton during a trip for the National Youth Administration in 1938, when I was asked to sit in on a class he was conducting in current events. He was using the *CIO News* as his text. J. E. Clayton was a graduate of Prairie View Agricultural College for Negroes in Texas. He was a minister and had taught in the segregated schools of his state. Following World War I, he acted as the agent dealing with several railways in persuading them to sell land to black people who established many small farms and rural communities in Texas and other southwestern states. As a result, he was widely known and respected among blacks and whites alike. Clayton was an orator of the old school, and could make the rafters ring. He said, "During World War I, if all the cattle raised by Negro farmers had been made into one big Texas Steer, he would be so large that his forefeet would be planted in the streets of El Paso, and his hind quarters would lap over into Texarkana, Arkansas, while his tail would fan the breeze about Aurora Borealis at the North Pole." He loved to tell jokes, usually with the rich white man as the butt of a prank pulled by some supposedly dumb colored boy just into the big city from off the farm.

Together, Clayton and Betton made a real team, and they came up with many ideas for things the union could do. Neither had a very high regard for Mr. Butler's ability. The black members often addressed F. R. Betton as *President* Betton. Clayton was loved by all: Whites as well as blacks would turn out by the hundreds to hear him speak. Clayton had a permanent free pass on all railways west of the Mississippi River, because of his land-selling activities. When there was a political campaign on in Texas, Clayton would be contacted by the politicians. He was an early supporter of Lyndon B. Johnson, and of Senator Tom Connally of Texas, ranking Democrat on the Senate Foreign Relations Committee, who called on Clayton for advice from time to time. Both Betton and Clayton were most conscious of race discrimination and were attracted to the Southern Tenant Farmers Union because it was truly interracial and pointed the way for a better life for blacks in the rural South.

During World War II, A. Philip Randolph, president of the Brotherhood of Sleeping Car Porters AFL, had just called the first march on

Washington and secured from President Roosevelt the executive order establishing the Fair Employment Practices Committee. He had been invited to address the annual convention of the STFU in Memphis. Two days before the STFU meeting was to start, political boss Ed H. Crump had forbidden Randolph to speak at a public meeting being held in a church on Beale Street. I insisted that Randolph come to the STFU Convention and speak. Clayton led a delegation to escort the distinguished civil rights leader to the union meeting place, which had been changed to a small Negro church on the outskirts of town. About a hundred delegates attended. They were soon joined by an equal number of plainclothes policemen and a few deputy sheriffs. Clayton made an introductory speech that lasted at least half an hour. The policemen were held spellbound as Clayton explained what the labor movement was about, and how great a man A. Philip Randolph was. Clayton afterwards introduced a special resolution and again spoke, making the policemen even stronger converts to unionism. The police lieutenant in charge came to me and said, "Mitchell, if you will help us organize, and have that man Clayton speak for us, we will march on City Hall."

J. E. Clayton was the organizer whose expenses were always the lowest. He traveled from town to town by train, as we said, free of charge. He had friends in every town, city, or rural community, who considered it a great honor to have him as their guest for as long as he would stay. Clayton once made a trip across to San Francisco from Houston, at an expense of $6.12—mainly for meals in some railway restaurant. He would sit up all night riding the day coaches, and spend his time talking and writing.

At the end of World War II, I got a letter from J. E. Clayton saying, "Please send me an official letter with the seal on it, naming me as the STFU Observer at the Founding Convention of the United Nations." Clayton had been in touch with Lyndon Johnson, then a member of Congress, and the senator from Texas, Tom Connally, who arranged for him to be the observer from the Southern Tenant Farmers Union. Clayton was the only person seated as an observer from a labor union at the founding of the United Nations. Neither William Green, president of AFL, nor Philip Murray, president of the CIO, was accorded such an honor.

The chief white organizers of the STFU during this period (from our Little Rock convention in 1941 to 1946, when we joined the AFL) included John F. Hynds of Forrest City, who helped rescue Clay East when he was mobbed on the courthouse lawn. Hynds was so angered by that attack that he abandoned his fresh meat peddling business, and started to organize for the STFU full time. As mentioned earlier, Hynds became the chief investigator for the union, filing claims for government subsidies, getting men and women out of jail, and filing laborers' liens with the Arkansas Labor Department.

Then there was David A. Griffin, sharecropper of Woodruff County, who became one of the union's best organizers and speakers. Griffin apeared on "Town Hall of the Air" in New York City and was in demand every year when the National Sharecroppers Week was on. Griffin's assistant in all local and county activity was Mrs. Flotine Hodge, who in 1937 wrote and produced before union audiences a three-act play called *The Southern Tenant Farmers Union Forever.* The play is about an Arkansas tenant farm family. The wife doesn't think too much of her husband's union activity. The planter landlord's family thinks even less. The maid in the planter's home is a secret member of the STFU and carries information she overhears about the planters' plans to break up the union. Forewarned, the STFU men thwart the planters' plot, the union comes to the aid of the tenant farm family, and the doubting wife becomes a strong supporter of the Southern Tenant Farmers Union *forever.*

During the latter part of 1940 and in 1941, I was again on leave, working for the National Youth Administration, and for three months I was an organizer for the International Ladies Garment Workers Union. J. R. Butler was still president of the STFU, while Blaine Treadway held the post of secretary. I was offered a permanent job by David Dubinsky, the ILGWU chief, and considered accepting it when I was implored by Betton and Clayton to return to the Southern Tenant Farmers Union. During this period, the STFU had made a proposal to the AFL for an affiliation which resulted in a controversy between Butler and me. I had met in Washington with my friend Frank P. Fenton, Director of Organization for AFL, and had also met with President William Green, to discuss the idea for a national farm labor union. This would include many federal labor unions in related fields, as well as the STFU, which would continue under its own name under the AFL umbrella. Butler, in view of our experience with UCAPAWA–CIO, demanded that the charter be given direct to the STFU only. I warned that this would not be possible, and sure enough, the AFL executive council rejected the application from the STFU for a charter, because, as the AFL said: "There did not appear to be a financial basis for the organization of a trade union among sharecroppers."

After drawing up a program with the help of Betton, Clayton, and other STFU leaders, which we called "Put the Man of the Land Back on the Land," I asked for an endorsement of the program at the Little

Rock convention in early 1941. The plan was well received and unanimously adopted. I was re-elected secretary by acclamation. However, in my program, I quoted what the AFL executive council had said about there being no basis for a trade union in southern agriculture, and added that one group of paupers—the sharecroppers—were trying to bargain with another group of paupers—the debt-ridden plantation owners. This phrase was repeated by the newspapers all over the South and played up as an admission from a long-time union leader that trade unionism would not work in the South.

While Butler had not made any objection to the program of land for the landless that we enunciated at the convention, he called a meeting of the executive council after the convention ended, and threatened to resign unless I repudiated the program that the convention had adopted. It was then that Betton and Clayton and the rest of the Negro leadership worked out a strategy for breaking this impasse. They called upon me to say that it had been a mistake to announce that there was no basis for a trade union in southern agriculture, and they promised in return either to put J. R. Butler in his rightful place, namely, as just the presiding officer of the STFU; or, if he proved recalcitrant, to elect a new president at the next year's convention. I settled for this arrangement.

Upon my return to office as secretary of the STFU, I found only 40 local unions holding charters, and less than 1,000 members enrolled. Butler, following the advice of Treadway, the Memphis printer and long-time member of the powerful International Typographical Union, had pulled every charter where there were fewer than seven paid-up members in good standing. This was not in the STFU tradition. People who attended meetings and otherwise supported the STFU were counted as full members, regardless of whether or not they had the money to pay dues regularly. The National Sharecroppers Week was netting $5,000 to $6,000 a year at this point. Then, there were special contributors like Mrs. Ethel Clyde, Mrs. Margaret Fleming, Mrs. Fiske Hammond, who could always be counted on to make special gifts when the union resources were exhausted. Butler had also found a new source of contributions in Mr. and Mrs. J. D. Overholt of Wooster, Ohio, heirs to the whisky fortune of the distiller of the then well-known brand of "Old Overholt," a blend of rye and bourbon whiskys.

Historian Carole S. Sweatt wrote of this period: "The distinctiveness of the Southern Tenant Farmers Union was the product of its hostility to capitalism, and its vision of the future. A member once predicted that the 'Union will speed up the day when a rope spun by God will be used to hang the planters.'" This proved to be inaccurate.

Plantations outlived the union, which barely survived a two-year affiliation with the CIO's United Cannery Agricultural Packing and Allied Workers of America (UCAPAWA), and limped forward during the early forties. She also added,

Most historians, including Donald H. Grubbs,* the foremost authority on the STFU have left the impression that wartime America saw the demise of the Southern Tenant Farmers Union. Although the STFU lapsed into a period of temporary stagnation, it is not entirely accurate to say that the Union ceased to function. Throughout the early forties, the STFU's top executives, H. L. Mitchell and J. R. Butler, continued to disagree about the goals, methods and philosophy of the Union. . . . By 1943, through diligent effort on his part, Mitchell had secured the support of the Executive Council, thus planting himself solidly as President of the Union.

On my return to the STFU, Betton, Clayton, and I launched cooperative market and purchasing associations in Arkansas, Missouri, and Mississippi, parallel to those of the Farm Security Administration. We opened up a new area heretofore untouched in northeast Alabama, in the Tennessee Valley Authority area. Forming alliances with the strongly organized trade unions in the TVA section, we assigned W. M. Tanner, a vigorous white organizer, to enlist the small farmers on the mountain plateau overlooking the big plantations alongside the Tennessee River. The plantations were peopled mainly by sharecroppers and black day laborers. South of the large town of Russellville, the members of the STFU formed a cooperative store in the Spruce Pine Community. Ailing John F. Hynds, our veteran organizer and investigator, was put on a pension by the union and assigned to operate the new store in Alabama.

The union's organizer in Alabama, W. M. Tanner, proved successful in signing up members and in establishing local unions. However, Tanner was also a minister, and sometimes the members could not distinguish Tanner's roles, one from the other. Religious conflicts arose for the first time in the STFU. There was also a lack of the interracial cooperation that had existed in Arkansas. Alabama's 150-year-old segregation patterns were more rigid than those in the younger areas of Arkansas and Missouri where plantations were larger and most land had not been in cultivation for more than twenty years. Just before the Eighth Annual STFU Convention in Sheffield, Alabama, in 1942, it was quite evident that W. M. Tanner was campaigning for the post of President, held by J. R. Butler. Betton and Clayton had spent some

Cry from the Cotton—The STFU and New Deal (Chapel Hill: University of North Carolina Press, 1971)

time in Alabama trying to unravel the problem. They had met Roy
Raley, then an assistant business agent of the Laborers Union,* who
also had a small farm on the plateau overlooking the Tennessee River.
Raley's wife also ran a small and unprofitable grocery store. Raley had
started the practice of giving job preferences to members of the STFU
whenever there was an opening in his local construction workers union
in the TVA area. Such STFU members, if they held a paid-up card, were
accepted without an initiation fee. Raley also worked closely with the
all-black Laborers local leadership and got the same kind of treatment
there for the black STFU members. So here was a new pattern that
boded fair for the STFU membership.

Many things happened in Sheffield. For the first time, there was
segregation of delegates at an STFU Convention. State law permitted
joint meetings, but required separation of whites and blacks. I didn't
realize that they were separated until the official photographer made
the convention pictures. The only white persons sitting on the side for
colored people were the office secretary, Ramona Wood, and two
distinguished visitors, Lillian Smith (author of *Strange Fruit,* a book
banned in Boston because of its interracial theme) and her associate,
Miss Paula Snelling, both from Clayton, Georgia.

The Central Labor Union welcomed the STFU delegates and provided banquets, but these too were segregated. Butler attended the
banquet for white delegates, and I the one for blacks. I was accompanied by the three women, who had refused to accept the segregated
arrangements in the hall.

On the final day before the nominating committee was to make its
recommendations, I went to Butler with the approval of Betton and
Clayton, to urge him to again accept the post of president. Butler
refused. He would accept renomination only if I stepped aside as an
officer of the STFU. The group then approached Roy Raley; otherwise
they feared that Tanner, with his solid support among the small white
farmers, would be nominated. All agreed that the STFU must not be
headed by a "religious fanatic" as Butler described the Holiness
Preacher Tanner. Raley agreed to serve only one term in the office, if
elected. He felt that his place was in the labor movement of the TVA,
and while an intelligent man, he lacked education and other qualifications to head a movement such as the STFU.

Roy Raley was elected president by acclamation, but not before
Butler had been named President Emeritus for life. Some of Butler's
most loyal friends were, to say the least, disappointed. Walking out of

---

*Also known as Hod Carriers or Common Laborers locals.

the convention hall, never to return, were organizers David A. Griffin and his friend, Flotine Hodge.

Early in 1942, following the STFU convention, Roy Raley and I attended a convention of the International Union of Hod Carriers and Common Laborers, in St. Louis. The president of the Laborers was Joe Moreschi. He had been elected by his executive board. The union itself had not even bothered to hold an election in twenty years. Raley and other delegates from the TVA area had introduced a resolution calling for recognition of members of the STFU by any and all local unions of the Laborers, with job preference and no initiation fees, to such applicants. I was also invited to address the convention and did so. The resolution was referred to the incoming executive board and was never heard of again. However, the plan for the transfer of union members by the STFU to other unions proved helpful during wartime, particularly when we started sending our members to work in New Jersey food processing plants.

The growers of food and fiber in the southwest saw the war as an excuse for importing cheap labor from Mexico to exploit in their "factories in the fields." Their representatives in Washington had already persuaded the federal government to enter into an international agreement with Mexico for the importation of thousands of workers for the anticipated farm labor shortages.

In Arizona, a special type of silk-like Pima cotton was grown. The cotton growers of this state and others from California, New Mexico, and West Texas enlisted the aid of the U.S. Army in bringing workers from Mexico into this country. They claimed that this special crop of cotton grown in 1942 was going to rot in the fields because of the lack of experienced cotton pickers. The growers demanded the immediate importation of 5,000 workers from Mexico. Spokesmen for the U.S. Army claimed the Pima cotton was needed as a substitute for Chinese silk used in making barrage balloons for directing field artillery.

A War Manpower Commission had been established to provide workers for all industry. On the commission were representatives of industry and agencies such as the U.S. Departments of Labor and Agriculture, the AFL and the CIO, as well as all major national farm organizations, the Farm Bureau, the Grange, and Farmers Union. (There were no specific representatives of farm labor.) The U.S. Employment Service had responsibility for recruiting all workers. The Farm Security Administration was assigned the job of transporting workers required in agriculture.

As soon as it became known that jobs were available in other areas of the country when there was no work in the mid-south (Alabama,

Arkansas, Mississippi and Missouri), the Southern Tenant Farmers Union demanded that American citizens be given the first opportunity for such temporary employment. The first move was to circulate petitions authorizing the union to represent the workers individually and collectively. Over 8,000 such authorizations were secured in 60 days. A wage conference was called in Memphis, Tennessee, on September 7, 1942. There were over 300 workers representing the petition signers in attendance at this meeting. The conference accepted the minimum wage fixed in the international agreement with Mexico—30 cents per hour, which was about twice as much as was currently being paid farm workers in the mid-southern states. The conference fixed a union rate of $2 per 100 pounds for picking cotton as the equivalent of the rates fixed for Mexican nationals. The union had thoughtfully invited representatives of all agencies of government concerned with farm labor to attend this wage conference. The U.S. Employment Service, the Farm Security Administration, and the War Manpower Commission each sent men to attend the well-organized meeting.

Ten thousand circulars were printed, and they were all distributed before sunrise on the morning of September 9th. The circulars advised plantation workers to remain at home until the rate of pay was established. The plantation owners were stunned. There were no arrests. There was not even a threat of calling out the National Guard to break the strike, as had been the pattern before. Circulars demanding the government fixed rate were not even torn down when they were posted on fences and barn doors around the plantations. Within two weeks, the cotton picking wage rate of $2 per 100 pounds was established in the mid-south states.

Then the union offered to supply two thousand experienced cotton pickers to harvest the Pima cotton in Arizona and other southwestern states, in November. At the insistence of the AFL representative, Frank P. Fenton, then director of organization, and the CIO representative, Clinton S. Golden, United Steel Workers of America (these two men were alternates for President William Green of the AFL and Philip Murray of the CIO), the Southern Tenant Farmers Union was invited to meet with the War Manpower Commission in Washington.

Among those also present at this meeting in early October was General Lucius Clay, who wanted assurance that the union could mobilize its members and transport them to Arizona as quickly as he could move troops. The union offered to assist the U.S. Employment Service in recruiting and then in transporting its members to Memphis, if the Farm Security Administration would provide trains for the trip to the West. In November 1942, after all the cotton had been harvested in the South, the STFU sent 2,000 workers west, with a capable union leader aboard each train. The first trainload arrived at a railway siding near Eloy, Arizona, to find no housing, no food, and no employers. The men and women refused to leave the train or let it move until an agent of the Farm Security Administration of the U.S. Government arrived. When the FSA men came, they quickly provided food, housing and then jobs at the promised rate of pay. There were similar foul-ups elsewhere. At McNary, Texas, the workers were unloaded from the train and transported by truck to a huge ranch where there was no housing, and the employer refused to pay the rate promised. The ensuing strike was settled by a young man from Austin, Texas, Clay Cochran, later Director of the Rural Alliance in Washington. Cochran sent this telegram to C. B. Baldwin, the FSA administrator in Washington: "Job issues settled, strike over, all quiet west of the Pecos."

Early in 1943, 500 more workers were sent to harvest fruits and vegetables in Florida. John Beecher, then a farm placement officer for the FSA, recalled how a trainload of workers arrived in Palm Beach. The men and women were all wearing a green union button; the emblem was a cotton boll with a plow, a hoe, and the letters STFU on it. Beecher was afraid that the Florida growers would refuse to accept the workers. However, the field bosses didn't learn for some days that they had union workers on the job. It was then too late to object.

The nation's large farm operators, mobilized by the American Farm Bureau, were determined that the farm workers should not become unionized as a result of the war emergency. Through their lobbying efforts, in 1943 a temporary law was passed by Congress that permitted the importation of foreign workers for employment in agriculture. At the same time, government agencies were prohibited from fixing wages and from providing transportation to any domestic agricultural worker, unless each individual worker had the written consent of his county agricultural extension agent to accept employment outside of the county in which he resided. This effectively ended the union's program of cooperation with the government agencies in providing its members with temporary work out of the South.

Several large-scale farm operators in New Jersey, claiming labor shortages, persuaded the U.S. Army to furlough men to work on farms. One of these operations was the Seabrook Farms of Bridgeton, which had a closed shop union contract with the Amalgamated Meat Cutters and Butcher Workmen of North America, AFL, that covered even farm employees hired for temporary work. In return for representation, each worker employed was required to pay 25 cents per week union dues. There is no record that any of the soldiers furloughed for farm work objected to the dues collections, but the Farm Bureau of New Jersey did object and stirred up the newspapers. The union leader was held up as a traitor to the country, hampering the war effort by insisting that his union contract be enforced. The problem was solved temporarily by the employer and the union agreeing that no more soldiers would be hired on Seabrook Farms.

By 1943, thousands of prisoners of war were captured in Africa and brought to the United States and put to work on farms all over the country. Theoretically, the employers had to pay the U.S. Treasury the current rate of pay for the use of the prisoners of war. Seeing an opportunity to get a cheap labor supply, food processing plant employers also made application for German war prisoners. However, local communities became alarmed at the idea of Americans working in the same plant with Nazi war prisoners. A young Jewish refugee from Hitler's concentration camps, the man who had been pilloried in the press for insisting that furloughed soldiers pay union dues of 25¢ a week, took action. Leon B. Schachter, business manager of Local 56 of the Amalgamated Meat Cutters, contacted the Southern Tenant Farmers Union. An organized migration plan was worked out whereby more than 12,000 workers from the mid-South were sent to work on temporary jobs in New Jersey and other mid-Atlantic states. The men and women were employed both in food processing and on the farm.

Workers were recruited by the Southern Tenant Farmers Union. Transportation was provided by the employers. Wages and working conditions, including housing, were the responsibility of Local 56, which held contracts in most of the plants and on one of the larger farms. The local and state employment services were bypassed by the unions. Local agents of the Employment Service in Arkansas had union representatives jailed on charges of "interfering with labor." Trucks and cars loaded with workers going to Memphis to board trains were turned back in Arkansas, Mississippi, and Alabama. The STFU protested to the War Manpower Commission and the Department of Justice that local farm workers were being held in a new form of peonage. The STFU's vice-president, F. R. Betton, termed the STFU project a new "Underground Railroad." The War Manpower Commission held that the organized migration arranged by the two unions was legal. The program continued throughout the war years.

Workers in the fields had found a new bargaining weapon. If the plantation owners refused to pay union wages, they told the boss they were going to the union and get shipped out to a job in New Jersey. Wage rates and working conditions continued to improve until the end of the war. The union started the practice of collecting its membership dues on the basis of three dollars annually. An economic basis for the organization was thus established for the first time. Negotiations for affiliation with both the CIO and the AFL were started.

16 Their Lives Were on the Line

Volunteers for the STFU

The STFU attracted the attention of many young men and women who were college students in the 1930s, as did the civil rights movement in the 1960s. While ours was not the first organization in the United States to attract such volunteer workers, it was certainly the first movement in the South to inspire young people *to put their lives on the line* on behalf of those less fortunate than they. The STFU perhaps had as many such workers in proportion to size as did the later civil rights organizations, particularly if one considers the fact that the activities of the union extended mainly into the cotton plantation country alongside the Mississippi River. While there were significant outposts in Oklahoma and Texas, the STFU was centered in the states of Arkansas, Mississippi, and Missouri.

There were differences between the students in the 1930s and those who joined the civil rights movement 30 years later. While many of those from both decades were from middle class and sometimes upper class families, those who came in the 1930s more often than not did so out of politically radical motives. Those who came in the sixties were motivated by a desire to help black Americans gain their rights within the capitalist system; the pioneers of the STFU days wanted to overthrow that system, which they were convinced offered little or no hope to those at the bottom of the economic heap. They had all grown up during the Great Depression. Some of them still looked upon the USSR as an example of a better world that was coming into being. True, there were some pretty sharp differences between those who proclaimed that they were socialists and those who admitted that they belonged to the Communist Party, but they both claimed that their goals were basically the same. Those who came to work for the STFU or to participate in related activities such as organizing support committees on their college campuses, including the annual Sharecroppers Week observance, did so because they were convinced that they too should be a part of a revolution that the sharecroppers were making down South. Even those who were democratic socialists did not see much hope of attaining the goal of a new economic system at the ballot box. Those who came and worked with the STFU, or who spent time at radical outposts in the South like Commonwealth College in Arkansas or Highlander Folk School in Tennessee, were as critical of the New Deal programs as was the STFU itself. Many of those who got their basic training as volunteer organizers for the STFU in 1935–1936 went into the CIO when it was formed in 1937 as an organization separate from the tradition-bound AFL.

The first to offer their services in organizing the Southern Tenant Farmers Union were not students, however, although most were college graduates. They were young people in their twenties who were already socialists. This group included Ward H. Rodgers of Oklahoma, by way of Boston Theological Seminary and Vanderbilt, and Evelyn Smith, a new member of the New Orleans local of the Socialist Party. Another who worked for and with the STFU was John Herling of the Strikers Emergency Relief Committee, a subsidiary of the socialist-oriented League for Industrial Democracy. Also there were Sidney Hertzberg, Aaron Levenstein, Aaron S. Gilmartin, Priscilla Robertson and her friend the photographer Louise Boyle, and Harriet Young. This young group was associated with Norman Thomas. Later, in 1940, came Mae Pearl Kelley, a LeMoyne College student, who worked as an organizer. Then there were others, who came to work with the union even in the Sixties.

The League for Industrial Democracy (LID), whose executives were Harry W. Laidler and Mary Fox, persuaded speakers such as Mary Hillyer and Jennie Lee while in Memphis to come for a visit with the sharecroppers in eastern Arkansas. As told before, Jennie Lee, a member of the British House of Commons, joined writers Naomi Mitchison and Zita Baker from England and led a march of STFU members out of Marked Tree, Arkansas, in early 1935. The young English women were about 30 years of age, like Howard Kester and me.

In 1937, a Quaker Work Camp was held on the Delta Cooperative Farm, which brought in about 40 students for a summer's work on this experimental project. Nearly all of the work campers afterwards visited the STFU office in Memphis, and attended meetings in Arkansas, and elsewhere. Among the first of this group to come to work for the STFU was Hazel Whitman from Middlebury College, a member of the same family that produced poet Walt Whitman. Another was Janet Frazier, of Bennington College, who had also been at the Delta Work Camp. These two had almost created a racial incident down on the farm by joining a fellow work camper, Prentice Thomas, a young black from

Howard University, on a stroll down the nearby Mississippi River levee. When she joined the work camp, Hazel was only 17, and when the group stopped for a visit at Norris Dam in the Tennessee Valley Authority near Knoxville, she discovered segregation. When she saw two drinking fountains, one labeled "white" and the other "colored," Hazel rushed over to see the colored water. After the work camp was over, the two college girls volunteered to work in the office of the Southern Tenant Farmers Union in Memphis. On arrival, Hazel went to get a room at the YWCA in the downtown section, thinking that the "Y" was the best place for a young girl traveling by herself. She was told that her room would be ready after dinner. When she returned to the lobby after eating in the "Y" dining room, some one in charge asked where she was from, and if she had a job. Hazel replied that she had been down in Mississippi on a farm, and now was in Memphis to spend the rest of the summer working for the Southern Tenant Farmers Union. The reputation of the STFU in the city was such that the young woman was summarily evicted from the YWCA, which we learned later was not affiliated with the national YWCA. Hazel, very upset, called my home and I went to rescue her from the perils of the YWCA. (This was not the last time that I rescued Hazel from such peril. In 1972, Dr. Hazel W. Hertzberg [nee Whitman], associate professor of history and education at Columbia University Teacher's College, was attending the American Historical Association meeting being held in New Orleans. Hazel had a reservation in a YWCA in one of the worst sections of America's most interesting city. I prevailed upon her to come and share my two-bedroom apartment in another section of town.)

Volunteers Hazel Whitman and Janet Frazier were first put to work in the STFU office in Memphis where they could be under the watchful eyes of Evelyn Smith, Howard Kester, and me. Their first assignment was to collect and arrange the newspaper clippings saved by the union, lodged in files, and scattered about the two-room office on Broad Street. I sent them to the stationery store where the Union had a credit account, to purchase a large scrap book. They bought the largest one in stock, about three feet wide by four feet long. They did an excellent job of arranging and cataloging the newspaper clippings, but the scrapbook was unwieldy. Every researcher who ever delved into the STFU files had a problem to find space to hold the book while reading the articles they were seeking. That problem was not solved until 1974 when the "STFU in the News" was put on microfilm and made available to college libraries that had already acquired the STFU Papers (1934–1970).

In 1937, discovering that Janet Frazier had some talent as an artist, we asked her to prepare a drawing for a new STFU emblem. It was to consist of a plow, a hoe and a cotton boll, to be surrounded by the words: "Southern Tenant Farmers Union." Janet worked on the design for several days, completed it, and proudly showed it to STFU organizer D. A. Griffin, who happened to be in the office that day. Griffin, without any regard for Janet's artistic sensibilities, plainly told her that she had gotten the plowshare on backwards and made fun of the earnest young woman's production. Upon returning to the office, I found Janet alone and in tears. I tried to console her by getting her a Coca Cola. That didn't suffice, so I took her for a ride through nearby Overton Park, and explained that while Griffin was right, he had no business to be so blunt about it. I prevailed upon her to rearrange the plow. Janet's emblem was used thereafter on Union stationery and was made into the Great Seal of the STFU, and all documents thereafter were stamped with the plow, the hoe and cotton boll.

At summer's end, the two girls traveled with Henrietta McGhee and Myrtle Lawrence (two sharecropper women), Griffin and me to New York City for National Sharecropper Week.

Hazel Whitman transferred to the University of Chicago to study economics, and was much influenced by Paul H. Douglas, noted economist and Quaker, who became U.S. Senator from Illinois. In 1938, Hazel returned to work with the union. She and Purnell Benson, a Quaker and also a student at the University of Chicago, developed a joint project of work and study. The plan was to convert the union leadership *and* the plantation owners to non-violence and peaceful co-existence. Hazel was also becoming active in the Young Peoples Socialist League. As usual, I was ready to try anything new, and encouraged the young people. Butler, the union president, who distrusted all forms of religion, was most critical of the project. Howard Kester, who had been southern Secretary of the pacifist Fellowship for Reconciliation, also had some questions.

Benson was the first to arrive and had done some field work in advance of Hazel's coming. Hazel was attending the Socialist Party convention in Kenosha, Wisconsin, and so was I. So Hazel hitched a ride with me to Muskogee, Oklahoma, where I had some meetings scheduled. Hazel was excited about going to Oklahoma, which she felt was the real wild and wooly West. The trip down was uneventful. We stopped overnight in a Kansas town, near the Oklahoma state line, and got an early start the next morning. We would stop for breakfast in Oklahoma. Hazel was haranguing about non-violence. Just as day was breaking, we drove over a hill onto the rolling plains. As far as one could see, the ground was ablaze with color. The bluebonnets had blossomed overnight. I stopped the car, thinking that my fellow traveler would be as awe-struck as I was. When I called her attention to the beautiful day, and the fields of color, Hazel's comment was, "That is nice, but Mitch, do you believe . . . ." When we arrived at the New Huber Hotel in Muskogee, Benny was already there. He and Hazel started talking while I registered for my room. The clerk asked, "Mr. Mitchell, aren't you going to register for your wife?" "Oh, no," I explained, "she is not my wife. I just drove her down here. She belongs to that young fellow she is talking to."

Also among the Quaker work campers was Barbara Howes, a Back Bay "proper" Bostonian. Barbara Howes was present at the St. Francis County Arkansas Courthouse in the fall of 1937 when Butler, as described earlier, was attacked by E. F. Bunch, the same riding boss who had led a mob attack on Clay East the year before. Barbara also arranged for several small bail bonds, posting her savings to free STFU members who had been arrested, usually on trumped up charges. Barbara Howes became a well-known American poet, with several published volumes of poetry to her credit. In 1978 one of her books was nominated for the National Book Award.

Another well-known poet who also knew Barbara Howes once said to me, "Poets are also necessary to movements such as the STFU." Forty years after she had worked with us, Barbara wrote, "The whole experience with the STFU was one of growing up out of the 'naive little girl from Boston' set-up. The several months down in Memphis, just like the earlier summer at the Delta Cooperative Farm, developed my understanding in a very important and valuable way."

I would add that we in the STFU benefited to a greater degree from our association with the gentle, lovely lady, Barbara Howes, than she did from us. One of her poems, composed especially for those who may read *Mean Things*, is included in "Songs and Verses," at the end of this book.

Prentice Thomas was another work camper who became a volunteer organizer for the STFU. He came and worked as an organizer for the STFU nearly every summer while at Howard. He had many adventures. He told several people that the most amazing thing to him about the STFU was the relationship between black and white members. Here in Arkansas and Mississippi where he spent most of his time, despite rigid segregation laws, he found blacks and whites working together, eating meals together, and often spending nights in each others' homes. Prentice Thomas became an attorney for the National Association for the Advancement of Colored People and worked in the New York headquarters for a time. From his experience as a work camper and as a volunteer organizer for the STFU, he had gained much insight into the lives of the people at the bottom.

It is possible that other students and young people who came to work with the STFU gained new insights as did Prentice Thomas, finding that both whites and blacks could forget their race prejudices and act together like men and women in the civilized world. In nearly every case that I know of, people who were actually associated with the union and/or worked in the Socialist Party, the CIO and the AFL always had a good feeling about our STFU. Here was something that they had a part in building; here were people in need to whom they could give a helping hand. Some of them became involved in labor, government, in business, or the academic world. They were part of the establishment, but I never knew a single one upon whom I ever called at any time for assistance who did not do everything he or she could possibly do to help. This was true no matter what we called ourselves, whether the Southern Tenant Farmers Union, or The National Farm Labor Union, or The National Agricultural Workers Union. They knew we were an integral part of their lives and times. Afterwards they gave the same sort of support to Cesar Chavez's United Farm Workers of America. And that too is part of the STFU heritage.

I recall Walter White's address to the Third Annual Convention of the STFU. He was then secretary of the NAACP. White said there had never been a lynching in any area where the STFU was organized.

Sharecroppers and the Law

Perhaps the greatest service provided by the STFU was advice-giving. Literally hundreds of letters arrived monthly from ill-informed and semi-literate tenants and sharecroppers requesting information on how and where to apply to the Farm Security Administration for loans, and for information regarding delinquent AAA payments. These requests were never ignored. Often we would send some one to investigate, or we would pass along the complaint to the proper government agency. As a result, hundreds of planters were forced to hand over to the tenants their proper share of the government payments.

Almost from the beginning, the STFU necessarily functioned as a legal agency concerned with the civil rights of its members. The fight to protect the constitutional rights to assemble peaceably and to speak freely never slackened from the day I retained C. T. Carpenter of Marked Tree, Arkansas, the first union lawyer.

C. T. Carpenter came from Virginia. His father had served with General Robert E. Lee in the Confederate Army. After the surrender at Appomattox, he followed Lee to Lexington where he completed his education and later helped build the law school at Washington and Lee University. After securing his law degree from the school his father had founded, C. T. Carpenter went west and settled in the town of Marked Tree, Arkansas. He often represented sharecroppers who had claims against planters, and at one time he was driven off a plantation near Truman by an irate planter with a shotgun in his hands. Carpenter had also defended strikers at the Singer Sewing Machine cabinet factory located in Truman. When Norman Thomas first came to Arkansas in the Spring of 1934, C. T. Carpenter accompanied H. J. Kreir, a socialist hardware store owner of Marked Tree, to hear the man who had already run twice as the socialist candidate for President of the United States. So, when the newly formed union needed a lawyer to free C. H. Smith from the Crittenden County jail, C. T. Carpenter was a natural choice.

Mr. Carpenter's most celebrated case was that of Ward H. Rodgers, adult education teacher, Methodist preacher, and union organizer, who was charged with Anarchy, Blasphemy and Barratry. Because of his successful work as the STFU attorney, the home of C. T. Carpenter was shot up one night by vigilantes. Later, his son Knight Carpenter was driven off the highway and into a drainage canal by a similar group of nightriders. Mrs. Carpenter was understandably frightened by these incidents, but C. T. Carpenter refused to be intimidated. He just took to carrying his revolver with him wherever he went. He was eventually forced by economic boycott to stop representing the union directly, but he continued his practice of law in Marked Tree. He died in an automobile accident while rushing to a trial of three black people involved in a lawsuit with a plantation owner.

The list of lawyers who served the cause of the STFU and its successor organizations is a long one. When Mr. Carpenter had to stop representing us, Herman I. Goldberger, of Memphis, took us on. Mr. Goldberger was a most courageous man who had even defended communists hounded by an ignorant, bigoted police chief. He was also killed in a mysterious auto accident, on the highway between Memphis and Nashville late one night in 1936.

Then came a young Republican, Newell N. Fowler, who became so involved in the union's legal affairs that he almost lost his divorce practice. Fowler defended Jim Ball, the black secretary of the local at Earle, Arkansas, who picked up a gun to defend his life. Fowler won that case in the state Supreme Court, when Ball's seven-year sentence was reduced to one year—the time he had already spent in jail waiting for justice. Fowler was also physically attacked by Everett Hood, a despicable deputy who had broken up union marches in the 1936 strike. Later, with the help of Pat Jackson in Washington, the union got Newell Fowler an appointment to the staff of the National Labor Relations Board in Denver and Salt Lake City. After a stint as NLRB atttorney, Fowler returned to Memphis, still wanting to represent unions. None would hire him because he lacked the "right" political connections; he became, instead, an employer representative in labor matters and prospered.

Attorney D. M. Moody of Little Rock represented the union at a trial in Forrest City, Arkansas, in June 1936. As noted earlier, Moody was the son of the courageous lawyer who first defended the Scottsboro Boys in Alabama. Moody was present when the plantation mob seized Clay East on the courthouse lawn in St. Francis County in 1936.

Attorney C. A. Stanfield of Hot Springs, Arkansas, came to the union's aid after this incident. Stanfield was also in court when Butler was physically attacked inside the same courthouse while attending the trials of several union members. According to the *Commercial Appeal,* Butler and the plantation owner E. F. Bunch became involved in an "altercation" in the courthouse. The altercation was witnessed by dozens of people, many of them union sympathizers and members. Aside from representing the STFU, Stanfield's chief claim to fame was that he obtained a hearing in the United States Supreme Court in the case of a man about to be deported to the USSR as a communist and an alien. The case was lost after the International Labor Defense, legal arm of the Communist Party, took over despite Stanfield's protest that he was the sole attorney involved.

Among the many other attorneys who served the STFU was Claude F. Cooper of Blythville, who also represented the Workers Defense League and the American Civil Liberties Union in cases growing out of the cotton choppers' strike in 1938–39. Three union members, Louis Johnson, his wife Beatrice, and an 80-year-old man, D. N. Johnson (no relation to the first two), were convicted in a local court on a charge of "Night Riding." These three had written on a union circular demanding $1.00 per 100 pounds for picking cotton: "You had better stay out of the fields, this means you." They were released on bond. The cases were appealed and finally dismissed.

Then in 1940 came K. T. Sutton, who had been practicing law in Helena, Philips County, Arkansas, where some twenty years before two lawyers named Bratton had represented the Farmers and Farm Laborers Association, the all-black organization wiped out in the Elaine Race Riot. Sutton was hired as the attorney for the STFU Legal Defense Committee, paid a monthly retainer and, when the union had the money, reimbursed for the actual expenses he incurred. K. T. Sutton challenged the constitutionality of the Arkansas practice of leasing prisoners to private plantation owners. He won that case and thus ended a form of slavery that had been abolished pretty much everywhere else in the South except in benighted Arkansas.

Another case handled by Sutton involved the residents of the once all black-owned town of Edmondson, Arkansas. Around the turn of the century, when the last Republican office-holders were driven out of Crittenden County by the Ku Klux Klan, some of them had clear title to some land. They eventually returned and established the town of Edmondson, which prospered and remained a black political enclave in white Crittenden County. In state elections, the white political machine sold its vote to the highest bidder. In the early 1930s a swift talking black man came to Edmondson proposing to gin the cotton of black farmers in the nearby area. He also wanted to set up a large mercantile business to be run solely by Negro personnel. These proposals sounded great to the town residents. The black entrepreneur was sold a tract of land on which to erect the cotton gin and a choice lot in the center of town to set up the store. The store building was erected, and in came a white man to operate it. The outsider had tricked his fellow black people into selling property to the white man, for whom he was just the agent. As the depression deepened in the thirties, the black farmers and residents of Edmondson began losing title to their real estate. They were in debt to the company store too, and soon the white man owned the whole town and much of the surrounding farm land.

An STFU local had been set up near Edmondson in 1935, and many of the Edmondson people became members. They asked for the union's help. K. T. Sutton was called in to handle their cases. The more Sutton looked into it, the harder it became to establish property rights. I made an appeal to the NAACP for help in this case. At one point, Thurgood Marshall, later the first black justice appointed to the U.S. Supreme Court, was in Memphis on an NAACP case, and conferred with Sutton and some of the Edmondson people. A few of the residents there were able to reclaim their homes, but most of the land had been swallowed up by the greedy white man.

At another point, I contacted the National Association of Legal Aid Societies, with an idea of establishing a Rural Legal Aid Bureau to provide free legal services to sharecroppers and farm laborers in the South. The top officer of the association met with me in New York, and there was correspondence afterwards, but the methods of the Legal Aid Bureau did not seem applicable for members of the STFU. The Legal

Aid Bureaus were usually set up by local bar associations, and lawyers contributed some of their time to such work. I knew that there were few members of the bar in the South who would offer their services to such a controversial organization as the Southern Tenant Farmers Union. There were too few Carpenters, Fowlers, Stanfields, and Suttons to be found.

However, there could always be found at least one lawyer willing to defend STFU members and advise them of their legal rights. Such a one was J. Ross Robley of Little Rock, who came to aid STFU members in the mid-forties when local planters and their retainers in the State Employment Service tried to stop the operation of the wartime out-migration of union members. George Stith, representing the union, was stopped in Pine Bluff from sending members out on jobs and was threatened with a jail term. Ross Robley was called in and won the case, establishing the right of the union to send its members to out-of-state jobs.

Then in 1947, after the Southern Tenant Farmers Union had changed its name to "National Farm Labor Union" and had affiliated with the AFL, one of the most remarkable of all lawyers, Alexander H. Schullman, came to aid the union in its battles with the DiGiorgio Fruit Corporation, the California Un-American Activities Committee, and Richard M. Nixon.

Almost from the time of my arrival in Washington in 1948 to open an office, Joseph L. Rauh, Jr., the famed civil liberties and labor lawyer, provided free legal advice and representation when needed before government agencies. One of Rauh's associates Daniel H. Pollitt cut his professional teeth as the attorney for our Farm Labor Union.

When the union turned its attention to Louisiana, the firm of Dodd, Hirsch and Barker made their services available to striking sugar plantation workers. Among the associates of C. Paul Barker was Jack Nelson. Some ten years later, his brother, Tom Nelson, became involved in aiding the Menhaden fishermen when they were organized.

Finally, the topmost labor lawyer in the Southwest, James E. Youngdahl, of Little Rock, became the friend, adviser, and legal representative of every group the union organized or tried to organize on the Gulf Coast in the 1960s.

After reading a draft of the above, attorney John P. Nelson, Jr., of New Orleans, wrote in August 1977:

You have brought to light the personalities of lawyers who at great personal sacrifice came to grips with truth. They heard the cry of the anguished and responded in a meaningful and effective way. Although frustrated and buffetted about by the higher paid and well entrenched establishment lawyers, their footprints to the halls of justice will be forever identifiable, thanks in a large measure to your recording for posterity their experiences.

The Alice and David Burgess Story

Some of those who came to help us were activist ministers in the tradition of Ward Rodgers and Howard Kester. David and Alice Burgess were volunteer church workers for the STFU when their 18-month old daughter was almost scalded to death. Alice remembers:

We had gone over on Saturday to spend the night with the Churchills. Arthur Churchill was also a minister and came in as director of a Quaker Work Camp. The Churchills were living in the manager's house on the Farm Security Administration Project called Delmo Labor Homes in Lilbourn, Missouri. They had a bathtub but no hot water system. We were due to leave there about six in the morning so that Dave could get back to East Prairie to preach there. Ruth Churchill was boiling water on the oil stove to give us a real first-class bath in that bathtub. She set the pail down on the floor. Her little girl and our Laurie were playing. Laurie was pulling a pull-toy, and backed into the pail of scalding water up to her neck. That was really a weird thing. Had I not been so young, I would have become quite hysterical, but nothing like that had ever happened. I didn't realize how serious it was.

We went to a local doctor at five o'clock in the morning, who was spending the night with his ladyfriend. This was common knowledge, so we did not waste time going to his home. He put sulphur salve all over the burns, wrapped her in a blanket, and told us she might live to get to Cape Girardeau, 50 miles away, and then she might not. Then we ran out of gas on the way to the hospital. At this point Laurie was going limp and going into shock. Once again, I didn't really comprehend. I just thought she was fainting. I remember feeling a little panicky, fearing the man at the filling station, which was closed, wouldn't believe our story that we had no money and that we had a child who was desperately ill of burns. The whole thing was frustrating. I thought: "Oh dear, what if he won't give us any gas?" but he did, and we got to the hospital. For five days we didn't know whether she would live. The winter was a rough one for me and also for Dave. She went back to the hospital for skin grafting later. It was about her hips that the burns were very bad. She was burned over three-fourths of her body.

Dave Burgess' family lived in Philadelphia. His father taught at Temple University. Dr. and Mrs. J. S. Burgess had been regular contributors to the Southern Tenant Farmers Union, almost since it started in 1934. In April 1939, when David was in his final year at Oberlin College, he had written to the STFU asking for a summer job as a volunteer. He subsequently went to Union Theological Seminary. In 1941 Dave met and married Alice, who had been at Berea College in Kentucky. They were first assigned by the Home Missions Board to the FSA migrant camp at Pahokee on Lake Okeechobee in Florida. Alice said they thought "that living with people and sharing their lives and their labor, and really identifying with them, was the sound way to work with people who were underprivileged." But then one day Dave lost his wallet, with all their ration cards and money. This was during World War II. Dave wired his parents for help. No matter how much they tried to live and be like the migrant farm workers, they couldn't really identify with the people in terms of finances and other material conditions of life. "When the wallet was lost, we could wire home for money." The migrants had no such resource to call upon.

In 1942, while following the migrant workers, as they followed the crops, Dave had spoken to a church group in a New Jersey town, and was told that the Southern Tenant Farmers Union no longer existed. I wrote to the young minister and told him that nearly 1,000 STFU members were right at that moment working in food-processing plants, some of them on the huge unionized Seabrook Farms near Bridgeton, New Jersey. Soon Burgess, with my encouragement, joined the organized migration project of the STFU and Local 56 of the Amalgamated Meat Cutters in Camden, N.J. His first contact with STFU members came when he joined a group of some 600 men working at the Campbell Soup plant in Camden. Said Dave:

> With this labor group, I learned my way. I learned the first things about unionism. I became a close friend of Leon Schacter, who was then President of Local 56 of the Amalgamated Meat Cutters. I wrote a column for the Union newspaper published by Local 56. I soon became a social worker, a negotiator, minister counselor and friend for this group of white and black men who were there working during the summer months for the Campbell Soup Company. Both blacks and whites lived in the same dormitory. There were seemingly good relations between them, but they had all sorts of grievances against the company, both petty and important, illusory and real, and I tried to help them. Then when the job was ended in the summer of 1944 we came to Memphis.

David had gotten an assignment from the Home Missions Board of the Congregational Church as a minister to farm labor, and was given a free hand to work with the STFU and its members. For three years, he was in Memphis, working out of the STFU office and living in a trailer provided by the Home Missions Board. Dorothy Dowe, then office manager for the STFU, remembers vividly the problems she had in taking care of Dave Burgess. Dave would arrive at the office on a bitter cold day wrapped up in a muffler and overcoat, probably having been persuaded by his wife Alice to don them before he left home. Then Dave would be working in the overly warm office, with shirt sleeves rolled up, and next he'd be strolling out on the street, minus even a jacket, with Dorothy rushing down the stairs after him with his overcoat. Once Dorothy came to the office late to find that Dave had lost his monthly salary check. He was down on the floor frantically searching the waste baskets, which as usual were filled with scrap paper and used mimeograph stencils covered with ink, as was David. Dorothy shuffled a few papers on Dave's desk and easily uncovered the salary check. As a child, David had rheumatic fever, and to overcome its effects he had an exercise program that included a two or three mile run every day. He had never given up this program.

Of his experiences with the STFU in the Delmo Labor Homes Project, he said:

When we moved on up to Wardell, Missouri, I first became acquainted with William "Bill" Johnson, the Southern Tenant Farmers Union organizer there. He was also the village blacksmith, as well as the head of the STFU Locals in Southeast Missouri. He was thoroughly reliable, and we had a good relationship. I leaned on him in a sense, and then he leaned on me. I would write things for him, and for the Union. Alice was pregnant at the time, and we both picked cotton, but Alice always picked more than I could. During the winter we moved to Memphis, and then I worked out of the STFU office. I traveled all over Arkansas and Southeast Missouri. I was helping F. R. Betton and J. E. Clayton contact former Union members who had dropped out. We often met at Betton's home near Cotton Plant, Arkansas. Often I stayed over night with Betton. I was also up in Southeast Missouri visiting other people and became acquainted with all of the people in this area who were a part of the STFU. . . .

Sometime in March, 1945, just before the death of President Franklin D. Roosevelt, there was a piece in the local paper up there, and there was a notice posted that the Farm Security Administration was about to sell, to the highest bidder, the ten farm communities known as the Delmo Labor Homes. I consulted with H. L. Mitchell, and we went up to see STFU organizer Bill Johnson, and worked out a strategy. We decided to first try the political route, so I went to Washington. I met Gardner (Pat) Jackson for the first time in Washington. Pat Jackson was then working for Jim Patton. [James G. Patton, President of the National Farmers Union]. Pat was very helpful, and with his help and that of H. L. Mitchell, I began contacting members of the Congress. I also went to the local Congressman from Southeast Missouri, Orville Zimmerman, who was very much pro big planter. I don't know whether he regarded me as a communist, or socialist, or just an agitator, but I was kept at a distance. We later learned that he was doing all he could against us. Senator William Langer of North Dakota and Congressman Frank Hook of Michigan were most helpful. They introduced an amendment to the law passed authorizing FSA to sell off such properties as the Delmo Labor Homes. Their amendment provided that the homes be sold to the occupants. This temporarily stopped the sale of the homes. There was also a bill before Congress to abolish the Farm Security

Agency or at least make it no longer a threat to the plantation interests. The American Farm Bureau was behind this move in Congress. . . .

Then they were about to sell the Delmo Labor Homes owned by FSA and occupied by our members. Frank Hancock, a former Congressman from North Carolina, was the Administrator, and the great Robert W. "Pete" Hudgens was Deputy Administrator. He advised us what to do. We sent a delegation of blacks and whites from the communities in Southeast Missouri. Bill Johnson helped me in the selection of men and women from each of the ten communities. With the Union's help, and that of the National Share-croppers Fund, we raised enough money to send a busload of people to Washington. We had tried to get folks, black and white, who could speak for the people in the buses. We put them out front as far as possible. We coached them on how to tell what the situation was, affecting their 600 families. We first talked to Frank Hook, who was on the Agricultural Committee in the House, and to Senator Langer, who was on the similar committee in the Senate. They had introduced a bill to sell the homes to the people who lived in them. After-ward, the group met with Pete Hudgens of FSA. He advised us to try to get some financial backing, from local people, their friends, relatives, and organiza-tions such as the Sharecroppers Fund—anyone so that we could raise a kitty of money. We worked out a plan where each family would put down $100 cash. This was difficult for most families—an extreme sacrifice, and impossible in most cases. We were also going to ask each family to pay $10.00 a month for eight years. We would pay off the total sum of $287,000 plus interest.

The first job was to organize a committee of so-called public-minded citizens. We started with Bishop Scarlett of the Episcopal Church in St. Louis. Then there was Henry Putzil, a prominent lawyer, and Mr. Missener, then head of the St. Louis Car and Foundry Company. We also had the help of Harold J. Gibbons of the Teamsters Union, and several other union people. Then there was Josephine Johnson, who was a Pulitzer Prize winning writer, and she was most helpful. (Miss Johnson had also assisted greatly in the project at Harviell started by Whitfield to house those from Homeless Junction). There was Ted Thornton, a classmate of mine at Union [Theological Seminary in NYC]. He was an Episcopal Minister in Kirkwood, and later died of cancer. Another was Charles Wilson, a minister in the City. Wilson was to become the first treasurer of the Delmo Housing Corporation, and he was followed by Wilder Towle. These men, and especially Bishop Scarlett, were most helpful to us in terms of making contacts with people with money. I went out and raised money. It wasn't very much, but it made the difference. I went to see Marshall Field in New York—the elder Marshall Field. I didn't have any clean shirts, so I stopped at a store, bought one and put it on in a taxi—a white shirt. Then I went in to see him. He said: "Well, Mr. Burgess, you seem to be serious." I think he put down $12,000 in a few minutes. Then I went to see Sherwood Eddy. He was a prominent YMCA and religious leader, who had persuaded my father to go to China in 1905. I said: "Sherwood, you've got to help me." He said: "I want you to go see Mrs. Emmons Blaine in Chicago." She was one of the original heirs to the McCormick fortune left by the McCormick reaper inventor. She put up an equal amount of money to whatever it was that Marshall Field gave. She matched it. The Teamsters Union in St. Louis, headed by Hal Gibbons, gave us some money at that time, and we got some from other sources. We eventually raised over $80,000 from outside sources. Thus we had the help of individuals like Pat Jackson, Sherwood Eddy, the union folks, and leaders of many national organizations. In the meantime we had to go back to Southeast Missouri to convince the people there that we were sincere, and not trying to cheat them. We finally won the battle late in November of 1945. The Farm Security Administration agreed to sell nine of the ten Delmo Communities for $287,000 to a non-profit organization which we formed.

Alice Burgess recalled:

Dave was going through this struggle as to whether he really was a pacifist and could change from the ministry to the labor movement. He finally decided that he would. The last thing he decided he wanted to do was to set up this corporation among the Delmo Homes so that the people could buy their own houses rather than having the landlords turn them all into company villages. You know—like a company town. Dave traveled a good deal, trying to raise money for a non-profit corporation. We moved into a typical small house on the East Prairie project in December of 1945. I went to a community meeting when Dave was away raising money to finalize this non-profit corporation which was to benefit all. Some character in the meeting came up with the rumor that Burgess was raising this money and putting it into his own pocket. I am from New England, and not accustomed to getting emotional. I was pregnant again— maybe this was part of what motivated me. I remember I got up. I was really red hot. I couldn't believe it was happening. I spoke up and told them off. They knew that Dave was away trying to raise money to save their homes for them. I remember saying that if he was out to make money in this life, we certainly wouldn't be there. Now that I am older, I can look back and see that it was an understandable suspicion of people, when an outsider comes and tries to help them.

Alice said that she and Dave sort of adopted one of the girls from the group, a Celia Parker. She came to live with them after they were in Greensboro, N.C. This girl's mother, Hazel Roach, who in the mid-70s was still living in the Delmo Homes, was considered by all to be a very sound person.

Burgess in 1946 left the ministry and the STFU assignment, to become an organizer among textile mill workers in North and South Carolina. By the mid-1950s, he was secretary of the Georgia CIO State Council, working out of Atlanta. Soon after the AFL-CIO merger, Burgess, sponsored for the post by Walter and Victor Reuther, became a labor attaché, and served at the United States embassies at New Delhi, Bangkok, and Jakarta. Before getting the job he was subjected to searching checkups by the FBI and the CIA. Burgess was not fully approved by George Meany's International Department (operated by Jay Lovestone, the early secretary of the Communist Party USA, who narrowly escaped from Moscow and Joe Stalin's executioners.)

While awaiting his new government assignment, Burgess was a guest of Victor and Sophia Reuther. Wanting to do something to repay the Reuther hospitality, Dave undertook to trim the high hedge that surrounded the back of the house where guard dogs were kept. Dave managed the dogs all right, but fell afoul of the electric hedge trimmer. As Victor Reuther reported, Dave cut the cord three times, and never did finish trimming the hedge.

David S. Burgess was one of the first labor attachés in the foreign service of the United States. He served at the Embassy at New Delhi for five years and was with the Peace Corps in Indonesia, and with Unicef in East Asia and at the New York headquarters. Following the rules of the United Nations, he retired at the age of sixty in 1977. He afterwards became a minister of his church.

Many of the people in the Delmo Labor Homes, people who were originally out on the highways in 1939, are still living in the community that Dave Burgess, the union, and its friends saved from the auction block and enabled them to buy.

17 Dorothy and the Union

"Are you the man 'who brooded over the fate of the sharecroppers while he cleaned the clothes of the planters'?" asked the slender young woman in her NYA office in Montgomery. She was quoting from Jonathan Daniels' recently published book *A Southerner Discovers the South.* I admitted that I was the man from Tyronza.

Dorothy Dowe was a native of Montgomery and her accent was very much that of a South Alabamian. Her brother Joe had an even more pronounced accent. Once when asked, "Where is Dorothy these days?" Joe drawled in reply: "She's up in Memphis wurkin foh the Suthen Ternant Fama's Union."

"Oh," said the inquiring friend, "this certainly is a day of specialization. I didn't know the southern turnip farmers even had a union."

Early in 1941, Dorothy and I met for the first time. I had come to her NYA office looking for help with a program I was trying to get under way. She was the youth personnel director for the National Youth Administration's projects for girls in most of the counties of South Alabama. Aubrey Williams, the National Youth Administration Director in Washington, appointed me a temporary consultant on rural problems. I was sent south to work out an idea suggested by some one in Washington. I was to look up young people who had been on the NYA program, to see whether they could be placed on farms of their own by the Farm Security Administration. During a few weeks in North Alabama, where I had visited an NYA project for young men near Haleyville, I found little interest in the proposal. The youngsters on NYA thought I was just another "nut from Washington." They asked questions like: "Are you going to help us find a girl?" "Do we get married before we apply for our farm?" and "How long will it take to get through all the red tape involved in getting a farm?"

The state director of NYA advised me to go to Montgomery and talk to the people in the regional office of the Farm Security Administration. Dr. John Bryan, the NYA director for Alabama, and also superintendent of Birmingham schools, told me to see "the efficient Miss Dowe of the NYA." Dorothy and I set up an NYA project for training young women high school graduates from rural areas. They were brought to Montgomery, sent to a business college in the mornings, and then worked four hours each day as file clerks and typists in the regional office of the Farm Security Administration.

When I returned to Washington to report, Aubrey Williams didn't think much of the project for training stenographers and office secretaries. He said there were already too many girls with such training then in Washington who couldn't find jobs. However, Williams was interested in the young woman who had set up the project. By the time the girls had completed their training, the Japanese had bombed Pearl Harbor and World War II was on. Every NYA trained girl who wanted a job was placed. Some of them worked in United States agencies, and were transferred to Washington.

Dorothy Dowe came from a family of Irish Catholic immigrants. Dorothy's older sister Leila had founded an incomparable dining place, the Blue Moon Inn of Montgomery. Many girls set their wedding dates so that the receptions could be held in this spacious pre-Civil War cottage, or on its grounds.

Dorothy graduated from Auburn University, and afterwards attended Tulane's School of Social Work. During the dark days of the depression when she applied for jobs and was asked to state her religion (then an integral part of every interview) she was not accepted. Finally, with the connivance of a county superintendent, she was given a job as a school attendance worker in a rural mountain area north of Birmingham. Her new boss listed her as a Presbyterian, since there was no Presbyterian church in the little town. However, she was advised to attend either the Baptist or Methodist Church whenever she was in town on Sunday. She went home most weekends. Assured of a job, she bought her first used car. When asked by the salesman how much she wanted to pay down on it, she replied: "I can't pay anything." She got the car anyway.

Dorothy was instructed by the superintendent not to give any attention to the few existing schools for colored children in the county. Said he: "If we pay attention to these schools, the first thing you know, the niggers will want new school buildings, school buses and supplies, just like the white folks." In defiance of these orders, Dorothy, as the county school attendance worker, called at the schools for black children whenever possible.

Social welfare agencies such as the National Youth Administration were the first casualties of the war. After getting a temporary job with another such agency that was similarly threatened, Dorothy accepted a job as a civilian employee of the U.S. Army. She was not only a trained social worker, but a person with years of experience as an administrator. So with typical military efficiency she was assigned to the typing pool at the Holding and Reconsignment Point in Montgomery. For days she sat with nothing to do until some stupid army officer with an equally stupid blank form would ask that she type it. She soon resigned from the Army job and applied for a job with the USO Travelers' Aid (United Service Organization). After a brief period at Columbia University in New York, she became the director of a Travelers' Aid unit at Grenada, Mississippi, where there was a huge army training center and soon an air base established too. Grenada (spelled that way in Mississippi) was 100 miles south of Memphis, and an equal distance from the state capital of Jackson. The Travelers' Aid bureau was overwhelmed by streams of young women coming to visit their husbands or boy friends, sometimes dragging young children along with them. Hotel and tourist accommodations were limited in Grenada. One of Dorothy's most difficult jobs as director of Travelers' Aid was finding any kind of housing for the transients or, for that matter, to find a place to live herself. At one point she was living in a small trailer in someone's back yard. Finally, she located a small apartment in an attic of a home.

When there were no volunteers to man the USO desk at the bus station, Dorothy took over and had to listen to the interminable hillbilly music blaring out of the juke boxes and radios. After a year of being subject to call twenty-four hours a day, she resigned and got a job as interviewer for the Memphis chapter of the American Red Cross. The salary, however, was much lower than she had earned with Travelers' Aid.

I then offered Dorothy a job in the union office in downtown Memphis, over another bus station. I gave her the title of "Assistant to the President" and about the same salary she received from the Red Cross. Dorothy listened sympathetically to sharecroppers and farm workers who came to Memphis to get advice and help. She answered their letters promptly and soon became known as "Miz Dorothy of the STFU." She was always finding amusing details in her work. Once she got a letter which read, "Dear Miz Dorothy: Here is my dues of $1.00, please make a racket [record] of it. [signed] Horse House." It was from a member named Horace Howes.

One of Dorothy's first jobs for the STFU was to make a compilation of the age, race, and sex of workers being sent to work on farms and in canneries out of the South. I had also undertaken to enlist black and white college girls for summer jobs, canning peas and other vegetables at the huge frozen food factory that operated on Seabrook Farms in New Jersey. The first group was preparing to leave by train from Memphis. Vice-president Betton was good at corralling the male, and the occasional female worker, sent out by the STFU, but the courtly black man found he could not control the lively young college girls. They were rushing here and there, getting off the coaches, going to buy candy or to make a last minute telephone call to say goodbye to "Aunt Emma and Uncle Dan." Neither Betton nor I was making any headway in getting the 200 young black women off on time. Then Dorothy took over. She got up on a coach seat, called the girls to order, and told them to stay in their seats. They were accustomed to taking orders from professors, so they obeyed and got quiet. Dorothy went from car to car, bringing order out of chaos. She won the admiration of F. R. Betton, whom she always called "Mr. Betton," since he called her "Miss Dowe."

We tried to maintain the pattern of interracial organization even for the college girls. I contacted some of the smaller and poorer white colleges to offer their students summer jobs. Some white girls made inquiries, but only black girls accepted the jobs. At one point, Dorothy and I made a tour of the colleges down through Mississippi, across Alabama and Georgia and South Carolina, arranging for some responsible person at each institution to handle recruitment and transportation. On an early spring day, while at Clark College in the Atlanta University complex, we met with girls and members of the faculty interested in summer jobs. Then a group of young men from nearby Morehouse College joined us. The spokesman, a round-faced striking-looking young black man with a powerful voice, wanted to know why the union didn't have jobs for men as well as women workers. I replied that there would be some jobs for young men in mid-July when the tomato harvest got underway and that the union would be glad to have applications from young men. Both Dorothy and I always believed that the spokesman from Morehouse College was Martin Luther King, Jr. I would have asked the civil rights leader if I had ever met him, but the opportunity never came.

After the end of World War II, some momentous changes took place in the union, and in the lives of Dorothy Dowe and H. L. Mitchell. At the 12th Annual Convention of the STFU in St. Louis, on December 12, 1945, Dorothy was elected secretary-treasurer of the union, which was renamed The National Farm Labor Union. A. E. Cox, who had held the title, insisted that since she was doing the work, "Miz" Dorothy should be given the credit. There was only one other woman at that time in the entire labor movement who held such a post. She was Bernice Heffner of the American Federation of Government Employees. Later, after we had joined the AFL, both Dorothy and Bernice were delegates to several AFL national conventions, but were usually placed on some innocuous rules or constitution committee, where they would pose no problem. At such conventions, as an International Union president, I was usually appointed to the committee on education, presumably because many farm workers lacked education.

Early in 1948 the union headquarters were moved from Memphis to Washington because the union needed help from organized labor, government, and the public. Sharecropping was coming to an end. The new tractor driven machines like the Rust Cotton Picker were coming into use. Since before the war, blacks as well as whites were migrating to the cities of the North and West seeking work or a better deal on welfare than they could get anywhere in the cotton fields.

F. R. Betton, the union's vice-president, and his assistant George Stith, both black, remained in the South and were always ready, willing, and able to take on any assignment for the union there.

Arthur C. Churchill, who had followed David Burgess as a minister to farm labor, kept the home fires going at the Memphis office, by then located on world-famous Beale Street. Churchill kept a diary of his activities and it is a valuable part of the STFU Papers. After leaving Memphis in 1954 he became a college professor. He retired in 1977 from

Defiance College in Ohio, where he was in the Political Science Department.

When the union office was moved to Washington, my wife, Lyndell, chose not to go with me. She had a good job as head of a department at Sears, Roebuck in Memphis. She had her church, friends, and family in Memphis. By this time, the marriage had disintegrated, so we agreed on a divorce. Still, we remained friends over the years. When anything happened in the family, we wrote or telephoned and kept each other informed. Our oldest son, Harry, graduated from the University of Tennessee and became an electrical engineer. He worked on the government's space program in Huntsville, Alabama, and later in Florida. After graduating from Memphis State University, our daughter, Joyce, became a high school teacher and married Joe Freeland, a newspaperman in Memphis. Sam graduated from the University of Chicago and became a professor of sociology. At this writing, I have six grandchildren.

With Dorothy, I entered into a relationship that has lasted over thirty years. Some time after our office was moved to Washington, Dorothy and I were en route to a union meeting in Superior, Wisconsin. We stopped at Fort Wayne, Indiana, and were married by one of our early STFU allies, Aaron S. Gilmartin, the first secretary of the Workers Defense League. Gilmartin had been jailed in Arkansas when he tried to get union members released on bail bonds. He was then the minister of the Unitarian Church at Fort Wayne. After an impromptu ceremony in the Gilmartins' livingroom, we drove on to Wisconsin to meet the dairy farmers, who had been in the union for about a year.

As mentioned, Dorothy has a great sense of humor—she early dubbed me "the Don Quixote of the labor movement." However, she was no Sancho Panza. Whenever there was an incident of bigotry against blacks or women, she was quite capable of mounting Rosinante and leading her own charge against the windmills. And she often did, especially after we moved to Washington.

18 Shirt Tail Union in the AFL

Peter Edson, a syndicated newspaper columnist, once called the National Farm Labor Union the "shirt tail of the AFL," while John Herling, a labor news reporter and editor of *John Herling's Labor News Letter* called me a "labor leader extraordinary." Wrote Herling:

> His Union has the largest jurisdiction in the country, but has never benefited from the New Deal, Fair Deal, or any government program. Mitch can also boast the largest number of non-dues-paying adherents of any International Union affiliated with the American Federation of Labor. . . . Mingling in the company where per capita payment of dues is king, H. L. Mitchell and his Union are notable for their lack of cash. Such a chronic financial deficit does not impair his ability to speak up for some of the poorest paid workers in the United States.

I had been in Washington early in the summer of 1946 and had paid a call at the headquarters of the American Federation of Labor, then at Massachussetts Avenue and 9th Street. I was told by William Green to be at the forthcoming session of the AFL Executive Council, which was to meet in Chicago at the Drake Hotel, August 12th. Mr. Green told me that the council would likely act on the application of the National Farm Labor Union for a charter. Green told me frankly that he did not know what the council would do, but that they would give us an answer, one way or the other. I had been in contact with prominent labor leaders in the AFL, such as Dave Dubinsky of the International Ladies Garment Workers Union. I had also written to John L. Lewis, who had just returned to the AFL fold with his United Mine Workers. Both Dubinsky and Lewis were members of the Executive Council—the highest governing body of the AFL.

The AFL was once described by its founder, Sam Gompers, as "a rope of sand held together by ties stronger than steel." The fifteen-man council was made up of the most important union leaders. They made the decisions, and officers like William Green carried them out. There was very little room for one-man rule of the AFL as a whole. Every international or national union was a law unto itself, and those with the most dues paying members, or the greatest number of organized workers in their trade or industry, were always the most important. The top officers of each union in the AFL gathered annually in convention, which always lasted a week or ten days.

While I had been lobbying the AFL, one of my associates, Barney B. Taylor, once in the Newspaper Guild, had been lobbying the CIO. The NFLU executive board had decided that the only hope of survival in the cold war already underway in the United States was to become a part of the organized labor movement. In view of the experiences the Southern Tenant Farmers Union had undergone, I did not have much hope of affiliation with the CIO, but Barney Taylor was able to enlist the interest of Allan Haywood, the CIO Director of Organization. At one point, Haywood practically offered to charter the National Farm Labor Union, but he had to withdraw his offer after consultation with Lee Pressman, the general counsel of the CIO. I had also had an off-the-record discussion with Lee Pressman at Pat Jackson's suggestion. Pressman had told me that CIO affiliation was impossible unless I agreed to go into Food, Tobacco and Allied Workers (FTA) and make peace with Donald Henderson. Henderson was still president of the FTA—formerly UCAPAWA, and he claimed jurisdiction over agricultural workers although he had few, if any, in his union. The CIO purge of the communist-dominated unions was still three years away. That ended any thought of going into the CIO, so we put all of our effort into joining the AFL.

A delegation from the National Farm Labor Union arrived in Chicago a day before the AFL executive council meeting and by pre-arrangement met with the International Secretary-Treasurer Patrick E. Gorman of the Amalgamated Meat Cutters and Butcher Workmen of North America, and with Leon B. Schachter, head of that union's Local 56 in Camden, N.J. Shachter's local had worked out the organized migration plan that provided jobs for a total of 12,000 STFU members during the war years. Though greatly reduced in point of numbers, that program was still going on.

In 1944 I had proposed that the STFU, Schachters Local 56, and the AFL cannery workers in California jointly apply for a national or international union charter; but Schachter, a man of great ability and an obvious comer in the trade union movement, elected to stay with the Amalgamated Meat Cutters. Pat Gorman, Leon Schachter, and Earl Jimmerson, president of the Meat Cutters International, agreed to accompany the Farm Labor Union delegation in its appearance before the Executive Council of the AFL.

At the appointed hour, our delegation—which included Barney Taylor, F. R. Betton, J. E. Clayton, and myself—entered the large room in which the powerful council was meeting. There we joined our friends of the Meat Cutters Union, already present. Betton and Clayton were both black. Betton was vice-president of the NFLU, and Clayton was one of our best organizers. I made my presentation, very briefly stating that the National Farm Labor Union would like to become a part of the AFL and undertake the organization of all workers employed on larger farms, ranches, and plantations in the continental United States and its possessions. Pat Gorman made a short but powerful plea, urging that the AFL extend its hand of brotherhood to that last man—the one who worked and lived down on the farm. Leon Schachter also told of the wartime cooperation between our two unions. There were no questions asked of our delegation or friends. William Green, AFL president, said to me, "We would like for you and your delegation to remain for a while, in the event there are some questions. The council will consider your application, and you will be informed in due course of its decision in this matter."

I thought at the time there would not be an answer for some days, and feared that it was likely to be negative. I thought: "What would the AFL do with or for the millions of people that nobody wants." Farm workers had so little in common with the highly skilled craftsmen, such as carpenters, machinists, boilermakers and others. Then I remembered the miners from whose ranks both John L. Lewis and William Green had come. And Dave Dubinsky, the garment worker, an immigrant and a socialist, had been friendly and had tried back in 1941 to get the STFU into the AFL. While out in the corridor, waiting for the morning session to end, I was called by Daniel Tobin, head of the Teamsters Union, and asked, "If the AFL grants your union a charter, will you want to include the dairy farms and plants in Los Angeles, or the 30,000 cannery workers we have in California?" I assured Tobin that the NFLU did not want anything that was already organized in another AFL Union—that no such claim would ever be made.

In less than an hour, William Green came to the door and handed me a letter saying that the AFL would issue a charter to the National Farm Labor Union, upon payment of a charter fee of fifteen dollars and the first month's per capita dues on its membership. In the meantime, Barney Taylor, trying to make himself useful, had contacted the newspapermen hanging about the pressroom, awaiting news of the AFL Executive Council action. He asked me to let him have the original letter so he could have copies made for the newsmen. That was the last I ever saw of the first official letter about the AFL entering the farm field. Newspapers like *The New York Times,* the *Washington Post,* and the *St. Louis Post Dispatch* gave it full play as a most significant development in the labor movement.

Later, George Meany, the AFL secretary-treasurer, wrote to advise me to pay per capita tax on the 8,000 members of the NFLU for the month of August, to insure full voting rights in the forthcoming AFL convention which would meet in Chicago, early in October. Incidentally, the dues required of national and international unions was only one-and-a-half cents for each member per month. Cotton picking time was approaching, and members would soon start paying dues. Our members were encouraged to pay their full year's dues every fall. During war time, country stores stopped their universal practice of giving away calendars to their customers. The STFU had taken over this service and was giving a calendar to its members whenever they completed their dues payments of three dollars a year. The annual calendars included all Jewish holidays too, and this was a source of amusement to visitors and sharecroppers alike as few of them knew such holidays existed.

Barney B. Taylor was a young man from Texas who, prior to World War II, had worked in the advertising section of the *Washington Post*. He became an organizer for the Newspaper Guild soon after it was founded by Heywood Broun, the nationally known columnist. Barney Taylor had some ROTC training in college and was given a commission upon enlistment in the army. Describing his war experiences, he claimed that he left New York Harbor at night, landed in Scotland at night, was taken by train to southern England, left on D Day for the coast of France, and landed at daybreak at Normandy Beach. He and his men waded ashore under fire. He saw only destroyed tanks, pill boxes, dead Germans, and some cows grazing. He kept going, although he was hit by a shell fragment. He captured the position he was ordered to take and held on until reinforcements came. A second shell broke his leg. He collapsed and was taken to a field hospital somewhere in France. When he woke up, surrounded by four tent walls, he was told that he would be evacuated to England at night, which was done. He was then put on the top row of a hospital plane, which landed first at Shannon Airport in Ireland, then at Gander, Newfoundland. He did not see anything at either place, since he could not move. The first thing he recognized was the Army Air Force Base near New York, where he landed. He had been there once before.

Captain Barney B. Taylor was finally awarded the Distinguished Service Cross by President Harry S. Truman after Taylor had started working for the National Farm Labor Union. Being a disabled veteran, he drew half pay from the army, and the Union paid him two hundred dollars a month for about a year. He made some field trips, and the union played up his rank and DSC award. His record doubtless protected him when he appeared as spokesman for the Farm Labor Union at hearings in Arkansas, Mississippi, and Missouri, held by the U.S.

Department of Agriculture to impose ceilings on the rates of pay received by cotton pickers.

Perhaps Taylor's most important service to the National Farm Labor Union was in October, at the AFL convention in Chicago. There he struck up an acquaintance with another World War II veteran, Henry E. (Hank) Hasiwar, and helped persuade Hank to go to California as our western organizer.

Soon after the AFL charter was received and the annual convention held, Barney Taylor decided to leave the NFLU and go to work for Americans for Democratic Action, the liberal political movement often referred to as "The New Deal Government in Exile." Apparently, that job did not last very long. The last anyone in our union heard, Taylor was serving as First Secretary at an American embassy in one of the Central American countries.

At the convention of the American Federation of Labor in Chicago, the two blacks in the NFLU delegation, F. R. Betton and J. E. Clayton, increased the minority representation in the convention by one hundred percent. Theretofore, only A. Philip Randolph and Milton P. Webster, president and vice-president respectively, of the Brotherhood of the Sleeping Car Porters, served as black delegates to annual AFL conventions. Racists and liberals alike awaited the report of the Resolutions Committee on the resolutions always submitted by the Pullman Porters' delegation, demanding an end to race discrimination in the AFL. Randolph would always make an eloquent plea to the delegates. All AFL delegates awaited his annual address, because they never knew when Randolph would accuse their own union of discrimination against Negroes.

I had attended past AFL and CIO conventions as an observer or visitor. At the New Orleans meetings in 1944, while seated as a fraternal delegate, I outraged southern AFL delegates by sitting at the table with Randolph and Webster on the floor of the convention.

At the Chicago AFL convention, which occurred less than two months after the National Farm Labor Union was chartered, very little attention was paid to the new affiliate with only 8,000 members. A. Philip Randolph and other socialists and ex-socialists in the AFL were considering the possibility of a farm labor party. Hank Hasiwar, a young ex-service man, had been prevailed upon by Socialist Party Labor Secretary Bill Becker to go to Chicago to lobby for the idea among the delegates. A. Philip Randolph had agreed to pay Hank Hasiwar's round-trip rail fare from New York to Chicago, on the pretext that Hasiwar would be working for the AFL convention's endorsement of a resolution to establish a permanent fair employment practices law. A meeting was set up at Professor Maynard Kreuger's home, near the University of Chicago. Hank and I had invited, and in some cases persuaded, democratic and republican "wheelhorses" to attend the unusual meeting at the home of the young professor who had been the Socialist Party candidate for Vice-President of the United States, on the slate with Norman Thomas, two years before.

In 1947 the AFL held its annual meeting in San Francisco. By that time the NFLU had launched an organizing drive in California, and was involved in the DiGiorgio Fruit Corporation strike that was to last two-and-a-half years. Hank Hasiwar, who had organized the DiGiorgio ranch, and I were the delegates to the AFL convention. I asked President William Green for permission to address the convention. So at one point between convention reports, when there was a lag in business, Green called upon me. He introduced me as "Brother Mitchell, the international president of that splendid organization, The National Farm Union, which is involved in a strike on California's largest corporation farm."

I then made a plea to the delegates, asking their financial and moral support for the 1,100 workers on the DiGiorgio Ranch who had "hit the bricks" over a month before. Hank Hasiwar and Fred West, the president of the Kern County Central Labor Union, had set the stage for financial help. They had already persuaded Hugo Ernst, president of the Hotel and Restaurant Workers International Union, to announce that his organization was giving one thousand dollars to the striking farm workers. This was matched by President Harry Lundberg of the Sailors Union of the Pacific. Others were inspired to announce gifts to the strikers, and hats were passed among the delegates so each individual could make a personal donation. All in all, the NFLU fared well at the 1947 AFL Convention.

One of the issues of the day was the Taft-Hartley Act, termed by William Green a "slave labor law." John L. Lewis had laid down his demand that the unions making up the AFL must refuse to sign the anti-communist loyalty oath, and they must then boycott the National Labor Relations Act, with its still intact provisions requiring elections to be held for the naming of a bargaining agent. The main provision of the law required that when a union won a majority of votes of all of the workers in the plant unit, the employer had to bargain for a contract. Lewis threatened to walk out of the AFL again if his proposal to boycott the new Taft Hartley Act was not accepted. Numerous delegates urged me to take a stand with John L. Lewis. I refused, saying: "John L. Lewis never in his life put principle above his own self interest." Lewis was swamped. The convention voted overwhelmingly against his proposed boycott of the National Labor Relations Act. The United Mine Workers left the AFL for a second time, and the National Farm Labor Union acquired its most distinguished "member." President William Green had been teased for being a member of the "Horn Tooters Union." He had joined the Musicians' Union when the United Mine Workers had previously been out of the AFL. I now offered William Green membership in the National Farm Labor Union, pointing out that most miners, when not digging coal, were subsistence farmers, and that he was therefore eligible. The grand old man accepted, and held membership in the NFLU until his death in 1952. William Green was the kind of man one could meet in a small town anywhere in America. Green was honest and upright, though he was never his own boss. He had been selected president to succeed the founder of the AFL, Sam Gompers, when the cigar maker died in 1924. After finishing grade school, Green had worked in the coal mines. He had served as a local and district union officer and finally became the secretary-treasurer of the United Mine Workers of America in the early 1920s. A Democrat, William Green had also been elected to the Ohio Senate, and he was the author of the first workmen's compensation law ever to be enacted by a state legislature.

Every time I met Green thereafter, the president of the AFL would say, "Brother Mitchell, how is my dues?" Often he would write out a check, sometimes adding a special contribution of his own, if his new organization was in dire straits. Green would always find time to meet with me. He put Betton, our vice-president, on the AFL payroll. He also paid the salary and expenses of William L. Becker for several months. He kept Hank Hasiwar on, paying his expenses even though there were questions about Hank's mileage reports. At one time during the Imperial Valley strike, the NFLU had nine full-time organizers. The AFL Executive Council ordered Green to slash the NFLU staff right in the middle of the strike. He did what he was told to do, cutting off those who were hired last. Only Hank Hasiwar and F. R. Betton were left on the AFL payroll. Later I persuaded Green to put on a new man in Florida. He was F. T. Riley, minister and sometime newspaper editor for the phosphate mine workers near Bartow, Florida.

We had organized several hundred fruit pickers in the citrus groves of central Florida around Lakeland, Orlando, and other such towns. I had convinced "Big Bill" Hutcheson, chief of the Carpenters Union, to recognize the local Farm Labor Union and enter into an agreement with our union for all grove workers hired by the Adams Packing Company, at Auburndale. The Carpenters Union owned citrus groves near Lakeland around the home for its aged and retired members. It was alleged that Hutcheson claimed the most productive orange groves as his own personal property and also that he hired the old-age pensioners living in the Carpenters' Home to pick his fruit at extremely low wages. Because of his personal holdings in the citrus area, Hutcheson had formed the Adams Packing Company. Eventually he agreed to unionization of the packing house, which employed nearly 2,000 men and women at the height of the season.

The workers were all members of an AFL federal labor union, a directly chartered and operated organization of the Washington office. Hutcheson as president of the Carpenters Union was the most powerful man in the AFL then. He was the representative of craft unionism. He was the man with whom John L. Lewis had a fist fight just before Lewis started the CIO. As a member of the ruling body of the AFL, Hutcheson was technically representing the workers he himself employed.

Often aged AFL organizers were assigned to Florida for the winter season, and others wanting a Florida vacation would get assignments for shorter periods of time. Except for those hired for the National Farm Labor Union, AFL organizers usually were men to whom some international union officer owed a debt for a past service, or he might be some rival whom the union leader wanted to get out of the way without making a martyr of him.

Our first organizer in charge worked closely with the field crews and acted as a kind of go-between with the plant manager of the Adams Packing Company who hired and assigned the men to the groves. There was on-the-job bargaining between the fruit pickers and management, and this had been quite successful for two years. The men would go into the groves, look over the condition of the trees, see the amount of fruit ready for picking, and set a price for which they would pick it. They would then sit down and wait while the organizer contacted the manager. The men always asked a few cents more per box than they actually expected to get. They were always able to make a deal. Sometimes the union organizer won a premium rate for the workers. The same situation prevailed in other groves where the men had organized a union. Sometimes the crew leader substituted for the union organizer.

Soon after F. T. Riley became the NFLU organizer paid by the AFL, the men employed by Adams Packing Company sat down in the groves. Riley was unable to persuade the manager to make any concessions. He didn't know what to do, so he stopped by the office of the Packinghouse Workers Federal Labor Union. The regular man was out of town, and his substitute, an old-time printing tradesman put on the AFL payroll in lieu of a pension, was in charge. Riley asked "Uncle Jim" Barrett what he should do. Barrett, probably dreaming about the past when his own union in North Carolina had met such situations by going on strike, advised the new organizer to put a picket line on the Adams Packing Company plant and Riley followed the old timer's advice. When the picket line appeared at the plant gates, every man and woman employed there came off the job. No one would cross the picket line, nor was the manager allowed in the plant. Two thousand workers were out because 85 or 100 fruit pickers could not get a square deal. The AFL's Southern Director, George Googe, later described what happened. Big Bill Hutcheson was on the long distance telephone, calling everyone concerned. He reached William Green, who said to him in his gentle manner, "Now Bill, why don't you get in touch with President Mitchell of the Farm Workers, this is a matter between two International Presidents. I am sure you can work out a settlement. President Mitchell is a splendid young man, and is most reasonable."

Hutcheson had no intention of contacting me. As far as he was concerned I was just the head of a pipsqueak union, so he demanded that Green fire Riley immediately. A few days later I was called in to see President Green. I remember that Green had several expense account reports sent in by F. T. Riley on his desk. Green asked, "Brother Mitchell, what is this man Riley doing on our payroll down in Florida? They tell me he is not a farm worker, but a minister."

I replied: "Mr. Green, Riley is the same kind of minister you are. He teaches a class at his church every Sunday, and if the minister is absent for any reason, then just like you would do, Brother Riley takes over and preaches the sermon. If he is ordained, he never mentioned it to me." I also said that Riley had worked in the phosphate mines and fruit groves too.

Without ever revealing what was behind the request, Green asked me to assign Riley somewhere up in Arkansas. I told him that Riley was a Florida man. His daughter was to graduate soon from high school in Bartow, and I doubted if he could be persuaded to leave his state. However, I suggested that Riley might be asked to make a survey and try to organize workers in the vegetable fields and packingsheds in south Florida. Green thought that would be O.K. Neither Hutcheson nor the strike was ever mentioned. It had already been settled on terms satisfactory to the fruit pickers, and anyway, the citrus fruit season was nearly over. Riley decided he would return to work for the Chemical Workers local in his home town. The episode was speedily forgotten.

At nearly every AFL Convention, Green would send for me and tell me: "I am going to call on you this afternoon, or tomorrow morning" and name the approximate time. I would be on the platform, and would always be introduced by President Green as "the International President of that splendid organization, the *National Union of Agricultural Workers.*" He seldom got the name of the "splendid organization" just right, but everyone knew that we were favored at AFL headquarters. The real reason was that the National Farm Labor Union never made trouble for William Green. We had no power in the AFL, and we were most appreciative of the president's interest.

In 1948, the NFLU scheduled its convention to be held in Cincinnati on November 12th through 14th, at the same time the convention of the AFL was meeting. William Green had accepted the NFLU's invitation to deliver the opening address, as he had when the union met in Washington early in 1947. However, this time Green was unable to come and sent a substitute, George Meany, the secretary-treasurer of the AFL. Meany looked over the group of about a hundred men and women, mainly blacks, some whites, and a few Mexican Americans from Texas and California. Showing his utter contempt for people who had, at great sacrifice to themselves and their members, raised money to attend their convention, Meany sneered: "I don't believe that the farm workers of this country can be unionized. I don't believe any of you want to be organized." These men and women, nearly every one of whom had been in a strike, on a picket line, had been hunted by nightriders, and had often been close to death itself, sat in stunned silence. Meany finished his tirade and stalked out. Once he had left the hall, which was owned by the Brotherhood of Railway and Steamship Clerks, delegates sought the floor. One man asked me: "Why the hell did you let that damned plantation owner in here?" I tried to restore order, and explained that since Mr. Green couldn't be present, he had sent Mr. Meany, the secretary-treasurer. Meany was a plumber who boasted that he had never walked a picket line, nor even been in a strike. Maybe he just didn't know what kind of people there were in the National Farm Labor Union. Some of us afterwards speculated as to whether or not he resented the black people in the NFLU, or whether Meany had just got up on the wrong side of his bed that morning. I did recall that once Meany had replied to a speech by A. Philip Randolph, asking: "Who the hell appointed you to speak for the Negroes?" Well, the answer was that Randolph and one other delegate from the Brotherhood of Sleeping Car Porters, were, for a long time, the *only* ones in the AFL to speak for the blacks.

The members of the National Farm Labor Union listed on the application for the AFL charter were as follows:

President, H. L. Mitchell   (White)
Vice President, F. R. Betton   (Black)

Secretary Treasurer, Dorothy Dowe	(White)
Second Vice Pres. George Stith	(Black)
Director Organization, Barney B. Taylor	(White)
Executive Board Members:	
Carrie L. Dilworth	(Black)
Mae Pearl Kelly	(Black)
J. E. Clayton	(Black)
A. E. Cox	(White)
John F. Hynds	(White)
W. A. Johnson	(White)

Thus, in 1946, long before the Civil Rights Movement, the NFLU had five black officers, six white, and in the tradition of its 1936 women's liberation movement, three women. Since Taylor was not an elected officer, the division was actually five of each race. Mae Pearl Kelly was the daughter of an ex-sharecropper family living in Memphis. She attended LeMoyne College and had worked part-time in the union office. She afterward went to the New York School of Social Work and we lost contact in the mid-fifties. Then there was Carrie L. Dilworth, one of the union's best organizers, who continued her activity into the 1960s.

Among the first members who came into the National Farm Labor Union as a result of our AFL affiliation were two dairy farmer locals in Louisiana. These people were farm owners, not workers. They were originally organized into the Teamsters Union by one Leo Carter, an international representative long considered by other AFL people in Louisiana as an "oddball." These small farmers were desperate. They were on the point of losing their farms and small herds of milk cows. Milk prices were low, and the federal milk marketing order in the New Orleans Milkshed gave little or no protection. Competitive milk was being shipped in from other states by truck and railway. The farmers, organized and led by Leo Carter, stopped the trains and dumped the milk trucks. Moreover they acted out in the open, in small towns like Amite and Hammond, directly on the Illinois Central Railway, and U.S. Highway 51. The dairymen who knew they had nothing to fear from local and parish, or even state police forces, were posed by an enterprising photographer with shotguns and rifles in hand, stopping trains, boarding the engines, and turning over out-of-state milk trucks. The redneck farmers of bloody Tangipahoa County had long been considered outlaws by the proper people of New Orleans. Back in the 1890s they had lynched cotton factors and bankers' agents who came into that parish to collect debts and foreclose mortages. The dairy farmers, however, had not counted on the "Feds." Their nemesis was

Herbert S. Christenberry, then U.S. district attorney of and for the New Orleans area. Later appointed a district court judge, Christenberry was to become widely acclaimed for his pro-integration decisions and court orders to desegregate public schools. However, his attitude toward unions was determined by his encounter with the little farmers led by the wild-eyed teamster Leo Carter. Christenberry secured convictions, and 91 men, including Carter, were sentenced to terms in the federal penitentiary for interfering with interstate commerce. The defense of the dairy farmer members in Louisiana cost the Brotherhood of Teamsters about $250,000, a huge sum for those days. So Daniel Tobin, the International's president, and the district vice-president, Dusty Miller, were happy to turn this group of farmers over to the new AFL affiliate. By that time, however, the dairy farmers had disbanded, and it required nearly two years of hard work on the part of a remarkable man, I. Lee Parker, to turn this situation around, to build a cooperative milk processing plant, and to work out a deal with a small milk distributor in New Orleans, whereby the farmers' milk was marketed as union produced, from farm to home.

Parker was an unusual organizer. He was a hunchback, ineligible for the armed services. While serving as an ambulance driver in World War I, some doctor convinced him that his spine could be straightened. An unsuccessful operation was performed after the war, and for over twelve years, Lee Parker was an invalid, confined to his bed. He was a native of eastern North Carolina and lived near Rocky Mount. He had bought a new Model "T" Ford just before his operation. His wife had never learned to drive, and his two children were too small. So, unable to drive himself, he arranged to have his car put on blocks out in the barn.

In the early days of the New Deal, when the first relief program was started, a welfare worker asked I. Lee Parker to interview some of the needy people. Word was passed around that people needing help could go to the Parker house and sign up for relief, but few came. Parker knew that there were hundreds of people out on the little farms, and in the coastal villages who were eligible, but who were too proud to ask for help. He asked the welfare worker to have a set of new tires and a battery sent out for his car. Lee hooked up the iron cage that had been made to enable him to sit up, and with the help of his wife he got into the car, and drove away to help others. He worked every day and soon rounded up many clients for the civil works program. He became a full-time supervisor for the WPA and traveled to and from Raleigh whenever there was need. Then in 1937, someone in Washington heard about the little man with the broken back in North Carolina, and he got a job with the agency that later became the Farm Security Administration. When FSA was about to fold, I. Lee Parker was hired by the United States Sugar Corporation at Clewiston, Florida, to recruit their supply of sugarcane cutters from the West Indies each year. This didn't last long either.

I. Lee Parker was recommended to me in 1948 by Nelson Cruikshank, former Farm Security Administration official, by then chief of the AFL Social Security Department, and one of my close friends and advisers. With Cruikshank's help, Parker was hired—with expenses paid by the AFL, and salary paid by the NFLU. At first, he was employed to head the farm labor recruiting and placement service, but the war was over and the program wound down. Instead Parker became a dairy farm organizer for the NFLU in Louisiana. He successfully reorganized the dairy farmers whom Leo Carter had led to federal prison. He helped them build their own milk cooling-and-holding plant, and found buyers for their milk in larger towns and cities. With the endorsement of the AFL in New Orleans, he helped put a small dairy distributor into a successful business. The Roemer Dairy advertised and sold its products as union produced, processed, and delivered. Lee Parker made the long-lived Roemer-Walker Dairy of New Orleans the leading milk retailer in the city.

Lee became ill and returned to his home in North Carolina. On a trip through the South investigating the rise of the White Citizens Councils in 1955, I stopped in Raleigh and learned of Parker's death, which had not been reported to the union. Soon after, Mrs. Parker received an unexpected $250 from the insurance policy the NFLU carried on all of its members.

The dairy farmers' organization lasted into the early 1950s. Because of new state and federal regulations requiring costly sanitary equipment for use in dairy barns most of the small farmers in southeast Louisiana just could not make the grade. They sold their herds and started growing other crops, or they abandoned farming altogether, and moved to nearby towns or to Baton Rouge or New Orleans. The only exception was in the all-union town of Bogalusa, Louisiana. There the dairy farmers organized, went on strike, and put a Borden Company subsidiary out of business. Since all the farms were in Louisiana, and the company operated only in the state, the federal anti-trust law did not apply. A local judge held that the farmers had a labor-management relationship to the company, and since the farmers were really workers employed by the company, they had a legal right to strike, picket, and boycott. Interestingly, the Louisiana Supreme Court upheld this specious theory. As a result of the strike action, the 40 farmers involved entered into an agreement with a small dairy processor, C. A. Stewart & Company, who also advertised these products as being one hundred percent union. The dairy farmers prospered, and well into the 1970s their local, composed of farmers, plant workers, and milk truck drivers, remained affiliated with the Amalgamated Meat Cutters.

The dairy farmers shipping to Stewart received the highest price set under the milk marketing order in New Orleans, and by 1970, the average union dairy farmer in this region had land, equipment, and a herd of cows valued at more than $250,000. The plant workers didn't always fare so well, but their wages kept pace with the cost of living. The C. A. Stewart Company prospered, because of its union connection in a town where nearly every worker belonged to a union.

At that time the Crown Zellerbach Paper Company was the largest industry in Bogalusa. In the 1960s when blacks were fighting for the right to vote, for equal accommodations, and desegregated schools, the issue in Bogalusa was the right to jobs. There were some bitter battles. Bogalusa was a center of the Klu Klux Klan, as well as the Congress for Racial Equality. The dairy plant workers were involved; the farm operators had too much work to do on the farm, and were not involved.

Our national union had a remarkable man on hand in Bogalusa— Clinton O. Cabe. Cabe was a member of that branch of the Cherokee Nation that hid in the mountains of western North Carolina, and refused to follow the Trail of Tears to eastern Oklahoma. According to local people, Cabe was a veteran of the Spanish American War, World War I, World War II, and would willingly have served in the Korean and Viet Nam conflicts also, if he had not been rejected as too old. No one really believed that this truck driver had actually lived at the time of the Civil War, but Cabe could tell stories of things that happened back then. C. O. Cabe got involved with the Bogalusa Ku Klux Klan in the mid-sixties. He stole the Klan roster, and with my encouragement, turned it over to the FBI. The FBI, copying the union's practice in the 1930s, promptly circulated the list to every residence and business in the city, and the Klan withered away. Two civil rights lawyers, Richard Sobol, representing the black workers, and James E. Youngdahl, representing the two international unions involved, eventually worked out an agreement for upgrading black workers which was accepted by the U.S. District Court, and racial peace was restored again to the town of Bogalusa.

In upstate New York, District 50 of the United Mine Workers of America had tried to unionize small dairy farmers but, finding the task unprofitable, they abandoned the membership that at one time extended into Pennsylvania, New Jersey, and Vermont. Our national union inherited this group with its legacy of defeat from the UMWA just as we had in Louisiana from the Teamsters. In the 1930s there had been a substantial movement among the dairymen in this area, led by a left wing organizer who was accused of being a communist. By the late forties, only the memory of Archie Wright's Dairy Farm Union remained. The organizer for our National Union was a dairy farmer from near Utica, New York. L. N. Gregory brought together a substantial number of small, insecure farmers, and for nearly a year our union had a growing membership in New York, New Jersey, Pennsylvania and Vermont.

Then one day in December 1948 I received a telephone call from an AFL organizer saying there was a revolt in the Duluth-Superior milkshed. The farmers had taken matters into their own hands and stopped the milk going from the farms into the processing plants over a wide area. Among the leaders of the striking dairymen was John L. Banks, Jr., a small farm owner, the son of a prominent banker in Duluth. The AFL man asked for help. I sent in one of our organizers who had just left Florida. It was 20 below zero when he arrived in Duluth. Picket lines were up around every dairy processing plant from the Iron Range in Minnesota to the small town of Wentworth, south of Superior, Wisconsin. The plant workers and milk truck drivers were honoring the picket lines. Our organizer called all parties together in the warmth of a hotel room in Duluth, and worked out a temporary settlement.

Under the leadership of John Banks and Karl Schimenek, the union expanded. Among those who joined the Dairy Farmers Union of Duluth-Superior was a large group of Finns on the Mesabi, or Iron Range, of Minnesota, north of Duluth. Most of them had started as ore miners, but had soon acquired small farms of their own, built dairy barns, and maintained small herds of cows. They belonged to both consumer and producer cooperatives and were members of trade unions. Many were also radicals, syndicalists, socialists, even communists. They supported the Minnesota Farm Labor Party from its start. Above all, they had a wonderful sense of humor.

On my first visit to Minnesota, we were sitting around the stove in a rural schoolhouse in early October and the men were telling jokes. One was about the weather. "What do you do in the summertime in Duluth?"

"Why, *that* day we play baseball."

The Russian-Finnish War was still a major topic of conversation. The men of Finland, armed with nothing but rifles, held the mighty USSR juggernaut at bay. For weeks the Russians were bogged down in the snow. According to one of the story-tellers, a man named Eino was the first of the brave ski troopers to return to his village when the resistance had been crushed. Eino joined some of the men gathered in the local bar.

"What do you do first when you get home?" he was asked.

"I go to bed with my wife."

"Then what did you do?"

"I take off my skis."

In the 1950s, dairy farmers in western Pennsylvania, eastern Ohio and West Virginia sought the help of the AFL. An organizer for the AFL who made his home on a farm near Charleston became interested. With the advice and assistance of Attorney Daniel H. Pollitt of Washington, an associate of Joseph L. Rauh, we decided that instead of setting up another organization of dairy farmers, it would be better to have the pro-union farmers who were in the already formed Tri State Milk Producers Association continue their membership, and take it over. Meeting in small groups, the men worked quietly for months before the annual meeting of the cooperative association that was to elect three new members to the board of directors. One of the directors was already a member and leader of the pro-union group, and his term would not expire until the following year. The group had selected its candidates for the board, and once they were elected, plans called for a vote affiliating Tri State with the Division of Farm Cooperatives of the National Farm Labor Union. The association claimed a membership of 4,500 in the three states. Normally, annual meetings were attended by 100 to 200 members, who dutifully voted for appropriate resolutions and elected the recommended slate of officers. Because of the union campaign, 1,500 to 2,000 farmers gathered in the baseball park. The directors of the association made plans for free barbecue with beer and soft drinks for all, plus entertainment by a popular hillbilly band. Politicians made speeches, and association officers were introduced. About 2 P.M. the crowd grew restless. Some of the dairymen said they had to get back to take care of their cows. They started yelling: "When are we going to have the election?" The slick secretary of the association, looking more like a big business executive than a farmer, came to the microphone: "In accordance with the rules and by-laws of this association, an election was held this morning at 11 A.M. here in this park, under the bandstand, and the members present voted unanimously for the election of the following directors. . . ."

The chairman took the stand and announced that "The business of the annual meeting of the association having been transacted, we stand adjourned, sine die." There was a near riot as the two officers made their getaway amidst flying beer bottles. Some of the farmers who were also coal miners said: "The next time, we will bring our rifles. The bastards won't get away with it again." Thus died "aborning" an effort by pro-union dairymen to take back their own cooperative association.

Under the Capper-Volstead Act enacted by Congress in the early 1920s, farmers are encouraged to form cooperative associations for marketing their products. The states are authorized to enact enabling legislation, and whenever such cooperatives have complied with provisions of the law, they are exempt from criminal prosecution under the nation's anti-trust laws. There were also provisions in the state laws whereby such cooperatives could enter into marketing agreements requiring their members to sell their products only through their association, and to permit percentage deductions from such sales for operating expenses of the association. Given the American proclivity for letting one person or a small group run an operation, these cooperatives rapidly turned into big business rackets, with the small producers being squeezed off the farm. This was a major complaint of dairy farmers in every area where small producers called upon a union for help. This was also true of fruit and vegetable growers in Louisiana in 1951.

Poultry producers were the victims of a new type of exploitation called "vertical integration." The production of poultry was highly organized by the companies that owned feed, seed, and fertilizer outlets. They made contracts with small land owners, erected buildings for production of broilers and eggs, and provided not only baby chicks from their hatcheries, but close supervision for the so-called independent farm operator. The poultry farmer wound up working on his own farm for lower wages than were provided by the national minimum wage law. Now and then there were revolts among these people. One such group that joined the National Farm Labor Union were the Jewish egg producers in New Jersey, near Atlantic City. These people were mainly garment workers from New York City who had gone back to the land in the 1930s under a program initiated by the American Jewish Committee. Many were socialists. It was apparent that the committee had it in mind to use the experiences acquired by such farmers in the soon to be founded State of Israel.

Nearly all of the small farmers who turned to the union for assistance had some connection with the trade union, or socialist movement, as witness the dairymen of northern Minnesota and Wisconsin. The dairy farmers of Ohio, Pennsylvania and West Virginia were often coal miners, also engaged in farming as a second calling. Even in Louisiana, many of the dairy farmers who turned to the union for salvation had worked in the paper mill at Bogalusa and were members of the well established trade unions. However, except for the 40 dairymen who were covered by a contract with C. A. Stewart & Co., the attempt to unionize the small farmers failed. Nearly all of the would-be farm unionists lost out to the privately owned collectivized corporate farm operation which was the wave of the future. Tomato growers in New Jersey and Pennsylvania contracted in advance for sale of their crops to processors such as Campbell Soup Company and H. J. Heinz Company. Citrus fruit growers in California, Florida and Texas, while nominally individuals, are members of associations, many of them cooperatives, but operating as corporate business structures. The American ideal of a small farm ownership with every man living in his own home with the proverbial vine and fig tree is, for all practical purposes, gone from this land.

19 Washington's Smallest Lobby

Ernesto Galarza appraised our union's activity in Washington:

From 1948 to 1960, two people ran the smallest lobby in the nation's capital. The headquarters of the National Farm Labor Union, AFL, later called the National Agricultural Workers Union AFL-CIO, were always located in some slum building in Washington. Operating out of the small office were H. L. Mitchell, the President of the Union, and Dorothy Dowe Mitchell, the Secretary-Treasurer.

While the President of the nation's poorest national union hounded and harassed and haunted the various establishments on behalf of farm laborers, Dorothy kept order in the organizational housekeeping. The bookkeeping chores of the Union's locals across the country came to her desk. Her typewriter produced memoranda addressed to the high and mighty of American politics. Such documents were usually first drafted by Mitch, but put in order, with correct spelling and good English by Dorothy, mimeographed, and then submitted to Congressional committees, the press, or anyone else who would read them. If there were intervals of low pressure between public relations campaigns in behalf of farm workers, the time was used to catch up on correspondence, like the letter from "Horse House" who asked her to make a "racket"[record] of his dues payment. In addition to the routine blizzard of such chores, Dorothy managed the frail finances of the Union and kept the bank balance just barely in the black. Just when the red ink threatened the Union budget, which happened about once a month, fund raising appeals would go out to individuals and organizations, and the extinction of Washington's smallest lobby would be postponed once again.

The life of the Union was remarkably like the daily lives of farm laborers in the Deep South and the Far West. From crisis to crisis in the face of the heavy weight of agribusiness, a hand was needed to keep the "racket" straight for the National Union. That hand was Dorothy's.

In 1949 the DiGiorgio strike was still in its early stages. We were seeking help from organized labor and legislation for the nation's farm workers, and all sorts of other things happened.

I was given the Clendenin Award for Distinguished Service to Labor, by the Workers Defense League. Among those who were at the presentation were two ministers. One was Arthur C. Churchill, the Congregationalist who, as we mentioned earlier, with his wife Ruth, had replaced David and Alice Burgess as minister to farm labor. The other was A. B. Brookins, one of the early leaders and organizers of the Southern Tenant Farmers Union. The two had ridden the bus from Memphis to Washington to be present when I got my "reward" as Brookins called it.

Among those on the program who paid brief tributes to me, was Charles Brannon, the Secretary of Agriculture in the cabinet of President Harry S Truman. Ralph Wright, an Assistant Secretary of Labor, also spoke. Senator Paul H. Douglas, a former professor at the University of Chicago, recounted the history of the STFU and the present National Farm Labor Union. Senator Douglas had a number of students who wrote papers about the STFU. Congresswoman Helen Gahagan Douglas of California (wife of Melvyn Douglas actor, and no relation to the Senator) said: "Mr. Mitchell is soft spoken, warm hearted. I have always considered him to be somewhat of a sainted man."

Dr. Mordecai Johnson of Howard University, then an all black institution, paid a moving tribute to the "one time orthodox organization of American Labor (AFL) that is reaching down to the last man of our land—the sharecropper, migratory worker, and farm laborer." The eloquent college president quoted Lincoln: "'I saw the last tyranny lifted from the back of the last man.' I believe that Mr. Mitchell and his union are trying to do that very thing."

I had been a direct action-ist for a long time. Back in the 1930s pamphlets on *The Plight of the Sharecropper,* speeches by Norman

Thomas, a documentary film by *March of Time,* studies of tenant farming by social scientists at the University of North Carolina, all helped to call attention to the injustices that were a way of life in the South. But it was the agitation of the Southern Tenant Farmers Union that brought into being the President's Commission on Farm Tenancy, in 1936, that a year later started the program of the Farm Security Administration that resettled and rehabilitated nearly a million farm families. It was incidents among the sharecroppers in Arkansas, including the near-lynching of Howard Kester, that led to Senator Robert M. LaFollette's committee investigating violations of free speech and the rights of labor. This investigation and its exposé of abuses against industrial and agricultural workers came directly out of a dinner meeting at the Cosmos Club organized by Gardner Jackson, then the STFU Washington representative. Southern political influence may have kept the committee from holding hearings in Arkansas, but the committee investigated labor warfare in California between farm workers and the Associated Farmers, Incorporated.

I was now in Washington as the only lobbyist for the nation's farm workers. I lobbied the Congress, the government agencies, and above all, the AFL and CIO. I tried to play off one branch of the labor movement against the other, to the benefit of the unorganized farm worker. I made proposal after proposal to AFL President William Green, and later to his successor George Meany. I always got a sympathetic hearing from William Green, and at least a hearing from George Meany. Walter Reuther, president of the CIO after 1952, accused me of exploiting him and his sympathy for the plight of the farm workers. Of course I was doing that very thing with everybody. In the process I made some people uncomfortable, and sometimes that was enough of a "reward" for me.

Within the AFL, there were lower echelon people always ready to give me a helping hand. The so-called "Farm Labor Mafia" within the AFL was made up of one-time Socialists and/or close friends of mine. Among these were Nelson H. Cruikshank, Bert Siedman, Peter Henle, and Lane Kirkland. They were the advisers and aides I could count on.

For about ten years, 1948–1958, I was a worker member of the Federal Advisory Council of the Bureau of Employment Security. We were a constant thorn in the side of that agency of the U.S. Department of Labor. We used the Federal Advisory Council position constantly to call to the attention of the public the plight of the nation's farm workers, and to the exploitation of Mexican nationals by the corporate farm interests, whether they were illegal aliens or imported contract workers. With Nelson Cruikshank's connivance, and the support of the remarkable Katherine Ellickson of the CIO, both fellow members of the Federal Advisory Council, we often won support from the public as well as the industrial employer representatives.

Also active on the "Hill," the union aligned itself with the powerful lobbies of the AFL, CIO, the Railway Labor Executives Association, the National Farmers Union, and groups such as the Catholic Welfare Association, and consumer groups, in behalf of exploited farm workers. With the support of these groups, we persuaded Harry S Truman in 1949 to appoint a Presidential Commission that in 1951 issued a monumental and historical report on Migratory Labor in American Agriculture. We enlisted the help of Senator Hubert H. Humphrey in a battle for extension of minimum wages, social security, and other social welfare legislation to some segments of the nation's farm labor force, and this was achieved over a long period of time.

Almost every year from 1942 to 1960 there was foreign labor importation legislation before Congress. Sometimes the farm labor lobby spearheaded by our union was able to modify the legislation or get better rules and regulations issued by the Labor Department. Usually the congressional mandates and regulations issued in Washington were honored more in the breach than in the observance; most of the time the corporate farm operators were in control of the actual administration in the farm areas.

On March 1, 1954, it seemed that the union was about to win a significant battle in the House of Representatives. The former chairman of the House Committee on Agriculture, Harold D. Cooley, of North Carolina, then ranking minority member in the Republican-controlled House, was for once on the side of the angels. Cooley was ready to submit a union supported bill to apply all standards required for Mexican nationals to domestic agricultural workers, and prohibit the importation of any foreign workers until bona fide offers of employment had been made to all available American workers. The Mexican Labor Bill was scheduled to come to the House floor shortly after noon.

Dorothy and I wanted to hear the debate. We were late in leaving the office. Since the time was growing near for the measure to be debated, we did not stop as usual at the office of Harold Cooley or some other friendly congressman to get a pass to sit in the reserved gallery. Instead, we went into the visitor's gallery, and took seats in the front row facing the well of the House of Representatives. There was a high solid railing, and Dorothy could not see over it. "Let's move up," she said, "so we can see as well as hear what's said." So we moved, followed by another visitor to the highest tier of seats. I then noticed a group of six people sitting to our left. I remarked to Dorothy: "It looks as though some of our Mexican friends are here to follow the debate on the farm labor bill."

An unidentified Congressman was holding forth. Whether he was discussing the pending legislation could not be determined. The members were coming in, and seats were being filled. Suddenly a young woman in the group on our left arose with shrill cries, and waving a flag in one hand and a pistol in the other, she yelled over and over as her gun went off into the ceiling and into the seats down front, "FREE PUERTO RICO! FREE PUERTO RICO!" The five men with guns in their hands were taking aim on members of Congress. Congressmen were being hit and falling, others were trying to hide under chairs. The press gallery, with two or three reporters, was to our right. The reporters hid under their desks. There was no place for Dorothy and me to take cover because the benches were very close together. I jumped up twice, thinking I should try to do something, and twice Dorothy grabbed my coat tails and pulled me back in my seat. Then the Puerto Rican Nationalists left. A former U.S. Marine officer, Congressman Van Zant of Pennsylvania, single handedly captured Lolita Le Bron and two of her male comrades. Three others left hurriedly down a back stairway. Two were caught trying to board a bus to New York. Only one of the six got away. According to official reports, there were only five, and all were captured, but I counted five men and one woman.

The doorkeepers for the House of Representatives were elderly men, unarmed and untrained, having been appointed to pay off a political debt. I left my card with one of the doormen and offered to give evidence as to what I had seen. I was never called. Over twenty years later, while up in West Virginia, I happened to mention this story to Don West, once an associate of Howard Kester at Vanderbilt Theological School. West told me he was a counselor to Mrs. Le Bron, who had been imprisoned all those years in a nearby federal penitentiary. I sent Mrs. Le Bron word by Don West that if my statement as to how she never shot a congressman was needed to get her out of prison, to let me know. I never heard anything from her.

Before Dorothy and I left the gallery of the House of Representatives, we checked the front row seats where we had originally sat down. Those seats were full of bullet holes. Upon our return to the Victor Building downtown on 9th Street, Callie McCloud, our office receptionist and typist asked: "What happened? You both look like you've just seen a ghost!" Perhaps we had, the ghost of Freedom for Puerto Ricans. The movement was buried by that incident, and by an earlier protest made by the "Independistas" when they tried to shoot Truman at Blair House.

Early in 1953, I had been named the worker representative of the United States, to attend an International Labor Organization Conference on Plantation Work, held in Havana, Cuba. Dorothy went along for the trip. Several things stand out in the recollections of those present. One was that the preliminary meetings held in the splendid building erected for the Cuban Federation of Labor (CTC) were always scheduled to begin at 10 A.M. but none of the Cubans ever arrived before 2 P.M. to start the meetings which then continued until six or seven o'clock. Dinner would be announced for 8 P.M. at some American night club, but never got underway before ten.

While I had been notified by the AFL president, George Meany, of my appointment, my expenses were to be paid by the United States government. This was in the days of the McCarthy Red Scare, and every person had to be checked and given clearance by J. Edgar Hoover's FBI. The conference was ready to begin, and my papers still had not cleared the State Department. Clara Beyer of the Department of Labor, and the head of the U.S. delegation, got busy when I told her I was going to leave Havana, after announcing the reason to the conference. Mrs. Beyer telephoned the Secretary of Labor, and/or the Secretary of State, and a cable was received giving me clearance, just before the conference opened.

The meeting in Havana was attended by people from all over the world where coffee, cotton, rubber, sugar cane and tea plantations existed. The entire delegation was invited to the President's palace to meet Batista. Soldiers surrounded the palace that was barricaded with barbed-wire. The palace walls were scarred by bullet holes. Europeans and American delegates felt the tension as we entered the building.

Adri de Ruijter, then general secretary of the International Land-workers Federation, and holding the same position with the Netherland Farm Workers Union, had stopped over in Washington for a visit with us and then accompanied Dorothy and me to Miami by car. From there we took the overnight steamer to Havana. There we were joined by two other labor leaders from Belgium and Denmark. The group stayed in the same small hotel on the main plaza in Havana. We, along with all the delegates to the ILO meeting, were standing about in line, awaiting the arrival of the "great man who held the presidency of Cuba." He made a grand entry surrounded by guards. Bulbs flashed as Batista's picture was made. Then as each delegate walked up to shake his hand, another picture was made. Perhaps 25 of the line had passed through. It was obvious that the Europeans, all of whom were members of social democratic parties in the respective countries, were alarmed. Dorothy solved the problem by announcing that she had no intention of shaking hands with that "greasy gangster Batista." She walked across the room to the head of the line that had already been through the President's reception. The relieved Europeans and I followed Dorothy's example.

The following day was Sunday. The "leaders" of the Cuban Sugar Workers Union announced a special trip to the Sugar Centrals, to view the mills, the people who worked in them, and the new workers' homes that had been erected by the American companies that owned the plantations. The Mitchells and our three European friends decided to skip the show being staged by Sr. Mujal, the head of the Cuban Confederation of Labor. Mujal, who was not even a Cuban but a Spaniard, was a dead ringer for the late Italian dictator, Benito Mussolini.

Our group rented an auto from Hertz and, accompanied by a guide who really was a sugar plantation worker, we went on our own to see the sights. We drove through several of the Sugar Centrals, saw the houses the companies had built for their favorite workers and supervisors and union officials, and then passed over to the back country roads, where 90 percent of the sugar workers actually lived in makeshift shacks of adobe, tin cans and paper boxes. After the Cuban Revolution, I remarked: "Had I been living out there on the back roads I would have followed Fidel Castro anywhere when he promised me a better life, no matter if he was a communist."

The following fall, in 1954, de Ruijter persuaded the Dutch Labor Party government to assign H. L. Mitchell for six weeks as a consultant to the Landworkers Union of the Netherlands. The Marshall Plan provided money for transportation, hotel and meal allowance, and paid me fifty dollars a day for my services as a consultant. There were sufficient funds for Dorothy to accompany me. After an all-night flight, we landed at Preswick Airport in Scotland in time for breakfast, served by a small Scotsman dressed in evening clothes. The next stop of the four-motor propeller plane was Schipol Airport, near Amsterdam. There we were welcomed by a delegation from the Landworkers Union, as well as a young cultural attaché from the U.S. Embassy, with an automobile ready to drive us to The Hague. Apparently Adri de Ruijter and his associates had other plans, and eventually we were rescued from The Hague and the Embassy. We moved to Utrecht, near the offices of the International Land Workers and the Netherlands Landworkers Union. Each day we were driven by car to see the sights important to union folks. Dorothy declared later that she believed we visited every polder and dike in all Holland. After visiting farms and admiring the cows and other livestock, we were turned loose to travel on our own to the Northwest, the area which had just recently been devastated by the North Sea pouring through the dikes. We visited the two-room cottage of a union organizer's parents; he told us how his aged parents were rescued by U.S. Army men in helicopters just before their home was inundated.

The invasion and occupation of Holland by the Germans in World War II was a popular topic, and everyone had a story to tell. One man told of hiding some escaping British prisoners of war in his attic while the Germans searched the countryside for them. Adri de Ruijter told of being jailed by the Nazi Gestapo on suspicion of being a Jew, because his nose was slightly hooked. He was able to prove that he had no Jewish ancestors. De Ruijter boasted that he had a relative, an Admiral of the Dutch Navy, named de Ruijter, who sailed up the Thames River with his fleet to bombard London during the seventeenth century.

After about four weeks in the small country of Holland, we left by train for Oslo, Norway, to attend the International Landworkers Congress. The Dutch told us tales of how arrogant the German customs officers were to travelers crossing the border. We were astonished when we reached West Germany to find the border guards downright meek. They merely looked at the U.S. and Dutch passports as they passed through the train, with smiles and apologies for having to disturb the travelers at all. After an all-night trip across Germany, the train stopped at the station in Copenhagen for a couple of hours, but the passengers saw very little of Denmark because it was pouring rain. We then took the boat train across the North Sea Channel to Sweden, and then traveled by railroad another fourteen hours up the long coast of Sweden and Norway, into Oslo. There the party was met by a delegation from the Land and Forestry Workers of Norway. Dorothy and I were the special guests of the Norwegian union throughout our stay. Knute Nakken, who was later to become president of Land and Forestry Workers of Norway, was our guide and almost constant companion. If either of us wished to mail a post card, it was Nakken's duty to take care of it. After dozens of lavish meals, we discovered a small restaurant in the basement of the hotel where one could buy coffee, rolls and other simple food. When Nakken located us there, he told us this would not do. We were expected to have our meals in the Viking Hotel dining room and not spend our own money. Besides, Nakken said, this place was patronized by ordinary workers who carried their lunches in their briefcases and stopped by for coffee. Thus was a mystery solved for the strangers in the land of Norway. We had wondered why everyone was always carrying a briefcase to work, even laborers roughly dressed for outdoor work.

In Norway especially, all Americans were held in high regard in those days. The U.S. armed forces had driven out the Nazi army of occupation, and had saved them from being overrun by the Red Army.

Besides, the U.S. had its Marshall Plan. Industries were being rebuilt, jobs were available. Furthermore, most Scandinavians had relatives living in the United States. Said the people of Oslo, "Norway has a permanent Marshall Plan. The Gulf Stream that starts off the U.S. southern coast, brings the warm waters to Oslo, and helps keep the temperature at a comfortable level." But sometimes it was 20 degrees below zero.

After the Landworkers Congress ended, Dorothy and I remained in Oslo for a few days. One Sunday we, along with our guide Knute Nakken, were invited to visit the home of one of the largest farm owners in Norway. Mr. and Mrs. Hendricksen welcomed our party. The United States and the Norwegian flags were up on the lawn of the large comfortable home. Mrs. Hendricksen was dressed in the colorful costume of her native province or village. She welcomed the visitors from America, serving a delightful Norwegian country-style dinner to her guests. Then the host showed the men about the farm, which in the United States would have been considered a family-type farm. There were perhaps 300 acres in cultivation and some woodland. However, Hendricksen was a large-scale employer, and his farm hands who lived in comfortable homes were all members of the Land and Forestry Workers Union.

We went by train to Stockholm, where we were guests of the Landworkers Union. I had told Ewald Janssen, the general secretary of the Swedish Landworkers, that I had a friend in Gavle, Yngve Moeller, who was an editor of a daily newspaper and a member of the upper house of Parliament. Moeller had made a cross-country trip with me in 1946 from Memphis to San Francisco. Moeller had been contacted and arranged his affairs to be in Stockholm for a reunion with his friends from the United States. During the Nixon era, Moeller was designated Sweden's Ambassador to the United States, but President Nixon refused to accept him.

After we visited the Landworkers headquarters and met officers of L.O. (the Swedish Federation of Labor), the Employers Association of Sweden invited the Americans to a special luncheon that lasted for about three hours. I had told our hosts that I was called "Mitch," and that I was unable to drink, but that Dorothy could drink for us both. It seemed to Dorothy that everytime she turned her head, some Swedish gentleman was raising his glass to her: "Mrs. Mitch, Skaal!" Then, that same evening in Stockholm, along with Yngve Möeller, we were the guests of the secretary of the Labor Party, a young man who had attended Wilberforce College in Ohio. The secretary, later to become the leader of the Labor Party and prime minister of his country, was Olaf Palme.

That night at the Stalmeisters Garden restaurant, the talk was of politics and the trade union movement. It continued for hours. Palme reported that the Swedish workers had under the Labor Party attained guaranteed wages, jobs, housing, security in their old age, and they were beginning to lose interest in the political party that had given them so much. What should be the next step so they could retain power? I asked: "Why not try socialism, and let the workers own and operate their industries and control their own jobs and lives?" The good social democrats were horrified at such a radical idea coming out of a trade unionist from the world's greatest capitalist country. We learned that less than 10 percent of Sweden's basic industry had been nationalized. I expressed my opinion that perhaps an even greater share of American industry was already state owned, and more than half was collectivized in corporations supported by the state.

After returning home, we were meeting one evening at the home of Gardner Jackson in Georgetown. It was here that Walter Reuther, newly elected president of the CIO, said to me for the first time, "Mitch, you were already a legend in the South when I was just a punk in an auto plant in Detroit." We were discussing the future merger of the AFL and the CIO. Reuther was assuring "Pat" Jackson and me that among the first things he would bring about was an organizing campaign among the nation's farm workers. Also on his list of priorities was a drive to unionize workers in the public employment sector—local, county, state, and federal government employees. Said Reuther: "It is the historic mission of the labor movement to organize the unorganized." I later learned that this was one of Walter's favorite expressions and came right out of his upbringing and the experience of his father, Valentine Reuther, as a Socialist Party and labor union organizer. Walter Reuther questioned me about George Meany, who had become president of the American Federation of Labor.

I told Walter Reuther the story I had heard around AFL headquarters of how George Meany, when he first came to Washington in 1940 as secretary-treasurer of the AFL, and having little else to do, spent his time reading every piece of correspondence and every document in the files of the AFL going back to 1886 when it was founded. I don't remember if I repeated the rest of the story to Reuther, which was that when George Meany had read everything in the AFL files, he was about to consign the numerous boxes to the trash. However, Miss Florence Thorne and her associates in the research department rescued the AFL records from George Meany and the trash man. Miss Thorne had been one of the secretaries of Samuel Gompers and wasn't about to let her idol's papers be thrown away.

I also told Reuther that I considered Meany a man of great ability, and keen intelligence, and that if he gave his word on any matter, it was always honored. I told Reuther of the time Meany addressed our convention of black and white delegates in Cincinnatti, and said he didn't believe farm workers could be, or even wanted to be, organized. I also said I didn't know whether this attitude stemmed from bigotry, or was simply an expression of the building tradesman's ideology. Meany's father had been a plumber, and he had become one too. And then, too, as was mentioned earlier, there was Meany's disturbing boast that he had never taken part in a strike, or walked a picket line.

On the other hand, Walter Reuther and his brothers Roy and Victor had been involved in the socialist movement and were also active in all of the efforts made by the automobile workers to organize from the time when they started to work in Detroit. Victor and Walter had both been subject to assassination attempts and had barely escaped with their lives. Walter was accompanied by a burly bodyguard when we met at Jackson's home in fashionable Georgetown.

When Meany and Reuther worked out the plans for the merger of the AFL and CIO into one central labor federation, I kept reminding Walter Reuther of his commitment to launch an organizing drive. Just before the merger convention in New York City in 1955, with the help of the National Sharecroppers Fund, and the encouragement of both A. Philip Randolph and Frank P. Graham, I started to make a survey of the rise of the White Citizens Councils in the South. Ku Kluxers in business suits, I called them.

Dorothy and I started south from Washington, making stops to call on friends of Dr. Frank Graham, like Virginius Dabney, the editor of *Times Dispatch,* who was away from Richmond on vacation. Then we stopped at Raleigh, North Carolina, to see Jonathan Daniels, editor of his family-owned newspaper, *The Raleigh News-Observer.* I told him of Graham's idea for all of the southern liberals to hold a meeting in Atlanta to start a backfire against the rapidly spreading White Citizens Council movement. Daniels said that if he should go down to attend such a meeting, it would be all over town before he boarded the train that Jonathan Daniels was going to Atlanta to meet Frank Graham and make the white folks send their children to school with the Negroes. Daniels promised a full play in his newspaper if such a meeting occurred. I next stopped in Charlotte, North Carolina, and had a visit with the editor of the *Carolina Israelite,* Harry Golden. He facetiously offered a plan for integration of schools, libraries, and other public accommodations. It was to have both blacks and whites stand up and never sit down. He claimed that no one objected to meeting and talking as long as they were in a vertical position. The editor of the *Charlotte*

Observer would do no more than Daniels. When we arrived in Atlanta, Ralph McGill, also an editor and a friend of Frank Graham, was not available. But I did see Dr. Benjamin Mays, president of Morehouse College and spokesman for educated southern Negroes. Mays wanted everyone who attended a proposed backfire meeting to pledge in advance to support the 1954 school desegregation order of the United States Supreme Court. He suggested that I visit George S. Mitchell, then executive director of the Southern Regional Council, and ask that the S.R.C. sponsor the meeting Graham and I had in mind. George Mitchell was willing to sound out his board of directors about calling a special meeting. However, he hadn't paid much attention to the rise of the White Citizens Council movement. In Georgia, there was a States Rights Party that performed the same function of opposing integration. I also visited Aubrey Williams in Montgomery and met Grover Hall, Jr., editor of the *Montgomery Advertiser* for lunch. In Birmingham, I called the editor of the *Birmingham News,* Mr. Van der Veer. Then I stopped over in Jackson, Mississippi, and ended my investigation in Memphis, where I attempted to persuade the editor of the Scripps-Howard paper, the *News Scimitar,* to assign one of his star reporters, my friend Clark Porteous, to do an investigation of the White Citizens Council. I made the mistake, however, of saying that what was needed was a crusading newspaper to go after these new Ku Klux Klansmen in business suits. Ed Meeman wasn't about to become involved in such a crusade for integration. The only newspaper editor in the South who was willing to even attend a meeting called by Frank P. Graham was Hodding Carter, Jr., of Greenville, Mississippi. Carter sent word to me that he would be glad to take part. I then prepared a report, relating the White Citizens Council to the 1948 Dixiecrat Party that fielded Strom Thurmond for President. My report was circulated widely at the merger convention of the AFL-CIO in New York City. Thurgood Marshall, then General Counsel of the NAACP, was present and sought me out, asking for several copies to be used by his organization. Later, at Walter Reuther's urging, I attended, along with Ernesto Galarza, the first annual winter meeting of the AFL-CIO Executive Council in Miami Beach. I remember Galarza's disgust at having to sit around in the plush hotel where the Executive Council was meeting, waiting to be even noticed by the powerful labor leaders. Finally, the newly named AFL-CIO Committee on Civil Rights met and considered my report and recommendations.

Among my recommendations was one that the AFL-CIO set up in the South a southern office on civil rights and launch a campaign of opposition to the White Citizens Councils' move to infiltrate the unions.

I had reported on the White Citizens Council operation among the rubber workers in Tuscaloosa, Alabama, led by Robert Shelton, Ku Klux Klansman, and similar activities in the United Steel Workers in Birmingham and in the automobile and rubber plants in Memphis. While my report was marked "Private" and "Confidential" and "Not for Publication," as soon as the Executive Council accepted it, George Meany's public relations men circulated it among the newsmen. George Meany announced that the AFL-CIO was going to name a southern director of civil rights, set up headquarters in Atlanta, and expel union members who became active in the White Citizens Council or the Ku Klux Klan.

Ernesto Galarza and I, en route to Washington by car, heard the news over the radio, and we both remarked simultaneously, "There goes another piece of work just shot to hell by George Meany." There was an immediate response by southern workers who supported the WCC. They threatened to abandon the AFL-CIO and set up a new movement. It would likely have materialized except for the fact that the organizers of the WCC movement were nearly as anti-labor as they were anti-Negro. An able young man from the United Auto Workers, E. T. Kehrer, got the lifetime job of civil rights representative in the South, and organized labor cooled off as well as the rest of the South after the civil rights movement of the 1960s finally broke the back of open opposition to integration.

Incidentally, the report I made listing the White Citizens Councils and their membership in each state became the basis of all sorts of reports, news articles, magazine pieces. My original report on the White Citizens Councils has stood the test of time. It should be noted that Walter Reuther's United Auto Workers provided the major share of money to finance this investigation and report.

As soon as the AFL-CIO merger occurred, the Industrial Union Department was established, with Walter P. Reuther as chairman. This was made up mainly of those unions coming from the old CIO, but important AFL unions like the Machinists also joined it. The National Farm Labor Union also became a part of IUD-AFL-CIO. I kept pushing Reuther about mobilizing the newly merged AFL-CIO to launch an organizing campaign among the nation's farm workers. With the help of friends like Lane Kirkland, Nelson Cruikshank, Peter Henle, and also Leon B. Schachter of the Meat Cutters, originally in the AFL, and newer friends of a like mind, such as Oscar Jager, public relations man for CIO, and the people in the United Auto Workers' Washington office, we prepared a report and a proposal that was submitted to George Meany. It was so well prepared and so phrased in the right terms that Meany read it all and then called me in. His verdict: "Mitchell, you have here a proposal that is essentially a CIO operation. I am not John L. Lewis. I have no organization like the United Mine Workers on whose treasury to draw. What you propose cannot be done by the AFL-CIO."

I immediately telephoned Leon Schachter and Victor Reuther. One or both suggested that I dictate a memorandum on this matter and thereafter keep a record of negotiations concerning an organizing campaign among farm workers. Leon Schachter suggested that I ask the Reuthers to support a proposal for financial aid to be made by the Industrial Union Department. I remember Schachter saying his international union, the Amalgamated Meat Cutters, now belonged to IUD and "We will be paying at least $25,000 a year in per capita taxes." I later suggested this in a conversation with Victor Reuther. So it turned out that early in 1957 an IUD grant of $25,000 was made to the National Agricultural Workers Union AFL-CIO. (We had changed our name again just before the merger of AFL and CIO.)

After my proposal for an organizing campaign among the nation's farm workers had been turned down by Meany, I developed another idea. Why not use the upcoming meeting of the International Landworkers Federation in Frankfurt, Germany, as a sounding board to encourage AFL-CIO to make good on its promises to organize the unorganized?

Going again to my friend Arnold Steinbach, in charge of international affairs in the U.S. Labor Department, I proposed that some way be worked out whereby I could make a trip of perhaps two weeks, paid for by some government agency. After several meetings and much telephone discussion, Steinbach finally came up with a small private foundation that might underwrite the trip. Nothing further was said of the sponsor. I notified my friends in Utrecht that I was coming to the founding convention of the International Federation of Plantation Agricultural and Allied Workers being held in Frankfurt.

Both Dorothy and her sister Leila decided to make the trip on their own, since there was to be only a roundtrip airplane ticket and per diem for one person. I had asked that I be permitted to make stops in England, Holland, Belgium, Switzerland, and Austria, prior to the meeting in Frankfurt. Dorothy and Leila arrived a week earlier at the small Hotel Cadogan in London, where we had stopped two years before. The Cadogan had been built by the Prince of Wales for his mistress, Lillie Langtry, about the turn of the century.

I was still in Washington, waiting for clearance, when they arrived in London. Both Steinbach and I were puzzled by the delay and blamed it on the FBI bureaucracy, which had cleared me two years before. I learned long afterwards that the delay was caused by the Central Intelligence Agency, which had supplied the money for my trip. I finally arrived in first class accommodations, via British Airways. A traveling companion on the overnight flight was a mysterious young man from Galveston, Texas, who claimed that his stepfather was the founder and still owner of the Leyland Motor Car Company. He expected to be met by his mother in her Rolls Royce. Undoubtedly a CIA agent, he was not met by his family, but was hustled away in a U.S. Embassy car. I rode the bus. On joining the ladies, I found they had been having a hilarious time shopping with British currency, and trying to communicate in their native Alabamese with the hotel's cockney staff.

Two days later, after making a call at the Embassy, and after lunching at an English club with the American labor attaché, Dorothy, Leila and I took off for Amsterdam. There we were not even met by the Dutch Landworkers, much less an embassy car. We arranged for accommodations at a downtown Amsterdam Hotel. While I rode a train over to Utrecht and renewed old acquaintances, the ladies took boat rides about the city, and visited the Rijksmuseum and other places of interest.

We then went to Brussels, and this time we were met by an Embassy car, driven by the chauffeur of an old friend, Oliver Peterson, who had been involved in the early days of the STFU in getting Ward Rodgers on the FERA (Federal Emergency Relief Agency) adult education program. Oliver's wife, Esther Petersen, a former labor lobbyist in Washington, and later an assistant secretary of labor under Kennedy and consumer affairs advisor to both Johnson and Carter, had planned an evening for the visitors. Leila Dowe reciprocated by inviting our hosts to be her guests at the famous Blue Moon Inn, if they ever came to Montgomery, Alabama.

Leaving Brussels for Zurich, we missed our plane, and rode the Wagon Lits Express across Northern France, arriving in Switzerland late in the evening. After several days we left for Austria, arriving in Vienna on a week-end. Our hosts of the Land and Forestry Workers Union had reserved rooms for us near the railway station in a typical third class hotel patronized by laborers. The next day, an Embassy telephone operator suggested that we go to a hotel near the center of the city. There our friends of the Austrian union found us on Monday. We had already seen the more obvious sights of Vienna, so we made a trip out to the Vienna Woods where we had dinner.

While being given a conducted tour of the agricultural areas of Austria, Dorothy, Sis, and I were on our way to visit the Esterhazy estate near the Austro-Hungarian border. The general secretary of the union had with him that day a young man who had picked cotton as a prisoner-of-war in Mississippi.

Before the group, traveling in a diesel-powered Mercedes-Benz, reached the Esterhazy estate, we stopped at a village restaurant. We were amused by a flock of geese wandering down the only street in the town. Pigs and dogs scampered about. The innkeeper took a long time serving lunch. The reason for the delay, we discovered, was that the innkeeper's wife, hearing that three of the party were from America, insisted on using her best set of china. She had to unpack and wash a full set of dishes before serving the distinguished visitors.

Before the first World War, Count Esterhazy had been the largest landowner in the Austro-Hungarian Empire. The Esterhazy family still owned thousands of acres just inside Austria. Across the border, Hungary had nationalized the Count's holdings and was operating a not-too-successful collective farm project, or so the Americans were told by Esterhazy's superintendent. It was apparent that the socialist officers of the Austrian Land and Forestry Workers did not share his enthusiasm for free enterprise. However, they represented the farm workers employed on the huge estate. The Americans were shown model homes built in 1890 for the workers, with brick walls three feet thick, impervious to either heat or cold.

Before returning to Vienna, the party made a stop on the shallow lake dividing the two countries, in which reeds grew higher than a person's head. Back in Washington some weeks later, we saw a TV program showing people escaping across the same lake when Russian troops invaded Hungary to put down the revolt in Budapest.

We were favorably impressed by the Viennese, and indeed by all the people we met in Austria. There was an openness and friendliness seldom found in those days when everyone wanted the tourists' dollars and had no time for anything else.

In Frankfurt, the three of us made a boat trip down the Rhine to Coblenz. Though it was ten years after the war had ended, there was still much evidence of destruction. One day the two ladies made a trip to Heidelberg, but I remained in Frankfurt to attend the founding congress of the International Federation of Plantation, Agricultural and Allied Workers. There I suggested that the word "plantation" be included in the name, in deference to the few delegates from the undeveloped countries of Africa and Asia who were present.

Also, I arranged a luncheon for the European representatives. To this group I posed the problem of the lack of concern shown by the American trade union movement in building an agricultural workers union. Some of my guests, suspecting that I was asking for finaancial aid, pointed that they were putting all available funds into organizing in Latin America, Africa, and Asia. I explained that the problem was not financial; the newly merged AFL-CIO had untold millions of dollars in the coffers of its more than a hundred national and international unions. I asked that the landworker representatives alert their trade union centers to urge that every visitor from the AFL–CIO be asked why it was that the labor movement in the most powerful country in the free world had not organized the two million or more farm workers.

It soon became apparent that the top leadership of the AFL-CIO was continually being embarrassed by inquiries made both at home and abroad from other trade unionists in the so-called "Free World." Needless to say, this sort of thing did not endear H. L. Mitchell to President George Meany and his lackeys in Washington.

20 The Hank Hasiwar Story

"Since human beings are out of season, and big Hank Hasiwar doesn't resemble a duck, it's reasonable to assume that he was marked for murder," wrote Victor Reisel in his widely syndicated newspaper column.* Undoubtedly Hank Hasiwar was the intended victim of assassination when James G. Price, the president of the Kern County Farm Labor Union, was gunned down in the home of Hattie Shadowen in Lamont, California, on the night of May 17, 1948.

Hank Hasiwar was a New Yorker, born and raised in the Bronx, in a neighborhood that was later called "Fort Apache." He was a tall, handsome fellow, near 30 years of age when he came to work for the National Farm Labor Union, AFL, in February 1947. Hank's parents were both immigrants from Germany, where they had been ardent social democrats. They were very upset when their party voted war credits for the Kaiser—after promising that in the event of war the party would call a general strike.

Hank's father, Frank Hasiwar, and his wife arrived in America

*May 18, 1948.

before World War I. Frank Hasiwar was a good mechanic, and he was promptly hired by Gar Wood, the builder of the first motor boats. Later Frank Hasiwar built a successful small business as an independent oil distributor, with office and plant in Yonkers, New York. Hank described his mother, to whom he was most devoted, as a German Haus Frau who prepared wonderful meals about which Hank boasted and which he often invited his friends to share, usually without prior notice to Mrs. Hasiwar.

After high school Hank entered Columbia University and became a student activist in the mid-1930s. After two years he was expelled as a troublemaker. He had picketed Dean Alexander's office when the president of Columbia, Nicolas Murray Butler (the students called him Nicolas Miraculous) accepted a bid to speak at Heidelberg University in Nazi Germany. Later it developed that the Dean was a member of a Nazi front organization called "The Friends of New Germany." There was a student strike, which arose not only over the pro-Nazi position of some college officials, but over the exploitation of the building service employees, especially the women who were paid between $8 and $9 a week as charwomen and elevator operators. Hank led a picket line of students in support of the strikers and collected funds for them. He was one of the leaders of the Socialist Club at Columbia, which numbered only 40 or 50 members but usually attracted 200 or more students to its meetings. In a poll of the student body at the university before the 1936 presidential election, Norman Thomas, the socialist candidate, led the field. Roosevelt came in second, while Alf Landon, the republican, barely nosed out communist Earl Browder for third place.

Hasiwar was so effective as an organizer and strike leader among the students and employees at Columbia University that when he was expelled, Local 94 of the International Union of Operating Engineers hired him. The Local Union represented skilled employees of hotels, office buildings, and of some colleges in New York City. Hank was employed as a "bird dog," hired to track down workers in small buildings, hand out applications, and persuade them to sign with the union. After having taken a leading role in a strike of hotel workers, he was hired as a regular organizer by the Hotel Trades Council, representing all unions in the hotel and restaurant business in the City.

When the Japanese bombed Pearl Harbor, Hank joined the army. He had his basic training at Camp Robinson near Little Rock (named for Senator Joseph "Greasy Joe" Robinson, the nemesis of the STFU), and soon became staff sergeant. He served in the 81st Infantry Division in the Pacific, was assigned to a military government team, and was sent to Japan after the 1945 surrender.

Emil Mazey, also in American occupation forces in Japan, later to be International Secretary of the UAW, once described Hank Hasiwar as "the only G.I. who served four years in the armed forces and enjoyed every day of it." Hank was called to Tokyo and there, without any guidelines, started to reorganize the Japanese unions, following a directive from President Truman "to foster the growth of democratic trade unions." He called in the emerging leadership of the workers in each industry and helped to draft their constitutions, by-laws, rules and regulations. One of his problems was the lack of reliable interpreters. Until he found an American Nisei, Josh Kawana, a student from the University of Chicago, he had to use Japanese communist trade unionists. Having been in jail for twenty years or longer, they were the only ones who had spent time learning English, but he found them untrustworthy.

During the year Hank worked in Japan in the group assigned to reorganize the Japanese trade union movement, he was constantly in conflict with the communist-led cadre in the military government, *and* with the craft unionists from the American Federation of Labor coming in from Washington. Both the communists and the AFL bureaucrats thought they had all the answers. But Hank successfully overcame the opposition, and the Japanese emerged with a new trade union movement based on industry-wide organizations similar to the CIO in the United States. Hasiwar came to the attention of other anti-AFL and anti-CP people when he wrote a letter to *Stars and Stripes* taking issue with some army officer who had condemned the United Auto Workers and Walter P. Reuther for the strike against General Motors.

Then came the inevitable conflict with the commander of the postwar government, General Douglas McArthur. Hank publicly accused the general of selling out the Japanese workers to the *Zaibatsu*—the old ruling power structure. Hasiwar was also active in the American Veteran's Committee, which had one of its largest chapters in Japan among the army of occupation. Soon, McArthur saw to it that the "troublemaker" was sent back to the states and given an honorable discharge. Hank, while waiting about for some sort of work, was a member of the 52-20 Club, collecting $20 for 52 weeks from the army. Meanwhile he spent his time writing a book about McArthur's role in occupied Japan. An editor of Harper's was interested enough in the manuscript to carry it home to read over the weekend. Unfortunately his five-year-old son found it none too interesting and made a bonfire of the pages. Since this was the only copy, Hank's expose of Douglas McArthur never saw the light of day.

When Hank's unemployment pay was about to expire, his friend Bill Becker, then labor secretary of the Socialist Party, cooked up a scheme to get him out to the AFL convention in Chicago in early October 1946. There he met Captain Barney B. Taylor and me, organization director and president, respectively, of the National Farm Labor Union. Together we persuaded Hank to come to work for the NFLU as our West Coast organizer. After some correspondence, and in spite of his disinclination to leave one or more girlfriends back in New York, Hank Hasiwar, our only professional union organizer and the most adaptable, came to Memphis to accompany me to California.

Hank arrived in Memphis one February day by railway coach from New York City. He had slept near a drafty window, and had a neck so stiff that he could barely turn his head. I assured him that once we were underway on the southern route through Texas, the warmth of the winter sun would banish the sore neck. It didn't work that way. It wasn't until we arrived in El Paso, 1,500 miles from Memphis, and halfway to California, that Hank heard about a chiropractor who helped Mexican workers employed in El Paso. This practitioner straightened out the sore neck in short order.

In California, I spent about two weeks driving Hank about, introducing him to people I knew in the state AFL and in the city central labor councils. Then one day I had to return to Memphis and, as Hank said, he was abandoned "with a suitcase, a portable typewriter, no means of transportation," and told to organize farm workers all of whom lived in rural areas of the state. Soon friends came to his aid. Wallace D. Henderson, once a socialist, then a vice-president of the Winery Workers' International Union, and his wife Esther took big Hank Hasiwar in tow. They found him a helper with an old jalopy. Here is the way Hank told the story:

His name was Venus. You know how the damned Okies are—Venus, Avis, Myra and so on—men or women, they all had the same names. I couldn't tell which was which. Just like the prairie dogs and the prairie bitches, they can't tell which are whiches. Venus Lewis lived in Orange Cove, 34 miles from Fresno. Wally Henderson would drive me out there, and Venus Lewis would drive me about to talk to the farm workers. We soon organized a huge grape ranch owned by one Zaninovich. I went and talked to the owner about recognizing the union. With Zaninovich was Bob Franklin, who was a representative of the Associated Farmers, the vigilante group organized by the big farm operators—Pacific Gas & Electric Co., Southern Pacific, and others—to prevent unionization of farm workers by use of any means, preferably by force and violence. Franklin pretended to be a more liberal type of Associated Farmer. He was trying to make them respectable, following the expose by the U.S. Senate Civil Liberties Committee headed by Sen. Robert M. LaFollette, Jr., of Wisconsin, whose report came out about the time of World War II.

Then I started in to unionize farm workers just like I would have employees

Hank Hasiwar (1948)

James B. Price, President of the Kern County NFLU local

James Price was shot (disabled for life), May 18, 1948, in connection with the DiGiorgio strike.

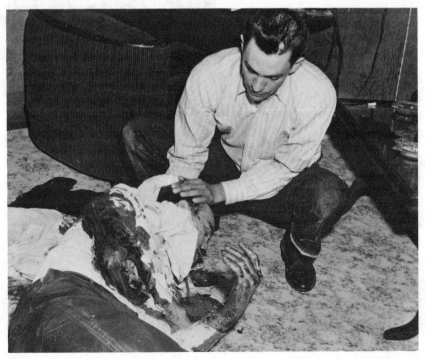

Above: Women workers were on the Di-Giorgio picket lines every day.

Right: Strike-breakers for DiGiorgio—deputy sheriffs were called in.

Left: Ernesto Galarza, 1948. *Right:* Alexander H. Schullman, Los Angeles attorney who represented farm workers in California, 1947–52.

in the automobile industry. When Zaninovich refused to bargain with the union, we called a strike, and put a picket line up about the big grape ranch where a new winery was under construction. For a few days, AFL building tradesmen from San Francisco and Fresno honored the picket lines of the farm workers. Then they put the pressure on, and we had to end the strike with a small gain in wages for the workers, but without union recognition.

Soon after, there was a new development. William Green, President of AFL, received a letter from Robert Lee Whatley of Lamont, California. Green sent the letter to H. L. Mitchell, saying that some farm workers in California wanted to organize. The newly chartered National Farm Labor Union AFL still had its headquarters on Beale Street, in Memphis, Tennessee. Mitchell wrote me asking that I look up Whatley. Bob Whatley was then near 70 years old. He was a one-armed socialist from Oklahoma, a follower of Eugene V. Debs. He was concerned about conditions among the people who lived in the towns of Arvin and Lamont. I met him at the "Smokehouse" in Lamont, a dirty old beer joint, but where one could get soft boiled eggs, which was all Bob Whatley could eat.

I learned that the primary employer was the DiGiorgio Fruit Corporation, that operated a 12,000 acre ranch producing fruits and vegetables. There was a large packing shed, and the Corporation boasted of having the largest winery in the world. There was a labor force of nearly 1,500 workers in the three operations of farm, shed and winery, which increased to 2,500 during the peak harvest season. About 80 percent of the workers were "Okies," a term applied derisively to all dust bowl migrants in the 30's whether they came from Arkansas, Iowa, Kansas, Nebraska or Oklahoma. Only 15 percent of the workers were of Mexican descent, and 5 percent were Filipinos. DiGiorgio did not employ Negroes.

The packing shed workers had the best jobs. They earned 80 to 85¢ an hour. Field workers earned slightly less. The skilled irrigation workers were paid $1.00 per hour for eight hours work, but were on duty 12 hours, without a break.

The towns of Arvin and Lamont were the locale of John Steinbeck's book and movie "The Grapes of Wrath." I was not about to move out there until I could see what kind of support I could get from the Kern County Central Labor Union. I did not want to get involved, or to involve the people, if we were going to get stabbed in the back by the building tradesmen again. I first went to see Bob Penzer, who was Secretary-treasurer of the Teamsters Local. Penzer was a very devout Catholic. He told me he felt he had to do something for people like those on the DiGiorgio ranch. "But," said Penzer, "the man you want to see is Fred West." Every Monday at noon, the Kern County labor leaders met for lunch at the El Tejon Hotel in Bakersfield. Usually there were 12 or 15 men who met, but sometimes as many as 25 came for the lunch. Any International Representative who appeared for the first time had to buy the lunches for all. Penzer probably paid the check that day for me, since I didn't have that kind of money to lay out. I went to the meeting, and I met Fred West. He looked like a hard guy—thin lipped, blue eyed, but sort of good looking. Reminded me of my father—cynical and kind of like a disillusioned socialist. I told him who I was, and he said, 'Oh, this is H. L. Mitchell's deal, ain't it?" I said "Yes, it is," and Fred West replied, "Good. That's all right, because the only people in the labor movement who have any brains are Socialists, anyhow." Later I learned that Fred West was once a "Wobbly," a member of the IWW, even though he was now business agent for the Hotel and Restaurant Employees. He had been involved in agricultural and cannery worker fights in Ventura, and Salinas, in the early 30's. Fred hated the farmers because he hated his father. His father was so motivated by making money that Fred West became a complete rebel. He was one of the most interesting human beings I have ever known. He was colorful and a most dynamic guy. He was also an alcoholic, but at this point he had sworn off. I only saw him once when he was on the booze, when he had a real bad deal, but the rest of the time he was a tremendous help. Fred once told me, "Don't worry about the farmers beating your brains out; worry about the building tradesmen stabbing you in the back." As long as he lived, he kept the building tradesmen off our backs in the Di-Giorgio strike. All of the time during the DiGiorgio strike, the building trades-men were complaining that we were disturbing the collective bargaining rela-tions in Bakersfield. This was because of the DiGiorgio Fruit Corporation's impact on the economic structure of Kern County.

Bob Whatley introduced me to a few key guys. Then we had a meeting in Lamont. At that time, Lamont had only a half-paved road in the town. There were some frame houses, but more wooden shacks, and tents on wooden plat-forms. There were about 3,000 people living in Lamont at that time. Most were dependent on DiGiorgio for jobs. Over at Arvin, most of the people were dependent on Joe Guimarra. He was also a huge grower in the area. Bob Whatley's brother had a flatbed truck. We put it back of the beer joint called the "Smokehouse." They strung up some lights for us, on a cord with bare bulbs. I was reading a new article out of *Colliers*. It was by Howard Whitman and was called "Heartless Harvest." I rolled into Lamont. The meeting had been set for 7:30. It was getting dark. I didn't see a damn soul. I said to myself "All the feeling about this thing is wrong." I was sitting on the platform of the truck. There was a big sandy area the size of a baseball field back of the Smokehouse, all empty. Then cars started coming, parking, switching off the lights, and I got up on the truck bed. There was no public address system. I spoke. I had that *Colliers* magazine in my hand. It sort of steamed me up. I read a little from that story "Heartless Harvest." Then I asked them to come up and sign with the union. I told them it cost a dollar to join, and dues would be $1.00 a month. I told them if they were going to join, to pay the $2.00. I was amazed. Everyone in that big field joined that night, and they paid. One of the first guys who came up was Phineas Parks. He was a Holiness preacher. This was our first meeting. We had other meetings too. Somebody told me about a lawyer there in Lamont who was an old time Socialist, who had also been a Wobbly (IWW). I went to see Wiley Doris. He was a character. He handled all kinds of cases, but mainly divorces. He was making money. He was a real old guy, with a shriveled hand. He looked like some character out of a Dickens novel. He said: "Hank, you need a loud speaker. I'll buy it for you." He bought the P.A. system, and then came out to a meeting and used it. All the Okies knew him because he handled their business of a legal nature. Wiley got up before them and said: "Now all of you ought to get in this damn union, because the more you make, the more money I can steal from you." That went over great, because they all knew that he was on their side. One night he invited me out to dinner. I always cut the fat off meat, but Wiley ate fat, read meat, and everything else they brought him. He was an alcoholic, but he didn't drink most of the time, but he sure did eat! He was a short little guy, and looked like a plum pudding.

We made full use of the P.A. system. Phineas Parks would start the meetings and whip them up. He would say: "My God, we need a Union! We got to stand up like men. The bosses are no more men than we are. They get into their pants just like we do, one leg at a time. These guys got so much money they buy Cadillacs so big that when they make a turn they need hinges on them." With local leadership like that, we had 2,000 members before the end of September. DiGiorgio didn't think we could organize so fast. They never bothered the workers. We had all the Okies and Arkies, but I was worried about the 250 local Mexican Americans employed by DiGiorgio. There were no Negroes. I was once criticized by Labor People down in Los Angeles for taking on a place where there were no blacks. My reply was: "Hell, I am trying to find a place to lay an egg, and I don't give a damn what color they give—white, brown, black or even green. I am looking for a place where I can get this movement going."

Zane Meckler, then the West Coast man for the Jewish Labor Committee, backed me 100%. There were others like Aubrey Blair from the Hollywood Film Council. He was Teamster too. Fred West was with us that night at the Weedpatch-Grange Hall when we took the strike vote. The Hall was jammed. We had between 800 and 900 people there, inside and out. The Kern County Sheriff, Johnny Lousalot was there too. He was in DiGiorgio's pocket. He owned a whorehouse in Bakersfield that was patronized by the Teamsters—not truckers—it was the business agents for the Teamsters Union who lived in town, or were just passing through, who stopped to get laid.

I had never worn a hat, but August in the San Joaquin Valley was hotter than Hell, and I needed one out in the sun, when the temperature often got as high as 110 degrees in the shade, except there was no shade to be found.

After the strike vote and walkout of about 1,100 Okies and Arkies from the DiGiorgio Ranch, there were problems from the 250 Mexican Americans, including 150 Mexican Nationals under contract, who provided a skeleton force that kept the farm operations going. I never wanted that strike. I was hoping we could hold the deal over until the following spring, but DiGiorgio put the pressure on. Phineas Parks was the first to be fired. Jimmy Price got the ax. Workers were coming to me saying: "Are you on DiGiorgio's Payroll? Are you selling us out?" Of course, that was normal. I was working out of the Teamsters Union Office in Bakersfield until they kicked me out for running up such a big phone bill.

About then I heard about a young Mexican-American, Louis De Anda, and went to see him. Later I married his sister, Delphina. De Anda was the first Mexican-American to become an officer in the American Air Force. He was an "Ace." Louis had shot down five German planes. When I met him, he was between jobs. We had a little money in the Local's treasury. Later he was paid by the State Federation of Labor. Neil Haggerty, the Secretary-Treasurer of the State AFL was a bullshit artist. Long on promises, short on performance. Anyway, we hired Louis De Anda, and we began to reach the Mexicans on the ranch. Louis would go to the ranch, talk to them in their homes, wherever they could be found. Later he used the loudspeaker Wiley Davis had bought for us. His sister Delphina had an early morning program on the Bakersfield radio. She would play records and sing Spanish songs, and in between commercials, she would broadcast the news about the union in Spanish. This was a big help, and the turning point. Her brother Louis wrote the spot news that she broadcast for us.

More guys got fired. We had taken the strike vote. We had sent letters to the Corporation. We had been strike sanctioned by the Kern County Central Labor Council, representing all Unions in the area. The State Mediation Service had sent Jules Medoff. Fred West, the President of the CLU, had even been out to the ranch and talked to the head foreman. The ranch boss claimed that all the workers wanted was Social Security. That idiot's name was Bob Newman.

I went over to see Fred West at his house. I said: "Fred, we got to go, there ain't no other way." Fred replied: "Well, let's all just commit suicide." He knew what was going to happen. We all knew it was going to be a rough deal. The first morning we put the pickets on we rolled everybody back. We couldn't get the Mexicans to come off the ranch and join us. Louis worked that PA and told them what the issues were. They didn't go to the fields for seven days. The Mexicans remembered what had happened to them when the Okies came in during the early 30's. The Mexicans went on strike then, and the Okies scabbed on them. They were afraid now it was just another deal to get the rest of the Mexicans out of the fields. Louis was making some headway. Then DiGiorgio got the County officials to declare the loudspeaker a violation of a county law. We lost much of our contact, though there were people going in and out and some of the local Mexicans came out on strike. Then we got rid of the Mexican Nationals there on contract.

H. L. Mitchell, working through William Green of the AFL in Washington, had persuaded the Secretary of State, George C. Marshall, to order the Braceros removed, as they were in violation of the International Agreement for contract workers to be employed on a job where there was a strike. The day after the strike meeting was held, and the men voted to put up the picket line, Mitchell arrived by train from Los Angeles, where he had come in by plane. Fred West met him at the railway station. West told me: "This guy looks like just another damn drunk—just like all the others that are Presidents of AFL Unions. He has come out here to sell out the members." Mitchell had been up two nights en route, and in addition had a severe flairup of ulcers. He was drinking milk, not booze.

Mitchell was also worried about how to raise money to support a strike so far away from his contacts in New York and Washington, none of whom believed anything ever happened unless the news was published in the *New York Times,* or the *Washington Post.* The picketing started October 1, 1947, and continued until April 1950. It was the longest picket line in the annals of farm worker strikes—both time-wise and area covered. To cover the main gates and the country roads leading onto the 12,000 acre DiGiorgio ranch required nearly 100 men and women. The Kern County Farm Labor Union 218 had a total of $2,800 when the strike was called. The National Farm Labor Union probably had even less. There was no strike fund. The money began to run out in a few days. The financial and moral support from the Unions in Bakersfield began to erode too. Fred West died suddenly. The cotton harvest was going on, and DiGiorgio strikers took to the fields. It lasted well into December. But by then, the AFL and the few CIO Unions in California had been mobilized.

W. J. "Bill" Bassett, secretary of the powerful Los Angeles Central Labor Union, told what happened at a meeting. The officers had met, and agreed to make a substantial donation to the Freedom Train. This was a private organization sponsored by Drew Pearson, newspaper columnist, raising money, foodstuff and clothing for European refugees, displaced persons in camps throughout Europe, seeking to migrate to Palestine. Bassett submitted his resolution to call upon all Local Unions in Los Angeles to support this worthy effort. A delegate from the Plumbers Union, who had relatives living near Bakersfield, got the floor on a point of order, and said: "Freedom Train Hell! We need to organize a Freedom Train of our own, and send our money, our food, our clothing, to 1,000 AFL union members—the farm workers now on strike against the DiGiorgio Fruit Corporation near Bakersfield!"

Some one offered a substitute motion to send a caravan of relief to the DiGiorgio strikers. This was the beginning of a tremendous effort on the part of trade unionists all over the country. Over a period of months, contributions in cash alone amounted to $250,000. That was the equivalent of several millions in the days of inflation and recession thirty years later when the capitalist system was on the brink of disaster. Food and clothing bought and paid for by the AFL Unionists totaled probably twice as much. Then there were Christmas parties. Hollywood stars came to Bakersfield and entertained the strikers, children and adults. Some of them visited the homes of the strikers. The movie "Poverty in the Valley of Plenty" resulted from these initial ventures. Congresswoman Helen Gahagan Douglas, once a stage star in her own right, and wife of Melvyn Douglas, a hero of the stage and screen, arrived with a delegation, including news broadcaster Chet Huntley, former Congressman Andrew J. Biemiller, and others less well-known. Louis de Anda, the youthful hero of World War II, who was brought up to consider women as inferiors, remembered Helen Douglas as the first woman he had ever met that he considered superior to himself and other men. People brought supplies and money to help the strikers. We had a huge tent set up behind the Baptist Church in Arvin. This is where we usually held our committee meetings, but our membership meetings were held in the Arvin Community Center, where Joseph DiGiorgio's statue was. I walked by that memorial to the great pioneer and developer of the grape industry in the Central Valley of California every day.

The second caravan bringing supplies to the strikers came from San Francisco. They had more than 100 cars and trucks in that one. We had asked them to donate flour. Jimmy Price was in the first car leading the caravan on the road to the main gates of the DiGiorgio ranch. I was in the second car, along with Neil Haggerty, the Secretary of the State AFL. He was there to show the other union people the picket lines. It was an impressive sight—1,500 to 2,000 people in that area turned out. Then a surprising thing happened. DiGiorgio had a countercaravan of strike breakers turned out to meet the one from the San Francisco Unions. Our people started yelling and throwing things at the scabs on the DiGiorgio trucks. They were about to dump those trucks. Neil Haggerty was scared. He said: "Hank, you have got to stop this thing before somebody gets killed." I got in the car with the mike, and directed the caravan into Arvin to the tent at the back of the Baptist Church. I asked people to refrain from any action. There they unloaded the food. Most of the people in the cars and trucks then joined the picket lines of farm workers at the DiGiorgio ranch. The same trucks of scabs would drive in one gate, and out the other. The people in those trucks were scared to death.

H. L. Mitchell who was present recalled how the DiGiorgio strikers were throwing things, trying to hit the scabs in the trucks. Soon DiGiorgio stopped his in-and-out-the-gate parade. He had about a dozen trucks, loaded mainly with wetbacks, or illegal aliens from Mexico, and supervisors from the ranch. At the most, 100 men were on the trucks running that gauntlet of over 1,000 strikers and another thousand sympathizers. It could have been murder that day.

I was operating out of an office at the Teamsters Union. I was making long distance calls everywhere, sometimes trying to answer two phones at once. Then I got some unexpected help. A lad by the name of Jim Wrightson came in. He was a Quaker, and during the World War II was a Conscientious Objector, and he was also a socialist. I turned over to Jimmy press relations, and the answering of letters and sending reports on activities to Washington and elsewhere. It was about this time that we changed hotels. Wrightson and I were staying at the Padre Hotel. The manager told us that our phones were tapped. We moved to the El Tejon Hotel, where the managers warned "Be careful on the phone." Even the maids were being paid by DiGiorgio. They searched the wastebaskets every day, which gave Jim Wrightson an idea. He posted a note to me on the dresser. It said: "John L. Lewis, United Mine Workers, has just sent $30,000." That went right to DiGiorgio. Lewis never sent a dime.

Soon after the movie made by the Hollywood Film Council was released, the Union sent DiGiorgio strikers everywhere to show "Poverty in the Valley of Plenty," and raise money for the strike. Jim Price went to both the Texas and Louisiana State Federation conventions.

Mitchell arranged to show the movie to the House Education and Labor Committee. John Lesinski of Michigan was chairman. We asked for an investigation, and the enactment of laws to cover farm workers as they covered industrial workers. A subcommittee was appointed. It included Cleveland Bailey, a Congressman from West Virginia, Tom Steed of Oklahoma, and Leonard Irving of Kansas City, who was once a Laborers Union Business Agent. These three were the Democrats. Thruston Morton of Kentucky and

Richard Nixon were the Republicans. Mitchell wrote me a letter describing each of the committeemen. "The last one is that S.O.B. Nixon from Southern California." This was in the Fall of 1949, and the hearings were held in Bakersfield.

When Helen Douglas and her group were up at Bakersfield, a reporter asked her what was the real cause of the strike. Helen answered: "If you had a wife and several children, could you live on $30.00 a week?" The Bakersfield paper played up to the economic interests of the area. We could get very little in the newspapers or on the radio after Delphina De Anda was fired. The Union then picketed the *Bakersfield California,* protesting its unfairness to the DiGiorgio strikers. Jim Wrightson had the idea. Jimmy Price led the picketing. They carried signs about "Citizen Keene." The Orson Wells movie about William Randolph Hearst was out about that time. Hearst was "Citizen Kane." The publisher of the Bakersfield paper was named "Keene."

The DiGiorgio strikers loved to picket. While DiGiorgio lost almost all of his grape crop in 1947, the next Spring he harvested some asparagus and potatoes. They put it on some non-union trucks. Jimmy Price led a group that followed the trucks to the Safeway Terminal in Los Angeles. They put up picket lines. The warehousemen were members of a Teamster Union. They left the Terminal. Some went out the windows. For two days nothing moved in or out of the Safeway Stores' largest warehouse on the West Coast. We also got help from the Retail Clerks and Meat Cutters in the Safeway and other chain stores. When you have 1,000 workers on strike, you have to have activity for them to take part in. So we picketed every supermarket we could reach, calling on customers to refuse to buy DiGiorgio products. They had several labels they used for fruit and vegetables. One was "Blue Flag," another "We grow the Best."

We didn't have enough money, nor did we have student volunteers, like there were in the 1930's and then again in the 1960's. The socialist movement was torn apart by factionalism in the 40's and 50's. The communists were never any help. The cold war was starting. They were too busy fighting HUAC and supporting Joe Stalin. Some representatives of the CP-led CIO Food and Tobacco Workers showed up but the pickets chased them away.

One of our leading people was Hattie Shadowen, a fantastic woman. She loved to picket. She and her husband worked in the fields before they got jobs in the packing shed. Hattie always had a bottle of beer the first thing in the morning. She was very nice looking, about 30 years old at the time. Her husband was a real thin string-bean type of Okie. Hattie was the boss in her house. She developed an interest in the whole struggle of organized labor. It was at her house that night when Jimmy Price was shot. An automatic rifle was emptied into the house through a window. Bullets from a Belgian gun were found. We were having a meeting. We all knew the strike was lost. We were trying to figure out what to do next. We were doing some good everywhere. The strike was having an impact. The strikers were fanning out over the San Joaquin Valley. They were talking Union everywhere. When those shots were fired, one hit an iron bar back of the sofa where I was sitting. Another struck Jim Price on his cheek, came out his ear. Some one made a picture showing him lying in a pool of blood. It could have been one of the Swearingens, or even that remarkable man Riley Watson who had a camera with a flash. Riley was an Indian from Oklahoma. His wife was one of the strike leaders too.

Earl Warren was Governor when that shooting occurred. He sent investigators, and had teams coming in to see us. He also offered a $5,000 reward for information leading to the arrest and conviction of the attackers. My wife Delphina and I were living in a house on the outskirts of Bakersfield. It was like a New York subway station, with people coming and going at all hours. Poor girl had never been involved in such a thing, and just didn't know what to do. We had gotten married in the early days of the strike, and went down to L.A. for several days.

Before Fred West died, there was that investigation by the California Legislative Committee on UnAmerican Activities, whose chairman was Jack Tenney. It started when State Senator Hugh Burns came along. Everyone knew Fred West was a "leftie and a radical," but they knew he wasn't a communist. Burns came down to conduct a little private investigation of his own. He was very much the McCarthy-type character. Fred West and I met Hugh Burns at the Padre Hotel while I was still living there. Everything I had was being continually searched and thrown about. They didn't even have the decency to put my clothes back in my suitcase. Burns asked me a number of questions—the same old crap they always asked. Burns didn't know a socialist from a communist. Fred West helped straighten him out on a few things, like why the strike was being conducted. It was not over wages. It was a fight for simple union recognition. "If we get union recognition," said Fred, "we'll get money later, but right now, all we want is recognition. We don't want a closed shop, or even a union shop. Just grievance machinery out on the DiGiorgio Ranch."

That was the whole issue. We didn't even ask for an increase in wages. Burns left satisfied that the strike was a legitimate one. How Jack Tenney received it was a different thing. Burns was on his committee. Tenney was a state senator from L.A. He was also a member of the Musician's Union. He wrote a song that was a big hit in the 1940's called "Mexicali Rose." He made his reputation in politics as an anti-communist fighter. Everybody was scared to death of him. We had this hearing in Los Angeles. They came to our hotel in L.A. and handed Mitchell and me subpoenas to appear before Tenney. When we appeared, the AFL guys were all there, officials for the State Federation, L.A. Central Council. People like Haggerty, Bill Bassett, and Roy Brewer, a Teamster who had led the fight against the communists in the movie industry were there. The Tenney Committee made a cute move. They called a guy who was an admitted member of the Communist Party, a painter named Frank Spector. They put Spector on just before we were called. Spector looked just like a Communist was supposed to look. He was short, dark, and had bushy, wirey hair. Tenney asked Spector whether the Communist Party supported the DiGiorgio strike. Spector replied: "The Communist Party supports all strikes of workers everywhere, and especially farm workers in Kern County." He also said: "Don't you remember, Jack, when you were in our faction, that the Party always followed that policy?" Spector was Secretary of the Los Angeles

Communist Party. His appearance was timed beautifully. *The L.A. Examiner,* a Hearst paper, came out in the early afternoon with banner red headlines saying "Communists support the DiGiorgio strike." Of course, that paper, nor any other, didn't report what Spector said to Tenney.

Previously DiGiorgio had made charges that the Farm Labor Union was communist, that its organizers were using communist tactics. We had threatened to sue him. I don't know if Tenney actually was a member of the Party, but they had supported him the first time he got elected to the legislature. He turned against them later. He was the one who started the red-baiting in the movie industry. Later on, the House Committee on UnAmerican Activities and the Senate Committee on Internal Security called many of the same people in Washington. Some were sent to prison for refusing to answer their questions.

Since we had been cleared by Hugh Burns, a member of the Committee, I did not know what the hell Tenney thought he had on us. I was getting letters most every day from H. L. Mitchell. They read a letter I had from him. Some of it was just personal, inquiring about my family. It was a very casual kind of letter, and ended by saying that Ackerman was checking into the John Reed angle. How did they get that letter? I thought I had torn it up and thrown it in the "john." It must have taken hours to piece it together again. On the stand I explained that John Reed was a labor contractor down in Texas, that Ackerman was the Secretary of the Texas Federation of Labor, and that he and the Labor Commissioners of the State of Texas had gotten out a warrant for Reed because he was recruiting Mexican Wetbacks and sending them across State lines to work on DiGiorgio's ranch where the strike was on. I added that this was a violation of the Norris-LaGuardia Act, a U.S. law. This ended my interrogation by the California UnAmerican Activities Committee.

Mitchell presented a formal statement on behalf of the Union, pointing out that the constitution of the Union prohibited persons from joining who owed their allegiance to another organization. This specifically applied to the Communist Party, the Ku Klux Klan and other subversive groups who were opposed to democratic institutions and procedures. He was asked if Norman Thomas was not a communist. He replied that Thomas was opposed to communism long before Tenney had ever heard of it. He was also questioned about the loyalty of Dr. Edward C. Lindeman, head of the New York University School of Social Work, who was also chairman of the National Sharecroppers Fund. The only thing that DiGiorgio got out of this hearing was the scare headline in the *L.A. Examiner.* A sop thrown to him by Tenney cited the National Sharecroppers Fund as a communist front organization. We tried to get the directors of the Fund to sue Tenney. No one was interested, nor did they care what some silly red-baiting committee in California said about them.

Soon after the strike started, DiGiorgio had all the workers living in housing on the ranch evicted. He had the Kern County Board of Supervisors ban the use of the loudspeaker. Seventy-year-old Bob Whatley was arrested for reading the Declaration of Independence over the P.A. A special committee was formed by W. B. Camp, once an AAA official in the Dept. of Agriculture, who found it more profitable to grow cotton on some acres he owned in Kern Co., and rent his worst land to the government under the subsidy program that STFU had exposed in the mid 30's as Socialism for the Rich. Camp and eleven other local businessmen then issued a pamphlet called "A Community Aroused," which showed pictures of homes of supervisors for DiGiorgio, and claimed they were homes of workers on his ranch. The Committee denounced the Union, but carefully avoided outright charges of Communist influence.

In the meantime, the Immigration Service would raid the DiGiorgio ranch every week, and pick up wetbacks (illegal aliens) but the company would replace them with others as fast as the border patrolmen could arrest them. Early in January of 1948, four pickets were jailed, charged with cutting down fruit trees. Bail was set at $15,000 each, but this was reduced when the Union attorney, Alexander H. Schullman, made an appearance in Court. The men were released on bail of $250. They were never tried, much less convicted. It was found that DiGiorgio had some diseased fruit trees cut down, and tried to make trumped up charges against Union members. The picket line was also attacked by ex-convicts hired by DiGiorgio.

I had a call early one morning from Tom Randall who said three men had been badly beaten and were taken to the Kern County Hospital. I was urged to stay away, because "All Hell is about to break loose." People who had been working elsewhere were taking the day off. They were going down to the DiGiorgio ranch to take it apart. I told Tom: "There is no way out—I am coming." First I went by the hospital, but the men were being taken care of and I couldn't see them. When I got to the picket line, the County Sheriff and his deputies were there, and the State Highway Patrolmen were already blocking the entrance to the ranch. Our people were milling around on the out-side. There must have been 1,000 men and a number of women too. About ninety percent of our folks had rifles. Some may have had pistols. The highway patrolmen were standing outside their cars with shot guns in their hands. The deputies weren't armed with rifles or shotguns, just pistols. There were about 15 State and county automobiles, maybe 25 men facing 1,000 Okies. Our people were waiting for me to come. They knew I would be there. As soon as I came up, I was surrounded. They began saying to me: "Hank, this is going to be it. We are going to settle this strike here and now." One of the things that worried me most was that we had a number of older women on the picket line. They were right in there. Some of them had clubs in their hands. I thought: "My God, if anything happens, these old women are going to catch it first." I thought: "This strike is not worth a lot of people getting shot, and some being killed." Then John Lousalot, the Sheriff, came up to see me and said: "Hank, you are the only one who can do anything." I said: "John, dammit, you are the one who caused this. You should have kept that caravan from coming out of the ranch. You know who beat up the pickets. You should have arrested them." He said: "This is going to blow, I'll do anything you want me to do, if you will stop it." The people were gathered about the Sheriff and me. One of the younger fellows walked up, looked straight at the Sheriff, and said: "John Lousalot, we are going to kill you first. We are going to shoot you dead." The sheriff had been arresting our people right and left. We had been bailing them out, paying a bail bondsman ten percent of the fines assessed against them. With the help of the older heads like Phineas Park, and Jim Price too, we got things calmed down, but there was still a division. Up until then there was a unanimity among the people. The real militants, who had done a real job in organizing, blamed me. John Shelton wanted to take me on. He had to be forcibly restrained. He was stopped by some of the older people, who told him that before he got me, he would have to go through them first. Then he simmered down. However, a lot of people came to me afterwards and said: "Hank, we should have gone after DiGiorgio that day." My reply was that there would have been a lot of people shot and killed, but they said that didn't mean a damn thing, we could have solved the problem then and there. But I kept saying, "We are fighting a long-term war, not just one battle." We were in a struggle that was overwhelmingly against us, anyway. I was concerned about the pattern for the future. If we had let this thing blow, high, wide and handsome, what help would it have been for other farm workers? This was the turning of the DiGiorgio strike. If the people had gone in on the DiGiorgio ranch, they would first have killed Sheriff Lousalot." I would have been shot down by his men. They would have broken through if they had to kill every state patrolman and deputy there. There would have been a slaughter on the ranch had they broken in. Every Okie, every Mexican, American or National alike, who was strike breaking there, would have died there, and a lot of good Union people would have died too. It would have been a wild one. I can still see those little old ladies with their glasses on. They were unafraid. They had clubs in their hands, and maybe guns too. After this march on the DiGiorgio ranch ended, the younger people drifted off. We set up a San Joaquin Valley Council. We organized and led strikes of cotton pickers, tomato pickers, and then we went into the Imperial.

The DiGiorgio Fruit Corporation turned to the National Labor Relations Board's general counsel for help in breaking the strike. Though farm workers were specifically excluded from benefits of the act, the NLRB filed suit in the U.S. Court in Fresno. Judge Hall ruled that the new Taft-Hartley Act required that he enjoin the NFLU for its use of the secondary boycott. Alexander H. Schullman, the able labor lawyer of Los Angeles, challenged this specious theory and tied up the National Labor Relations Board in litigation for several weeks. Said Al Schullman 30 years later: "Our argument was that you cannot impose sanctions on those not benefited by the Act. We appealed the Court's decision enjoining the union, to the National Labor Relations Board, and they held that we were right." After a Washington hearing on the NLRB injunction at which attorney Schullman appeared on behalf of the union, the DiGiorgio Fruit Corporation decided not to appeal the Board's final ruling.

Then there was Nixon and this congressional committee. Three days before the congressional committee arrived in Bakersfield to conduct its hearing, DiGiorgio sued the AFL, the AFL state federation, the Hollywood Film Council, H. L. Mitchell, Ernesto Galarza, Hank Hasiwar, and the NFLU, for $2 million each, claiming that the movie *Poverty in the Valley of Plenty* was libelous. The hearings of the House of Representatives subcommittee were held in Bakersfield on November 12, and 13, 1949. We still have the record of proceedings—edited by Nixon and other members—which shows that Nixon dominated the hearings, held by a subcommittee led by a Democrat, Cleveland Bailey, who was sympathetic to the NFLU. Nixon took over to show what he could do before an audience that had some growers in it. He was preparing to run for the Senate against Helen Gahagan Douglas. This was a good campaign opportunity for him. His deviousness comes out in his cross-examination of witnesses, but Galarza put him down forcefully. The subcommittee went to Bakersfield with a democratic majority, under a Democratic administration in Washington, probably to come up with a report that would support the strike, but then back in Washington, Representative Werdel, who was not even on the subcommittee, substituted a report written at the behest of the DiGiorgios and passed it off as the subcommittee's report. It was Werdel who put the report into the *Congressional Record*.

Hasiwar recalled:

The first time I met Richard Nixon was at the bar in the Bakersfield Inn. Neil Haggerty and I were there, at the end of the first day's hearing. We were sitting at a table. We didn't invite him over. He came over and sat down. Haggerty said "Hello" to him. Nixon said: "You guys are making quite a presentation. I think you have the case on your side." A few other remarks were passed, and I made one like—"I hope we have, but I don't think the facts are going to be accepted fairly by you." He sort of laughed. My general impression at the time was that Nixon would have made a good attorney in a prosecutor's office, if he didn't steal the place blind.

As I recall the next day's incident—he said that he just thought we were communists, but now he knew we were not. Just looking at this guy Nixon made me so angry! I knew that he didn't play a straight role. He had treated a lot of straight-forward farm workers whom I knew very well as criminals. Seeing the way this guy Nixon treated people who had suffered and sacrificed in this strike I guess it all just boiled over. I figured the son of a bitch should have a good poke in the nose. I didn't give a damn if he was a Congressman, or anything else. I felt that what he was doing to these people was terrible. I would have loved to flatten him, but I was stopped. Nixon came walking across the room. He walked like Charlie Chaplin with his red flannel underwear on. Mitchell and I were standing near each other. We were waiting for Ernesto Galarza, who always had a dozen things to do before he could take time to eat lunch. Then Nixon said to me and Mitch: "If you get into another hassel with these big growers, and they accuse you of being communists, just come to me, and I will straighten them out."The bastard had it coming, and I was about to let him have it. Mitchell, Haggerty and Al Schullman, one or all of them, stopped me. That guy Haggerty was always scared out of his beans every time I moved.

Ernesto Galarza recalled the way Richard Nixon cross-examined the six or seven witnesses who appeared for the union: "The thing I remember about Richard Nixon was the way he played to his audience. That room in the Bakersfield Inn was filled to capacity with growers from all over the state, who came to see the union raked over the coals, and Nixon was in his glory. I remember his face. Every time he made a point, like scoring the union for bloodshed or subversion, he would look up at his audience to see how he was doing."

It was not only a grower crowd at the hearing. There were actually twice as many farm workers there at all times than there were growers.

The pickets were kept on at DiGiorgio's ranch for part of 1950. Though no one knew it, the boycott was damaging DiGiorgio. Joseph DiGiorgio died, and his nephew Robert took over the empire created by the Sicilian lemon-picker. Alexander H. Schullman maintained contact with the younger DiGiorgio. At one point, Robert DiGiorgio indicated to Schullman that the Corporation might well have signed a union contract had the token pickets been kept on, and the boycott continued. However, the AFL refused to continue its support of a strike that the California labor movement considered lost. But the DiGiorgio strike had succeeded in spreading the idea of a farm workers union to all of the San Joaquin Valley.

Hasiwar goes on:

In the fall of 1949, the Associated Farmers felt sure that the attempt by farm workers to organize was dead for another twenty years. They held a meeting, and reduced the wage being paid for picking cotton from $3.00 per hundred pounds to $2.50. This meant a loss to pickers of at least $1.00 per day. Led by the dispersed DiGiorgio strikers, caravans began to roll through the west side from Bakersfield north to Stockton. Ernesto Galarza and I, by then the only Farm Labor Union organizers in all of California, became involved. Twenty thousand or more men, women and children engaged in picking cotton were called out on strike. The caravans would clear the ranches of pickers in one area. The rates would go up, and the caravans would move into an adjoining area and repeat the same operation. The State Mediation Service was seeking a way to bring about a settlement. The best they could do was get the principal cotton growers in California to agree to pay the high rate, and promise to recognize and negotiate with the union the next year. However, by 1950, huge cotton picking machines were in the fields. Workers were needed only to supplement the mechanical pickers.

That Winter of 1950 there was starvation in the farm worker camps. Children were dying of malnutrition—the polite name for starvation. The union and its friends back East enlisted the attention of *Colliers,* then a national magazine with a huge weekly readership. *Colliers* sent Lester Velie, one of its roving editors, to California. Velie wrote a series of articles called "Americans Nobody Wants." Velie later became a labor reporter for *Readers Digest.* Some claimed that he was unfair in exposing the likes of Hoffa and Fitzsimmons of the Teamsters and similar phonies in the AFL-CIO. Perhaps Velie's close association with our union had set a standard for labor organizers in Velie's mind that few others ever attained. Back in Washington, this series of articles set the stage for Mitchell to call on President Harry S Truman for the appointment of a Presidential Commission on Migratory Labor in American Agriculture. This commission made a thorough study and issued its monumental report in 1951.

In January 1950, the 16th Annual Convention of the National Farm Labor Union met in Fresno, California (counting from the first organizing meeting of the STFU in 1934). Here the union faced up to the problem created by the entry of hundreds of thousands of poor people coming from Mexico every year and being exploited by corporate farm operators on both sides of the Mexican border. *The New York Times* had given good coverage to the DiGiorgio strike; San Francisco Bureau Chief Lawrence Davies, along with his wife, attended every session of the union convention in Fresno. Afterwards they told us how impressed they were with the democratic conduct of the convention, delegates and officers alike. The Los Angeles bureau chief of *The New York Times,* Gladwin Hill, decided to do an article on farm labor and the illegal alien from Mexico.

Among those to attend the Fresno convention was William L. Blackstone, the one-time cotton patch preacher, the Arkansas organizer and STFU representative on the President's Committee on Farm Tenancy in 1937. Hank told of making a pre-organization trip through the Imperial Valley where he came across Blackstone:

I met Gladwin Hill in El Centro, and traveled with him to Indio, in the Coachello Valley, and found Blackstone in the migrant camp there. Blackstone gave Gladwin Hill the first clear picture he had ever had of the farm workers' view of the whole illegal alien problem. After three hours talk with Blackstone, Hill said he understood for the first time what the employment of wetbacks was doing to the whole farm labor structure in this country. Hill decided that he would tell his people on the *New York Times* that this thing loomed so large that he needed a staff of people to really expose the situation among farm workers.

The contact with Gladwin Hill coincided with an important event in my personal life. After having first driven down to meet the *New York Times* man in El Centro, there came a call from my sister-in-law that my wife, Delphina, was having a baby and wanted me. It was a 300 mile trip back. I must have done more than 1,000 miles in less than 24 hours. I got so damn tired that I was rolling off the road. I would ride off into the desert, come back onto the highway again, trying to make myself stay awake, but finally had to stop and sleep for an hour. I got to Bakersfield at 8:30 in the morning. The baby was born at 8:00—I was only a half hour late. After seeing the baby, Eugene, I returned to the Imperial Valley the next day. One thing about Delphina, she could understand. Del was Mexican, and she knew I was helping her people, although she regretted my being away all the time.

The Imperial Valley was home to the members of the Union. This was where they came back to live during the Winter time. From here they went to harvest fruits and vegetables; first to Phoenix to work in the Salt River Valley, then up as far north as Firebaugh in the San Joaquin Valley. After the melons were harvested, they would come back to the Imperial. They were all skilled workers, they knew the melons, and if given a fair rate, they could make a decent amount of money. They worked in crews and had their own deal. They did not work with labor contractors. We had just one area-wide Local Union for all of the Imperial Valley members. El Centro was the County seat for Imperial. There the Labor Council for the Valley had a three-story building with a hall in it. They gave us an office in the basement. We also got hold of an apartment across the way from the Union Hall, where we could put up all our guys like organizers, who came in later.

The organizing campaign for the melon strike was underway for a year. I was really trying to play this one right. I was not going to let them hurry me on this one. I had learned a lot in three years in California. I was getting clearances from the State Federation of Labor, the El Centro Central Labor Council and getting our organizers oriented. I had Ernesto Galarza in there with me. The members thought he was Jesus Christ. After the first few months, Ernie spent full time there in the Imperial. Bill Becker was working with us again, Mitchell got him on the AFL payroll some way. There was also Carl Lara, an electrical worker from Salinas. We also had my brother-in-law, Louis De Anda, with us from time to time. We had every Mexican-American farm worker in the Union, and tied in close one way or the other. We had almost 5,000 people in the Union.

The basic issues were well defined and understood by every one of our members. The local labor people, the townspeople, little businessmen, professionals and growers and their Imperial Valley Association knew what we wanted: The first preference in employment. Hire our workers who were local residents, then if there were not enough workers for the jobs, certify and bring in Mexican Nationals under the International Agreement between the U.S. and Mexico. Don't knock us out by flooding the area with wetbacks, or combination of illegals and nationals from Mexico. The business people knew that money earned by Mexican Nationals, whether contract workers or illegals, was being sent right back across the Border.

Before the strike came, we got clearance from Central Labor Council. We sent letters to all the growers. We called in the State Mediation Service to try to avoid a strike. After the growers did not answer, we put them all on the "Unfair List." As far as the American Federation of Labor was concerned, we were authorized to strike.

When our people went on strike, they all quit work at the same time everywhere. When everybody quit, they went directly to their regular meeting place. They had their own speakers. We would get information out to them as to what was moving and where, then they would go talk to people, telling them not to go back to work. They all enjoyed picketing, especially when we were picketing the Mexican Consul at Calexico. That SOB was the right arm of the enemy, the Imperial Valley Farmers Association. He was really shook up at the fact that he, a representative of the Republic of Mexico, was being picketed by Mexican American workers.

We were having meetings all the time, trying to pull things together. About 5:00 o'clock one morning, I was sleeping on a cot in the Labor Temple. One of the strikers came and woke me up. He said there was big trouble in a labor camp just outside El Centro. He said Bill Swearingen was there already, so I went out to the camp, and found four or five big trailer trucks loaded with men. We had about twenty pickets blocking the entrance to the camp, which had a wire enclosure. The sheriff's deputies were there. Our pickets were circling. Cruz Urquidez was talking to the wetbacks in the trucks. He was telling them that they were taking jobs from the Mexican people in the Imperial, and asking them not to do it. What the hell could I do? Had the deputies not been there, those bastards would have driven right over the pickets. The driver of the first truck came to me and said: "You have to allow ingress and egress, or we will run over those pickets." The pickets weren't about to move. If they had tried to run over the pickets, then Cruz would have shot somebody or got shot himself.

Suddenly I had an inspiration, and said to the truck driver nearest the pickets—"You are under arrest, I am making a citizen's arrest." There is a citizen's arrest law in California. If you see a crime being committed, it's your duty to make such an arrest. I had heard of this law at the time of the Jim Price shooting. I arrested them all, drivers and strike breakers they had brought in from Mexico. We carried them all to the Border Patrol, the Immigration and Naturalization Service. A new activity developed. All our members started making citizen's arrests of illegal aliens who were taking jobs in the fields. One day, the Chief of Police at El Centro called me, and said, "For Christ sake, Hank, why are you sending these people to me—take them to the Border Patrol." He went on to say that there were a couple of women there with forty wetbacks, whom they wanted him to put in jail. There was not enough room in the city jail for aliens. With everybody in the union going out and arresting wetbacks, soon there were none in the Valley.

Carl Lara had already sealed most of the Border crossing points, with his baseball bat brigade, proving when necessary that they meant business. Lara and his brigade slept so little their eyes were swollen from lack of sleep. Sealing the entry points and making citizen's arrests were the greatest demonstrations of what people can do on their own.

At the office back in Washington, I received a telephone call from Willard Kelly, then Chief of the United States Border Patrol, asking me to come over to the INS (Immigration and Naturalization Service) office at the Justice Department building in Washington. Kelly was enthusiastic, and told me that this was the best thing that had ever happened. He had already alerted the border patrolmen from Brownsville, Texas, to San Diego, California, about how union members were arresting illegal aliens. Chief Kelly wanted us to get the AFL and CIO in all the border states to take similar official action in bringing the illegals to the Border Patrol, who would put them across into Mexico. Of course, none of the other unions in the AFL or CIO were directly concerned. Soon after the Imperial Valley was cleared of illegal aliens from Mexico, a bill was introduced by a congressman from Texas to prohibit the arrest of an illegal alien except by a uniformed border patrolman. This became known in Washington labor circles as the "Hank Hasiwar Proviso." It was included in the McCarran Act revisions of the Immigration laws.

In summing up what happened, Hank said:

There was another thing that helped solidify the entire Mexican-American community behind the Union, and the strike in the Imperial. Casey Zuniga got going on organizing, and became known all over the Valley. His real name was Casimiro, but everyone called him Casey. He sometimes worked in the packing sheds, and since such work was not considered agricultural, Casey was eligible for unemployment pay. He was working as a volunteer for the Union. He wasn't paid anything. Sometimes the Local would buy gasoline for him. Casey picked up some unemployment checks. He was charged with collecting unemployment pay while working out in the fields, and was jailed. It was a phony charge. Here is what happened. On the first day of one of my infrequent trips back home to Bakersfield, just to see what my family looked like, Delphina woke me about 3:00 in the morning. Zuniga's wife had just called. Casimiro was in jail. She was very upset. I got dressed and went right back to the Imperial Valley, 300 miles away. I contacted that wonderful woman, Lolita Grande, who was the organizer for the Hotel and Restaurant Employees Union. Lolita was always at the El Centro Labor Temple every morning at 7:30. I asked her to get the bail bondsman, and we got Casey out of jail by nine o'clock. That sort of thing had never happened to a Mexican in the Imperial Valley. Casey's case never came to trial. Usually if a Mexican got jailed in the United States, it was about like it was in Mexico. They were in jail forever. Then I turned around and drove back to Bakersfield to spend a few days with my family, and take a little rest.

Soon after I came to work for the Union, Mitchell persuaded President Green of the AFL to put me on an expense account. The National Union was supposed to pay me a salary of $200 a month, and sometimes it did. However, the most important thing was the AFL payment of weekly expenses. Several times Mitchell was called into AFL headquarters to explain all the traveling done by farm labor organizers paid by AFL. Soon after the time I made the trip to take care of Casey Zuniga, he was called in by William Green, and asked how an organizer could be on the road for so many miles in one day, and do any work for the Union. Mitch told the AFL President that I was a most unusual organizer, so devoted to my work that I often would keep going with less than four hours sleep a night. He told Green why that particular trip had to be made, and how Casey Zuniga was bailed out of jail. Green accepted Mitch's explanation, and my expense account was paid.

During the Imperial Valley Strike, the C.I.O. Fruit Tramps in Packinghouses organized in Local 78 refused to honor the picket lines of the Mexican-Americans. Most of these C.I.O. members were Okies, and they were the aristocrats of agricultural labor. They had a union contract for several years, and good wage rates, but they were soon to face field packing of fruits and vegetables by contract workers and illegals from Mexico. Once the jobs were back in the fields, they had no recourse under the National Labor Relations Act, and soon saw their Union wither away on the vine.

After the Mexican-American workers in the National Farm Labor Union, which they called "SANTA" for Sindicato Agricolo de Trabajadores Americanos, had cleared the Imperial Valley of wetbacks, the U.S. Secretary of Labor, Maurice Tobin, broke the strike by certifying the need for contract workers from Mexico. Tobin, the former mayor of Boston, was undoubtedly the most political person ever to occupy the post of Secretary of Labor in any President's cabinet. He had come to Southern California, and met with the growers. Ed Pauley, the oil multimillionaire, had ridden back to Washington with him on a plane. Pauley was the Democratic National Committeeman, and chief bagman for the Truman administration. He had raised millions for the Democratic Party in 1948. Overnight, 7,500 certified Mexican Nationals were brought in under cover of darkness and installed in the labor camps. In spite of the law that said that a labor shortage could not be declared while a strike was in progress, there was nothing that the Union could do, except protest.

Joseph L. Rauh Jr., the famed civil liberties attorney who was also Washington Counsel for the United Auto Workers, had long been the attorney for the National Farm Labor Union AFL. Mitchell asked Joe Rauh and his staff to prepare the papers, and suit was to be filed in the U.S. Court in the District of Columbia, to enjoin the Secretary of Labor, who was clearly violating the law in authorizing the importation of Mexican Nationals to be employed as strike breakers against American citizens. Attorney Rauh and Mitch had a final meeting with Maurice Tobin, Secretary of Labor. Rauh told Tobin, after an hour's talk: "Mr. Secretary, you have a choice. Who do you want to sue you— the growers in the Imperial Valley, or the Farm Labor Union of the AFL?"

Mitchell said Tobin was squirming, jumping up from his big desk, rushing to the bathroom as if he had a case of diarrhea. He would return, combing his thinning black hair, to argue some more. Apparently there was a telephone in the toilet, and Tobin was in direct contact with the Imperial Valley Growers Association. In the meantime, the Assistant Secretary of Labor was over at the AFL headquarters awaiting the arrival of ailing William Green. Finally Green came in, and Ralph Wright persuaded the old man to contact Mitchell and beg him not to sue the Secretary of Labor. Green called Mitchell in Secretary Tobin's office, and said: "Brother Mitchell, please don't sue the Secretary of Labor. You know, the Department of Labor is *our* Department, and it would be bad for the labor movement generally for one of its National Unions to sue the Secretary." Mitch told Green that unless the Secretary agreed by noon to withdraw the Mexican Nationals being used as strike breakers, the suit would be filed. He asked Green to talk to Tobin in behalf of the Union. Then Tobin made another trip to his private bathroom, and was gone for a long time. He came back smiling, saying: "All right, Mr. Rauh, Mr. Mitchell, you have won. The Nationals will be moved from the Imperial within 72 hours."

Thinking we had won a great victory, Mitchell rushed out to telephone me and Ernesto Galarza of the Secretary's agreement. Galarza was in the El Centro office, and answered the phone. He said: "Mitch, the melon season is over. Our members are all heading North for the harvest about Firebaugh. You have won a Pyrrhic victory. Last night there was a meeting of the strike committee. We have called it off as of today."

This ended the Union's four-year struggle in California to establish a viable organization among farm workers. In the Imperial, everything had been done to assure success. The community was all for the Union, the workers had cleared the Valley of illegal aliens. The only thing lacking was an honest Secretary of Labor. Maurice Tobin dashed the hopes of the farm workers there for another fifteen years, by acting as strike breaker for the corporation farmers.

Soon I was transferred to Louisiana, and only Ernesto Galarza was left to carry on the battle for the domestic farm workers in California. The Imperial Valley was the place. I had the feeling that after going through so many strikes, building up organizations and seeing them torn apart, that this was it. We would have won, had it not been for the government breaking the strike. We all felt that way. Our guys were the only ones who really understood people and knew what it took to form a farm labor organization. This was because we were all basically socialists. It takes a socialist to organize people, unless you want to hammer the people in, like the Teamsters do today. They get workers into a union by economic pressure. They force people into unions. They sell the workers out. The union can also go the race or nationality route. That's what Cesar Chavez has done.

I have always disagreed with this highly nationalistic approach. I think Chavez is wrong, but then Cesar Chavez never really came up through the labor movement. He doesn't have the socialist ideals. He was trained by one of Saul Alinsky's men, Fred Ross, as a community organizer for the Mexican people. We came out of the socialistic movement. We had basic knowledge, every one of us. In the end, people learned from us. There were no Anglos, no Okies, no Blacks, no Mexicans, just human beings working for a living in a hard harvest. We had no race or nationality problem because we approached people on the basis that they were workers—that they were human beings first, last, and always. We didn't even discuss such things. It never occurred to us. We were just a group of individuals trying to help others get together. We believed people were more important than an organization. Maybe that's why we failed.

21 Ernesto Galarza: Man of Fire

Once again a delegation from the National Farm Labor Union was at the United States Department of Labor to see secretary Maurice Tobin, one of the first of the Boston Irish Mafia to make it in Washington. It was in the early 1950s and the strike of farm workers in the Imperial Valley of California, the first to occur there in nearly 30 years, was over. The young attorney, Daniel H. Pollitt, who had just joined Joseph L. Rauh's law firm, recalled that the delegation consisted of H. L. Mitchell, NFLU president, Ernesto Galarza, the union's research and education director, Monsignor George C. Higgins of the National Catholic Welfare Conference, and Gardner Jackson, the man led around on a leash by an underdog. There may have been others.

Here's how Dan Pollitt remembers it:*

We all walked in there. The Secretary's office was a large corner room with lots of exposure, thick rugs, and a huge desk behind which sat Maurice Tobin. Galarza walked across the long room to confront the Secretary of Labor with these words—"Mr. Secretary, you could sleep twenty farm workers in here very comfortably."

And Mr. Secretary replied very belligerently: "The last time I saw you guys, I thought it was understood that everything said was confidential, and the next I knew there was a press release."

It was obvious the Secretary was trying to intimidate us, but Ernie Galarza wasn't intimidated. He replied, "Yes, Mr. Secretary, you went back on your word. If you go back on your word again, there is going to be another press release. Just what have you got to hide?" I didn't know what to say or do, but then Father Higgins interrupted the exchange, saying something pleasant and trying to placate everybody at the meeting. Here was the Secretary of Labor, a big Democratic politician formerly Mayor of Boston, who had been chairman of the 1948 Democratic Convention the year that Harry S Truman nosed out Thomas E. Dewey for the Presidency of the United States. I had never even seen a cabinet officer before.

The bracero program operated under a law that said that contract workers from Mexico could be brought in, but the Secretary of Labor had to first certify that there was a shortage of American farm workers, and that the

*Joan London and Henry Anderson, *So Shall Ye Reap* (Crowley, 1970).

270

importation of braceros from Mexico would not decrease the wage rate or working standards of Americans. The law provided that the Secretary of Labor had to give all interested parties an opportunity to talk about it before such importations could be made. The Secretary had failed to do any of this, and had therefore violated the law. . . .

Sometime before Joseph L. Rauh had prepared the papers to be filed in the U.S. District Court, Rauh and his young associate Dan Pollitt were still prepared to sue the Secretary of Labor. Just as the meeting was about to end, Gardner Jackson asked Tobin if he had to clear everything he had agreed to with Edward Pauley, the national committeeman from Souther California. The secretary was again infuriated, for Jackson had hit home. He was referring to the well-known connection between these two: Tobin and Pauley had returned to Washington in the same plane, and the secretary had paid off part of the political debt by approving the importation of several thousand Mexican nationals to break the NFLU's strike of Mexican-American workers in the Imperial Valley.

Pollitt also recalled that most of the delegation who met with the secretary of labor then went on to the Willard Hotel Coffee Shop for lunch, and there they were joined by Marquis Childs of the *St. Louis Post Dispatch,* one of the most highly respected newspaper columnists of the time. All during lunch, Childs made notes on what the delegation told him about their encounter with the secretary of labor.

Pollitt said, "Here I was, a brand-new lawyer on my first assignment, and I had met with a member of the President's Cabinet, and I had lunch at the Willard with the Nation's best known news reporter. The National Farm Labor Union had few members and no economic or political power, and yet they could get a hearing in the highest echelons of the United States Government."

Years later Ernesto Galarza wrote about me, "Mitchell, a Southerner with the outward appearance of perpetual relaxation, said with a touch of literary elegance: 'Poor folks have poor ways.'"

Galarza would have had the union base its appeals to the public on angry confrontations with the bureaucrats like Maurice Tobin. I, known as the man with the soft approach, knew that the real enemy was the corporation type farm operator, and not his allies in government agencies. I was continually calling upon Galarza for more direct action in the field which I could use in Washington with the liberal and labor establishment that reached into the Congress and sometimes to the White House as well. This was the difference in our approach.

Ernesto Galarza was undoubtedly the most remarkable man ever in the farm labor movement in the United States. He was born in a mountain village in the state of Nayrit, Mexico. His mother was of part Indian heritage. His father was an overseer of an hacienda owned by absentee German landlords. Before Ernesto was six years old, the perils of the Mexican revolution of 1910 were swirling about the countryside. Like thousands of other Mexican people, the Galarza family fled to the United States. Crossing the border was no problem in those days. The problem was how to earn a living once they were across. Most of the refugees joined the migrant stream from Texas across what is now New Mexico and Arizona to the fruit and vegetable fields of California. The Galarza family eventually landed in the Mexican Barrio of Sacramento.

When he was a teenager, Ernesto had a summer job as a farm worker and lived in a labor camp alongside a ditch bank. While he was there, a child of another harvester died, his illness caused by the contaminated water from the irrigation canals. Someone had told Ernesto of a law to enforce better conditions for farm workers and of a commissioner of Immigration and Housing who was sympathetic. Ernesto peddled his bicycle 20 miles to Sacramento to see Simon J. Lubin on behalf of those who were ill and dying on the ditch bank. The men Lubin sent to investigate found Galarza's charges to be true, but as a result of his exposé, he was fired from his job. The Commissioner told young Ernesto that the farm workers ought to organize to secure better wages and living conditions. Galarza never forgot what Commissioner Lubin told him, though a number of years passed before he was able to do anything about it.

In the winter months, when young Galarza attended school in town, he got to know many kinds of people. He became friendly with one of the old-time members of the Industrial Workers of the World. The old Wobbly taught him much about life, and why things were as bad as they were. Another person who was kind to the young Mexican lad living in the Sacramento slums was a woman who followed the world's oldest profession. She allowed him to keep the money for returning her large collection of beer bottles, which she placed in a corner of the fence for him, but warned him never to come into her yard. Ernesto earned money also as a part-time messenger boy for Western Union. Soon after he entered high school (an unusual achievement for a member of his group in those days), he attracted the attention of his teachers. They encouraged the bright young Mexican-American boy to complete his education. With their help, he won a scholarship to Occidental College near Los Angeles. He graduated with honors. Once, years later, when invited along with Hank Hasiwar and me to have lunch with union supporter Margaret Fleming at her home in Pasadena, Galarza questioned his hostess about her neighbors. Ernesto was interested in knowing if such and such families still lived where he had once mowed their lawns to help pay his way through college.

Galarza was awarded his master's degree at Stanford University and in the early 1930s entered Columbia University in New York, from which he received his Ph.D. some years later. In the depths of the Depression he held odd jobs teaching, and in 1935 he became an employee of the Foreign Policy Association. Somewhere along the way he became a member of the New America group led by Dr. Harry F. Ward of Union Theological Seminary, who sought to translate Marxian Socialism into American terms. In 1939 Ernesto Galarza went to work for the Pan American Union (now known as the Organization of American States) in Washington. He soon rose to be director of Labor and Social Information for the Pan American Union. He traveled widely throughout Latin America and came to know most of the political and labor leaders who arose on the scene, even into the 1960s. Though he never met Fidel Castro, he believed the Havana lawyer had neither a program nor a philosophy for Cuba. It was Galarza's opinion that the cookie pushers in the U.S. State Department actually drove Castro into the arms of the Communist Party. Prior to the accession of Castro, the Communist Party in Cuba had been a minuscule organization, with no influence.

At one point Galarza was on a mission to Bolivia, where the tin miners were on strike. Ernesto tried to assist the workers. He and his wife Mae had made plans to settle down in their own home on the banks of the Potomac, looking forward to a secure life in the Washington bureaucracy, but they agreed that Ernesto should denounce the anti-labor role of the United States in the Bolivian crisis. This decision changed the course of their lives.

In 1946 Ernesto Galarza resigned from the Pan American Union. He was later to tell a congressional committee: "I resigned voluntarily, on account of illness. I suffered a stroke of *nausea* when I observed at close quarters the betrayal of the Bolivian tin miners and farm workers by the United States Department of State." He reported that a coalition government representing the tin barons, large landowners and communists was formed in Bolivia with American approval.

Galarza appeared at the first convention of the newly chartered National Farm Labor Union AFL, which was held in January 1947 at the Mount Vernon church, just across from AFL headquarters in Washington. While AFL President William Green was the principal speaker, perhaps the most significant address to the convention was made by Ernesto Galarza, who challenged the new AFL affiliate to organize Mexican-American farm workers. I asked him to come to work as an organizer. In about a year a program was worked out whereby Galarza was financed jointly by the AFL and the Robert Marshall Civil Liberties Fund. He was to make a survey of conditions among the nation's farm workers. Moving to California, he started his research project and assisted in the DiGiorgio strike then underway.

Ernesto Galarza and Hank Hasiwar worked well together, although there were never two more different people. Hank was an activist; the new "Director of Research and Education" was a sociali scientist. Galarza loved the title given him in lieu of a regular salary by the union president. Though he afterwards was elected vice-president, and later secretary-treasurer, he always preferred the title "Research and Education Director."

Galarza often became exasperated with both Hank Hasiwar, the professional organizer, and me, with my flair for publicity in behalf of the nation's farm workers. However, when he wrote of the long-term effect of the Southern Tenant Farmers Union and its successor organizations, Galarza was most objective.

In its dreamiest moment the STFU . . . regarded itself as an articulate organization of men moving irresistibly toward revolution. It was much less. None of the resources or levers of power were passing into its hands. Nevertheless it showed how, in a society like America's, power that cannot be transformed, can be resisted and .contained. It was a message that came through lightly in the soft speech of men like Mitchell, but one that became so magnified that it was still echoing in the marches of the Delano strikers thirty years later."*

The meeting with Tobin, and later with Marquis Childs, showed how the National Farm Labor Union with no economic or political power could yet get a hearing in the highest echelons of government. By combining the soft approach with appeals to the public through the news media, we disarmed the opposition, and brought pressure to bear to attain many things. Galarza would have had the union concentrate its activity on assembling information and then bring the facts to public attention in an angry confrontation with the bureaucrats. I always urged Galarza to get the masses of people moving on issues that directly affected their lives. Strikes and demonstrations for wages and better living conditions, action in the field, I knew, meant more in Washington than any number of thoroughly documented reports. Galarza never understood what Hank Hasiwar and our successor in the farm labor field, Cesar Chavez, instinctively knew—that "Green Risings" come

*Ernesto Galarza, *Farm Workers and Agri-Business in California, 1947–1960* (University of Notre Dame Press, 1977), p. 12.

into existence only when men are moving irresistibly toward revolutionary changes in their lives.

In 1953 Ernesto Galarza and I were attending a meeting of the newly formed United States-Mexico Trade Union Committee, which tried to work out some sort of reciprocal program for the braceros who were being imported into the U.S. by the thousands. The meeting was described in a dispatch dated December 14-16, 1953, by *The Industrial Worker,* a newspaper published by the radical native American syndicalist movement in the United States, the Industrial Workers of the World (IWW). Reported the journal:

> The AFL was represented by H. L. Mitchell, President of the National Farm Labor Union, and Ernesto Galarza, the Vice President of the same; Jerry Holleman of the Texas Federation of Labor, looking like a refugee from a millionaire's club . . . and some others. The CIO sent its second string: O. A. Knight, a midwestern Justice of Peace type, President of the Oil Workers International; Timothy Flynn, who resembles a harness bull on his day off; the old ward heeler, R. J. Thomas (one-term President of the United Auto Workers); Schwartz, the CIO's Latin American expert with the brain of a burlesque comedian; Frank Sternback of the Puerto Rican CIO looking like a fugitive clothing merchant . . . and others. For the Mexicans, there was the usual collection of criminals and hangers-on that are usually found about the Mexican Federation of Labor (CTM) as well as representatives of a number of independent organizations.
>
> Fidel Velasques, General Secretary of the CTM (who opened the conference), spoke slowly with that conviction of his own importance often found in protestant bishops, and with the careful enunciation of a clandestine drunk.

The article described the response of O. A. Knight, who was sorry that some American employers are cruel heartless men who exploit Mexican farm workers, and went on:

> H. L. Mitchell said he was glad to be there, and having traveled down to Mexico by automobile, and seen the poverty of the Mexican peasants, he could understand why they all wanted to come to the United States. On hearing this, the representative of the National Confederation of Peasants straightened his imported English gabardine coat and said that he was only a poor peasant. He hoped it wouldn't be taken amiss if he pointed out that through the unselfish and unstinting efforts of his organization, the living standards of the peasants had been raised to the level of the urban worker. One of the translators belched, and the "poor peasant" looked at him suspiciously. "The peasants never had it so good," he continued. "They just go to the U.S. for a lark." The rest of the assembly stared fixedly at their hands, and said nothing. The "poor peasant" said that in closing he wished to remind the gathering of the slogan of his organization: "Peasants of America Unite."
>
> Then another spokesman for the CTM asked why in hell they were meeting

here in the first place. A CIO man replied sadly that nothing could be done as long as the Republicans are in. A Mexican Senator said then that the Mexican worker has faith in his government, and confidence in its laws, but a CIO respondent said that the CIO does not have a touching faith in its government, and that results will come from direct action. The Mexicans looked shocked.

Easily the most outstanding personality at the conference was Ernesto Galarza of the AFL Farm Workers Union. His faded khaki shirt, open at the neck, as he pleaded with the Mexican leaders for cooperation in an organizational drive among the braceros contrasted sharply with the hand-painted ties of his bored and restless audience. This was the only important and concrete accomplishment. Among the papers the janitor swept out of the conference room were two copies of the Readers Digest, and a Hopalong Cassidy comic book. Most of the group from the United States, including the Mitchells, were there because the AFL and the CIO sent them, and paid their expenses. The only bona fide representative of farm workers on either side was Dr. Ernesto Galarza, who held a doctorate in anthropology from Columbia University.

One of Galarza's main contributions was in fighting the bracero program. This subsidy to growers, in the form of a captive labor force, erected a virtually insuperable barrier to the unionization of farm workers in the southwest. The program, which was started in 1942 during the wartime emergency, was continued for 22 years as a result of the powerful growers' lobby. So for almost a quarter of a century, over 4 million Mexican temporary workers were brought across the border under an international agreement to harvest U.S. crops. They not only displaced domestic farm workers, but they froze or cut back wages and working conditions. This was not supposed to happen according to the rules drawn up between the two countries. Galarza pointed out that it *was* happening. After running up against the growers' control of the bracero situation in the NFLU's Imperial Valley Strike, Galarza was reluctant to put more American farm workers in the position of losing their jobs to braceros brought in as strike breakers.

Instead, he began to investigate the operation of this giant giveaway program from the point of view of the braceros themselves. They were doubly jeopardized. First, since they spoke no English, it was hard to find someone to complain to. And second, if they did complain, they were sent home, thus losing their chance to earn badly needed American dollars. Galarza entered their camps, listened to their grievances, and won their confidence. He collected facts documenting violations of the international agreement. His 1956 report "Strangers in Our Fields" exposed widespread violations of the Labor Department's rules on pay, food, housing, and health standards for braceros. At first his charges provoked angry rebuttal; then red-faced officials began a series of reforms. Galarza's crusade was a step in the right direction, even if it didn't win jobs for American Workers or get rid of the bracero program outright. It would take ten more years and massive lobbying to do that.

Galarza in the meantime went on attacking almost everyone connected with the bracero program. He exposed the collusion of the officials of the California Farm Placement Service, a state agency, with private growers. He wrote stinging challenges to all representatives of the power structure, from the governor to the indifferent top labor men. This angry crusader stepped on a lot of toes.

His ten years, more or less, with the union exhausted this fiery Mexican-American, but gave him the material for several books. His book *The Merchants of Labor* was an expose of the bracero program, written partly from his own frustrating experiences. In *Spiders in the House and Workers in the Field* he described the machinations of several congressmen—especially Richard Nixon—hampering the NFLU's DiGiorgio strike. His 1977 book, written on the eve of his retirement, *Farm Workers and Agri-Business in California: 1947-1960,* sums up his entire experience as well as his tireless research into the subject.

This unusual man has also written books for children in Spanish. With his wife Mae, a teacher, he has been almost as interested in bilingual education, and education generally, as he has been in farm workers. All the issues important to the Spanish speaking community are important to him. His portrait and biography appear on posters in classrooms for Spanish-speaking children in the southwest. As a leader of his ethnic group, his example is used to inspire the young. He wrote of his own young days growing up in Mexico and Sacramento in his most appealing book, *Barrio Boy.*

Dick Meister, labor news reporter, published an article in *Rural America* in April 1978 that sums up the life of Ernesto Galarza:

Ernesto Galarza had a frustrating career as a labor organizer, but the experience, like everything else that happened to him, contributed to his progress as a writer. Whatever rebuffs he met in action he surmounted by writing about them. It can be truly said of him that he had the last word.

The shining black hair has turned white; the fierce, penetrating glare has softened; the words once shot out in sharp, intense indignity now flow at a soft, slow pace. It's impossible to believe, but Ernesto Galarza insists on it. He is retired. *Retired.*

At 72, Galarza has decided there will be no more organizing. No more slashing speeches against those who oppose what he thinks right for farm workers and his fellow Mexican-Americans generally. No more scholarly writing painstakingly documenting his bitter charges and angrily demanding reforms. No more teaching. No more controversy.

If Galarza maintains his resolve, he will silence what has been one of the loudest and, surely, most unusual of the voices that have been raised to demand economic and social justice for the farm worker. Galarza holds a Ph.D., has written a half-dozen books and numerous pamphlets and articles, and has taught at all levels, from elementary school to university. Yet he also has been an active union organizer, a key leader in laying the groundwork for the emergence in California of the farm labor movement led by Cesar Chavez.

22 Revolt in Rural Louisiana

The Strawberry Rebellion

In February of 1951 hundreds of desperate small farmers swarmed out on the highways of southeast Louisiana and stopped the movement of strawberries going to market. The farmers brought an end to all sales of the crop, including berries sold on roadside stands.

Because Louisiana's strawberries were the first to reach the market in the early spring, the growers normally received a premium price. However, in 1951 they were being offered about 6 cents a pint. The same berries were being sold to the consumer for 25 cents in the New Orleans supermarkets.

There were in 1951 about 4,000 farmers in Louisiana producing strawberries as their main cash crop on an average of three acres per farmer. They planted, cultivated and harvested the crop. The work was done by the family except for the picking or harvesting, when some workers outside the family were hired. The farmers then delivered the berries to a local handler who prepared them for shipment and loaded them on refrigerated trucks or in railway express cars. The strawberries were then sold at public auction in Hammond, Louisiana. This town was known as the strawberry capital of the nation. At the auction that was conducted each evening, there were only a few buyers, representatives of chain stores like A. & P. and Safeway, and some others who were buyers for fruit markets in Chicago, Baltimore, and New York. The little farmers knew they were being defrauded of the product of their labor and of the labor of their wives and children. Prior to the auction each day, the buyers would be seen meeting in the coffee shop at the Casa de Fresa Hotel in Hammond, next door to the log cabin where the auction took place. Individual farmers had often overheard the buyers agreeing among themselves as to the top prices they would pay for the berries at the evening auction. The prices offered had dropped from $4 per 24-pint crate the year before to a low of $1.50. This was the point of no return. The farmers went on strike and stopped the sale of strawberries.

While the strawberry production lapped over into adjoining parishes (i.e., counties), the center was in "Bloody Tangipahoa Parish," so called from an armed revolt back in the 1890s when cotton growers stopped the foreclosure of mortgages and forced-sales of their farm land, livestock, teams, and farming tools. The mortgage holders were mainly "cotton factors" in New Orleans, who lent money to farmers at high interest rates, then purchased their crops and sold them for their own profit. The city of New Orleans still had its own militia and sent heavily armed men to Tangipahoa Parish. The farmers fought pitched battles with these defenders of the big-city cotton factors. Thereafter there was fear and hate between city and country folk. Since then there had been a few uprisings of small farmers. One revolt occured in the late 1930s when a lawyer named Jimmy Morrison led a strawberry farmers' protest and afterwards got elected to Congress regularly, and was still serving his district in the 1950s. A dairy farmers' strike in 1946 has been described in an earlier chapter.

In 1951 after the farmers around Hammond had forced the strawberry price up to about $3 per crate, some started thinking about a permanent organization. They turned to the Louisiana Federation of Labor, which in turn called in the National Farm Labor Union of which I was president.

I could not get down there at the time, so I asked for help from the AFL and one of our long-time western associates, George Webber of El Paso, was sent in to help. We chartered a Fruit and Vegetable Producers Local that soon had a dues-paying membership of over 1,000. This was an unheard of development in our small national union, and Hank Hasiwar, our best organizer, was sent in to take charge of the situation.

On arrival in New Orleans, Hank first tried to locate Reverend Vincent J. O'Connell, a pro-labor activist of the Catholic Archdiocese. Hank left word at several places that he wanted to see O'Connell and asked that he telephone him. Instead, Father O'Connell arrived late in the evening at Hank's motel. The priest was an unusual man of wide experience. O'Connell came from a "lace-curtain" Irish family of Philadelphia and had received one of the best possible educations. He was a student at Munich when Hitler's *putsch* failed. In Rome, he saw the fascists in power under Mussolini. He was in Madrid when Franco led the revolt against the loyalist government. He was a surprise to Hank, who, though a lifelong Catholic, had previously met only establishment-oriented priests. Hank brought out a bottle of bourbon and offered the priest a drink. They talked throughout the night until the whiskey expired. O'Connell outlined his plan to organize both the small farmers and the sugar cane plantation workers and thus change the power structure of Louisiana.

Prior to Hank Hasiwar's arrival, the Fruit and Vegetable Producers Local had already worked out an arrangement for a one-desk selling agency. An expert sales manager, John Simpson of Hammond, had been hired full time at $20,000 a year. Simpson had also been promised a bonus or a percentage on all sales in excess of the fixed cost of production of fruits and vegetables he would sell for the farmers. The strawberry farmers were organized into some 35 units that covered the entire area. Each group elected its own leaders and had three representatives on the Executive Board. In the membership were several smaller cooperatives engaged in the business of handling the fruit for their members. These included the First Hungarian and Second Hungarian cooperatives, both operating out of the town of Albany, west of Hammond. There was also a strong vegetable growers' cooperative, composed mainly of black farmers, which joined. There were about 30 independent handlers who operated for profit. Most of them immediately signed with the union, making an agreement to handle only union members' products. There were a few holdouts among the handlers who defied the union early in the season. Hasiwar came in just at the right time, when direct action was required. He set up picket lines of farmers around the recalcitrant handlers' places. At times the going got rough. At Denham Springs a handler got a court injunction enjoining the union men from picketing his place of business. Hank mobilized the wives and children of the farmers to take over the picketing. Soon the handler was brought into line and signed the union's agreement. While the union was picketing a handler in the town of Ponchatoula, an out-of-state trucker insisted on going through the lines to have his truck loaded. The union pickets then would not let his truck out of the loading yard. Finally the driver came out alone and promptly got into a fight with two of the union's toughest characters— Louis Edwards, who was sergeant-at-arms for the union when the general meetings were held at Hammond, and Cassell Jones, a strawberry farmer and part-time construction worker. The trucker was knocked into a hardware store showcase. Edwards and Jones were arrested and thrown in jail. The following day the union arranged for a bail-bond for them, but they had to pay for the store showcase. Edwards and Jones reported to the executive board on the horrible conditions of the Ponchatoula jail. The executive board promptly made a donation to the town fathers to repair the jail so that it would be more comfortable if other union members were hauled in. None were.

The union also set up a credit union as soon as the strawberry season was over. A small percentage of each member's receipts was set aside as his credit union deposit. The union dues, which amounted to $24 a year, were still paid on a volunteer basis, but an average of 2,000 members continued through the year 1952. The National Farm Labor Union extended its insurance program to all of its new Louisiana members.

Every evening during the harvesting season, the union's executive board would meet just before the doors were opened to the buyers. There were 105 members of the executive board. In practice, any strawberry farmer—regardless of race or nationality—who was a member, who happened to be in Hammond, was automatically seated on the executive board while he attended the auction. It was soon noticed that the largest number of union members at the towns of Independence and Amite had Italian names. There the Baciles, the La Marcas, Guzzardos, and Loscarros led the list. In Albany the names of members were harder to spell because they were mainly of Hungarian descent. French names such as Broussard and Bourg were as common as Edwards, Jones, and Felders that predominated in Hammond.

John Simpson, the one-desk selling-agency manager, would have reports on strawberry prices from all over the country. He would advise the executive board members what he considered a fair and reasonable price to demand that evening for the day's strawberries. Usually the men accepted Simpson's recommendations. However, now and again there would be some stubborn farmer among them who thought they they ought to get more. Sometimes the figure was set so high that the buyers would not bid in the auction. Then Simpson would close the auction and get on the telephone, calling the fruit auctions in Baltimore, Chicago, Cincinnati, New York and Boston. He would tell his contacts that he had so many carloads headed their way by rail or truck and could deliver them on a certain date, if they would buy the lot. Simpson was so good at his job that by the end of the second strawberry season, the Louisiana berries were bringing in an average of $9 per crate. The farmers increased his salary to $25,000 and gave him a higher commission.

Recognizing that they had to have accurate bookkeeping, Leon

Porier, a young certified public accountant, was also hired to keep a continuous audit on the operations of the Fruit and Vegetable Producers Union.

The strawberry farmers got involved in politics. They set up their own political action committee, got out the vote in the primaries, and in the general election of 1952 endorsed Adlai Stevenson for President. Louisiana went Democratic that year by a narrow margin—by just about the same number of votes cast by the strawberry farmers. The state did not again vote Democratic in a general election until Jimmy Carter was elected President in 1976.

The union was making inroads throughout the state. There were some vegetables such as zucchini squash, cucumbers, and that table delicacy, shallots (which some people who are not French persist in calling "multiplying onions"), which were specialties of Louisiana. Shallots are grown in only two places in the world. One of these areas is some 40 miles north of New Orleans, and the other is in a river valley south of Paris. The chefs of both cities know the value of shallots, in cooking as well as in making salads. The shallot growers were quick to join the union, and they were followed by the cabbage growers west of the Mississippi. There was even talk of organizing a sweet potato cooperative near Opelousas, 150 miles to the west.

Due to O'Connell's influence, both the rural priests and the organized labor movement in Louisiana were cooperating with the farmers. O'Connell's plan, to bring social change to Louisiana, really appeared to be working. The small farmers were on the march. The union local was in reality a huge umbrella over small cooperatives. It was a movement that was bound to succeed. The politicians recognized it. Hank Hasiwar recalled that he and Lester Felder, president of the local, and George Forestal, the secretary-treasurer, were all invited by the governor, Earl K. Long of Louisiana, to come in for a visit.

Said Hank:

> We went to see Earl Long in the Governor's mansion. Long was sitting on a couch in the living room. There was a big fireplace, with a fire going in it, and the Governor was chewing tobacco and spitting juice into the fire. He had on a pair of black boots, which must have cost $150 to $200 at that time. He was wearing gray slacks and a white shirt. He just sat back, and said: "I think you boys are doing a hell of a good job, and I am with you all the way." He had asked a number of questions. I was impressed by the guy's attitude and approach. He knew every trail in the strawberry country. I remember a phrase he used: "I am glad you are doing this work because we are not letting those sapsuckers (the opposition) bleed you dry."

Hank also told about the local starting a newspaper called *The Union Farmer* "edited by an old guy who was once a Trotskyite, but was then a devout Catholic. The paper came out for about six months, and then the editor died. It was never revived. We had too many other problems at that time."

The FBI was likely called in to investigate the strawberry farmers at the time they started the action out on the highways. The Department of Justice sent in a special investigator in early 1953, soon after General Eisenhower was sworn in as president. Herbert Brownell, who had directed Eisenhower's campaign, and had subsequently been appointed Attorney General of the United States, was quite aware that the strawberry farmers had caused the Republicans to lose Louisiana in the recent election. About that time there was a charge pending against General Motors, alleging a conspiracy to violate the anti-trust act. However, Charles Wilson, former president of General Motors, was in President Eisenhower's cabinet and had already announced that "What is good for General Motors is good for the country." He saw to it that GM's case was dropped as soon as the Republicans came into office.

The strawberry farmers had no defenders inside the Republican Party, so they were prosecuted by the U.S. district attorney for conspiracy to violate the Sherman Anti-Trust Act. Hank Hasiwar, along with all the local officers, was indicted as well as the Fruit and Vegetable Producers Union. Our national union was not named in the indictment, which was announced in Washington but was assigned to U.S. District Court Judge Herbert S. Christenberry in New Orleans. We called on Daniel H. Pollitt, whom we designated as our "general counsel" in lieu of any kind of payment for his services, for advice. He had worked as a clerk in the law office of a federal judge in Washington and for a brief period had represented the National Federation of Milk Producers Cooperatives. Dan helped us work out a complete reorganization plan for the Fruit and Vegetable Producers Local. He prepared the papers and got them ready to be filed in the secretary of state's office in Baton Rouge. Lester Felder, the local president, was sent to Baton Rouge and instructed to file the papers, get a receipt, and keep everything in the office records. The union's lawyers, Joseph L. Rauh, Jr., Daniel H. Pollitt, and C. Paul Barker, all met with lawyers for the Anti-Trust Division of the Department of Justice. At their instruction, I wrote a detailed letter to Judge Barnes, head of the Anti-Trust Division, giving every fact in the matter. The attorneys for the Department of Justice then made an agreement with our lawyers, that a plea of *nolo contendere* would be accepted. They would recommend that a light fine be assessed against the local union, and other charges would be dismissed.

But no one counted on Judge Christenberry. (This was the same man who as U.S. district attorney in New Orleans had previously sentenced 91 striking dairy farmers to the federal penitentiary for interfering with interstate commerce.) At a preliminary hearing in his chambers, the results of an investigation were revealed. The local had not filed its certificate of incorporation with the secretary of state in Baton Rouge, to comply with Capper Volstead Act. Someone had blundered. Some thought the local's president, Lester Felder, had been paid off. In any case, there was no record of compliance with the law. Christenberry refused to accept the settlement worked out in Washington. The case of the 3,600 small strawberry farmers would go to trial in open court. Christenberry then asked if Hank Hasiwar had not also been involved in organizing the sugar cane plantation workers and calling a strike. The judge announced that if the law permitted him to do it, he would send the union organizer to prison for the rest of his life.

What actually happened was a severe punishment indeed. Hank was fined more than any of the local people. He was also given a two-year suspended sentence and forbidden during that period to take part in any further union activity. Thus Hank was lost to the union and to the labor movement. He joined his brother and his father in the oil distribution business in Yonkers, New York, where he still works today. Even worse than the loss of the best organizer for the farm labor movement was the complete destruction of the Fruit and Vegetable Producers Union. Soon the strawberry farmers gave up and quit, and California's frozen strawberries were shipped into Hammond. We knew there was a conspiracy on the part of the establishment in Louisiana to destroy— with the assistance of the United States District Court Judge Herbert S. Christenberry—the militant strawberry farmers' organization. They also succeeded in destroying a local industry. In the 1950s the strawberry crop produced was valued at over five million dollars. Twenty years later, sales of strawberries were less than a million dollars. Hammond was no longer the nation's strawberry capital. The center for production of strawberries by then was in California.

The Cane Mutiny of 1953

The first recorded attempt by farm workers to organize anywhere in the United States occurred on the sugar cane plantations of Louisiana on both sides of the Mississippi River in 1880. The *American Cyclopedia* of 1880 reported that

. . . this was not an uprising of blacks against whites, but one of employees and against employers, in the Parishes of St. James, St. John the Baptist, and St. Charles. During the month of March, Negroes went from plantation to plantation, requiring others who had not joined their movement to desist from work and to even leave these parishes. They rode about in armed bands, broke into cabins and frightened the inmates, took quiet laborers from their work in the fields and whipped them. Louisiana's Governor Wiltz issued a proclamation, but it had no effect on the rioters, and the militia was called out and sent to two or three points of disturbance. The ringleaders were arrested without bloodshed or difficulty and were brought to New Orleans, tried and imprisoned.

There were occasional flareups among the lowly sugar cane field workers over the 75 years that followed the strike of 1879. However, the real "Cane Mutiny" occurred when several thousand plantation workers voted to go on strike October 12, 1953. While the 1953 mutiny was led by the Sugar Cane Field Workers Local of the National Farm Labor Union, the strike was initially financed by the Roman Catholic Archdiocese of New Orleans.

Hank Hasiwar, the NFLU organizer, had come from California to organize for the union in Louisiana. In an oral history interview with me in early 1975, he told of being called in by Archbishop Francis Rummel, who put him through such a grilling that Hank said he knew exactly how the victims of the Grand Inquisition felt when they were interrogated before being put to torture. Finally, Hank became so exasperated with the Archbishop that he said to the elderly man: "Dammit, whose side are you on anyway?" Thereupon the Archbishop ceased playing the devil's advocate and gently asked Hank what he needed in the way of funds to see that no plantation worker's family went hungry during the strike. Hank did some quick calculating and replied that the local union would need $7,000 to keep going until I, as president of the NFLU back in Washington, could get out an appeal and receive funds from other unions in the AFL and CIO. Archbishop Rummel told Hank to wait until the following day, then go to see the pastor of the large church in Houma, about 60 miles west of New Orleans. Hank said he thought maybe the Archbishop was going to arrange for him to get a few hundreds for the union strike fund. He was totally unprepared for what occurred in the pastor's study the next day at Houma.

After Hank had identified himself to the older man, who was from Holland, and whose name Hank could never remember, the priest opened a desk drawer and began counting out twenties, tens, fives and one-dollar bills. The money was arranged in seven piles of $1,000 each. It was then put into a large paper sack. Hasiwar was asked to sign a receipt and was dismissed. Hank later learned that the priest at the large church in Houma was treasurer of the Catholic Charities for the Archdiocese of New Orleans. He got in his car, tossed the bag of money in the back seat, and took off for the union headquarters in Reserve. Hank was so excited at getting so much money that he felt he must have a beer. He stopped at the first roadside beer-joint and had two beers. Suddenly it occurred to him that he had left all that money in his car, and had not even locked the doors. However, Hank was lucky. No one going in or out of the beer-joint had been curious about the contents of the grocery sack in the back seat of the car. Hank arrived safely at the union office in Reserve, where the more practical secretary-treasurer, Frank Lapeyrolerie, received the Archbishop's money and deposited it that afternoon in the Bank of Reserve. So thanks to the Catholic Church, no striker's family went hungry that fall of 1953.

Two large mass meetings were held on Sunday, before the "Cane Mutiny" got under way the next day. One was held on the grounds of a church near Paincourtville (shortbread town), whose pastor was Father Maloney, a Josephite priest. The other was held in a roadside beer-joint near Houma, by an unusual character named Picou, who was black. Picou always opened each union meeting by rapping on the table with his loaded revolver. The organizer assigned to the Houma area was Joe Guidry of Lafayette; he was a graduate of the University of Southwest Louisiana, and had been teaching in an agricultural school. Joe had abandoned his teaching job when he first heard of the union. During World War II, he had been a bombardier, and his plane was shot down over the wilds of New Guinea. He and his crew bailed out and were led to safety by a native whose language they could not understand. During the days' long march, the men kept trying to assure their guide that once back at an American base, they would reward him. The guide kept repeating: "Want Push-em-Pullem." When they arrived at the base, they discovered that what the guide wanted was an accordian, to make music for his tribe. Joe Guidry was a French-speaking Cajun who was equally fluent in English. Hank used Joe as translator, since many of the field workers knew only Cajun French. This was equally true of both blacks and whites.

Prior to the mutiny, there had been many attempts to reach an amicable settlement with the sugar cane corporations and other large producers. Charles Logan, an advisor to the Archbishop, had intervened. Logan, then a leading labor consultant in New Orleans, boasted that as regional director of the NLRB in the early days of the Wagner Act, he had organized more workers in his region than all of the AFL and CIO staff organizers did. It was Logan who arranged a meeting between the Archbishop and the sugar cane growers. The growers were respectful to a prince of the church to which most of them belonged, and they promised to consider the Archbishop's plea that they just meet with a representative group of plantation workers. Once they were out of the chancery, however, none of them even replied to the Archbishop's offer of mediation.

The first days of the strike were more like a holiday. Instead of picketing, the men, their wives, and children all gathered about the rural churches, lodge halls, and other places where they had been holding meetings. They came in the early morning and left in the late afternoon. There was much preaching and praying, and singing of union songs and spirituals. Spencer McCulloch, a labor reporter from *St. Louis Post Dispatch,* sent to Louisiana to report the strike, could find no news, certainly no violence. In the beginning, there were expressions of sympathy from the sugar refinery workers organized in the CIO. The Godchaux Sugar Refinery Workers at Reserve gave the striking plantation workers $500, and each individual worker was called upon to make a personal donation. Students in New Orleans took to the street, taking up collections for the plantation workers. The Reverend Louis J. Twomey, Director of Human Relations at Loyola, mobilized labor union support and came out to attend meetings to encourage the strikers.

The Reverend Jerome Drolet, pastor of a church in the midst of the cane fields, who already had a reputation as a "Picketing Priest," came to Hank and offered his services for 30 days of his vacation to lead the picketing. Instead, Hasiwar suggested that Father Drolet go on with his original plan to visit his family in Illinois and then to call upon some of the top leaders of the AFL and CIO and ask for contributions to the strike fund. Drolet was most successful. He visited Pat Gorman, secretary-treasurer of the Meat Cutters in Chicago, and got a $1,000 donation, with a promise of more to come when it was needed. He next called upon Walter Reuther in Detroit, who said he would ask the UAW executive board to donate $5,000 if Drolet would persuade A. J. Hayes, president of International Association of Machinists, AFL, to contribute the same amount. Both the AFL and CIO affiliates came through with the $5,000 asked by Father Drolet. He also persuaded the International Ladies Garment Workers' president, David Dubinsky, to make a substantial contribution, and the Amalgamated Clothing Workers came through with an equal amount. While Drolet was out raising money for the union, back in Louisiana, there were some "Mean Things" happening in the sugar cane land. A back-to-work movement, led by International Representative Sutton of the United Packinghouse Workers of America, CIO, was started in a sugar mill owned by the Godchaux Sugar Corporation, which had been closed by the strike of field workers and the union sympathizers in the mill.

The other sugar corporations started bringing in strike breakers from distant areas unaffected by the strike. The Southcoast Company bussed field workers from Oaklawn plantation on Bayou Teche, 80 miles from the strike area. Some shotgun blasts were fired at the buses and trucks loaded with strike breakers, so they refused to work. The sugar corporations then arranged with a compliant U.S. Labor Department for the importation of 500 cane cutters from the British West Indies. This time, we were able to nip this strike-breaking tactic in the bud. The Latin American representative of the AFL, Serafino Rounauldi, and I called on the labor attache at the British Embassy in Washington. Together, we stopped the importation of British West Indians. The larger sugar cane companies began evicting the families of their workers on strike. The evictions were brought to a halt in many places, at least temporarily, by the labor law firm of Dodd, Hirsch and Barker of Baton Rouge and New Orleans. Nearly every man in this large law firm was set to work in behalf of the sugar cane plantation strikers. Among the lawyers then associated with the firm was John P. Nelson, Jr., who as the legman rushed from court to court, filing actions to delay the evictions. But then the lawyers of the American Sugar Cane League and the sugar corporations struck back. The anti-labor lawyers sought and obtained a local court injunction, prohibiting the union from striking during sugar cane harvest time. These actions by the employers were based on a specious theory first advanced by Richard M. Nixon, that since Congress had failed to include the nation's farm workers under social welfare legislation applicable to other workers, they therefore had no right to join together and act in concert. A local Louisiana judge expanded on the Nixon doctrine, holding that agricultural workers were also prohibited from striking when the state's principal crop, sugar cane, was being harvested.

Judge Hawkins, in handing down his decision, stated that he did not recall whether he was basing his decision on evidence presented in his court or on his own personal knowledge, derived from past employment as a supervisor for a sugar cane corporation. This decision was immediately appealed to the Louisiana Supreme Court which, with one dissenting vote, upheld the lower court's ruling. The injunction was so broad that attorney C. Paul Barker said that he was actually prohibited from advising the union and its members of their legal rights. I urged that we take a leaf from the experiences of the Industrial Workers of the World (IWW) in its free speech fights, and that we fill the jails of Louisiana with people defying the injunctions. We had successfully followed the IWW precedent in Arkansas in the past. However, since the peak of the harvest season was past, it was decided that the strike should be called off, that the sugar cane mutiny be postponed to another time. As Frank Lapeyrolerie made clear, the strikers would not have minded going to jail, but their families were all threatened with eviction from the cabins, many of which had been occupied by their forefathers in the days of chattel slavery. These were the only homes they had ever known. Thanks to the initial gift of $7,000 given to the union by Archbishop Rummel, and to funds raised by Father Drolet and the rest of us, no worker or his family had gone hungry during the 30 days the strike lasted.

Though we knew it would take time, we decided to appeal the Louisiana court injunction to the United States Supreme Court. I went to see the chief attorney for the AFL and asked for financial aid in paying the costs of filing an appeal. But the strike was over, and the AFL lawyers had no interest in fighting a lost cause. Joseph Rauh and I went to see Arthur Goldberg, who was then general counsel for the CIO. Goldberg said that though the case involved an AFL union (the National Farm Labor Union), the CIO would finance the appeal if our attorney would assure him that there was a chance of getting a reversal by the Supreme Court. Rauh said he could not give that assurance. Arthur Goldberg was later to become John Kennedy's Secretary of Labor. He served for a brief time on the Supreme Court, and finally he was chosen to be President Johnson's Ambassador to the United Nations.

So neither AFL nor CIO would act on the sugar cane field workers' behalf. However, we still had an ace-in-the-hole in the person of Daniel H. Pollit, one of Joe Rauh's associates, and later professor of law at the University of North Carolina, Chapel Hill. Pollit felt so strongly about this injustice that he found a way to cut the legal and financial bars of access to the Supreme Court. Since our union had no money to pay even the costs of printing a brief, several plantation workers joined in filing an appeal *In Pauperis*. It was known as *Picou et al. v. Southcoast Sugars Inc. et al.* Daniel H. Pollitt wrote the brief, Dorothy cut the stencil, I ran it off on the mimeograph machine, and we all three carried the required number of copies to the office of the Clerk of the United States Supreme Court. The case was accepted on the basis of a pauper's oath. About two years later the United States Supreme Court considered it. Justices Black and Douglas wanted to hear argument on why the sugar cane workers couldn't strike during harvest time. These two jurists, who nearly always voted on the liberal side of every question, considered Richard Nixon's theory so far fetched that though the case was "moot," they felt that it should be aired openly in court. The Cane Mutiny came to an end in the highest court of our land, and the Supreme Court of Louisiana was ordered to set aside the injunction it had upheld.

23 AFL-CIO and the Farm Workers

In 1958 the Industrial Union Department of the AFL-CIO made a grant of $25,000 to the NAWU to enable us to lay the basis for a broad organizing campaign among the farm workers. It had been possible for Dorothy and me to spend two months in California with Ernesto Galarza surveying the situation there. There were small groups of farm workers, mainly Mexican-Americans, with whom Ernesto had maintained contact. The leaders of these groups had been trained to assemble information to be used to attack the officialdom of the state and national employment service and the abuses in the "bracero" program under which more than 100,000 Mexican Nationals were imported into the state each year. Galarza considered this of greater importance than a frontal attack on the employers and labor contractors who still employed native American farm workers at lower rates of pay than were guaranteed contract workers from Mexico. I proposed to Galarza that he develop a program of hiring halls controlled by the union, and that he seek out small farm operators with whom he could develop a program of direct benefit to the workers. Galarza did not like this approach. I deferred to his judgment and we returned east. We stopped in Hammond, Louisiana, where we had spent the previous summer trying to revive the fruit and vegetable producers' union that had been smashed by an anti-trust suit upon the advent of the Eisenhower Administration.

After this grant, arranged for us by Walter Reuther, expired, we began to have serious money problems. The executive secretary of the National Sharecroppers Fund, Fay Bennett, was so deeply involved in the organization of the prestigious National Advisory Committee on Farm Labor that the monthly grant of $1,100 was being sent to the NAWU in dribbles and was always at least a month in arrears. There was no money in the union's treasury to meet expenses. Devoted organizers like George Stith could no longer be paid. Ernesto Galarza's $400 a month salary ended with the expiration of the Reuther grant. Had it not been for small savings Dorothy had made over the years, we and the union would have gone under before 1959. In desperation, I sent out appeals for funds. Two union leaders, old socialists John P. Burke, president of the Paper Pulp and Sulphite Workers, and Patrick E. Gorman, secretary-treasurer of the Amalgamated Meat Cutters, came through with $200 a month each. Eventually, Reuther's United Auto Workers sent us $600. On this we survived. I also persuaded the State Federations of Labor of both the old AFL and the CIO to let us use lists, or to make mailings containing an appeal for funds to celebrate the union's 25th anniversary, which was to be held in Memphis in the fall of 1959.

George Meany, president of the AFL-CIO, continued to evade the issue of an organizing campaign among farm workers. Letters and telegrams requesting meetings to discuss the problem sent to Meany by me, by A. Philip Randolph, by Walter Reuther, all were brushed aside. A strong labor committee that included Reuther, Randolph, Charles Zimmerman, a vice-president of the International Ladies Garment Workers Union, and Leon B. Schachter, then a comer in the leadership of the Amalgamated Meat Cutters International Union, had made no visible impression on the stolid Meany.

The AFL-CIO Promises Aid to Farm Workers

Early in the year an event occurred that was the culmination of a long public relations campaign. This campaign began with the meeting that we of the NAWU had held with Walter Reuther in Pat Jackson's living-room a few years before the merger of the AFL and CIO. Walter Reuther made a promise that night and I found ways to hold him to it throughout the following seven years.

So, on February 5th and 6th of 1959, a public inquiry into the plight of the nation's farm workers was held in Washington, by the National Advisory Committee on Farm Labor, a prestigious organization made up of the liberal establishment. It had grown out of the National Sharecroppers Fund, established first in 1936 to raise money to keep the Southern Tenant Farmers Union alive in the South. Among those taking part in this unusual inquiry was Eleanor Roosevelt. A. Philip Randolph, who was then the best known civil rights leader, was chairman of the dinner meeting the first day. Helen Gahagan Douglas was the narrator of a drama called "Out of Their Poverty." Among the speakers introduced by Mrs. Roosevelt were James P. Mitchell, Secretary of Labor under Eisenhower, and John M. Seabrook, president of Seabrook Farms of Bridgeton, New Jersey. Both men endorsed the extension of the minimum wage law to workers on larger farms. Jack Seabrook humorously described the dealings he and his father had with

Local 56 of the Amalgamated Meat Cutters for the past 15 years. Sea-brook advised the group not to send "do gooders" out to convince farmers, but to send farmers like himself, who had learned that there were profits to be made by a unionized force of better paid farm workers.

William F. Schnitzler, then secretary-treasurer of the AFL-CIO, in an address to the group pledged that the "manpower and resources of the AFL-CIO would be put into an organizing drive to unionize the nation's farm workers." Schnitzler departed from his text to praise the National Agricultural Workers Union and its indefatigable leadership. In this regard, he may have been speaking for some of the members of the AFL-CIO executive council, but he was not necessarily speaking for Meany who had at last been brought to bay by the nation's mobilized liberals. Frank Graham and Norman Thomas were those who con-tinued to keep the AFL-CIO on the ball following this promise of active aid in organizing farm workers. Without continued support by Reuther and Randolph, the organizing would never have gotten underway.

Walter Reuther was aware of the plight of the NAWU and sought a solution. The AFL-CIO executive council had increased its per capita tax by one cent and allocated money to support an organizing campaign among farm workers, based on a program which we had worked out. Reuther and Randolph proposed that the AFL-CIO put both Ernesto Galarza and me on the payroll as organizers. This Meany refused to do. He had not forgotten the questions raised by European trade unionists as to the lack of organization of American farm workers. Meany also held me responsible for the formation of the National Advisory Com-mittee on Farm Labor, which had mobilized public opinion so effec-tively that he was forced to move in the farm labor field, much against his will.

It was at this point that Meany told Randolph and Reuther that he would not have Mitchell involved in the campaign even as a file clerk. Reuther again repeated his saying about my having been a legend in the South while he was still just a punk in an auto plant. Later Meany was to agree that Ernesto Galarza would have a part in the AFL-CIO organizing campaign. Soon after this meeting with Randolph and Reuther, I was told by Reuther that the best thing to do was to work out a merger with the United Packinghouse Workers. He suggested that I go out to see Ralph Helstein in Chicago.

We'd had some problems with this union earlier. As soon as the AFL-CIO merger became a reality, the National Agricultural Workers Union had picked up two local unions of sugar mill workers in Louisi-ana with over 500 members. The affiliation of these workers brought on a bitter jurisdictional dispute with the United Packinghouse Workers of

America (UPWA), once a CIO affiliate. As a precondition for launching an organizing campaign, the NAWU was required by the AFL-CIO to turn these workers over to the UPWA. About this time I wrote to Ernesto Galarza that it seemed to me that the labor movement would like to see us go away, or be swept under someone else's rug. Nevertheless, I went to Chicago and met with Helstein, who claimed he had not even been informed by Reuther of such a proposal. He pointed out that his own organization was then losing members. The stockyards were being shut down and moved to the rural areas. Helstein agreed that he would take in farm workers if Reuther would see that money and other resources were placed at his disposal. "However," said Helstein, "we are eventually going to merge with the Meat Cutters, even though negotiations are now at a standstill." It was then that I went to see Patrick E. Gorman at the new headquarters of the Amalgamated Meat Cutters, out on Sheridan Road. Gorman was willing to make a place on his organizing staff for me and Galarza, but would promise nothing more. In 1956 there had actually been a plan for a three-way merger, involving United Packinghouse, National Agricultural Workers and the Fur and Leather Workers. The Fur and Leather Workers had been one of the unions expelled by CIO as communist dominated. Pat Gorman, the maverick of the labor movement, defied the establishment again and took them in. Since it was known that we had been the first group to break away from the CIO on the communist issue, our coming into the Meat Cutters would have been good public relations, even though we represented few dues-paying members. Gorman told me to discuss matters with my friends Leon Schachter and Harry R. Poole.

AFL-CIO Enters Farm Field

Soon after I returned to Washington from Chicago, I was called in by John W. Livingston, a former UAW Vice President who was then director of organization for the AFL-CIO. Livingston told me that his department had drawn up a budget of $150,000 for a year's operation of an agricultural workers organizing committee. I protested that this was entirely too much, that there were only a few of us who had experience in the field and we were unaccustomed to such sums. I suggested an alternative of perhaps $50,000 for the first year, and that the balance be held in reserve to be used in the event of strikes. Jack Livingston said that the Executive Committee of AFL-CIO would likely cut it down to half the amount he was requesting, so why not ask for the whole amount? Under those circumstances, I agreed. The next problem was naming a campaign director. Livingston said Reuther told him to contact Norman Smith, once a United Auto Worker organizer whom I had known back in Memphis in 1937. Smith had been beaten nearly to death by Ford and Firestone company police while attempting to organize the Ford plant in Memphis. He had often been over in Arkansas to speak at STFU meetings. I had not heard from him in over twenty years. It seemed to me that if Norman Smith, one of the old timers from the UAW, was acceptable to Walter Reuther, I could not object. I suggested that the campaign be based in Stockton, California, an area in which we had had some success and where Galarza had developed good local leaders. One of them, Raul Aguilar, had been working there for the past few years. It was also near Delano, where the Filipinos led by Philip Vera Cruz had won a partial victory in 1952, when they struck the huge Schenley grape ranch. I was assured by Livingston that Meany would agree to Ernesto Galarza being made assistant director, and that he, Livingston, would see that deserving organizers in California and elsewhere would be put on the AFL-CIO payroll. I figured that as long as our monthly grant of $1,100 from the National Sharecroppers Fund was forthcoming, we could keep an office open in Washington and continue lobbying activity in behalf of farm workers.

Conflicts in AFL-CIO Organizing Committee

Soon after the campaign was launched in California, problems of conflicting jurisdiction arose. It had been agreed, or so I thought, that all farm workers organized by the new Agricultural Workers Organizing Committee would come directly into the NAWU, and those workers who were in related agricultural industries such as canneries and packinghouses would be turned over to UPWA, headed by Ralph Helstein. Galarza began making reports of how the UPWA staff was moving in to take over all workers being organized. He indicated that Norman Smith was actually favoring the Packinghouse people over the Agricultural Workers. I protested directly to Smith, to Livingston, Reuther, and others. Smith froze all dues collected from members, cutting off even the small income we had been getting from a few local unions remaining in California. When next I met Randolph and Reuther, there was an interesting development. Walter Reuther said George Meany had agreed that $7,500 a year of AFL-CIO funds could be set aside, and that the Industrial Union Department which Reuther headed would match this amount. This could be used to pay me a salary. I would also be furnished an office and a secretary by the IUD, and continue as a spokesman, and as a kind of "tribune in Washington for the nation's farm workers." I told Walter that I could accept as reality what he said that the IUD would do, but that after even one year, I feared that George Meany might rescind his offer. I asked Reuther if his IUD would underwrite the proposed operation. "No," said Walter, "the AFL-CIO money would be given to one of Dr. Frank Graham's organizations and channeled that way to you." I could surmise that this would be the National Advisory Committee on Farm Labor. It was a huge amount—$15,000. I had never had a salary of more than $4,800 in a single year, and often not half of that was actually paid to me. Reuther said he would send me a letter saying that United Auto Workers would guarantee the amount for a period of years, in the event either AFL-CIO or the IUD reneged on the arrangement. Such a letter was eventually sent me. It is in the STFU Papers. The amount mentioned, however, was $7,500.

I talked to Leon B. Schachter after this Reuther proposal. He advised me to accept the offer, but I told him that I was tired of the frustrations of Washington. I also said I didn't want to become involved in a battle with Fay Bennett over the control of either the National Sharecroppers Fund, *or* the National Advisory Committee on Farm Labor. She was Executive Secretary of the fund and devoted to the cause she served. She had many fine personal qualities, but the ability to get along with subordinates was not one of them. I had no intention of ever being placed in such a position. Schachter said he would talk to Gorman again, and that if Galarza and I would come with the Amalgamated, we would be paid a salary and given an expense allowance, but that we should not expect the Amalgamated Meat Cutters to launch a drive to organize farm workers. Said Leon: "We don't even spend the money needed to organize meat packing plants, which are a part of our basic jurisdiction, but if you will help organize meat departments in the large chain stores with whom we have national agreements, you will be Pat Gorman's favorite organizer. Pat has never let an organizer go yet, so all you have to do is to keep trying." This later proved correct.

One evening in June 1960, Harry R. Poole, destined to become president of the Amalgamated in the mid-1970s, and Leon Schachter came to Washington. We had dinner and spent the evening at my home on 37th Street NW, on the edge of historic Georgetown. It was agreed, as Ernesto Galarza afterwards put it, "to submerge" the Agricultural Workers into the Amalgamated Meat Cutters and Butcher Workmen of North America AFL-CIO. So after being one of the smallest of the international and/or national unions, we joined one of the largest in the AFL-CIO. My work continued much the same as ever, but though I was low man on the totem pole in the Meat Cutters, the pay was regular, and I continued for nearly twelve years. Among those I helped organize were the pogy boat fishermen or the "Sharecroppers of the Sea."

24 Down South Again

One day a roly-poly man about five feet tall and about as broad, rolled into the Washington office of the National Agricultural Workers Union. My door was open, and he asked me: "Where is Ernesto Galarza? He promised to meet me here at 9:30." I replied that Ernesto was always a few minutes late, but that I was sure he would be in soon. The next question fired at me was, "What the Hell are you drinking so early in the morning?" I said I had ulcers and was drinking milk. My visitor pulled out a container from his coat pocket, and said, "Mix this with your milk. It will go down easier." I gave him a questioning look, and he introduced himself. He was Emil G. Conason, a doctor of medicine and a chemist who had worked on the Manhattan Project in World War II. He was a friend of both Ernesto Galarza and Pat Jackson, but I had never heard of him before. He told me that the container he had just given me held Amino Acid, a rich protein more highly concentrated than milk or any animal source. He and a colleague had just developed this powder in a laboratory set up by the Schenley Distillers in New York City. So I tried out the remedy and could detect no taste. He later sent me a keg of the Amino powder and I used it. We continued talking, and among the things he said was that there was only one way for me to cure my ulcer, and that was to get rid of the union, and let some one else assume the responsibility I had been carrying for so long. Dr. Conason was right. The final steps were taken in August 1960, when our National Agricultural Workers Union was merged into the Amalgamated Meat Cutters. Within a year the ulcers were gone, and I was back down South again, at the age of 54.

When Dorothy and I returned to Memphis, I called a meeting of the leaders of the remaining locals of the NAWU nearby. A group of men and women, most of whom were much older than I, came to meet me. I soon realized that conditions on the cotton plantations had radically changed in the twelve years since I had left the area for Washington. Only the older people remained in the rural communities, and only a few still had a place on the cotton plantations. There was year-round work only for a few tractor drivers and most anyone who could drive a car could soon learn to ride a tractor and pull the multi-row culti-vators and mechanical cotton pickers. The labor of women and children was almost at an end in the cotton fields. Some were still employed to chop cotton in the spring and to glean the fields after the mechanical cotton pickers had harvested 90 percent of the crop. There were a few old-time members of the Southern Tenant Farmers Union who held on in Arkansas, Mississippi, and Missouri, and most of them were drawing social security benefits. Obviously they could not pay the dues charged by the Amalgamated Meat Cutters and Butcher Workmen of North America. However, our National Sharecroppers Fund had agreed when we joined the Amalgamated Meat Cutters to make a special grant of $300 a month to enable us to continue the $250 death benefit insurance plan we had for these older members of the union.

So they were all given free membership cards. Since it was hopeless to undertake an organizing campaign in the cotton plantation country, we turned our attention to south Louisiana. There, in Bogalusa, we still had a small local of dairy farmers and dairy plant workers. There were also good contacts in the sugar cane country and in the rice mill towns like Crowley over in the southwestern part of the state.

The vice president and district director for the Amalgamated, Sam Twedell of Dallas, came to meet me in New Orleans to pave the way for the Agricultural and Allied Workers Union Local 300, as we now called our union, to come into the state. There were already three other local unions of the Meat Cutters in Louisiana, and the officers of the large one in New Orleans feared the entry of another. They were also concerned about the new organizer, who had been the president of a national union. I tried to assure them that I had no intention of inter-fering in any way with their organization. I pointed out that if we were successful in unionizing agricultural workers and related industries in the rural areas, they would find it easier to organize the chain store employees in the smaller towns. I also said that eventually their local union would likely become the home of the organized workers who first joined Local 300. This proved to be true twelve years later.

Among the first people whom I contacted on arrival in Louisiana was Frank Lapeyrolerie of Reserve, Louisiana. Frank was the man who had helped Hank Hasiwar organize the sugar cane plantation workers in 1952 and had become secretary-treasurer of the Sugar Workers Local that led the strike in 1953. Frank was a native of the plantation country alongside the Mississippi River. He was highly regarded by both blacks and whites in the area. The white power structure turned to him when the cooperation of the Negro people was needed. But Frank Lapey-rolerie was his own man. He owed no one a thing. Instead, others were indebted to him for past favors. He was active in the Catholic Church and a leader of the Knights of Peter Klaver. He had belonged to the NAACP and had mobilized people to vote for their own interests long before the civil rights movement started. Frank told me when I went to see him that the reason we failed to win the strike in 1953 was not just the court injunctions that enjoined even the lawyers from advising the union men of their rights, but the strikers' fear of being evicted from their homes on the plantations.

We decided that we would first undertake to organize the rice mills and get a plantation worker housing program started. So I made headquarters in the town of Lafayette. There, 70 percent of the population was Catholic, and many spoke only Cajun French. Like most ethnic minorities, the Cajuns told many stories among themselves. One of the first things I did in Lafayette was to rent a post office box downtown. The streets were narrow and had many twists and turns, so for a long time I would get lost every time I went to the Post Office for my mail. This reminded people of the story of a stranger who lost his way in the maze of Lafayette streets and asked a little Cajun boy,

"Where is Theriot Street."

The boy replied, "I dunno."

The man commented, "You are pretty dumb, aren't you boy?"

"Maybe so," said the child, "but I ain't lost like you are."

Over in Crowley, 20 miles away, there were nearly 30 rice mills. At one time, our union had contracts with several of the mills, so I contacted two former rice mill workers, Earl Wilson, a black, and Gene V. Collins, a white. Gene Collins had been named for Eugene V. Debs. His grandfather and grandmother had lived in the socialist-sponsored New Llano Colony near Leesville. Gene's father had been a rice mill engineer, and Gene had also served as his assistant in the mill owned by the Godchaux family. He was now a deep sea diver and was constantly being called out to help salvage ships, or to do some work for the army engineers on their drainage projects. Earl Wilson had been involved in an attempt by the Teamsters Union in the late forties to organize the rice mills. Wilson and the Teamster organizer Leo Carter had led a protest march on city hall and won voting rights for the black people of Crowley in 1947. Wilson now had a job with the city. With the help of these two men, we called meetings and soon had over half the rice mill workers signed up.

I had never had anything to do with elections conducted by the National Labor Relations Board. I went to see the labor union attorney who had been so helpful when the sugar cane plantation workers went on strike in 1953. C. Paul Barker wanted a large retainer and a guarantee of his expenses from the Amalgamated Meat Cutters. This I knew would not do, so I called on James E. Youngdahl who had been an organizer for the Amalgamated Clothing Workers Union in Louisiana a few years before. Jim was in Little Rock with a new law degree doing uninteresting work on behalf of a large firm that included a former governor of Arkansas, Sidney McMath. He came down to help me, with only his expenses assured. The rice mill operators association had already employed the firm Kullman & Lang of New Orleans to represent them. This law firm was one of several in the South who sold employers a package deal guaranteed to defeat any attempt to form a union.

Sam Lang, who was once regional attorney for the National Labor Relations Board, had set up the firm. He surrounded himself with young lawyers who had also worked for the government agency concerned with workers' rights. These men all had ties within the NLRB. So Kullman & Lang always knew every move a union was making. The anti-union campaign would start with the employer or manager of the plant calling the workers together with an attorney from New Orleans present. There was a set speech, about how unions were all rackets, out to get the workers' money. They were told that each man would have to pay a huge initiation fee equal to a month's wages, and each month thereafter he would have to pay dues, and then there would be fines assessed against members who failed to attend meetings, even if there was illness in a worker's family. This was followed by a series of letters signed by a top company official, which was sent to each employee's home. One of these would tell of a strike where violence occurred and many people had been killed or injured. Then the night before the election was scheduled to be held, the company would invite each worker and his wife to a dinner paid for by the company. At this dinner meeting there would be scare speeches, and a movie called "And Women Must Weep" would be shown, depicting a trailer house with bullet holes in the doors and windows. A baby in the cradle covered with red paint ended the film. Without it actually being said, the impression was left that this had all occurred in a recent strike, and that the union people were gunmen and killers of children.

I had petitioned for elections in 26 of the rice mills; 16 elections were actually conducted by the NLRB, of which the union lost fifteen. The others were called off in the face of this kind of campaign of fraud and misrepresentation by the employers. The one mill where the workers voted union was quite small. The company could not afford to pay the fee charged by Kullman & Lang. Edwin Edwards and his brother, who were lawyers in Crowley, represented the small rice mill owner. Edwin

Edwards later became Governor of Louisiana. I remember Gene Collins and I going to Edwards' office to discuss a contract. Edwards warned us humorously that if we worked out a contract, our members' dues would likely have to be paid in rice. He said the employer had promised to pay his fee in that commodity, and the workers were now required to take a portion of their wages in rice. A contract was signed, but soon the employer closed down. The secretary-treasurer of the Rice Millers Association, who had been in high school with Gene Collins, called him and said he would like to know if the union was going to continue its campaign in Crowley. The man said that the retainer charged by Kullman & Lang was so high that the association was broke, and the smaller millers just could not pay any more such fees. This was my introduction to the workings of the National Labor Relations Board, an agency established to assure industrial workers of their right to organize and bargain collectively with employers. The law had been amended, and some of the current employees of the regional office had been corrupted. Many of the lawyers employed by the New Orleans NLRB were bucking for a connection with the anti-labor law firm of Kullman & Lang.

We soon moved on to Lake Charles, Louisiana, in the southwest corner of the state. Lake Charles was a strong union town. The petrochemical industry and the building trades were all unionized. The year before, the Amalgamated Meat Cutters had narrowly lost an election in the Louisiana State Rice Milling Company there. In Lake Charles, I met big Charles Stanfield, and his partner, Willie Berry. Stanfield had supported his black partner for the office of president of the Lake Charles local, which was composed of packinghouse workers and some chain store employees. The packinghouse had been closed down, so Charlie lost out as secretary-treasurer and business agent, and Berry was no longer president. Stanfield had just been hired as an organizer by a large local union in Arkansas, but his family was still living in Lake Charles, and he saw them sometimes on weekends. He provided me with lists of names, and together we worked out a plan to get Willie Berry to help me organize the rice mill where many of the workers were blacks.

I also attended the meetings of the Lake Charles Central Labor Council, composed of all the unions in the area. I asked for their help. The council passed resolutions in favor of our campaign and some individuals tried to help, but the building tradesmen withheld their support. I recalled what Fred West in Bakersfield once told Hank Hasiwar: "Don't worry about the employer, just watch the building trades unionists. They will stab you in the back." The aristocrats of labor were afraid of me, even in Lake Charles. They remembered how we had denounced the State Federation of Labor for sponsoring a special "Right to Work" law against farm workers in 1955, as almost its first act following the AFL-CIO merger.

It was Victor Bussie, the newly elected president of the state AFL-CIO, who introduced it in the state legislature and lobbied for the anti-union right-to-work law. This was done with the support of the Sugar Cane League, the Farm Bureau, and other farm representatives in return for repealing a similar state law applying to industrial workers. Bussie openly made a deal to trade off the rights of the sugar cane workers, the rice mills, and other agricultural industries.

However, he didn't know about people like Ernesto Galarza, Pat Jackson, and me. We reached Frank Graham, Norman Thomas, and Mrs. Roosevelt. A national public denunciation of AFL-CIO for its anti-labor actions in Louisiana hit the press. The AFL-CIO executive council had the item on the agenda at its summer meeting, and tried unsuccessfully to counter the bad publicity caused by the Louisiana incident.

The Lake Charles rice mill election was held, and the union gained a few more votes, but not a majority. Kullman & Lang was not involved. The company lawyer was a local man, Everett Scott, a fairly decent guy. About the same time, the union won an election in a small rice drying mill with about 15 employees. The union won hands down, but the employer, who was away at the time of the election, returned and filed a complaint with the Labor Board, claiming that the workers were agricultural and therefore exempt from protection by the NLRA.

Shortly thereafter, the union won a contract with Leading Dairy, a Lake Charles milk producer, without even holding an election. Under the law, an employer and a union of his employees could enter into a voluntary agreement if the union showed by signed cards that it represented a majority of the workers. This was done at Leading Dairy. We started advertising the product of this small dairy as all-union. Some of the families of the labor union members cooperated in buying union milk, but the "building tradesmen" sabotaged our program.

We were called upon by a group of young drivers and plant employees working for the Borden Company of Lake Charles. All the men signed up. Again we tried to get the support of the Lake Charles Central Labor Council. A committee was appointed to call on the plant manager at Borden. It was headed by a building tradesman. He allegedly paid a call on the plant manager, but reported that Borden Company demanded that we go through an election. This time the firm of Kullman & Lang was called in for the first time in Lake Charles. The round of letters was sent to the workers and their families. Young wives were called and told if their husbands didn't leave the union, they would be attacked out on their routes. The company called the families to the final dinner, and showed the movie "And Women Must Weep." I filed charges against the company for misrepresentation of the union. By that time I had sworn statements that our union had never been charged with or responsible for killing babies. The whole film was a fiction based on a strike that occured in a plant where nearly all of the employees were women. The head of that union was a grandmother. The thugs portrayed were hired by the company. The NLRB finally set aside the Borden Company election and outlawed the use of the fake film. This took over a year. In the meantime, the Borden Company had been picketed and boycotted. The most active union supporters had been fired. There was no point in going through with another election, and besides, Willie Berry and I were busy organizing the "Sharecroppers of the Sea."

25 Sharecroppers of the Sea

"Git that extra man off my back!" was the slogan of 1,500 pogy boat fishermen whose leaders sought us out in Lake Charles, Louisiana, and wanted to organize a union. Nearly all of them were black. They were menhaden or pogy fishermen in the Gulf of Mexico. They came to the gulf coast every year in May and worked until the fish disappeared in late October. These fishermen had a burning grievance. Either the boat captains, or the companies that owned the boats and the fishmeal plants along the coast, deducted from each man's share of the catch, a part of his earnings to pay the cost of hiring an extra man or two on board each of the large fishing boats. Theoretically, each boat had a crew of seventeen men—a captain, a first mate, a pilot and fourteen fishermen. The boats would leave port each Sunday afternoon and remain out until they had caught a load of fish. Sometimes this took nearly all week. Sometimes there would be a man or two who failed to show up at sailing time. The captains would hire an extra man or two on the boat, and penalize each fisherman, including the mate and pilot, by deducting from their share of the catch enough money to pay the extra man or men. Often these deductions would run from $50 to $100 per man, every two weeks. The men resented this system. It was worse than anything I had ever heard of in the cotton plantation country where often the "deducts" got all a man made, so I dubbed the pogy boat men "Share-croppers of the Sea."

One Sunday afternoon, a group appeared at the home of Willie Berry, the assistant organizer, to tell their story. (I had persuaded the secretary of the Meat Cutters, Pat Gorman, to let me hire Berry and pay him $75 a week for his salary and expenses.) We warned the men that their employers would probably hire the notorious firm of Kullman & Lang and that they would be subjected to a campaign of lies. One of the fishermen said, "Pieces of paper won't scare us. Let them send their letters; we will just throw them in the water." And that is what happened. Kullman & Lang met its match in the pogy boat men. The lawyer for the Smith family boats was Tom Kerrigan, labor relations specialist for a huge New York corporate law firm, Putney, Twombley, Skidmore and Hall. I once asked Tom why his name was not on the firm's letterhead. He said, "The Irish name I have would never fit in with those of the aristocratic founders of the firm."

At that time there were three Smith brothers—Harvey, Gilbert, and Otis—all operating fishing boats and plants on the Gulf of Mexico. Harvey had plants and a dozen boats at Cameron, Louisiana, and Sabine Pass, Texas. He was a rather mysterious fellow who was seldom seen by outsiders. Gilbert Smith operated the Smith Company boats and plant at Moss Point, Mississippi, near Pascagoula. Although he looked like a punch-drunk prize fighter with his cauliflower ears, Gil Smith was a gentleman and family man.

The other brother was Otis H. Smith, who came down to Abbeville, Louisiana, and built a five-million-dollar modern fishmeal plant at Intercoastal City. Otis was the intellectual of the Smith family. He was the first to recognize and enter into a contract with a union for his fishing boats operating out of Lewes, Delaware. Before coming to Louisiana, for 25 years Otis Smith was mayor of Lewes and a political power in the small state where the Dupont family reigned. Otis Smith had a reputation for dealing fairly with everyone. At one point there was an attempt by blacks to integrate an all-white beach at Ocean City, Maryland. Otis Smith owned a tract of land near Lewes, and he promptly made it an open bathing beach, inviting all comers, black and white, to use its facilities. His support from blacks was thereafter assured. Otis had a large farm and a huge modern home that overlooked the town of Lewes. He once told me that his wife Hazzel (two Z's, believe it or not) and he did not know how many rooms it had. Hazzel was a great horsewoman who bred and raced horses. There was a story that Otis Smith became sympathetic to unions after an experience he had with an organizer for the Fur and Leather Workers. That union had tried to organize the menhaden fishermen in the early forties. When the organizer came to Smith's office and Smith refused to recognize the union—so the story goes—the Fur and Leather worker belted him. Thereafter, any union organizer who came to see him and behaved like a gentleman was received kindly by Otis H. Smith.

The Smith family owned over half of the menhaden fishing boats and plants in the United States, and also had holdings in Peru and Chile. The family holdings were reported to be worth more than a hundred million dollars, but Otis Smith was a man of simple tastes. While his wife remained in Lewes, Delaware, Otis lived in a trailer house near the new plant south of Abbeville. He did his own cooking, but he needed help house cleaning. One of the Cajun women who also worked in the fish plant gave his trailer periodic cleanings. One day when Otis was away, Hazzel called him at the trailer and the cleaning woman answered the phone. Hazzel arrived soon afterward, took one look at the cleaning woman, decided that she was no rival for Otis's affection, and caught the next plane back to Delaware.

The fishermen voted solidly for the union in elections that were held on all but three boats. Kullman & Lang's propaganda had no effect whatever on this group.

The National Labor Relations Board, the Fishermen, and Me

Until I started work in Louisiana as the agricultural representative of the Amalgamated Meat Cutters, I knew little about the government agency that guarantees non-farm workers their right to form unions and requires the employer to bargain collectively. The menhaden fishermen had voted overwhelmingly for our Agricultural and Allied Workers Union Local 300. However, those captains and/or companies who were represented by Kullman & Lang simply refused to bargain with the union. I filed unfair labor charges against the employers, as is provided under the National Labor Relations Act. Because of their close relationship with the regional office of the NLRB, Kullman & Lang delayed the proceedings for long periods. K & L hired ambitious young lawyers who had served their apprenticeship with the NLRB in New Orleans, paying them well for beginning lawyers and promising membership in the firm which represented employers all over the southeast and southwest; this could lead to great wealth and power. These young men were so corrupted by their ambitions that they used every connection they had in the NLRB and all they had learned to break unions and deny workers the rights guaranteed by law. Unable to make any headway in the regular procedures of the labor board, I filed charges against Kullman and Lang, alleging that the law firm was engaged in the business of selling services to employers who wished to deny their employees rights guaranteed by the National Labor Relations Act.

My unprecedented action in filing unfair labor practice charges against the most prominent and prestigious management law firm had no effect on Kullman & Lang. They knew they could beat the rap. But the regional director was frightened, and so were some labor lawyers and even union organizers. Many came to me expressing their fear that if NLRB procedures were challenged, the whole Act could be overturned by the Supreme Court. But when the regional director for NLRB in New Orleans finally acted and dismissed the charges, I appealed to the NLRB in Washington. Later on I had an off-the-record meeting with an old friend of the STFU days in Washington. He was Frank W. McCulloch, chairman of the National Labor Relations Board under the Kennedy administration. My charges against Kullman & Lang were allowed to die, but after that there was quicker NLRB action on the fisherman cases. Another time I filed charges against an agent of the NLRB alleging that he was discriminating against fishermen because of their race. When this charge was dismissed upon appeal to Washington, another crisis was precipitated when a young woman lawyer in the Appeals Section of NLRB tried to force a hearing on the charge of racial bias.

However, the union won an NLRB decision against the Louisiana Menhaden Company, a client of Kullman & Lang whose boat captain had fired his entire crew after they voted solidly for union representation in an election held by NLRB in 1964. The men were awarded a total of $30,000 in back pay. The award itself attracted little attention outside the area, but George Powell, the NLRB trial examiner, in his decision recommending the back pay award, referred to a fisherman who appeared as a witness in the formal hearing held by the NLRB in Louisiana. The Associated Press quoted from Powell's decision:

You would expect a bunch of fishermen-witnesses in a labor dispute to be simply dressed, even on the rough side. But here was this one character, in a National Labor Relations Board hearing in Louisiana, who showed up in style. Extraordinary! He was dressed in a tuxedo coat and trousers with a pearl pin in the coat lapel. He wore a red tie. His feet were enclosed in brown cowboy boots! I can only surmise that he was told he was to appear in a *formal* hearing.

I Meet a Future Vice-President of the USA in New Orleans

One day in August 1964, I was working in my home in Lake Charles, pounding away on my typewriter, when I had a phone call. A strange voice said, "Mitchell, I hear you have won some Labor Board elections on the Smith Boats." Thinking that my caller was a newspaperman, I replied that the union had just ended an organizing campaign on the Gulf Coast. Fifty-four NLRB elections had been held on a boat-by-boat basis, and the union had won 51 of the elections. The caller then said, "I am the attorney for the Amalgamated here on the East Coast. I know the company lawyer and all of the members of the Smith family. They own more than half of the boats where you won your elections."

He said he was coming to New Orleans that weekend on some other business, and if I would come over, we could talk about union matters, and perhaps he could give me some help in working out contracts for the fishermen. I protested that I was only an organizer, and that I had no authority to hire lawyers. The caller said: "I know Pat Gorman and that he would never let you retain a lawyer." He asked me to come over to New Orleans on Friday to meet him Saturday and talk about the matter. He assured me that no cost would be involved, and he could help get a good contract. Since I did not even know who the caller was, I asked him to please tell me his name again. He replied, "This is Ted Agnew," and he repeated that he had been the attorney for the Amalgamated Meat Cutters in Baltimore ever since he finished law school. He said he had just been elected chief executive of Baltimore County. He also added that he had negotiated the first contracts with the Smith fishing companies on the east coast.

I agreed to meet Mr. Agnew in New Orleans and told him I would be staying at the St. Charles Hotel, one of the oldest in the city. Agnew then asked me the names of other hotels in New Orleans. I named the Roosevelt, the Monteleone, and the Royal Orleans that had just opened in the heart of the French Quarter. He asked me to spell the name of the Royal Orleans and said that his secretary would make reservations for him.

Never one to miss a chance to get free help for the union, I flew to New Orleans on Friday, attended to some business, had dinner with my friend Father Louis J. Twomey of Loyola University, and went back to my room at the St. Charles Hotel in the early evening. I called the Royal Orleans and asked if Mr. Agnew had registered. The clerk said he had no reservation for an Agnew. Thinking that Agnew had been delayed, I waited until the following morning, and when I had not heard from him by nine o'clock, I called every hotel and motel in downtown New Orleans, but could not find him. I waited impatiently for two hours, then checked with the airlines and found I could get back to Lake Charles soon after noon. I packed my bag and was ready to leave when the phone rang. It was Agnew. He apologized for being late and said he was downstairs. I asked if he had just arrived in New Orleans, but he said no, he had arrived early Friday afternoon. He asked me to meet him downstairs and would tell me all about it while I had lunch and he had breakfast. He waited for me near the house phones, and there I met the future Vice-President of the United States. He was an attractive, well-dressed, youngish-looking, middle-aged man.

While we ate, we talked about what he could do to help me get contracts for the fishermen. We also talked about politics. He said he was a Republican, and I asked why he was not a Democrat since he held such liberal views. He said there were many Democrats in Maryland; sometimes they would fight among themselves, and a liberal Republican could then get elected. He said that was what happened in Baltimore County, and again when McKeldin, a Republican, had been elected Governor. Agnew said he might happen to be elected governor if that circumstance should arise again, and that he might even serve a term in the U.S. Senate, but that was probably as far as he would go. He said neither party would ever consider a Maryland politician for Vice-President, because the state had such a small number of electoral votes.

He asked me to stay over night, so we could go out on the town. He had been accompanied by a friend, and if we ran into anyone from Baltimore, he was going to introduce "Susan" as my "niece." He also asked me to telephone my wife and to tell her that in the event "Judy" called, she should report that we were out visiting some fishing camps where there were no telephones. He had left my Lake Charles telephone number with his wife. I made no comment, and did nothing about the matter. We walked over to the French Quarter and met Susan in one of the exclusive gift shops on Royal Street. She had selected an expensive piece of antique jewelry as a souvenir of her trip. Agnew pulled out a big roll of bills and tossed a couple of hundred dollars on the counter to pay for the gift.

I met Agnew again in New York City with the attorney for the Smith Company, this time at the offices of Twombley, Putney, Skidmore and Hall. Harvey and Otis Smith were both present. The meeting began with the two lawyers telling each other all the dirty jokes they had heard since they had last met. I noticed that Otis Smith's slightly bald head would flush when an especially dirty joke was told. I could take them or leave them, and I never could remember one long enough to repeat it.

Afterwards, Smith told me that every time these two legal characters met, they spent an hour telling each other dirty jokes, then another hour conducting business, and they charged him and the union the full rate for the two hours they spent together.

The Smith company lawyer, Tom Kerrigan, was a star football player when Columbia University had a team. He was also the attorney for his University. Later he became U.S. District Court Judge in Connecticut, a result of his close relationship with Spiro T. Agnew, Vice-President of the United States.

After Nixon and Agnew were elected, it seemed that every time I picked up a paper, Airforce Two would be landing in New Orleans. Agnew made numerous trips to New Orleans to meet with a nonexistent Southern Republican Committee, and once it was announced that he was in New Orleans to meet with the editorial staff of the *Times Picayune*. Then Nixon unleashed the Cambodia bombing. Even the students at staid Tulane, Loyola, and lesser known colleges in New Orleans were aroused. One night a group picketed Vice-President Agnew's hotel. Two students were in back of the Royal Orleans, at the motor entrance, when Agnew came out, entered a limousine, and with a police escort headed uptown. The two students jumped in their Volkswagon and gave chase. Agnew's "limo" and the police car were seen entering the exclusive millionaire's street, Audubon Place. There, guards permitted only residents or their guests to enter. Chains were strung across the entrance, and armed guards were always on duty. The students saw Agnew enter the home of an oil millionaire. No one had been at home there for some time, but servants were always on duty. After a few hours waiting and watching, the Tulane students grew tired and went to bed. The next day, one of the editors of the so-called underground newspaper *Nola Express* called and told me about this incident. I told him about my meeting with Agnew in New Orleans six years before, and suggested that perhaps it had been nothing more than a rendezvous with "Susan" or another such person. While the newspapers never ran the story, the tale spread throughout the French Quarter.

One day at lunch soon after that, Dorothy and I were watching the news on a television program called "Midday." Since there was no visiting celebrity that day, the woman who ran the program was interviewing the manager of the Royal Orleans. In her enthusiastic way she inquired, "And isn't it true that our Vice-President is a most frequent guest at your hotel?" The manager, an overstuffed middle-aged gentleman, reared back and replied:

"Oh yes, every time Vice-President Agnew comes to New Orleans, he stays at the Royal Orleans. We have a special suite reserved at all times for Mr. Agnew. He comes quite often."

The interviewer then said, "Cherchez la femme." (Find the woman.)

I have often told this story about Agnew, and I usually add: "Ted Agnew was a likeable character. He was just an honest crook, trying to make a fast buck. Richard Nixon tried to steal the whole country, but Agnew, the son of Greek immigrants, only wanted a big share of it for himself."

Mistaken for Advance Agent of the Civil Rights Invasion

In the summer of 1964, Willie Berry, Howard Harrity and I were in Pascagoula, Mississippi. We were joined by an organizer for the Amalgamated Meat Cutters, Melvin Tyler of Crisfield, Maryland. Melvin Tyler had been the first organizer of the fishermen on the east coast. In nearby Moss Point, there were three large fish plants. The National Labor Relations Board had held a hearing that day at the county court house in Pascagoula. Just as the sun went down, we drove over to the black part of town to meet with some of the leaders of the International Longshoremen Association. Their hall had once been a garage or warehouse with wide doors at the front. Several of us were sitting in the doorway. Melvin Tyler and I were white, the others were black. We were talking about ways in which we could be sure that the union won the forthcoming NLRB elections. I noticed cars driving very slowly past the open doorway. I assumed it was just idle curiosity on the part of some residents and paid scant attention. When we started to leave, a car loaded with uniformed men drove by, and a voice yelled at us: "Is there any trouble over there?"

Willie Berry thought the men were concerned because big Howard Harrity was with us. "There's no trouble here, officer," he said, "this man is with me."

Tyler and I went to my car, and I noticed as we got in that the car loaded with police was just across the railroad tracks at the edge of the black section of town. I told Tyler I thought they were going to stop us, and if so, to let me do the talking. I had been in and out of Pascagoula and Moss Point for weeks and had seen the entire police force of the town, and even the highway patrol contingent, in the Holiday Inn where they always ate. I felt sure they would recognize me. As soon as I drove by, they blew the siren, passed us, then stopped in front of us. The officers jumped out and surrounded us. I got out immediately, asking what the problem was. They wanted to see my driver's license and my car ownership certificate. I was driving an Oldsmobile like all others leased by the Amalgamated Meat Cutters each year for every organizer on the staff. I even had a car identification card with me. Two of the men got into the back seat. They as well as the others were heavily armed.

Pistols, shotguns and even a machine-gun were in the car that stopped us. They said they were taking us in for questioning. We drove up to the back of the county courthouse, which was attached to the county jail, and were taken inside. Tyler was told to sit down in one room, and I in another. We were being watched by the men who had arrested us. Soon a tall young man, the chief deputy sheriff of the county, came in. He was in plain clothes and the others were in uniform. The chief deputy asked me what I was doing in Pascagoula. I told him I was there trying to organize the fishermen into our union. He then asked to see my union credentials. I showed him the car that identified me as a bona fide representative of the Amalgamated Meat Cutters and Butcher Workmen of N.A., AFL-CIO. He then said: "Mr. Mitchell, your being over there in the colored folks section of town after dark alarmed Constable Jones, who patrols that beat. You know there is an invasion of dangerous and heavily armed men moving toward Mississippi, and Constable Jones and his men thought you were the advance agents of the civil rights invaders."

He apologized for disturbing us, and said that he had been an assistant business agent for the Electrical Workers Union, and he would be pleased if we would get our business all done during daylight hours hereafter. He said, "You know, the colored people are afraid of white men coming into their part of town these days." Then Constable Jones and his men came in to apologize, saying that they were all members of unions, and had it not been for the unions, they would still be working in the Pascagoula shipyards and other industries for just the minimum wage that the law required the employers to pay. They were very sorry that they had mistaken union organizers for advance men of the civil rights invasion.

This was the summer of '64, when thousands of young men and women came into Mississippi to help their fellow men secure their legal rights. And while they were a danger to the outworn southern way of life, they were armed only with ideas—never with guns. I thought: "Twenty-five years before, no one would have cared about two older men going into the Negro section of Pascagoula, unless they knew we were union organizers." Times had changed, and they were to change even more in Mississippi.

The finest man among all of those who surfaced when we organized the fishermen on the Gulf coast was Howard V. Harrity. He was six-and-a-half feet tall and weighed nearly 300 pounds. He was big, black, and bald. Harrity was born in Alabama, but as a child had been taken to upstate New York. He attended school in Plattsburg, New York, and at the age of 15 he ran away from home and joined the famous all-black

9th Cavalry regiment. He was stationed at Fort Bliss before World War I. His cavalry unit was ordered into action against Pancho Villa, whose insurgents had raided and shot up a U.S. border town. Soon after, the commanding officer learned that his big young trooper was only 15 years old, so Harrity was discharged and sent home. Harrity moved to New Jersey and for years followed the construction trade. He finally became a menhaden fisherman on a Smith Company boat. Later, he moved his family to Ferandino Beach, Florida, and continued his life as a fisherman. He was involved in the first attempt of the fishermen to organize a union. He was working on a boat off the Gulf coast, when he and his crew first heard the radio broadcasts the company was making. They alleged that the Fur and Leather Workers was a communist union. He said he tried to hold the men in line, but it was no use, and the movement died. He had heard about the organization of the fishermen up on the east coast, around Lewes, Delaware, and Chesapeake Bay, but the union had not yet gotten down South. Then when southern fishermen started talking union, he was the cook on one of the Smith boats, working out of Sabine Pass, Texas. He attended the first meeting and helped Willie Berry sign every fisherman going out of that port. Here, all of the crew were blacks, even the captains. They had the worst boats in the Smith fleet, and as a result they caught the fewest fish. In addition to this, captains were stealing from the men, and Harrity was determined to put a stop to it. One Sunday, Willie Berry went to Sabine Pass for a special meeting. Berry told the fishermen that the white man, Mitchell, was going to put them all in a farm union headed by himself and a black French fellow from Reserve, Louisiana, named Frank Lapeyrolerie. Berry proposed that a local union run by a fisherman be set up at each port. Berry's proposal sounded good, but the more Harrity thought about it, the more doubtful he was. He wondered where the fishermen would get enough money to pay a business agent in each port. Who would take care of the union while the men were all back home during the six or seven months no fishing was being done? He raised some of these questions with Berry privately, but Berry had no answers. Howard Harrity then telephoned me and asked me to come to see him. A few days later I went over to Port Arthur, where he lived. and we spent the day talking. I told him that this was the first I had heard about setting up a half dozen small local unions. Actually I had been talking to Willie Berry about his becoming the business agent for the fishermen and being paid by the local union for his services. But Berry wanted no further responsibility for men who put out to sea in the big motor boats. He wanted an organizer's job with the international union, and had been talking to both Sam Twedell, the vice president and district director, as well as to Sam's son, "Big Dick" Twedell. He had convinced at least Big Dick of Dallas that he was the man who could get things done with the black people in District V, composed of Arkansas, Louisiana and Texas. "Big Dick" was always talking about "Trades Labor Movement" instead of the Trade Union Movement, and he was slated to inherit his father's job when the old timer retired.

I arranged for a meeting in Chicago to discuss whether there should be one large union, or six small ones. I persuaded Howard Harrity to fly up with me for the meeting. Harrity, the solid trade union man, was my ace in the hole. We went in to see Pat Gorman, whose office door was always left open, and anyone in the building, from the janitor to the president, could just walk in without an appointment. Harrity's first words to Gorman, after I introduced him were, "Mr. Gorman, my name is Howard V. Harrity, I am black Irish, you know."

Patrick E. Gorman, the sentimental "Man of Eire" who wrote songs and poetry and sometimes published both in the International Union journal, replied: "I am Pat, Howard, so you just call me by my first name." Howard Harrity was a hit with everyone he met in Chicago, from the woman who ran the cafeteria to the Executive Vice President, Harry R. Poole. After a discussion of the fishermen's problems, it was decided that the name of the local should be changed to "Fish, Seafood, Agricultural and Allied Workers Union Local 300," and that when the next election was held, a fisherman would be proposed as president. Harrity, who had some experience in serving as treasurer of a laborer's union, said he would have no part of a job that required him to handle money. In due course, Howard Harrity became president of Local 300, and Frank Lapeyrolerie remained as secretary-treasurer until 1973, when the local came to an end. Willie Berry was hired as an organizer by the international union and was sent to work in Arkansas and Mississippi, where the union was trying to organize some poultry plants. He was quite successful as an organizer. He knew how to persuade people to sign cards, and how to keep them in line until the election was held and won. Sometimes he was even successful in helping to negotiate contracts, but I had the same experience with Willie Berry that I had with some others. Once the union was established, Willie Berry would often start an internal squabble among the members. Sometimes he succeeded in undoing what he had already done so well. My friend, Leon Schachter, arrived in Chicago soon after everything had been settled, including Berry's appointment, and Schachter took me to task for allowing a man to shoot up to the top in the international union without having earned the job.

I soon learned that my estimation of Howard Harrity was correct. I turned over to him the job of representing the fishermen with the boat captains. He helped organize the first of the fishmeal factories, and took part in a campaign to organize the huge rice mill in Abbeville, Louisiana. One day we were meeting with Otis Smith, who, for all his liberal ideas, was quite cagey when it came to his family money. He was not about to give anything to his fishermen or factory workers either. Howard Harrity took the lead.

"Now Mr. Smith, you pay these men more, and *you* are going to profit. Let's work out a bonus system. For every additional thousand fish a boat catches, you pay all the union men an additional two cents per 1,000. The first thing you know, your boats will be bringing in more fish than your plant can process."

The bonus system worked. Soon, fishermen who had been earning $1,500 for a season's work, were taking home $5,000 a year, and finally they earned as much as $10,000 for five month's work. At that point, I turned my attention to other things, and let Howard Harrity and Otis Smith, the two fishermen, carry on. I knew nothing about the fish business, and they did. The black man and the white man, the big fisherman and the millionaire, became fast friends. Otis Smith once said to me: "Mitch, if Howard Harrity had been a white man, there is just no telling how far he would have gone. He probably would have made a million dollars."

I told Smith, "I think Harrity is one hell of a good union organizer in any case, no matter what his race."

In the early spring, Howard Harrity went to the eastern shore of Virginia to meet with union members who came south each year to work on the fishing boats in the gulf. While there he was involved in an accident. His hip was badly injured. Whether it was due to improper medical care at the time, or to the disease perhaps already being present, Howard Harrity became a victim of cancer. He had a series of operations, therapy treatments, and long stays in the hospital. The Smith boat companies had no health insurance plan, so who paid for his care? It was paid for by Otis H. Smith, his one-time employer, and by H. L. Mitchell, his friend in the union. Smith gave several thousand dollars and I a few hundred. Every payday, the captains and crews of the Smith boats chipped in to help Howard Harrity. For a time it appeared that Harrity was on his way to recovery. One night he was down at Morgan City, Louisiana, waiting for the big fishing boats to come in. When his landlady called him the next morning, she found that the big fisherman had gone to another Port.

26 Sugar Cane Land and Sister Anne

In 1965, the union turned its attention away from the menhaden fishing industry towards projects affecting sugar cane plantation workers. Somewhat earlier, Frank Lapeyrolerie, Father Louis J. Twomey of Loyola University and I had been delegates to a conference in Washington called by President Lyndon Johnson. There we raised the issue of training programs for farm workers as well as housing for rural families. We were told that Louisiana had refused to enter into agreements with the federal government to secure funds for manpower training programs of any sort. These were the days when southern state legislatures, governors, and members of Congress were boycotting the federal government, even to the extent of refusing funds for welfare programs.

Learning that there was money available for direct grants to non-profit organizations, a plan was worked out whereby Father Twomey's Human Resources Department of Loyola, applied for and secured the first government grant for a manpower training program in Louisiana. Frank Lapeyrolerie was named as the coordinator of a tractor driver training project. It was soon found that the basic need was for adult education. Tractor drivers knew how to ride a tractor but they could not read an oil gauge on a $50,000 cane-cutting-and-harvesting machine they were operating. The Tractor Jockey's Project was enlarged and expanded to the entire community of Reserve. Here, grown men and women went back to school to learn reading, writing, and arithmetic. The grants from the federal government permitted a small stipend to be paid the trainees. Then in 1966 we started the program to build a hundred houses in the sugar cane country. The first ten houses for workers were built by ten families pooling their own labor on a self-help basis. The first self-help homes in Louisiana were completed in the town of Edgard, in St. John the Baptist Parish. Others were built in or near the town of Reserve. Among the first homes erected on the east side of the Mississippi River were those to house families still living in cabins built for slaves on the San Francisco Plantation. The manager of the old sugar cane plantation and sugarmill was very much in favor of the plan to erect new houses for families living on the plantation. At one point he promised that if his employees would build new houses uptown, he would have a bulldozer destroy the old slave quarters. The San Francisco Plantation House is one of the show places for tourists on River Road, but in the mid-70's, two miles behind the mansion to the old sugar cane land and mill, one would find the old slave quarters, still occupied, and with no improvements made in over 100 years. What happened was that as soon as the sugar cane workers got off the plantation and into decent homes, they found better jobs in construction or in one of the industries that expanded rapidly along the river. They were no longer interested in the low wage rates required by the U.S. Department of Agriculture under the Sugar Act—wage rates, by the way, that were designed to benefit the large corporations such as Tenneco Oil and the Jim Walter Corporation, each of which owned large tracts of sugar cane lands, mills, and refineries in Louisiana. A new batch of people, poorer than those who left, were moved into the slave quarters and put to work by the owners of the plantation.

Along with the housing program for sugar cane plantation workers, we also launched an organizing campaign in 1966. Frank Lapeyrolerie and I appeared every year at the annual wage hearings held under the National Sugar Act, and we mobilized other spokesmen for the workers. This was very much resented by the representatives of the American Sugar Cane League. Since most of the sugar cane field workers were now tractor drivers, we set up a Tractor Drivers Union within Local 300, and called a tractor drivers' holiday on the day the Sugar Wage Hearings were held. I announced to the news media that there was going to be a walk-in and sit-down. This became confused with the civil rights demonstrations that were still occurring all over the South, and we received widespread publicity. The New Orleans TV stations ran specials on the plight of the sugar cane workers. They even filmed a meeting of the union with the message that a group of blacks and whites were planning a massive organizing campaign among the plantation workers. Meetings were held all over the area. Sugar cane field workers were becoming bold enough to take part openly. They were encouraged by some of the Catholic priests in rural areas.

In Franklin, Louisiana, in the heart of the sugar cane country on Bayou Teche, Father Francis J. Ecimovich opened the church-owned school building for union meetings. This courageous priest had been the one who served the papers on Leander Perez, the political-boss, oil millionaire and leader of Louisiana's white segregationist movement, excommunicating him from the Catholic Church. Father Frank had been attacked and beaten severely in his own church by Leander Perez's thugs because he had served the papers, which were sent by Archbishop Rummel. Ecimovich had been sent to Franklin, where he would be out of harm's way, but he continued to involve himself with social problems. He launched the St. Jules Credit Union, started a housing project for poor people, and supported the work of the courageous husband and wife team, Bernard and Rose Mae Broussard. Rose Mae ran the credit union and Bernard was involved in the consumer cooperative movement. Father Frank's home became the center for students who came in during the late 60's and early 70's. He was finally called in by his superior, the Bishop of Lafayette, and given his walking papers in the form of a transfer out of Louisiana to Pine Bluff, Arkansas.

Each year the union would get the tractor drivers signed up, have them attend meetings, elect their own officers, and attend annual wage hearings. They were slowly improving their working conditions. Each year I would propose to the Amalgamated Meat Cutters that formal demands be made on the employers for union recognition and, if recognition was not granted, that we be given strike authorization. Each year someone would pull the rug out from under the plantation workers. Once Secretary-Treasurer Pat Gorman, hearing that 5,000 men would be involved, counted up the cost of paying each one $25 a week in strike benefits in a strike that might last a year, and said, "Hold off another year."

Then in 1968 Sam Twedell retired, and his son "Big Dick of Dallas" succeeded the old man as vice president and district director. We filed a petition with the NLRB for an election among the plantation workers, knowing full well that the regional board would reject it because of the exclusion of agricultural workers under the Act. Twedell, at my request, fired off telegrams to the companies involved, supporting our demands. Soon after, there was a merger of the United Packinghouse Workers of America into the Amalgamated Meat Cutters and Butcher Workmen of North America. Once the refinery workers were in the same union and paying dues, the field workers were abandoned.

As soon as the National Labor Relations Board in Washington had formally refused to hold an election, out attorneys filed a suit in the U.S. District Court in New Orleans challenging the constitutionality of the exclusion of farm workers. Unfortunately, this action was assigned to U.S. District Judge "Tut" Mitchell, a man who was noted for his ties with sugar cane and other corporations. Alexander H. Schullman, of Los Angeles, who had the idea for a test case, thought that the case should be filed in District Court in Washington, but Dick Sobol, a civil rights attorney who had won case after case in the federal courts of New Orleans, thought this was the best place. Our principal attorney, Jim

Youngdahl, went along with Sobol. Judge Mitchell delayed a hearing on one pretext after another. Sobol was also pressured by the United Farm Workers in California, who never wanted to be under the National Labor Relations Act, to drop the case. Cesar Chavez wanted a state law to guarantee the rights of farm workers in California to organize and bargain collectively. I never believed that any kind of social welfare legislation, even if it could be adopted, would ever be administered fairly for workers by state bureaucracies, nor did I believe that if California passed a law that 49 other states would ever do the same.

Involved in our test case over the rights of farm workers were two of the union's best friends. One was Frank W. McCulloch, who was then chairman of the National Labor Relations Board. We were suing him. Frank had headed a delegation to Arkansas in 1935, and later was administrative assistant to Senator Paul H. Douglas of Illinois. Douglas and McCulloch were always ready to help the nation's farm workers. The other person who was about to be involved was Ray Marshall, then professor of economics at the University of Texas. Marshall was to do an economic study of the sugar cane industry and appear in federal court on behalf of the sugar cane field workers. Ray Marshall later became secretary of labor in President Carter's cabinet.

The United Packinghouse Workers of America held contracts with all of the smaller sugar mills in Louisiana. While the workers in those mills had often appeared to favor the organization of field workers, their leaders usually were opposed. The leaders feared that if the field workers organized a union, and began to get better wages and working conditions, the employers would refuse to improve conditions for the mill and refinery workers. With these members now in the Amalgamated, there was more at stake than when Secretary-Treasurer Gorman's only fear was that the Amalgamated's strike fund would be diminished.

The new district director, "Big Dick of Dallas," found that the sugar refinery workers numbered nearly 2,000 dues-paying members, and they had union shops in Louisiana, and dues were collected each month. He decided that if he went along with me and Lapeyrolerie, he not only risked a strike by the new members, but the workers in the sugar mill and refineries would suffer a loss in wages too. There was a meeting that fall in Chicago, at the end of which several of us were called into the office of the president, and there Big Dick told me that his heart bled for me, but that he had to tell me the Amalgamated just wouldn't go along with the organizing drive among sugar cane field workers at that time. Dick said that I should join "Little Shank" (Ed Shanklin) the UPWA organizer and try to get the rest of the sugar mills in the state organized. It was at this point that I gave up hope that the Amalgamated Meat Cutters and Butcher Workmen of N.A., AFL-CIO would ever do anything about farm workers in Louisiana. I tried to interest the United Farm Workers in organizing the tractor drivers and other field workers on the sugar cane plantations. Cesar Chavez decided against it since the UFW was so involved in California that it could not go into other areas at the time. So, as early as 1968, I began thinking of retiring as an organizer for the Amalgamated Meat Cutters.

Early the following year, I was invited by the Southern Students Organizing Committee (SSOC) to attend a conference on radical history of the South. The meeting was held in Atlanta, at Emory University. SSOC had been set up by southern college students who were active in the civil rights movement. It was an offshoot of the Students for a Democratic Society (SDS), one of the most radical of all student movements. SSOC had adopted as its emblem the Confederate battle flag, with black and white clasped hands superimposed over the stars and bars. I had just received a copy of the 1936 *March of Time* film on 16 mm* and we were about to show it when an old fellow with long hair and whiskers like Ho Chi Min stood up in the back of the room, and asked: "Is that H. L. Mitchell up there?"

It was Claude Williams whom I hadn't seen in thirty years! The film included a re-enactment of the beating of Claude Williams and Willie Sue Blagden. I invited Claude and his wife Joyce to have lunch with me and my other guests, Virginia Durr and Anne Braden, and they accepted.

Virginia Durr was the Alabama woman who had led the fight to outlaw the poll tax as a requirement for voting. She was also the sister-in-law of Supreme Court Justice, Hugo Black. She was reported to have sometimes written personal letters advising Justice Black on important civil rights issues before the Supreme Court. She and her attorney husband, Clifford Durr, once federal communications commissioner under FDR, lived near Montgomery, Alabama. They, along with E. D. Nixon, an early civil rights leader in the area, got Rosa Parks out of jail after she defied the segregation laws and started the Montgomery bus boycott. Anne Braden was the long-time Secretary to the Southern Conference Educational fund, which grew out of the Southern Conference for Human Welfare that first met in Birmingham, Alabama, in 1938.

Summer Work Project for Students

It was at this radical history meeting in Atlanta that I got the idea for a Southern Students Summer Work Project to be conducted in Louisi-

*See page 102 for a transcript of the film.

ana, among the sugar cane plantation workers. A group mainly recruited from the ranks of the SSOC leadership was interested in spending a summer working with the union in Louisiana. However, we had to have money to finance the project. I attended a board meeting of the National Sharecroppers Fund held in Virginia, where a project was being undertaken to help some black small farmers. NSF was so involved, and its funds so completely committed, that it could do nothing about the proposed student project in Louisiana. One of the down-to-earth NSF board members, Vera Rony, a former secretary of the Workers Defense League, asked me if I knew Andrew Norman. I recalled having met Norman and his wife one night at the home of Sidney and Hazel Hertzberg at Palisades, New York. Vera and I telephoned Andrew Norman, and he agreed to put up $2,500 if we could find an equal amount elsewhere to finance the summer project for students in Louisiana. Vera Rony and I appealed to people we both knew who had been contributors to various causes. We got $1,000 from another foundation and varying amounts from individuals who thought our summer project offered more constructive work for students to engage in than taking over college campus buildings. One of the leaders of our sugar cane field workers organizing committee was Thomas Harris. He offered to provide the students with an old house he owned in the town of Thibadoux, Lousiana. The next problem was to find a director for the summer project. We selected Sister Anne Catherine.

Sister Anne Catherine

Anne Catherine Bizalion was a Rural Dominican nun, the young Mother Superior of a convent on the edge of the town of Abbeville, Louisiana. Although born in Germany, she had grown up in Grenoble during the Nazi occupation of France. Her earliest recollections were of gunfire between the German army and the partisans helping people escape across the border into the freedom of nearby Switzerland. Sundown was curfew for the youngsters who grew up during the war. There were few relationships outside her immediate family. The young girl turned inward and became a nun. She came to the United States by way of Quebec. In the mid-sixties there was a new stirring within the Catholic church. Sister Anne Catherine's order was one of the first to abandon the strict practices that had been a way of life since the Middle Ages. Sister Anne Catherine graduated from the University of Grenoble in France, before entering the convent. In the 1960s she became a student again and received a degree from Tulane's School of Social Work with the highest scholastic honors and in record time.

I first met Anne Catherine in 1967 when we were about to organize

Otis Smith's new fishmeal factory south of Abbeville near the intercoastal canal. With the help of one of the women in the office, I had a
complete list of employees of the Seacoast Products Company's factory. We had tried to hold a meeting and get all the men and women
together. But the whites would not attend a meeting in the black section
of town, and the blacks were afraid to go into the white section. One of
my friends, Art Emery, who was working for the Southern Consumer
Cooperative in nearby Lafayette, told me of the Rural Dominican
Sisters Convent, where the cooperative had once used a room for a
meeting place, and of Sister Anne. So I went to see her one day at her
office downtown. She was then director of the Head Start program in
the area. I was told I would find her at home. She was living in a small
house on the edge of the black section of town. I expected to find a nun
properly dressed in her long black flowing habit with a veil. I found a
young woman out in the front yard dressed in a skimpy blouse and
shorts, working on her knees among her flowers, with her prominent
posterior turned up. I asked her if she knew where I could find Sister
Anne Catherine. She stood up and said, "I am Sister Anne Catherine."

I told her who I was and that I wanted to use a room at the old convent for a meeting of the fish factory workers. She invited me in for a
cup of coffee. There I met her companion, a fiery little Cajun woman,
Lorna Bourg, whom Otis Smith once described as more of a nun than
Sister Anne Catherine had ever been. Anne Catherine and Lorna agreed
to let us use the main room of the convent on a night agreed upon. They
also said they would attend the meeting. I sent letters to each of the
sixty-odd fish factory workers, stating the time and place. Nearly all of
the workers turned out. Not knowing much about the religious practices of nuns, liberated or otherwise, I asked Sister Anne if she would
give the invocation. She declined to do so and pointed out that one of
the black men present was a minister of the local Baptist Church. He
was called upon.

I explained to the workers that if a majority would sign cards with the
union, we could then proceed to contact the employer and ask for recognition and a meeting with a committee chosen from their number to
negotiate a contract. Nearly every man and woman signed a card that
night. Some took extra cards and promised to get absent workers to
sign too. They all knew about the fishing boat men who were also in the
union. The fact that the convent was a common ground, where they
knew no outsiders would be present, and both white and black, male
and female, had been made welcome before, was a deciding factor for
the union.

It turned out that Otis H. Smith would not agree to recognize the

Former slave quarters, San Francisco Plantation, Reserve, La (1967). Houses like this were still occupied by farm workers in the mid'70s. (photo by Betsy Berleson)

Self-help housing being built, with union sponsorship, for the use of sugar cane plantation workers. (photo by Lynn Franklin)

Above: Executive Board, Agricultural and Allied Workers Local 300, Reserve, La. Left to right: Vice-President Howard V. Harrity, Secretary-Treasurer Frank Lapeyrolerie, A. E. Cox, President H. L. Mitchell, Gene V. Collins, Leonard Carter. (photo by Lynn Franklin)

Lower right: Sister Anne Catherine, Rural Dominican nun who became director of the Southern Mutual Help Association. Left to right: Robert Carter, child-care specialist; Lorna Bourg, assistant to SMHA director; Rev. Murphy Wright, board member of SMHA; and Sister Anne Catherine. (photo by Lynn Franklin)

Howard V. Harrity, organizer of Gulf Coast fishermen. (photo by Lynn Franklin)

union until an election was held by the National Labor Relations Board. An election was held, and the union won with only five dissenting votes being cast.

In early summer a group of workers in the huge Louisiana State Rice Milling company plant at Abbeville came to me saying that they too wanted a union. With Howard Harrity, Frank Lapeyrolerie, Art Emery and others, we first tried contacting the rice mill workers house-to-house. It was a very slow procedure. Only a few cards were signed. So I returned to Sister Anne Catherine and arranged for the use of the convent grounds for a meeting on a Sunday afternoon. In the meantime, someone in her Head Start office borrowed an R. L. Polk Company City Directory from the Chamber of Commerce. I hired two girls from her office to go through the big book listing every man, his wife, name and occupation, in and near Abbeville. We soon had a list of all employees of the rice mill for the past two years or more, including supervisors. All were invited to come to the meeting at the Dominican Sisters Convent. Almost 150 of the 200 workers employed in the rice mill came to the meeting. Most of them signed cards. We found that some were supervisors, and these were the most articulate in denouncing the evils of the company. Several other meetings were called, and a house-to-house campaign was organized. The union was striking at the heart of the establishment in Abbeville. The Godchaux family owned the rice mill. They had a huge family home there. Without warning, Sister Anne Catherine was fired from her job as Director of the Head Start Program. It was an outstanding project with both black and white children attending and their parents fully participating. This was unheard of anywhere, even in South Louisiana, where the Catholic Church under the leadership of Archbishop Rummel of New Orleans had already desegregated church schools. A young black who headed the Parish Community Action Association, had been the one to fire Sister Anne Catherine. The entire staff of Head Start, black and white, paid and unpaid, walked off the job. They put up picket lines about the local office and likewise picketed the director's Office in Lafayette. Sister Anne filed a suit against the Community Action Association director, and was called in by the Bishop and ordered to remove her name from the case. With their economic support cut off, it appeared that Sister Anne and Lorna would be forced out of South Louisiana. I raised some money to tide them over for a few weeks. Then the Students Summer Project started. Sister Anne Catherine was named as the director, and eventually I induced Fay Bennett, executive secretary of the National Sharecroppers Fund to put Sister Anne on the payroll as the Louisiana representative of NSF.

Sister Anne Catherine was invited to present a paper at the annual meeting of social workers in New York. Thinking that this would be a good time for her to meet the people with whom I had worked, I suggested that she, Lorna and Father Frank Ecimovich, all go to New York city, contact people in foundations and also wealthy individuals. Bernard and Rose Mae Broussard also decided to go, so a group of five arrived in New York City. I asked Beth Biderman, former NSF secretary to set up meetings for the group. Sister Anne made a speech to the social workers convention on "By-passing the Establishment."

In 1969 the students started arriving almost as soon as the delegation of Louisiana folks returned from New York. They made a preliminary survey, and we had another tractor driver holiday when the U.S. Department of Agriculture held its annual hearing to fix a minimum wage that was "fair and reasonable." Nearly everyone presented a statement. A new element was then introduced into the proceedings. Three of the group of students held a meeting on the plantation of Southdown Sugars owned by the Tenneco Oil Company, which also possessed hundreds of thousands of acres in California and other states. The three young men had been in touch with the farm manager of Southdown Sugars and had told him of their plan to hold a meeting with the farm workers and to help them set up a self-improvement program to repair the shacks in which they lived. The student volunteers were arrested and thrown in jail at Houma, Louisiana, on the same day that the spacemen first landed on the moon, June 21, 1969. As soon as word reached me that these youngsters were in jail, I called union attorney Tom Nelson and an ex-newspaperman, Lynn W. Franklin. Then I recall talking to the bureau chief of the Associated Press in New Orleans. After giving him the facts, I remarked that three men could go to the moon, but three equally dedicated young men could not even get on a corporation owned plantation in the sugar cane country. This became the lead line of the story, and it appeared not only locally, but all over the country. Tom Nelson, Lynn Franklin and I were ready to take off for Houma when I got a call from Henry Pelet, a sugar refinery union leader. He said these three young students were about to be put into the bullpen with other prisoners, and he was especially fearful for the safety of Jay Youngdahl, who had long hair. The jailhouse was notorious for sexual assaults on young men. I urged Pelet to arrange for a bail bondsman to get the men released. He called back in a few minutes to say that the arrangement had been made, the men were free, and were heading for New Orleans.

One of the youngsters was David Papen, a former Holy Cross brother who had been teaching in a school in New Orleans and helping to run the grape boycott for the United Farm Workers. Gordon Johnson of Chicago, a student from Oberlin College, was another. The third was Jay Youngdahl, the son of James E. Youngdahl, union attorney from Little Rock. Thereafter the three were jokingly known among their friends as the "jailbirds." Soon after this occurrence, Lynn Franklin and his wife Pat invited the "jailbirds" to spend a week-end with them. Pat was an artist who was teaching at Tulane. Lynn had a sailboat and was often out on Lake Ponchartrain. One evening the four men returned from sailing. The young brother, Dave Papen, was the first to enter the Franklin house, and he almost had a heart attack when he saw what he thought was a nude woman in the entrance hall. Someone had placed a life-sized statue of nude Pat Franklin in the hall. It is possible that Gordon and Jay had arranged it to frighten "Brother David" as he then called himself. But they've never admitted it.

Lynn Franklin, who had been a reporter on the *New Orleans Times Picayune,* wrote an article that was never published about the trials and tribulations of Sister Anne Catherine, whom he termed "the Joan of Arc of Louisiana." I never saw her that way. To me, she was first of all a lovely woman who had the ability and personality to have made her mark anywhere. Though she abandoned the "habit," she remained a Rural Dominican nun.

Soon after the first student group left the sugar cane land, we called together a group comprised of nuns, priests, union organizers and plantation workers and set up an organization that I named "The Southern Mutual Help Association." This organization was set up to continue work we tried to do in the Amalgamated Meat Cutters and Butcher Workmen of N.A., AFL-CIO. Those involved included Frank Lapeyrolerie, who conducted the first manpower training program in Louisiana, organized the first self-help housing program in the state, and founded the St. Johns Federal Credit Union. Also included were the Broussards, mentioned earlier: Rose Mae, who managed the St. Jules Federal Credit Union, and her husband Bernard, who had been in the Southern Consumer Cooperative Association and in every other movement for social betterment in that area. Then there was Father Francis J. Ecimovich, pastor of St. Jules Catholic Church, who developed the housing project in his parish, conducted cooperative farming and marketing projects, and whose rectory housed and fed student workers and sometimes union organizers like me. Thomas Harris, the leader of the black community in the town of Thibadoux, and Henry Pelet, a sugar cane refinery worker of Bayou Le Fourche, both joined. There were also courageous plantation workers like Gustave Rhodes, who was among the first to join the union. Sister Anne Catherine was named director, and her assistant was Lorna Bourg. Later Father Vincent J. O'Connell, the man who helped Hank Hasiwar in the early 1950s and got kicked upstairs, returned to Louisiana, and took up where he had left off some years before. There were countless others. The Southern Mutual Help Association was chartered under state law as a nonprofit organization, and with leadership such as the above, health clinics, adult education projects, self-help housing and benefits of a similar nature came as a result of the organization that replaced the Agricultural and Allied Workers Union in the sugar cane land, after I left Louisiana in 1973. At every wage hearing held by the U.S. Department of Agriculture, Sister Anne Catherine and her helpers were there to demand increased wages and better working conditions for tractor drivers and others living on the plantations. By 1978 the minimum wage for plantation workers had increased to over $3 per hour. "With an organization like the SMHA," some said, "who needs a union?"

27 A New Career

"What a wonderful thing for the young people of this country," wrote Priscilla Robertson in 1972 when she first learned that I was visiting college campuses, talking to the students, and persuading historians and librarians to order the sixty reels of microfilm of the *Papers of the Southern Tenant Farmers Union*. Priscilla's letter continued: "Every generation thinks it invented the world, but ours was more political than the current generation, or so it seems to me."

I had received this letter in the mail just as I left home to appear at the University of Alabama in Tuscaloosa. I was having lunch with the chairman of the History Department when I thought of the letter and opened it and read the above to Dr. John Ramsay. He asked if this was *the* Priscilla Robertson, author of *Revolutions of 1848:* "Her book is required reading in all of my classes in European history." I recalled that Priscilla had sent me an autographed copy when her book first came out about fifteen years earlier. Dr. Ramsay then talked about

Priscilla's father, Preserved Smith, a famous historian at Cornell University. Professor Ramsay's voice indicated that this just-retired union organizer had risen in his estimation because he was a friend of Priscilla Robertson.

Priscilla Robertson of Louisville, Kentucky, and her photographer friend, Louise Boyle from Ithaca, New York, had spent the summer of 1937 working with the Southern Tenant Farmers Union and living in the crowded home of organizer Myrtle Lawrence. The two women attended union meetings nearly every night and always on Sunday. Louise Boyle's picture of a group of sharecroppers attending a union meeting under the bridge across U.S. Highway 70 near Forrest City caught the spirit of the interracial movement as no other photograph ever did, before or since. Priscilla had written an article about their summer project, but it was not published until 1970 when it was included in the STFU Papers.

One day a student named Tom Becnel, from the Louisiana State University at Baton Rouge, came to see me in Metairie, a suburb of New Orleans. He asked me to read a paper he had written about sugar cane plantation workers' strikes in Louisiana that dated back to the 1870s. I said, "Tom, you must have done a lot of research for this paper."

"Oh no," he replied, "it took me a lot longer to write it than to do the research work." He explained that the university library had copies of every newspaper in the state on microfilm, and since he knew the approximate dates of the sugar cane field workers revolt, he just read the newspaper accounts on microfilm. He asked me where the Southern Tenant Farmers Union papers were, and I replied that they were all in the Southern Historical Collection of the University of North Carolina, at Chapel Hill. I wondered if such a collection consisting of maybe 100 file boxes could be microfilmed. He was sure they could be.

Since it was obvious that the Amalgamated Meat Cutters would never try to unionize the plantation workers in Louisiana, or anywhere else, I had begun to think about an early retirement. I thought that Dorothy and I would move to Chapel Hill so I could work on our union papers, and perhaps do a book. However, there were complications. Dorothy's sister, Leila Dowe, had sold the famous restaurant "The Blue Moon Inn" and had retired some time ago. The new owner, Cecil McMillan, held a retirement party for "Sis," which we attended. I said at the party: "You know, Sis, when we retire, we will just come to Montgomery and live with you in that nice new home you have built." "Sis," who was some ten years older than we were, held us to that promise, at least to move to Montgomery. I knew I could not afford to commute between Montgomery and Chapel Hill, 500 miles away. This was especially true since the Amalgamated Meat Cutters and Butchers of N.A. AFL-CIO had decided that I was entitled to retirement pension credit only for the eleven years I had worked as an organizer for the Meat Cutters. This would amount to 22 percent of my highest average salary. I was low man on the totem pole. "Big Dick of Dallas" tried to persuade Pat Gorman and the executive board to honor the verbal commitment to include my previous 25 years as a union official. But officialdom stood firm and held that the written agreement we had signed to submerge our national union was all that counted.

So in 1973, I retired, taking the small pension from the Meat Cutters, which was less than I received from social security. With Dorothy's social security, and the interest on investments she had made, and income from some property she had inherited, we thought we would have enough for us to live frugally in Montgomery. Some other benefits accrued as a result of the Amalgamated organizers forming a union of their own. The benefits included a supplement to Medicare, dental and vision coverage, and a prescription drug program that covered any medicine prescribed by a doctor. We could get such medicine upon payment of a fifty-cent fee for each prescription. The big union gave me a good deal after all.

Prior to my retirement I had been invited to speak to students at the University of Indiana at Fort Wayne. An historian, Louis Cantor, had just written a book which he called *Prologue to the Protest Movement* published by Duke University Press, about the highway demonstration of evicted sharecroppers in southeast Missouri in 1939. My "lecture" was surprisingly well attended. There must have been at least 300 students and faculty members who turned out from both Indiana and Purdue Universities, which had adjoining campuses. I was interviewed on radio and television, and the Fort Wayne newspapers gave full coverage to my visit. Later that fall I visited Oberlin College near Cleveland, Ohio, where Gordon Johnson, one of the three students jailed in June for trespass on the Southdown Plantation, was finishing his undergraduate work. While at Oberlin, I also arranged for a work-study group to return to Louisiana the following spring to make a house-to-house survey of living and working conditions of sugar cane plantation workers. These college "kids" did a bang-up job under Sister Anne Catherine's direction. The father of Amy Gladstien, one of the students, was an economist, and he permitted his daughter to use a computer to analyze the results of the survey. The printout, when presented by the students at the 1970 public hearing on sugar cane wages, impressed the USDA officials and even the cane corporation people. Usually the corporate representatives came to the wage hearings armed with statistics proving that the sugar workers over the years had received wage increases of over 300 percent. Our reply was "So what?—300 percent of nothing is still nothing." But now we had documentary evidence of wage rates, housing, and other living and working conditions that could not be refuted.

Upon learning about microfilming from Tom Becnel, I had asked him to get the names and addresses of companies that performed such services. Eventually he sent the addresses of Bell and Howell, Eastman Kodak, University Microfilms, and The Microfilming Corporation of America. I sent a letter of inquiry to each of these companies. Within a few days I had a telephone call from Jean S. Reid of the Microfilming Corporation of America, a subsidiary of *The New York Times*. She thought her company would be interested in filming the STFU Papers on a commercial basis. She asked if the papers belonged to the university and said something about their paying a royalty to owners. The papers were only on loan to the UNC Library. My sole interest at that point was to find if I could get a copy of the microfilm for my own use. She was sure that if MCA undertook the job, I would be provided with a negative and a positive copy. She asked me to meet her in Chapel Hill. We set a date and then met with the director of the Southern Historical Collection, Dr. Isaac Copeland, and worked out a tentative agreement. I made a draft of the terms we had discussed, and asked Daniel H. Pollitt who was teaching at the law school at UNC-Chapel Hill, to put it in legal terms. Pollitt drafted the contract that provided a 20 percent royalty to the Rural Welfare Association that we had incorporated to hold all property of the STFU and its successor organizations. Fortunately for us, the officers of the Amalgamated Meat Cutters had no interest in the old office furniture we had in both Washington and Memphis, or in the old union files dating back to 1934. At Howard Kester's suggestion when he had arrived in early 1935, we had saved every letter that came in, and made a copy of every reply, and had one or more copies of nearly every document issued or received by the union over the past 35 years. Also in these files were thousands of letters from sharecroppers and farm workers themselves, about their day-to-day problems. The history professor from the University of North Carolina who first found the STFU papers housed in an old building on Beale Street in Memphis, said this was the greatest find of all time. Said Dr. Patton: "Important people such as statesmen had always saved their correspondence, but no one before had ever collected the letters of poor people."

We didn't really know why we had saved those things, but there they were. Soon *The New York Times'* lawyers had dotted a few "i's" and crossed a few "t's" in our proposed contract, and the agreement was signed. A graduate student from Columbia University, Daniel J. Singal, later a professor of history at Tulane University, was hired by the Microfilming Corporation to prepare the guide to the STFU Papers. With the cooperation and constant work of the staff of the Southern Historical Collection at the UNC Library, the papers were put in chronological order. Newspaper clippings were removed because *The New York Times* did not want to become involved in a controversy with some other newspaper or magazine publisher. I asked for and was given a leave-of-absence from the Amalgamated to work in Chapel Hill on the papers. After nearly a year's hard work on the part of all, the filming of the *STFU Papers* got underway. I wrote a draft for the "Introduction to the Guide" and called the collection "The Archives of the Rural Poor or the STFU Papers." I also arranged with Ben Wall, the secretary-treasurer of the Southern Historical Association, to provide a complete list of the association's members.

It was then suggested that I attend the annual meeting of the Southern Historical Association, to be held in 1971 at Houston, Texas. There was a panel on the "Southern Tenant Farmers." A paper was read by Donald H. Grubbs, whose new book *Cry from the Cotton—the STFU and the New Deal,* had just been published by the UNC Press. Louis Cantor, the author of *A Prologue to the Protest Movement,* also gave a paper. Dr. August Meier, of Kent State University, who was editing books about Negro History and had reprinted Howard Kester's *Revolt of the Sharecroppers,* was the commentator. Dr. Meier took the two young historians—Grubbs and Cantor—to task because they failed to emphasize interracial aspects of the Southern Tenant Farmers Union. A man in the audience got up and said: "I would like to hear what Leland Mitchell, who is here, has to say about these presentations." This was my grade-school classmate at Halls, Tennessee, now the famous Civil War historian, Dr. Bell Irvin Wiley, of Emory University. No one had called me by my given name in at least 30 years, except members of my own family. Not wishing to embarrass the young historians, and also being grateful to them for the things they had said in both their scholarly papers and in books, I was a bit evasive in my reply: "It seems strange to sit in a meeting, and hear myself discussed."

Then Dr. James Silver, who had spent many years teaching history at the University of Mississippi and had been discharged when he wrote the book *Mississippi: The Closed Society,* asked me a very pointed question. "Mr. Mitchell, what would have happened in 1939, if you had told your members camping along the highways of Southeast Missouri, as these historians suggest, to lie down on the highways and block all traffic with their bodies?"

"If I had made such a suggestion," I answered, "no one would have paid any attention to me, for they would have known that if they actually had lain down on the highways, they would have been run over and killed." I added that 1939 was nothing like 1971.

Dr. Bell Irvin Wiley introduced me to every prominent historian at the meeting. I also met for the first time that indomitable woman, Kate Stokes Born, then a part-time teacher at Memphis State University. She too introduced me to everyone she knew, and she knew a great many people attending the Southern Historical Convention that year. I afterwards sent out a huge mailing to all members of the Southern Historical Association, offering the *STFU Papers* for sale. To some of them I added a line saying that I was planning a trip to their vicinity, and if they would like to have me do so, I would be happy to stop over at their university to speak to classes or the student body. I didn't mention fees or even travel expenses. I was still on the payroll of the Amalgamated Meat Cutters, and Jean Reid had worked out an arrangement with the Microfilm Corporation whereby they would pick up the tab for expenses I incurred that the Amalgamated would not pay. In 1972, I started out on a tour that took me through Atlanta, Georgia; Columbia, South Carolina; Chapel Hill, North Carolina; Charlottesville, Virginia; and on up to New England, as far as Gorham, Maine. At some of the universities where I spent a day or two, someone would hand me a check with an apology for its being such a small honorarium. Others in charge of the arrangements would tell me that in due course, their university would send me an honorarium. They would ask for my social security number, and correct home address. I had never before heard the term "honorarium." However, as a rule, I learn things fast. So that winter when Jim Silver called me to come to the University of South Florida, I asked about the honorarium. As I recall, he agreed to find a couple of hundred dollars in addition to my round-trip plane fare. So it was, thereafter. Sometimes it was more, sometimes less. Incidentally, Jim Silver reminded me of how he, then a slim young black-haired professor from the University of Mississippi, climbed the dark stairs on Broad Street one day to find the office of the Southern Tenant Farmers Union and invite me to come to Oxford, Mississippi, to speak on a program he was arranging. I agreed, but I never heard anything more. Jim now said that he had duly reported the visit to the university president, who advised him that H. L. Mitchell was much too controversial at that time to be a guest speaker at the university. Dr. James Silver was determined to carry out a commitment he had made to me nearly 30 years before. Incidentally, the University of Mississippi very likely still considers me too controversial a person to darken its doors. However,

Mississippi State University at Starkville, the home of the South's agricultural power structure in the 1930's, has acquired most of the STFU papers on microfilm.

I was able to place more than 60 sets of the microfilm edition of *The Archives of the Rural Poor or the STFU Papers* in academic and public libraries in the United States, and several more in other countries. The successors to the organization men of *The New York Times,* who once dressed in gray flannel suits, were not always appreciative of my efforts to place their product in libraries in this country and in foreign lands as well. Sometimes the newcomers would question the value of having the old man with contacts on more than one hundred of the nation's finest colleges and universities claiming commissions as well as royalties on these sets of microfilms. I became a fixture at many of the historical associations' conventions. Once I appeared at an annual meeting of the Organization of American Historians, to find a large table set aside, with a hand-printed notice: "This table reserved for Mr. H. L. Mitchell of the Historic Southern Tenant Farmers Union," so that is how I got the designation: "H. L. Mitchell, Co-Founder of Historic Southern Tenant Farmers Union." At least, I was one of the eleven white and seven black men who founded the STFU, and that's what I'd like to be remembered for. Just how "historic" the organization was or is, I leave to the historians.

28 In Memoriam

A Tough Old Radical—America's Conscience

When Norman Thomas died at the age of 84 in December 1968, an Arkansas newspaper editorial termed him a "Tough Old Radical," but he was more than that. He was America's conscience. "There are no lost causes," he said, "only causes that have not yet been won." Norman Thomas put his life on the line for every worthy unpopular cause of his time. He made "sharecropper" a household word, and the Southern Tenant Farmers Union almost as well known.

When terror struck the cotton fields of eastern Arkansas, and night-riders were on the prowl, breaking up union meetings, burning churches, shooting up the homes of union leaders, while men were being beaten, jailed, and a few killed, Norman Thomas came back to Arkansas to make his powerful voice heard. In the village of Birdsong he was manhandled and driven out of Arkansas. Thereafter, for nearly 25 years, he came back to speak at union meetings. As much as any other man he helped stir the lethargic AFL-CIO leadership into action in behalf of farm workers. Also, in the mid-1960s, when he was past 70, he was down south again, involved in the civil rights movement.

Early in 1968, I had my last visit with Norman Thomas. He was crippled and almost blind, but as mentally alert as always. He invited me to have lunch with him and we talked about old times and old friends. He thought it was great that I kept up with so many of our mutual friends. After an hour's talk, he apologized for having to leave to keep an appointment uptown with the Secretary-General of the United Nations. I hailed a taxicab for him.

In 1976 W. A. Swanberg's biography, *Norman Thomas: The Last Idealist,* was published. It described the details of his life, but the author never explained what Norman Thomas' life was really about, his belief in socialism and in the cooperative commonwealth of the future. Perhaps the author, who was also the biographer of Henry Luce, founder of the *Time-Life* empire, never knew that it was Thomas' belief in socialism that made him the idealist he was, as well as the voice of all that was best in America.

Latter Days of Gardner (Pat) Jackson

One night in early 1944, Pat Jackson was in New York with a physician friend of ours, Emil G. Conason. Pat had been drinking, and then he had a few more as the two drifted from one bar to another in Greenwich Village. At one point they ran into some of Joe Curran's boys, one of whom was known as an ardent supporter of the Communist Party. Joe Curran was founder and president of the National Maritime Union, CIO. Jackson called them all a bunch of phonies, and there were angry replies by the Maritime Union men. Dr. Conason persuaded his friend Jackson to leave and put him to bed at the old Earle Hotel on Washington Square. Soon after being left alone, Pat got up and returned to the street, where he again met the NMU group and was beaten almost to death. Jackson suffered the loss of one eye, and it was more than a year before he could return to Washington and resume his career in behalf of the underdog.

Early in 1940, Gardner Jackson had been asked by President Roosevelt to investigate the connections between John L. Lewis and William H. Davis, an oil multi-millionaire from Alabama and Texas. Davis was selling oil through Mexico to Nazi Germany and Fascist Italy. Conason knew about this assignment from the President. We—Conason and I— once speculated whether Pat Jackson on his second foray into the Village that night had revealed what he knew to the NMU men, and whether the communists had not tried to kill him for that reason. Both John L. Lewis and his Mexican counterpart, Vincente Toledano, president of the Confederation of Trade Unions of Mexico (CTM), were known to have been associated with the disreputable William H. Davis. When Emil Conason was in City College of New York, he was an organizer for the Young Communist League. He was involved when Jay Lovestone was general secretary of the Communist Party USA, and he knew that murder for political purposes was sometimes carried out.

Before I wrote the first letter to President Harry S Truman in 1949, asking that a second presidential commission be formed to investigate the plight of the nation's farm workers, I talked with Pat about it. He drafted the letter for me, then helped me line up support among liberals in and outside the Administration, and in the CIO. After I received the reply from President Truman saying that the matter was under consideration, I submitted a list of persons I thought should be members of the commission. Pat did the same. Only one of those I recommended was selected. He was Robert E. Lucey, the Archbishop of San Antonio, whom I had met a year or two before when visiting in Texas. Peter Odegard of the University of California, recommended by Jackson, was also named to the commission. Odegard and Jackson were involved in selecting Varden Fuller to be the executive secretary of the President's Commission on Migratory Labor in American Agriculture.

For some reason, Pat Jackson and I were the ones who met the train bringing Archbishop Lucey to Washington for the first meeting of the President's Commission. We were both unaccustomed to meeting and greeting Archbishops of the Roman Catholic Church. We talked about whether we should call him "Your Grace," "Your Excellency," or whatever. When Lucey got off the train, Pat asked him, and his reply was: "You can just call me 'Archbishop' if you like. Some of the people down in Texas call me 'the Arch,' and others call me worse names than that."

It was after the Presidential Commission had made its report, and soon after the Democrats had won back control of both the House and Senate, that I had a telephone call from Pat. He said: "I just ran into Lyndon Johnson here in the Senate Office Building. I tied into him and asked when he was going to do something for the American farm worker. Lyndon replied, 'Now is the time.' He said we should go see Pete Williams, and tell him he said the issue of migrant farm workers is a natural one for him to take up." As he rambled on about other matters, it was obvious to me that Pat had been drinking, but I realized that this was of utmost importance.

Lyndon Johnson, Majority Leader of the Senate, had told us to see the newly elected Senator Harrison Williams of New Jersey, and he was telling Williams that the farm worker question was a major issue for him to handle. I lost no time once Pat stopped talking. I called AFL and CIO people. I contacted Williams' office directly and asked for an appointment for a group of us to meet with the Senator. The meeting was set up. Since Senator Williams had been placed on the Labor and Welfare Committee of the Senate, we proposed that a subcommittee on Migratory Labor be made permanent and that Williams be made chairman. We also arranged that one of our group, Attorney Daniel H. Pollitt, should become Acting Counsel for the subcommittee. And so was born a special committee in the U.S. Senate for the nation's farm workers, because Pat Jackson and Lyndon Johnson met out in the hall on "The Hill." Interestingly too, Pat could not remember the incident at all. He accepted my word that he was responsible.

As described earlier, I met Walter Reuther at Pat's home in 1952, to discuss an organizing campaign among farm workers. It was before the merger of the AFL and CIO occurred. The Jackson home was a meeting place for many of the older New Dealers and for those who were, or wanted to be, in the upcoming Democratic Administration of John F. Kennedy and Lyndon Johnson. Pat Jackson had worked with young Kennedy in his first campaign for Congress. After Kennedy's election to Congress, I met him once at the Jackson home. As I recall, Jack Kennedy was there to consult Pat about a Georgetown house for his family. Later, the Kennedys bought a large house on N Street NW, several blocks from the Jackson home.

I often found the Schlesingers, as Pat called them, "Papa Arthur" and "Young Arthur," at the Jacksons' home. Dr. Schlesinger, Sr., was a Harvard professor, and Dr. Schlesinger, Jr., wrote books about the New Deal and became an assistant to President Kennedy. Also a frequent guest at the Jacksons' was the novelist John Dos Passos. Dos Passos had been associated with Pat in the Sacco-Vanzetti Defense Committee. As Dos Passos grew older, he became more and more conservative, but even so, I found him a delightful person. At one point, Joe Rauh, an outstanding civil liberties and labor attorney, was involved in a defense of playwright Arthur Miller, who was accused of being a communist by the Senate Committee on Internal Security. Pat and I met Miller one day in Rauh's office. I did not, however, meet Mrs. Arthur Miller, as Pat so formally called Marilyn Monroe.

However, not all of Pat's friends were prominent or famous. Sometimes he would strike up an acquaintance with some down-and-out person on the street and bring him home for dinner and a talk. For nearly a hundred years the city of Washington had no representative government, and the District of Columbia was run by the Congress. From time to time, the voiceless and non-voting citizens of the nation's capital would organize. Pat Jackson was always involved. He would appear before the congressional committees to speak for these underdogs too. Sometimes Pat Jackson was called the unofficial mayor of Washington.

Pat spent most of his days going around from office to office on Capitol Hill or to the many government agencies. Taxi fares were cheap, and Pat always started his day with a pocketful of nickels and dimes for making his numerous telephone calls. Usually he telephoned me at least once a day, if we were both in town. At his home, he had a favorite chair next to the telephone. I recall that one night after numerous calls, someone asked his wife, Dode, if Pat didn't get a sore arm from holding the telephone so long. "Oh yes," said Dode, "I usually have to massage his arm every day, and you know, Pat has a callous on his ear caused by the telephone." Pat strenuously denied the allegations.

If anyone wanted to find someone in government or in the AFL or CIO, they asked Gardner Jackson. If he didn't know the person, he knew someone who did. Soon after General Eisenhower became President, and in the economy drive afterwards, there were stories going around among the employees of the government. One we picked up was that someone called the Department of Defense and asked the telephone operator, "Do you have a Sexour there?" Her reply was, "Lord no, we don't even have a coffee break since this new administration came in." But Pat said that in fact "There is a Colonel Sexour over there, I know him."

In an editorial in the *New York Post* on April 17, 1965, James A. Weschsler said, "He was the gentlest agitator, the troubled troublemaker, the friend of the lonely have-nots, and the conscience of many of the powerful. When he died at 68, they didn't stop the presses anywhere. Yet for nearly 40 zestful years, Gardner (Pat) Jackson was both a legend and a meaningful presence in the battle against injustice."

Arthur Schlesinger, Jr., in *The New Republic,* wrote about his own and his father's friend:

He began as a student defending President Alexander Meiklejohn against conservative attacks at Amherst. As a reporter on *The Boston Globe* he organized the Defense Committee for Sacco and Vanzetti. In New Deal Washington he constituted a one man farmer-labor party. If he could get no one to work with him in combating the indignities of the world, he would cheerfully set out to do it by himself. . . . He cared so deeply about people and injustice, he forgot things other people care about, like power, prestige, money.

The 40th Anniversary of the STFU

In 1974, some of the survivors of the sharecropper and farm worker struggles of the 1930s, '40s, '50s, and '60s, met in Little Rock to celebrate the 40th Anniversary of the founding of the Southern Tenant Farmers Union. They were joined by friends and supporters who had been with us through the years.

Clay East and I were the only ones left of the 18 founders of the STFU. Clay was living in a mobile home in a Tucson, Arizona, trailer park. He and his wife Belva came to Little Rock for the meeting and to take part in a session held a day later by the Arkansas Historical Association at Camden. After leaving the Arkansas scene in 1936, Clay operated gas stations and grocery stores in Arizona until he retired in the early 1970s. He said he had played the stock market in a small way and accumulated a little of this world's goods. During World War II he worked in an aircraft plant near Phoenix and helped organize a union in the International Machinists Association. He was still a socialist.

J. R. (John Russell) Butler was also at the anniversary meeting. As president of the STFU in 1942, he refused re-election because of his disagreement with me over my pragmatic approach to current problems, which he termed opportunism. He became a skilled machinist, and as a member of the IAM (International Association of Machinists), helped organize new plants in Memphis during the war years. He prospered during this time and bought an apartment building where he occupied a small unit and rented the rest. After retirement he moved to Phoenix, Arizona, and lived there until his death in 1975. Butler was a very private person, and while we knew that he had been married, it was not until after his death that we learned he had two children. At the anniversary, Butler joined Evelyn Smith Munro, our first office secretary, in conducting (perhaps for the last time) the "Ceremony of the Land." The closing lines are, "Speed now the day when the plains, the hills and all the wealth thereof shall be the people's own, and free men shall not live as tenants of men, but become the faithful keepers of one another, and the good earth—our home."

After leaving the STFU, Evelyn Smith had an active career in various social enterprises, and she had married David Munro, in New York. During World War II Munro was involved in public relations work for the Office of Price Administration headed by another advertising man, Chester Bowles. For a few months Evelyn edited a Washington News Letter for the STFU, perhaps pointing the way for our eventual establishment of our main office in Washington. After the war ended in 1946, Dave Munro returned to college and received his doctorate at the University of Michigan. Later, they moved to California where Evelyn was education director of ILGWU in the western states. At one point, she was conducting interracial day care centers and she came in conflict with the rank reactionaries of Orange County who tried to convict her of being a communist. After all, she had been a socialist, worked for the STFU, been a labor organizer—any of these was sufficient grounds for a Nixonite to brand her a communist in those days. Evelyn and Dave Munro had three daughters. From time to time, Dave received assignments to teach in foreign countries. The Munros were at the University in Santiago, Cuba, when the Cuban Revolution led by Fidel Castro broke out. Later, they were at an African University when there was a revolt in Biafra. After returning from their adventures abroad, Evelyn became a writer for the education extension service of the University of California at Irvine.

George Stith, who was among those who played a great role in building the STFU, also attended the anniversary meeting. Stith served the union in nearly every capacity, because he was very capable, loyal and dependable. After serving as an organizer in California and Louisiana, Stith retired from union activity and learned the welder's trade. He was employed by a company near his home town of Gould, Arkansas. In 1978, at the age of 62, he became a minister. As he said, he had always preached to people about the union, and now he was talking to them in the same way in the small churches he served.

Frank Lapeyrolerie of Reserve, Louisiana, the black man who led the sugar cane plantation workers' strike in 1953, and later built housing for plantation workers, formed credit unions and conducted manpower training projects, was also at the 40th Anniversary meeting in Little Rock. Frank continued his activities until his death in September 1978. He was attending a meeting of the Council on the Aging when suddenly he was stricken with a heart attack and died instantly. He was a kind and gentle man.

Presiding at the 40th Anniversary meeting was A. E. Cox, one of the 1936 founders of the Delta Cooperative Farm in Mississippi. He was accompanied by his wife, Lindsey Hail Cox, a registered nurse who first came to the co-op farm intending to remain for a summer. Instead, she married "Gene," and stayed in Mississippi for 30 years, until the family was driven from the state by the White Citizens Council of Holmes County.

Ernesto Galarza, 1969

American Historical Convention, New Orleans, 1972. Left to right: John Beecher, H. L. Mitchell, Howard Kester. In the background: "Labor Documents in Microfilm," STFU-NFLU papers featured in MCA booth display.

H. L. Mitchell at the University of California-Irvine, 1971. (photo by Evelyn Smith Munro)

Fortieth Anniversary of the
Southern Tenant Farmers Union

Ceremony of the Land, Little Rock, Ark.,
1974. (photos by Bradley Smith) STFU ceremony written by Howard Kester and Evelyn
Smith was first performed at the 3rd Convention, Muskogee, Oklahoma, January 17,
1937.

Left: J. R. Butler and Evelyn Smith Munro
officiating.

Clay East

Sidney Hertzberg and Carrie L. Dilworth

Left to right: H. L. Mitchell, George Stith, A. E. Cox

Others who were at the celebration were the following:

Tee Davis and his wife, Elizabeth. Davis served seven years for trying to defend his home from an intruder who failed to identify himself.

There was Mrs. Carrie Dilworth. She was still living in Gould, Arkansas, in 1978, though not in good health.

Mrs. Fannye Booker of Holmes County, Mississippi, one of the leaders of the STFU and a resident of Providence Farm, was also there.

Sidney Hertzberg, who founded *National Sharecroppers Week* to raise money to aid the Southern Tenant Farmers Union was there.

Making pictures as he had done in the Little Rock Convention in 1938, was famed photographer (*Life Magazine,* etc.) Bradley Smith, Evelyn S. Munro's brother. Alfred Baker Lewis was there. He once offered to raise money to buy an armored car for the STFU. I sent him word to please send the money, but leave the car in Boston. Lewis afterwards became treasurer of the NAACP.

James Loeb, a former Ambassador and White House Aid to President Kennedy, was there. At one time Jim was treasurer of the *National Sharecroppers Week* and in 1943 was incorporator and board member of NSF.

There were many local people from Little Rock and Memphis who one way or another were associated with the STFU, and they came too. The AFL-CIO state president, J. Bill Becker, came; and Nick Zonarich of AFL-CIO from Washington, and Steve Coyle, the International vice-president of the Amalgamated Meat Cutters, from Chicago, came.

Among those who wanted to be at the 40th Anniversary meeting, but couldn't make it was Howard Kester, whose wife had died a few years before. Buck Kester had retired after a long career as an educator. He had been dean of students at Montreat College, near Asheville, N.C., and lived nearby in High Top Colony, near Black Mountain. Kester died on July 12, 1977. I attended a memorial service held at the Blue Ridge Assembly Chapel near Kester's home. The services were conducted by Will Campbell, the director of the Committee of Southern Churchmen, which was founded by Kester and others in the summer of 1934. Four generations participated in the memorial service. They were Kester's grandson, Graham Neale, Tony Dunbar, Will Campbell, and me. Then at the suggestion of the conductor, all of his friends who gathered there stood and gave a round of applause which reverberated over the Blue Ridge Hills for the orator, the preacher, and the radical prophet—Howard Kester.

We heard from a good many more of our old-time organizers and friends in late 1977, when our association of Members and Friends of the Southern Tenant Farmers Union distributed nearly $1,000 left over from microfilm sales and from speaking engagements I had made at twenty colleges and universities. Checks were sent out to nearly 40 of the surviving members of the STFU and its successor organizations, whose names and addresses were still known. Most of these were people who were also entitled to a small death benefit on a group insurance policy we carried for them. So in December 1977, we received many cards and letters from those who received checks.

One of the most interesting was from Mrs. Corinne Partlow, the last secretary of the Edmondson, Arkansas, local of the STFU. She was born in April 1908. In her letter she described affairs in the town of Edmondson, which the STFU had fought to save from the greed of the plantation owners and restore it to its original black owners. All of the letters are presented as they were written:

Edmondson, Ark.
Dec. 23, 1977

Mr. H. L. Mitchell

Dear Sir:

Mr Mitchell your Letter & The check came as a great Surprise to me as the old saying is it left me dumfounded not noeing what to say However it found me well & That $25.00 was Just what I needed for Xmas I got me a dress & several other items Oh I thank you one million times & would Kiss your hands if I were clost enough Mr Mitchel Edmondson have come a long ways we have a colored mayer Clifton Minnis We colored people have built a City Hall we have the post office in it but of course the white people are wanting to move It but I am praying that they dont We ceniour Citizens Meet 5 days a week in it we eat 1 meal we piece quilts we quilt we nit Caps make hats them that can We sell these things to try to Keep our orginazion going on sometime our money runs Just about out we are trying to build a room to the City Hall for ceniour citizens only but have no succeded yet we have a Fire Truck We have city water also here in Edmondson Now street Lights I have Rhumatism but I don't stop going I got a Christmas card from Mr A.E. Cox Well I say Thank you again Mr. Mitchell Wishing you & yours a Merry Xmas & a Happy New Year & may you live a long long time and God Bless you forever

FROM Corinne Partlow
P.O. Box 103
Edmondson, Ark. 72332

Dear Friend Mitch

My writing hand is hampered by inherited arthritis, but I want to thank you promptly for most pleasant Holiday surprise. Thank you for both enclosures. When I returned to Mfs in the 50's and obliged to find work for myself and home for my father, I was most grateful to become employed by the Mfs Academy of Arts where I found friends who treasure the same values. Frances G. (see enclosed) taught classes there. As it happened, he died from brain tumor the same day as Presley, but his passing was literally buried on back page of paper. So I'm sending your $25 gift, which will be matched by his partner, to promote a scholarship. What better investment than our constructive youth?

All best wishes,

M. V. [Margaret Valiant]

Margaret Valiant once introduced me at the Unitarian Fellowship in Memphis as one who was good at getting money from rich widows up North to help poor folks down South. Margaret was the daughter of a Mississippi plantation owner. She attended a conservatory of music and spent a year in Italy, where she auditioned at La Scala Opera House. She became ill, lost her voice, and returned to the United States in the darkest days of the Depression. She became a worker for the Planned Parenthood Association in New York City and lived with its founder, Margaret Sanger. For a brief time she was in the chorus line of the Ziegfield Follies. Later, she collected folk songs with Charles H. Seeger, Peter Seeger's father. She worked for the Resettlement Administration, during which time she wrote and produced a play which was performed at the White House. She became a friend of President and Mrs. Franklin D. Roosevelt.

I first met her in 1939, when we were both working for Aubrey Williams, administrator of the National Youth Administration in North Carolina, and later in the Washington office. Margaret was the organizer of the Youth Philharmonic Orchestra directed by Leopold Stokowski. She discovered Arthur Fiedler and was able to persuade the N.Y.A. to employ him. She returned to Memphis in the mid-fifties, worked for the Memphis Fine Arts Commission, and also at a public radio and television station. She was the first white person to move into an all black public housing project in Memphis. In 1977, she was still carrying on the battle for human rights, taking the liberal position by telephone, on radio and TV talk shows.

Mr. H. L. Mitchell   Edmondson, Ark.

Dear Mr. Mitchell   Dec 2, 1977

I am well as a woman of my age can be. I was really surpriced to get the money & I thank you so much I am sorry I was so long about writing but I dont write no more so I have to get some one to write for me but Mr. Mitchell you new just what I needed most I just love you & am glad you were thinking about me Love to your family & Happy New Year

FROM PHEBIA BELL

Edmondson Ark.

Thank you Thank you Thank you

Mrs. Bell was then 85 years old. She was born June 11, 1892.

Pine Bluff, Ark.
Dec 18 1977

Mr. H. L. Mitchell
I receive your letter and the check I thank you very much I am sorry to tell you tee die on the 16 of november he had ben sick so long I am style live in my home it is very lonesom But the lord nose bes & I will strive to stay in tuch with you by writing I no it will be a said Xmas with me we had be married 44 year that has ben a long time & thank you Very Much for the check Because I rely need it & wish you a Merry Xmas and a happy New year From Elizabeth Davis
pine Bluff Ark 6014 W short Ave

This letter is from the widow of Tee Davis, a sharecropper who lived and worked on an Arkansas plantation. One night he and his wife were awakened by a man knocking on his door demanding that "You black S.O.B. come on out here!" Tee asked who wanted him. The intruder refused to identify himself and knocked the door down. As he did, Tee fired at the man, slightly wounding him. It was a deputy sheriff. Tee Davis was jailed, tried and convicted of "assault with intent to kill." The Southern Tenant Farmers Union and the Workers Defense League provided legal defense for Tee Davis. Appeals were made to the Supreme Court—to no avail. Tee Davis served seven years on the Cummings Prison Farm in Arkansas. Tee Davis and his wife attended the 40th Anniversary of the founding of the STFU in Little Rock in 1974.

Route 3 Box 241
Russellville, Ala.
Dec. 30, 1977

Dear Bro. Mitchell,
Many Thanks for the Check for $25.00. I was surprised and very thankful to receive it.
I am doing pretty good Considering my age and Condition. My eyes have almost failed me and am crippled with Arthritis almost beyond getting about. Hope you have a happy and prosperous New Year

Fraternally yours,
A. A. Tiggs

A. A. Tiggs, of Russellville was Secretary of the STFU Local at Russellville, organized in the early 1940s. He was one of the leaders of the Alabama Co-operative Association that operated a cooperative store in the town of Spruce Pine, Alabama. He was born September 9, 1892—and was past 85 years of age at above writing. Mr. Tiggs died in early 1978.

Wentworth, Wis
Dec 18 1977

Dear Mitch:—

It was sure nice to hear from you and the check was sure a surprise. I am really enjoying my old age. Do a lot of hunting and fishing and made 3 trips to Europe in the last seven years. Please keep me on your mailing list. I Like to get your newsletters. I was very glad to hear that you carry on as you do. More power to you. Greet all my old friends as you see them. My wish for you is the Biggest measure, plumb full of Good health and Happiness.

Yours truly
Karl Schiminek

Karl Schimenek was born June 1906. He was one of the leaders of the Minnesota-Wisconsin Dairy Farmers. His family came from Norway, and apparently he has made several trips to the old country since retirement.

Southern Tenant Farmers Union
C/o
Mr. H. L. Mitchell

Thanks very much for the check for $25.00. My daughter is writing this note. My sight has just about gone, but thank the Lord, I feel pretty good. May God Bless you,

George Burnett

George Burnett lived in Tillar, Arkansas. He was nearly 84, born January 1894.

29 Nostalgia, Meet Reality

There have been many changes in agriculture in the past 50 years. The harvest hand and the migrant worker are rapidly being displaced by machines. Today, machines are used to plant, cultivate and harvest most fruits and vegetables. The Agricultural Experiment Stations maintained by the United States Department of Agriculture developed the cotton picking machine that displaced hundreds of thousands of family farmers and hired workers. They are now doing the same for other crops. If not already in use, the machines are on the drawing boards. The manufacturers of farm implements are prepared to make and sell them as soon as there is enough of a demand.

In 1950 there were 200,000 farms in the state of Alabama. By 1970, there were only 61,000 farm units of all kinds in the state, and of these only 17,000 had owners who earned their living from the land as productive farmers. The story is the same everywhere. However, there is a discernable revolution underway in the rural areas of this country. Workers from the industrial areas are returning in ever-increasing numbers to the rural community. In some cases, one member or more of a family owns a small tract of land, and the family living is earned from industrial jobs, to which the workers may commute, sometimes as much as a hundred miles daily. Others, on retirement, return to the land or to small towns to live on union-negotiated pensions or, in many cases, social security benefits. Often, the return to the land is made to escape the problems of city living. Sometimes the back-to-the land impulse is due to nostalgia provoked by stories told by the parents or grand-parents who migrated to the cities in the '30s, '40s, and '50s. Few of these new rural dwellers are productive farmers. Even if they eventually learn how to farm, nearly all lack the capital to buy or rent extensive tracts of land, or to acquire the costly machines needed to make a living on the farm today.

In February 1976 an editorial appeared in the *Pine Bluff Commercial* entitled, "Nostalgia, Meet Reality." It was written by Paul Greenburg, a Pulitzer Prize winner, and tells the story much better than I can, so here it is in full.

Nostalgia, Meet Reality

A few years ago, a fellow was driving us around the back roads on a tour of the place where he had grown up. The only landmarks were the abandoned shacks that dot the roads of the rural South. After the umpteenth one, he turned and said: "You know, there used to be a family living in every one of those places. Sad, isn't it?"

Forty-two years ago, Harry Leland Mitchell was organizing the people who lived in just such houses around Tyronza, Arkansas. At its peak in 1938, his Southern Tenant Farmers Union would have 31,000 members. It had a powerful dream of a prosperous society of smallholders rooted in the land. And it had even more powerful enemies.

It was the high point of H. L. Mitchell's organizing days, and when he came to Pine Bluff this week to lecture, one might have expected him to look back longingly and explain why the old dream would work even now. One would be disappointed. H. L. Mitchell isn't likely to confuse nostalgia with a policy.

Yes, Mr. Mitchell can trade stories with the best of 'em. He can talk turnip greens and brozene. He has a remarkable memory for names and places forty years back; he still has a vivid recollection of the time Huey Long came up here from Louisiana and put Hattie Caraway, that poor widdur-woman, in the United States Senate. But those days are long gone, well gone in many respects, and in any case beyond reviving. What about his union's old dream? "Hell," he replies, "you can't unscramble eggs."

The old dream is enjoying something of a revival these days among campus theorists and others who never had to live through the reality. But it becomes increasingly difficult, almost impossible, for the small—the really small— farmer to compete with the economies of scale available to agribusiness.

H. L. Mitchell traces the great exodus of farm workers back to their failure to get a fair share of federal subsidies under the first Agricultural Adjustment Act. But in the end the most powerful enemy of his union was not any political figure, or even the political system, but the progression of technology. It is a progression that continues today as fewer and fewer hands are required to farm more and more land, and more crops are harvested by machine.

Sad, isn't it? But perhaps not as sad as the reality that was sharecropping. Mr. Mitchell knows the economic and political bondage it spelled, the endless debts to the company store, the lack of education, the sight of votes being trucked to the polls—a tradition that continued until lately.

The Southern Tenant Farmers Union was too close to the reality to gloss it over with fancied hopes. "We were probably the only organization," Mr. Mitchell recalls, "that ever encouraged its workers to leave." When the opportunity arose for wrk outside the sharecrop system, the union urged its members to take it, and not dally.

H. L. Mitchell always did have a sharp eye for reality. That may explain his life-long aversion to communism, even when a little compromise with it might have furthered his career in the union. Even now, when he hears the Chinese communes cited as a model, he wonders why it's always the secretary of the Communist Party who winds up as the boss. And why, instead of the will of the people flowing up through the table of organization, it's the boss who sends the orders down. Ever the happy provacateur, he compares that system to the kind of "grass-roots" policy-making favored by the American Farm Bureau.

One would have liked to have been there in 1948 when H. L. Mitchell was asked to support Henry Wallace's presidential campaign. Mr. Mitchell remembered Mr. Wallace from 15 years before as the Secretary of Agriculture who purged the tenant farmers' friends from his department, and how he suppressed the news that federal subsidies were going to those who owned the land but not those who worked it. When you start doing farm work at the age of eight, going to school only when no work can be found, and grow up with all the other aspects of the sharecrop system, you *remember*. Yep, one would have liked to have been there when H. L. Mitchell was asked to support Henry Wallace for anything.

At 69, Mr. Mitchell has had a long acquaintance with the American tradition of agrarian demagogues. He finds the current crop, mainly George Wallace, disappointing, to say the least. The old-timers, the Bilbos and Vardamans and Huey Longs, did have a grasp of the economic interests of their barefoot constituency, says Mr. Mitchell. Though their drive for power might have obscured that fact. George Wallace has the words and culture and prejudices down pat, says Mr. Mitchell, but there's no substance to any of it. Which strikes us as pretty accurate diagnosis of the Wallace Syndrome. In the language of the political scientists, ol' George is all status politics and no issues.

Mr. Mitchell is too much of a realist, and apparently always has been, to go for empty ideology. Whether it comes from the politically ambitious or young crusaders against the clock. He's more interested in controlling economic currents than waging a futile fight against them. H. L. Mitchell still speaks of the danger of monopolies and the need for competition, but he won't take refuge in nostalgia, or confuse economic illiteracy with a last redoubt. He doesn't pretend to know the answer, but he does seem to have a pretty sure grasp of what the answer isn't, which is an impressive sight these days.

Nearly all of the small farmers who turned to the union for assistance had some connection with the trade union, or socialist movement, as witness the Scandinavian dairymen of northern Minnesota and Wisconsin. The dairy farmers of Ohio, Pennsylvania, and West Virginia were often coal miners, also engaged in farming as a second calling. Even in Louisiana, many of the dairy farmers who turned to the union for salvation had worked in the paper mill at Bogalusa and were members of the well established trade unions. However, except for the 40 dairymen who were covered by a contract with C. A. Stewart & Co., the attempt to unionize the small farmers failed. Nearly all of the would-be farm unionists lost out to the privately owned, collectivized, corporate farm operation—the wave of the future. Tomato growers in New Jersey and Pennsylvania contracted in advance for sale of their crops with processors such as the Campbell Soup and H. J. Heinz companies. Citrus fruit groves in California, Florida, and Texas, while nominally owned by individuals, are members of associations, many of them cooperatives, but operating as corporate business structures. The American ideal of small farm ownership, with every man living in his own home with the proverbial vine and fig tree, is, for all practical purposes, gone from this land.

Sharecropping scarcely exists anywhere. A tenant farmer like Buddy Chadwick, of Pine Bluff, Arkansas, who is also president of his County Farm Bureau and who rents land from retired owners living in the town or cities, and farms 3,000 acres of cotton, rice, and soy beans, is a far cry from the hundred sharecropper families once needed to farm the same acreage. In 1976, Chadwick had an investment of a quarter-of-a-million dollars in machinery alone. He, his brother, and three other men planted, cultivated and harvested the crops grown on his rented acreage. Chadwick said that all five of the workers drove tractors with air conditioned cabs, and his brother had stereo in his tractor cab as well. Conglomerates like Tenneco Corporation and the Jim Walters Housing Corporation are models of capitalistic enterprise.

The solution to the farm problem does not lie in trying to turn back the clock to the eighteenth century ideal of small farm ownership. It remains the same as it was in the 1930s when we in the STFU had a dream that large-scale privately owned plantations could be made into cooperative farming units owned and operated by and for the farmers who did the actual work on the land. Instead, the farms, ranches and plantations have grown larger. The land is owned by corporate enterprises whose objective is to make a huge profit. For over 40 years they have been subsidized by the U.S. Treasury. Labor from Mexico and the West Indies has been provided, while labor-displacing machines have been developed by other agencies of government. The taxpayer and consumer have paid for the capital investment in land, machinery, and labor a hundred times over. Eventually agriculture, America's largest industry, must be socialized and operated for the benefit of those who work on the land and those who consume its products. This I believe is the real wave of the future.

What Life has Meant to Me

Since that hot night in July 1934, when eighteen men met to form the Southern Tenant Farmers Union, I have never known what it was to be bored. I have gotten tired. Sometimes I have been discouraged. Sometimes I have been very angry. I have never met a man or woman that I could not really have liked. I could not hate the plantation owners of Eastern Arkansas, nor their retainers who often wanted to take my life, and a few times damned near succeeded. I could not hate the deputy sheriffs nor the plantation riders who broke up union meetings, beat up men and women, and even killed a few. I felt sorry for them all, for they too were the victims of a system they did not make. I could never hate the politicians who supported the programs, or the bureaucrats who administered the programs that had built-in discrimination against those who were at the bottom of the economic heap. However, I have always believed that it was my job, no matter where I was, to expose injustice, to stir up controversy among complacent people. I believe that if "mean things" are brought to light, then something may eventually be done to correct them.

I don't believe there is another world to come, and I am glad there isn't; to live to be one hundred is enough. I have never accumulated any of this world's goods. I never built a lasting organization of people; I never had the problem of exercising power justly because I never had any power. There will be no marble-faced building erected to the memory of H. L. Mitchell in Washington, or anywhere else, and I am glad.

When I shall have lived out my life (100 years, more or less), I have asked that my body be cremated, and that my ashes be scattered in the wind over Eastern Arkansas. Then, if any one of the plantation owners or their descendants who know of me still survive, may they some day look up to the sky, and if something gets in their eyes, they can then say: "There is that damned Mitchell again."

*   *   *

December 5, 1978

Dear Mitch,

Thanks so much for coming to Tulsa—we've enjoyed all conversations and the time you've spent with us.

We appreciate the work you've done in your life and the work you're still doing. Let 'em call us a bunch of young idealists—and we'll include you.

Thanks so much,

THE STUDENT'S PROGRESSIVE CAUCUS
(Univ. of Tulsa)

Linda M. Overbey
Joanne Magnis
Scot W. Boulton
Charles Sackrey
Toni Byrd
Brian D. Hunt
Gail Chambers
Roger D. Horne
Rob Bracken
David E. Pugh
Cathy Bradford
Randall Griffin
Abdullah Essa (Somali)

30 A Selection of Songs and Verses
FROM THE FARM LABOR MOVEMENT

HUNGRY, HUNGRY ARE WE

by John L. Handcox

Hungry, hungry are we
Just as hungry as hungry can be,
We don't get nothin for our labor,
So hungry, hungry are we.

Raggedy, raggedy are we,
Just as raggedy as raggedy can be
We don't get nothin for our labor,
So raggedy, raggedy are we.

Homeless, homeless are we
Just as homeless as homeless can be
We don't get nothin for our labor,
So homeless, homeless are we.

Landless, landless are we
Just as landless as landless can be,
We don't get nothin for our lrbor,
So landless, landless are we.

ROLL THE UNION ON

by John L. Handcox

It was in nineteen hundred and thirty six
And on the ninth of June
When the STFU pulled a strike
That troubled the planters on their thrones.

The planters they all became troubled,
Not knowing what 'twas all about,
But they said, 'One thing I'm sure we can do,
That's scare them sharecroppers out.'"

We're gonna roll, we're gonna roll,
We're gonna roll the Union on;
We're gonna roll, we're gonna roll,
We're gonna roll the Union on.

If the planter's in the way
We're gonna roll it over him,
We're gonna roll it over him,
We're gonna roll it over him,
We're gonna roll the Union on.

If the boss is in the way
We're gonna roll it over him
We're gonna roll the Union on.

If the governor's in the way
We're gonna roll it over him
We're gonna roll the Union on.

Thad Snow, who owned a large cotton plantation in southeast Missouri, actually invited the union to send an organizer. John L. Handcox, who was chosen to go, afterward sent me this poem:

OUT ON MR. SNOW'S FARM
or
The Kind of Man We Like To Meet

Early the second Monday in June,
I walked up to Mr. Thad Snow's Home, all alone,
And introduced myself to Mr. Snow,
One of the best men in SE-MO, I know.
He says to me, something for labor ought to be done,
And you are perfectly welcome to go on my farm.
He pointed me out some of the hands in the field,
Told me to talk with them and see how they feel.
Then he asked me what else he could do
To help put our labor movement thru.
I told him his help would be much if he didn't object
For the labor on his farm to join our Union as such.
I walked over Mr. Snow's farm in all ease,
For I knew that Mr. Snow was well pleased.
I sang. I talked and rejoiced as I went,
For I knew I had gotten Mr. Snow's consent.
This is the kind of men we need, you know,
Men that are in sympathy with their labor, like Mr. Snow.

Note: Please fix this up and send Mr. Snow a copy.

John L. Handcox

COMING IN TO MEMPHIS
[From Marked Tree]

by Naomi Mitchison

This-here is the end of a world,
Full of the gloomy and endless wailing
Of the propertyless great-grandchildren of slaves.
Poverty here tooths the eroded banks,
Silts up the furrows with sand,
Picks at the boards of cabins.
This is the end of my kind of world.
Oh Challengers,
Oh Movers of the new thing in the human spirit,
Is it the beginning of yours?

GOODBYE TO THE SOUTHERN TENANT FARMERS UNION
[With Zita Baker]

by Naomi Mitchison

We turn our backs on Marked Tree and the grim miles of cotton.
Forgive us, McKinney and Moskop, Brookins and Stultz forgive—
You-all, think friendly of us, not quite gone and forgotten.
We are needing your forgiveness as you need to live.
Here we are, warm, well fed, security round and through us
White like an English blanket, we running away.
Forgive us, Mitchell and Kester, who never knew us,
Only the faces we turned you, the talk of a day.
We with our pound-bought dollars, each in turn buying
Romance or beauty or struggle, all there is to be had,
Now they carry us safe off, while you maybe are dying.
Forgive us our trespasses, we sure do need it bad.

WE BELIEVE

by Harriet Young

We believe
That a gun is no defense
In the hands of a hungry man.
That battleships are no defense for a people ill housed.
That anti-aircraft guns are no defense
Against the poisonous fumes of discontent and disillusion.
These are the things we believe:
That a free nation is one whose people gain each year
More share in all its goods.
That free speech, free press, voting, free assembly
Are but the framework of democracy
The sturdy props on which we build
The strong, the spacious House
With room for all,
With work and food for all,
With full security,
With space for growing.
We have the sturdy props,
We have the ground-plan,
the building is begun.
We have a stake in its completion.
The building must go on.
This is our defense,
This is our democracy.
This is our land.   1938

RED EMMA PASSES AT TORONTO
[1940]
by H. L. Mitchell

Red Emma passes at Toronto, the newspapers say.
But the death of a woman of seventy
Is scarcely news today,
When cities are bombed and rivers of red
Are flowing and workers are dying across the sea.

Who was Emma Goldman and why did they call her red,
Why she was hardly a lady even by the standard of today
Though once she was young and beautiful, that too had passed away
Not long ago she stirred workers to thinking
And that was the reason she was red.

Red Emma was proud of that title, which she held to her dying day.
This great woman was deported, America should claim her today
For war and its carnage she hated, and always raised her voice to say
That American workers had nothing whatever to gain that way.
She stirred people to thinking and that was the reason she was a Red.

Emma Goldman knew no master, no one ever possessed her.
And in prison as in exile she bowed to no authority
She held no beliefs but one and that was—people should be free.
In a world that is in shambles and tyrants triumphantly have their way
We are better off now for the free spirit of Emma Goldman is alive even today.

> So Red Emma passes at Toronto, the newspapers say.
> But the death of a woman of seventy
> Is scarcely news today
> For cities are bombed and rivers of blood
> Are flowing and workers are dying across the sea.

Written upon reading about the death of Emma Goldman (1869–1940), the Russian anarchist and pacifist. Deported from the United States because of her opposition to World War I and later persecuted in Russia by the Bolsheviks, she fled to England and eventually became a British subject. Her autobiography *Living My Life* is one of the most remarkable documents of all time.

BALLAD OF THE DI GIORGIO STRIKERS

Pickets standing on the line
Looking down the country road,
Saw a lonesome stranger coming
And he said his name was Joad.

Now the stranger stood beside us
And his face was pale and thin,
Said he'd like to join the Union
So we said we'd let him in.

Thursday night he came to meeting
And he raised his snowy head,
With a voice like Resurrection
Spoke, and this is what he said:

"There's a fence around Creation,
There's a mortgage on the sun,
They have put electric meters
Where the rivers used to run."

"God Almighty made the valley
For a land of milk and honey,
But a corporation's got it
For to turn it into money."

SHERIFF PEACHER'S STOCKADE

by Barbara Howes

We had heard about it, of course;
Rumor sketched the inmates clearly—
        Their alarm, their rage,
        Penned in the coop
        Till dawn-work-morning.

We trudged up a bent path—
The fossil grass limp, puffs
Of cotton dangling . . .
        We smelled danger.

        Then came upon
Friends: purple, white, jaune—
        Gérard; my dear;

Others—we *are of* all
        These people, who
        Travelled so far . . .
        I do remember.

Written especially for this book. [Paul D. Peacher was convicted in 1936 of holding thirteen STFU members in slavery.]

Index